MAUD RUSSELL (1891-1982) was the daughter of Paul and Maria Nelke, German immigrants who settled in London in the 1880s. An important patron and collector of modern art, she was portrayed by Matisse, Sir William Nicholson and Cecil Beaton – among others. She was an avid reader and disciplined writer of letters and a diary, which she kept for forty years from 1937-1977, providing a rare social record of her times. Marriage to Gilbert Russell, a cousin of the Duke of Bedford, brought her into contact with the leading writers, artists, musicians and politicians of the day, many of whom stayed with her at Mottisfont Abbey, her country estate in Hampshire. She was unfortunate enough to live through both World Wars, suffering from anti-German sentiment during the Great War and helping her Jewish relations to escape Germany in the 1930s. From 1943-45 she worked on secret propaganda activities at the Admiralty. After her husband died, Maud formed a relationship with the Russian artist Boris Anrep, sponsoring his Modern Virtues mosaic floor near the entrance of the National Gallery.

EMILY RUSSELL is Maud's granddaughter. She read English at Manchester University and has a Masters in Criminology from Middlesex University. She worked for Amnesty International, the Howard League for Penal Reform and the Campaign for Freedom of Information before becoming a journalist and eventually moving to Chile. She now lives in Santiago with her partner and two children.

Following page:
A composed 20-year-old Maud by John Singer Sargent.

A CONSTANT HEART

The War Diaries of Maud Russell

1938 -1945

Edited by

EMILY RUSSELL

THE DOVECOTE PRESS

In memory of my mother, Anne Russell, and
for my children Tom and Nicole

'Many happy returns to my own perfect friend, wife, companion,
mother and old monkey and everything else I like.'

GILBERT TO MAUD
December 7, 1934

First published in 2017 by The Dovecote Press Ltd
Stanbridge, Wimborne Minster, Dorset BH21 4JD

ISBN 978-0-9955462-3-3
Text © Emily Russell/The Maud Russell Estate 2017

Emily Russell has asserted her rights under the
Copyright, Designs and Patent Act 1988 to be identified as author of this work

Typeset in Sabon and designed by The Dovecote Press Ltd
Printed and bound in India by Replika Press Pvt. Ltd.
All papers used by The Dovecote Press are natural, recyclable products
made from wood grown in sustainable, well-managed forests.

A CIP catalogue record for this book is available from the British Library

1 3 5 7 9 8 6 4 2

Contents

Foreword

JOHN JULIUS NORWICH

During some twenty years perhaps, in the fifties and sixties, Maud Russell would invite us regularly to Mottisfont. For me it was, quite simply, the most desirable country house in England. It was known as 'Mottisfont Abbey'; in fact, it had never been an abbey at all; what it had been was an Augustinian priory, founded as early as 1201. (It was always popular with pilgrims to Winchester, since it was fortunate enough to possess the little finger of John the Baptist.) Inevitably, it was dissolved by Henry VIII; and Henry passed it on to his Lord Chamberlain, Sir William Sandys. Now Sandys didn't really need it, since he was already owner of the Vyne, near Basingstoke; but he set to work at once to convert it into a magnificent gentleman's residence. Fortunately, and unlike most of his contemporaries similarly employed, he did not begin by tearing down the old building; instead, he turned the nave into his new mansion, adding wings on each side. In our bedroom part of the upper wall was cut away, revealing part of a soaring gothic arch. The thirteenth-century cellarium – the storeroom, or pantry – still exists today.

The atmosphere of Mottisfont was, however, anything but monastic. Thanks largely to Gilbert and Maud, who had bought it, loved it dearly, and lavished their ample funds upon it, it was as comfortable as a house can be; and in those years domestic staff were not yet a problem. You were greeted at the door by a butler; your suitcases were taken to your room by a footman and unpacked by a maid; and in no time you were sitting in that glorious long drawing-room, frescoed by Rex Whistler, with its blazing log fire and its beautiful Steinway (regularly tuned), sipping the whisky sour for which the house was famous.

And then there was Maud, who epitomised that wonderful and all too rare combination – considerable wealth and boundless generosity. At first sight there was nothing particularly remarkable about her: medium height, quiet country clothes, immaculate hair, a soft, gentle, slightly breathless voice, with a tendency to repeat what you had just said before answering. The guests tended to be literary (Raymond Mortimer, Lord David Cecil, one or two struggling young authors) – or musical; there was always someone to sit down to the piano – Eddy Sackville-West, perhaps, or Burnett Pavitt, who represented Roche Pharmaceuticals and played like an angel. He and I used to tackle endless duets; he was as superb a sight-reader as I was a rotten one. Ian Fleming was never there in my day; he and Maud had drifted apart, and in 1952 he had married Ann Rothermere. Boris Anrep I saw only once, when I was staying somewhere else and dropped in one afternoon. He was never invited to the main weekends, probably at his own request; he would have been a fish out of water and he knew it.

I don't remember very well what we did during the day: there must have been bracing country walks, if only to counteract the gargantuan breakfasts and lunches. What remains clearly in my mind is the fact that the beds were all carefully turned down after lunch to allow for an hour's siesta. And then, in the summer, there was the enormous pleasure of afternoon tea on the lawn, under some of the most magnificent trees in England, watching the Test flow by; a proper tea too – large silver tea-pot with burner underneath, wafer-thin cucumber sandwiches and, always, a particularly delicious chocolate cake with jam inside. When it was over we would stagger to our feet and play croquet for an hour or so before it was time to dress for dinner.

I loved Mottisfont so much that when Maud moved out I seriously considered trying to form a syndicate to buy it – or at least to rent it from the National Trust, to which she had very sensibly left it. My plan was to have four young couples, each of whom would have the right to go for three weekends out of four, taking it in turns to invite a fifth couple to stay for the fourth weekend. It could, I think, have worked; but before I could do much about it another tenant took it on, with fairly disastrous results, and I gave up the idea. But there: it would have been a sad anti-climax after the Russell golden age. Perhaps it was just as well.

Maud was an intensely secretive person – none of her regular guests, for example, was allowed into her bedroom – and none of us, so far as I know, had an inkling that she kept a regular diary. But how lucky we are that she did: for here is one of the last fascinating pictures of English upper-class life in both peace and war. How lucky we are, too, that she had a granddaughter – a granddaughter who found the diary, who has edited it brilliantly to a manageable size, and who sets it now before us.

Introduction

When I was young my grandmother Maud Russell accused me of snooping. I had left the drawing room after a family lunch on the pretext of needing to use the bathroom, and sneaked up the stairs to explore the top floor of her elegant London flat overlooking Hyde Park. I ran along the long passage, finding closed doors on either side that I dared not open, and returned to the drawing room within what I thought were barely a few minutes. 'You've been snooooping,' she said.

Almost half a century later, I have spent the last few years snooping into her life – big time. I have buried myself in the diaries that she kept for 40 years from 1937 to 1977; read correspondence between her and my grandfather Gilbert Russell; and tracked down and contacted relatives I had not known existed of Maud's father, my German Jewish great-grandfather Paul Nelke.

So who was Maud Russell and why the fascination? The daughter of wealthy German immigrants, Maud was an English patron of the arts, discriminating art collector and discerning society hostess. She was an outsider who found a place in society through her wealth, education and marriage but who never completely fitted in, remaining an enigma to many. Together with her husband Gilbert Russell and after his death in 1942, she entertained leading politicians, high society figures, writers, musicians and artists in London and also at Mottisfont Abbey, their 2,000 acre estate in Hampshire.

Her circle of friends included members of the fashionable intellectual and artistic groups of the late nineteenth and early twentieth centuries, such as the Souls, the Coterie and the Bloomsbury Group, and also the 'Bright Young Things' of the 1920s and 1930s. Among these were Margot Asquith, wife of the Prime Minister H.H. Asquith; the high-society beauty Lady Diana Cooper; the writer and art critic Clive Bell; and the photographer Cecil Beaton. The novelist Ian Fleming, who invented James Bond, was an intimate friend and probable lover. She later formed a close relationship with the larger-than-life Russian artist Boris Anrep, a known womaniser, becoming his staunch ally and companion until his death in 1969.

Intensely interested in arts and letters from a young age, Maud sat for Henri Matisse and amassed an important modern French art collection, including works by Picasso, Modigliani, Derain and Braque. Among her notable contributions to the arts were her commission of the *trompe l'oeil* murals by the artist Rex Whistler in the drawing room at Mottisfont; the gift of Mottisfont – originally an Augustinian priory founded in 1201 – to the National Trust; and her sponsorship of the last of four mosaic floors by Boris Anrep in the National Gallery. On a less public scale, she was a committed supporter of classical music and young musicians. She held musical evenings at home, was involved with the Haydn-Mozart Society, sat on the fundraising committee for Covent Garden and backed promising performers. She was a serious reader and counted many writers in her circle including Cyril Connolly, Raymond Mortimer, Harold Nicolson and Stephen Spender. Later in life, she said reading and writing her diary were her greatest pleasures.

Maud Julia Augusta Nelke was born on 7 December 1891 in the bed of the actress and former royal mistress, Lillie Langtry, at 18 Pont Street in Knightsbridge which her parents were renting. Her father, Paul Solomon Nelke, was a stockbroker and racehorse owner who came from a well-established Jewish family in Berlin. Her pretty and petite German mother Maria, a Christian, was the daughter of Carl Conrad, the Master of the Mint in Frankfurt and, after unification, in Berlin.

Paul began travelling to London and New York for business in the early 1880s and became naturalised British in 1885. He formed the broking firm Nelke, Phillips & Bendix with two partners in 1888, going on to make his fortune by taking large positions in risky ventures. One of his clients was Winston Churchill, whose brother Jack worked for the firm for a number of years. After marrying Maria in Berlin in early 1891, the couple moved to London to set up their home.

Maud and her sister Kate, who was two years younger and known as Kitty, had a sheltered and privileged Edwardian childhood. They grew up in the family's six-storey mansion in Cadogan Square, Knightsbridge, where outings to the theatre, concerts and art galleries were everyday treats. Relaxed weekends and holidays were spent at the family's large country house and farm, Wood Lea, in Berkshire, conveniently close to Ascot for Paul to indulge in his passion for horse racing. Paul was also fond of gambling. According to an obituary notice, he was once described as the 'best bad [card] player that ever lived'.

Paul and Maria were keen for the family to assimilate into English society as quickly as possible and usually spoke and wrote to each other and their children in English. The girls were brought up in the Church of England and no expense was spared on providing them with the best education of the day, both at home by governesses and at exclusive private schools. Maud's first school was run by Edith Lyttelton, the wife of politician Alfred Lyttelton, who were both members of the Souls. Later she studied at Queensgate and then at Miss Wolff's in South Audley Street where Vita Sackville-West, the poet and novelist, was her main rival for the annual composition and oratory prize.

The school year was broken up by long trips to the continent involving outings to historic churches and museums and, on one occasion, a formal introduction to the pope. The governess of the day would accompany them to impart classes for an hour or so in the mornings and to act as chaperone. A typical day in Cannes, for example, was an hour or so of Italian lessons in the morning, tennis practice, golf lessons at the club after lunch, tea at Rumpelmayers and finally a violin class in the evening.

Serious, sensitive and intellectually active, Maud soaked up this exposure to culture and learning, and her deep interest in the performing and visual arts shaped her life until her death.

Among her closest childhood friends were Felicity and Iris Tree, the daughters of the prominent English actor and stage manager Sir Herbert Beerbohm Tree and his actress wife Helen. Other friends from her early childhood that continued into adulthood were the Vansittart family, whose eldest son Robert became an influential British diplomat. 'Van', as he was known by his friends, is best known for his staunch opposition to appeasement in the years leading up to the Second World War. Maud later credited him for being instrumental in the provision of visas to England for her German Jewish relatives in 1939.

Despite the silver spoon, the young Maud felt that the family were regarded as foreigners in England. She was also concerned that her mother's few English friends would result in a lacklustre introduction to society. She need not have worried. After spending some months in Germany and France to perfect both languages, Maud was presented at court on 4 March 1910, Coronation Year, and the great Russian ballerina Anna Pavlova danced at her 'coming out' ball.

An heiress, Maud was a striking, petite woman with her father's dark colouring and looks and a fashionable dress sense. Today many of her evening gowns from the 1920s and 1930s are held by the Victoria and Albert Museum. From 1910 onwards she drew a stream of suitors and, like so many of their generation, a number of her admirers were killed in the First World War. Of these, she was particularly fond of Major John 'Buzz' Archdale-Porter, whose family owned the Bell Isle Estate in County Fermanagh, Northern Ireland. Among other suitors were the diplomat Sir Cecil Dormer, who was Britain's Minister to Norway from 1934-41 and Ambassador to Poland's government in exile from 1941-43; and the distinguished Gallipoli war correspondent Ellis Ashmead-Bartlett.

Through her close friends at the time, Phyllis Boyd (later to become the socialite Phyllis de Janzé), the heiress Nancy Cunard, and Clare Tennant, the oldest child of Edward Tennant and Pamela Wyndham, Maud went to the wild parties held by the Coterie – also known as the 'Corrupt Coterie'. It was in these years that she met the Coterie's leading light Lady Diana Cooper – or Lady Diana Manners as she then was – and her husband-to-be Duff Cooper, a member of Winston Churchill's inner circle in the 1930s. Although she recalled her friends having affairs with the attractive, eminent young men they met at these parties she does not seem to have had a particularly riotous time herself. She was a 'shy young woman' while the men she was seeing 'did not belong to that wild world,' she later wrote.

The outbreak of the First World War was particularly difficult for the Nelkes, not only because of their German roots and family ties. In 1912, their younger daughter Kitty had married Count Anton ('Tony') Apponyi, a Hungarian aristocrat descended on his mother's side from the Hapsburgs, and the couple were living in Hungary, an ally of Germany. While Maud nursed wounded British soldiers in a hospital in Brighton, Kitty set up a hospital for Hungarian soldiers in an outbuilding at the Apponyis' estate Jablonica, occasionally visiting Tony at the front where he served with the Royal and Imperial Hussars. Although letters got through, the Nelkes did not see Kitty – said by Maud to be her parents' favourite – and her young children for five years.

As the war continued, the Nelkes suffered from growing anti-German sentiment. In 1917, after being an active member of the London Stock Exchange for 30 years, Paul was not re-elected; the fact his son-in-law was fighting for 'the enemy' did not help his case. Paul sold the broking side of Nelke, Phillips & Co. and continued to operate privately. He was joined by two former partners, Hermann Marx (a relative of Karl Marx) and Julius Stern, both also of German Jewish origin.

It was at a dinner party during the war that Maud met her future husband Gilbert Russell. He was on leave in London from his post as a captain in the Intelligence Corps on the Western Front, where he was responsible for interrogating German prisoners and had seen service in the trenches.

Within less than a month and after meeting just seven times, the couple were engaged. It was a love match on both sides and went on to become a strong marriage.

'Here is some news for you – I am engaged to the most delightful of creatures, by name Maud Nelke,' my grandfather wrote on 31 December 1916 to his sisters Diana and Flora. 'Do not be alarmed when I tell you she is a German Jewess for I know you will like her. Also the idea of marrying a German in war time tickles me immensely.'

Although born in England, Gilbert did not think Maud was like other English women. 'Not an English girl at all – a foreigner – in fact an Oriental or Jewess,' he told his sisters. 'Very feminine and well dressed – rather highly strung type, but with the most direct nature I've ever seen. No humbug or snobbery or social ambition.'

The fifth of six brothers and sisters, Gilbert came from a prominent Whig family that was proud of its liberal, reforming tendencies. His great-uncle, Lord John Russell, promoted the 1832 Reform Bill that brought in a broader and fairer electoral system, before becoming Foreign Secretary and then Prime Minister. His father, Lord Arthur Russell, a brother of Hastings, 9th Duke of Bedford, worked as private secretary to his uncle John and later represented Tavistock as Liberal MP for over a quarter of a century.

Gilbert's French mother, Laura de Peyronnet, was the granddaughter of Comte Pierre-Denis de Peyronnet, the chancellor at the Court of Charles X. A clever, learned woman, Laura held a literary salon at their home in Audley Square attended on occasions by the Stephen sisters, who became after marriage Virginia Woolf and Vanessa Bell. Reminiscent of the Nelkes, she did not speak to her children in French for fear it would be detrimental to her husband's career.

Now aged forty-two, Gilbert had studied at Balliol, Oxford, before joining the Grenadier Guards and fighting in the Anglo-Sudan and Second Boer wars. On resigning his commission in 1906, he worked as a financier, initially for Lord Revelstoke at Barings Bank and then independently, travelling widely and living in Paris for a number of years. He did not care much for society and enjoyed poking holes in other people's prejudices. He smoked heavily, enjoyed Club life and found gambling 'a fascinating amusement'. His humour was widely admired and, according to Maud, 'he was by far the wittiest person I have known. Voice, enunciation, pauses, unexpectedness, all built up his wit.'

A loyal family man, Gilbert was unpretentious and warm-hearted. He doted on his two spinster sisters Flora and Diana and was close to his younger brother Conrad, a farmer and the devoted admirer of Lady Diana Cooper; his older brother Claud, a diplomat; and his eldest brother Harold, a lawyer and naturalist, who died in 1926. After his marriage, he extended the same affection to Maud's family.

Maud and Gilbert married on 14 March 1917 in a small wartime wedding in London at St Andrews Church, Wells Street, in Marylebone. Sixteen years younger than Gilbert, Maud always said her liberal outlook was nurtured by the Russell family. 'G. used to call me his child wife and that is really what I was for some years – gentle, quiet and obedient to the Russell influence,' she wrote later.

The newly-weds settled into a large Georgian house in Cavendish Square where they lived until 1937 when the block was bought by John Lewis for its Oxford Street department store. They then moved to Princes Gate, overlooking Hyde Park. They shared the same sense of humour and many private jokes, a love of travel and were both interested in leading active and sociable lives. According to Maud, they never quarrelled. Their first son Martin was born in 1918, their second Raymond arrived four years later in 1922. Then, in 1924, Maud's niece Alexie came to live with them as her parents, who were living in Hungary, were experiencing financial and marital problems and thought the five-year-old would be happier with her young cousins in England. Exotic pets such as Sharkey the snake, Anthony and Cleopatra the armadillos and a crocodile completed the household.

After the war, Gilbert worked as the London agent for the New York bankers Salomon until 1921 when his father-in-law Paul helped him set up the merchant bank Cull and Co., with three other partners, Anders Cull, Hugh Micklem and Hermann Marx. The company quickly prospered through entrepreneurial investments, mainly in the natural resources sector. As the business grew, Maud and Gilbert began leasing grand country houses, such as Heveningham Hall in Suffolk and Blickling Hall in Norfolk, to get the children away from London during the holidays and to entertain their friends. The only blot on this happy life was Gilbert's failing health. His first serious asthma attack occurred in 1928 and poor health dogged him ever after. By the time these diaries open he is a semi-invalid and Maud is living an increasingly independent life.

Already knowledgeable about the arts at the time of her marriage, in 1924 Maud joined the Contemporary Arts Society and, over the next decade, began her own art collection, becoming one of the foremost collectors of modern French art among her generation in Britain, according to the art historian and critic Richard Shone. As she pursued her own interest in the arts, so her circle of friends widened to include other collectors, artists, critics, writers and musicians.

Previously portrayed by artists such as John Singer Sargent, Sir William

Nicholson and the sculptor Frank Dobson, in 1937 Matisse agreed to draw Maud's portrait. He seldom accepted commissions and in order to win his consent she had to show she was worthy of his interest by adding a Degas to her growing collection. Maud found Matisse boring company as she sat for him over five days in his Boulevard Montparnasse studio in Paris, but her view of him improved at a lunch she held for him afterwards in London, described retrospectively in these diaries.

Maud was never comfortable with the two Matisse portraits (three others were discarded directly after the sitting) and at first they were not hung at all. In the 1960s she found an obscure place for them on the stairs of her London flat and eventually lent them to Southampton Art Gallery (1977-1985). Large charcoal drawings, Matisse's thick, black, confident lines show an austere, unhappy face close-up. They 'make everything else look silly,' she noted in her diary in 1947.

Over the years, she would occasionally show the Matisse drawings to visitors. The poet Stephen Spender saw them in 1961. 'Stephen looked attentively and searched for whatever it was Matisse could have seen. He then came out, surprisingly, with a likeness in the tragic drawing to Theodora in the mosaic in [the Basilica of] San Vitale and I immediately saw it myself: the mournful ageing face and pinched expression. "He saw and drew a byzantine look you have," he said.'[1]

With an active and curious mind, Maud loved lively company and keeping pace with new ideas, courting and keeping the friendship of younger people throughout her life. Among these in the 1930s were Winston Churchill's son Randolph; the painter and fencer Ian Campbell-Gray; and the dashing young Reuters journalist Ian Fleming. Ian would go on to play a crucial role in the Naval Intelligence Division at the Admiralty during the Second World War, possibly gaining a foothold there through introductions from Gilbert, before becoming a famous novelist in the 1950s. As my grandmother later recalled, he had the 'handsome looks of a fallen angel' and his dynamic personality was 'stunning to newcomers'.

The circumstances of Ian and Maud's first meeting are not clear. The Russells knew Ian's grandparents, the Scottish investment banker Robert Fleming and his wife Kate, staying with them at Joyce Grove in Nettlebed as early as 1922. On 17 December 1931 Kate attended a matinee performance, organised by Maud, in aid of the British Hospital for Mothers and Babies at London's Phoenix Theatre. On the same day, Maud notes in her engagement

1. Russell, unpublished diary, October 11, 1961.

diary 'Meet I.', possibly referring to her first meeting with Ian and added later. A few months later, on 11 February 1932, Maud invited Ian to her home in Cavendish Square: 'Cises, Dixons, Guy Dawnays, Peakes, Pamela G., Ian Fleming. On to Embassy,'[2] her engagement book records. The use of his full name indicates it is the beginning of their friendship. Thereafter she refers to him once as 'Ian' and then almost always as 'I.' both in her engagement book and in the diary she began in 1937 (he used to write to her as 'M.'). She was 40, he was 23. There was a strong mutual attraction: for a few years he was the person she saw most outside of her family circle. He became a regular guest at the Russells' weekend house parties and Maud used her influence to get him a job at Gilbert's bank Cull and Co. (where he was overlooked by the partners and soon grew bored). Intelligent, well-connected and cultivated, Maud was a mentor for Ian, while he was the admiring, intimate confidante to whom she could open up.

Although not specifically confirmed by Maud's diaries, it's likely they became lovers in the 1930s and the affair continued intermittently over the next decade or so. It was relatively common among Maud's circle for women to have admirers, or even lovers, and the relationship was discreet and did not draw much attention – although it led to speculation after the war. Despite her discretion, there are various clues that are suggestive of a love affair. To me the most telling evidence is a small envelope with a black lock of hair inside that I found among her papers. On the envelope, Maud has written a simple 'I.'s' in pencil.

These war diaries reveal the importance of Maud and Ian to one another. They show how Ian was a major support to Maud after Gilbert's death in 1942 and pulled strings to get her a job in the Admiralty's wartime propaganda division. She, in turn, provided him with an escape from the stresses of his top-secret work at the Admiralty. Maud was his 'comfort during the war' he told Sefton Delmer, who ran the Political Warfare Executive's black propaganda activities.[3] She always noted the dates of Ian's often lengthy trips overseas and she would be among the first he would contact on his return. 'You're the one reason I want to see London again. I have missed you very much,' he wrote to her from Colombo in 1945.

2. Cyril ('Cis') and Anne Asquith, diplomat Sir Pierson ('Bob') Dixon and his wife Ismene, Guy Dawnay and his wife Cecil, Conservative politician Osbert Peake and his wife Lady Jane Capell, Pamela Paget who was married until 1935 to Lord Glenconner (Christopher Tennant), and Ian Fleming.

3. Russell, unpublished diary, May 22, 1957, account of conversation with Sefton Delmer.

Another important man in Maud's life was the Russian artist Boris Anrep. Born in 1883 in St Petersburg to Russian nobility, Boris first studied law but turned to art under the influence of his friend the artist Dimitri Stelletsky. Sensitive to religious imagery and symbolism, Boris was inspired to work as a mosaicist after visiting the Roman and Byzantine mosaics in Ravenna.

Boris became close friends with the English painter Henry Lamb while studying at the Académie Julian in Paris, and through him met Augustus John and the Bloomsbury circle of artists and intellectuals. In 1912, the writer and critic Roger Fry, one of the Bloomsbury Group, asked Boris to select the Russian exhibits for Fry's Second Post-Impressionist exhibition in London, and in 1913 Fry wrote the foreword for the catalogue of Boris's first one-man show at the Chenil Gallery in Chelsea. These connections were instrumental in helping Boris obtain many important commissions in England, including works for the Tate Gallery, the Bank of England, the National Gallery and Westminster Cathedral over the next five decades. He began to visit London frequently for work while maintaining a studio in Paris.

An impressive figure due to his large size and gregarious personality, Boris led a Bohemian lifestyle and was attractive to women, gaining a reputation for always sustaining relationships with two women at the same time. Lady Ottoline Morrell described him as 'clever, fat, good-hearted, sensual, but full of youthful vitality and Russian gaiety.'[4] He wrote poetry, enjoyed cooking and was a lively story-teller and keen tennis player (competing in the Wimbledon doubles in 1920). Of himself, he said: 'I abandon myself to an unreasonable pleasure when I can cause joy even if it is a joy from a popping cracker.'[5]

Under family pressure, in 1908 Boris married a Russian girl, Yuniya Kitrovo, with whom he was having an affair, and she accompanied him to Paris. There he fell in love with Helen Maitland, who was a former girlfriend of Henry Lamb and close friend of Dorelia John. She moved into the marital home in 1911 and had two children with Boris; Anastasia in 1912 and Igor in 1914. It was only on the outbreak of the First World War that Yuniya left this odd setup to return to Russia to work as a nurse.

Boris also went back to serve his country in the Imperial Russian Guard, leaving Helen and the children in England. While on leave in St Petersburg, he began an intense romantic liaison with the Russian poet Anna Akhmatova.

---

4. R. Gathorne-Hardy (ed.), *Ottoline. The Early Memoirs of Lady Ottoline Morrell*, London 1963.
5. Anrep, letter to Maud, December 30, 1934.

Boris always insisted that it was only a 'warm friendship' but Akhmatova was apparently bitterly disappointed when he left Russia for good in 1917 and dedicated over 30 poems to him.

Having obtained a divorce from Yuniya, Boris married Helen in 1918 to ensure the legitimacy of his male heir and they set up home in London. True to form, he invited to live with them his latest lover Mariya Volkova (known as Maroussia), the 18-year-old sister of his brother Gleb's wife. Despite having agreed to the arrangement, Helen was unhappy living in a *ménage à trois* and, to Boris's rage, began an affair with Roger Fry. She eventually left Boris for Fry in 1926. After their separation, Boris returned to Paris with Maroussia, and set up his studio at 65 Boulevard Arago in the Latin Quarter.

Maud met Boris in June 1934 while staying at Budd Farm, the country home of their mutual friends the politician and lawyer William Jowitt, and his wife Lesley. Boris had made a mosaic floor for the Jowitts' Mayfair house in 1922, and was visiting from France. When he returned to England the following December he got in touch with Maud: 'Dear Mrs Russell, I am back in England till the 8th of January. Shall I see you? Or, rather, may I see you?' Maud was in bed with an unnamed ailment but agreed to receive Boris on December 21. Boris amused her with his expansive chatter as he sat by her bedside and he returned for another visit on January 5 while she was still laid up. She was attracted by his vitality, while he noted in her a 'great capacity for response to anything warm and alive.'[6]

They saw little more of each other, however, until he arrived in London in 1940 after escaping from Paris on the same day as the Germans entered the city. The development of their acquaintance into an intimate relationship is described in these War Diaries. An expressive, emotional man, Boris soon declared his love for Maud while she grew to love him too, but more slowly, causing him considerable despair. 'When I met B. I was having a holiday from normal life, just as he was,' she recalled in her diary in 1962. He courted her patiently and lovingly, entertaining her over lunch in Soho, doing odd jobs around the flat and meeting her at the bus stop outside the Admiralty on her day off to help her with her bags to Waterloo, where she took the train alone to Mottisfont. In turn, she worried about his lack of an occupation during the war, eventually offering to sponsor Boris's fourth and final mosaic floor at the National Gallery, *The Modern Virtues*, which was completed in 1952.

It turned into a thoroughly modern love affair that lasted over 25

6. Anrep, letter to Maud, December 30, 1934.

years until Boris's death. There was never any intention to marry (in fact Boris remained married to Helen) and they lived independent but closely connected lives after he returned to Paris in 1946. On Maroussia's death in 1956, Boris became more reliant on Maud and he eventually settled permanently into the top floor of her flat in Hyde Park Gardens.

The painter Duncan Grant commented later to Richard Shone that it was remarkably courageous of Maud to take up with Boris given his reputation as a womaniser. But Maud seems to have had few causes for jealousy except for Boris's dedication to work: 'Two years ago when B. went back to mosaic life in Paris I felt I had a formidable rival. And I was right. And so it is. And I must bow to my rival,' she recorded in her diary in 1948 when a restless Boris was eager to return to work while they were on holiday in Italy. Boris worked tirelessly until the age of almost 80 when he retired after fixing the mosaic for the Blessed Sacrament Chapel at Westminster Cathedral, his last major commission.

Although different in many ways, Boris shared with Gilbert a warmth, gaiety and expressiveness that Maud depended on to brighten up her often sad and serious reflections on the world and also her own life. Both men were also persistent debunkers of falsity and affectation, something which she also intensely disliked.

Maud's reputation as a notable hostess established itself at Mottisfont Abbey, which lies in a setting of great natural beauty in the River Test valley in Hampshire. Founded in the twelfth century as an Augustinian priory, the house developed over the centuries into a Tudor and then a Georgian mansion and exudes an atmosphere of magical calm. A stream ripples beside the house, a pristine natural spring rises in the garden and ancient trees – including England's oldest plane – dot the grounds. In Maud's time the 2,029-acre estate, including 490 acres of woodland, provided excellent pheasant shooting while the Test's crystal-clear chalk streams are still world-renowned for their trout fishing. A perfectionist, Maud laid on lavish meals, copious drink and a convivial atmosphere to round off a day of walks, tennis and croquet, or shooting or mushroom picking when in season. She was an excellent hostess, drawing out her guests with tact and skill, while rarely holding forth herself.

When the Russells bought Mottisfont in 1934 it had been uninhabited for many years and needed a complete overhaul. Maud worked with the architects Easton and Robertson and with an eye for the building's history, chose pale shades, marbling paintwork and marble chimney pieces to create a light, neo-classical look. Influential garden designers were brought in to do the garden: Norah Lindsay designed the box-edged parterre on the site of the old priory cloister in front of the house; Geoffrey Jellicoe put in the Lime Walk, reminiscent of a cloister, at the back. Later, in 1938, Russell Page recommended shrubs.

There was one room that Maud and Gilbert left for later: the original entrance hall and largest space in the house, referred to by Maud as the 'big room'. It was unattractive with fake wooden panelling done in plaster, according to Maud's account of its renovation.[7] After giving some thought to the matter, in 1938 Maud commissioned the artist Rex Whistler to redo the room. A member of the 'Bright Young Things', Rex had come to the attention of fashionable society at the age of just 21 for his light-hearted mural of a romantic landscape for the Tate Gallery restaurant in 1927. He was also an accomplished book illustrator, theatre designer and portraitist. Rex's extravagant rococo style was not aligned with Maud's own interest in modern art but she would have been attracted by his skill as a draughtsman and the sense of fun that imbued all his work.

'I spoke to Rex Whistler, who was a friend, and first mentioned as a possibility a kind of modern Gothic, in other words 1938 Gothic, decoration. This idea was eagerly taken up by Rex Whistler, who began to make out his suggestions and sketches on any odd envelope he happened to have in his pocket or on a bill,' Maud recorded. The concept perfectly suited a house that was founded in the medieval era and which had incorporated the features of different periods over the centuries. It was also coherent with Maud's treatment of the rest of the house, including Lindsay's parterre and Jellicoe's lime walk and their references to the building's history. Over 10 months in 1939, Rex created a spectacular architectural illusion of gothic pillars and high vaulted ceilings in what is now known as the Whistler Room. The overall effect is discreet – reflecting Maud's own character and taste – and shaped a stylish drawing room that alluded to the house's medieval beginnings but with a modern, minimalistic touch.

Today Maud would be mortified to learn that she has been depicted as Rex's least favourite client. Writers on Rex have vilified her as 'tyrannical', 'feeble', 'too anxious for critical approval', 'not generous' and lacking in restraint.[8] There is, however, little evidence that Rex shared these views of

---

7. Maud Russell, untitled and undated typed document on the creation of the Whistler Room, written mainly in the third person with amendments inserted in Maud's handwriting. Maud Russell Family Estate.
8. Thomasson, *A Curious Friendship*, p. 358; Olivier, unpublished journals, 17 October 1938; Whistler, *The Laughter and the Urn*, p. 228; and (the last two) Cecil and Cecil, *In Search of Rex Whistler*, p. 184.

Maud although, by the end, he had clearly had enough of the commission. 'I am just finishing this wretched room . . . It has been the longest and most arduous and most boring of any that I have done,' Rex wrote on October 21, 1939 to Henry Paget,[9] the younger brother of the socialite Caroline Paget with whom Rex was unhappily in love.

For her part, Maud was genuinely fond of Rex, despite her exasperation at his habit of not answering letters, or failure to turn up for appointments or meet deadlines. 'Sat. morning Rex finished the room and left,' she wrote in her diary on November 5, 1939. 'He left quickly and I felt as if a loved person had gone for ever or as if part of the house I was living in had been suddenly pulled down.'

So what happened? In essence, although Maud and Rex agreed on the room's gothic architectural style, they had different ideas for the murals on the walls. 'Some of [the] sketches seemed to have too Georgian a flavour and I turned down the use of colour in the panels, preferring grisaille,' recalled Maud. Furthermore, while Rex was inspired to paint landscapes, Maud insisted on trophies, despite his attempts to persuade her otherwise. Maud's hesitation in sticking to her original choice of trophies delayed completion of the room, as did the slowness of one of Rex's workers, Victor Bowen,[10] and additions to the original project, such as wall lights and ermine curtains. Maud also attributed the delays to Rex's failure to spend sufficient time at Mottisfont, possibly because he was distracted by his efforts to win the affection of Caroline. To compensate, Maud offered to pay him an extra £300 (over £18,000 in equivalent 2016 prices) but Rex only accepted £100 for the additional work (see Maud's diary entry on 5 November 1939).

It was Rex's close friend, Edith Olivier, who set the tone with her unsympathetic depiction of Maud in the journal she was writing at the time, thus shaping the now widely accepted view of the relationship between Rex and Maud, and of Maud's own personality. An older woman and writer, Olivier hosted a circle of young writers, artists and musicians at her home in Wilton and doted on Rex. Although living close to one another and moving in similar circles, the two women were not friends and Maud found Olivier intimidating. Olivier, meanwhile, thought Maud

---

9. The Rex Whistler archive, The Salisbury Museum.
10. Letter from Rex Whistler to Osbert Sitwell, May 3, 1939: 'Mr Bowen who is working for me at Mottisfont keeps clamouring to know when he may start on your ceiling at Renishaw. He is the slowest worker in the world (as I am finding to my terrific cost) but rather accomplished I think don't you?' Rex Whistler archive, The Salisbury Museum.

'rather a feeble little woman – afraid of her own taste. Trying to be in the correct art fashion.'[11] Maud was establishing herself at the time as one of the premier English collectors of modern French art and it is possible that Olivier felt threatened by the younger woman's growing position as an art patron and hostess. As the Mottisfont commission dragged on Olivier naturally sympathised with Rex's predicament and accused Maud of 'ignorant interferences' and 'taking the advice of every weekend guest'[12] – among other criticisms.

The diaries and Maud's written recollection of the making of the Whistler Room provide a more balanced picture of the Mottisfont commission, filling in a number of gaps in the information available up until now. I also hope that the portrait of Maud provided in this book will help to dispel the impression that she was a weak, ungenerous character who was easily swayed by other people's opinions. On the contrary, she was an assertive connoisseur of the arts, who knew her own mind, and who was generally ready to help those around her – as is made clear by her diaries.

Fortunately experts agree that the result of Rex's labours at Mottisfont is first-class. Laurence Whistler asserted that it contained 'at least his most notable achievement in *trompe l'oeil*,'[13] while Hugh and Mirabel Cecil affirm that the room 'has a harmonious coherence and subtlety which is particularly attractive.'[14]

Nor was the commission all conflict and misery. As these war diaries reveal, memorable afternoons were spent with Rex in the 'big room' as he worked. He also took pleasure from sneaking in colour to the panel of an urn in a *trompe l'oeil* niche while Maud was away in London. 'It was a complete surprise to [me] but Rex Whistler had so obviously enjoyed painting it that [I] did not like to get him to wash it out,' wrote Maud in her memoir of the room. In addition, he painted smoke billowing out of the urn in a playful reminder of Maud's dislike of bonfires, and placed objects around it that represented her: books, a musical instrument, letters and a black evening glove. The Latin proverb *Magna est veritas et prevalebit* ('Great is the truth and it will prevail'), almost certainly chosen by Maud, is 'inscribed' on the vessel and aptly reflects her fighting spirit as war approached and she helped her Jewish relatives flee Germany. Rex's sympathetic and teasing representation of Maud's interests and fears in the

---

11. Olivier, unpublished journals, October 17, 1938.
12. Ibid., June 3, 1939.
13. Whistler and Fuller, *The Work of Rex Whistler*.
14. Cecil and Cecil, *In Search of Rex Whistler*, p. 188.

smoking-urn niche suggest that while Rex found the work tedious, he did not dislike his patron.

The Second World War broke out while Rex was painting the room (poignantly documented in an inscription on top of one of the pilasters saying, 'I was painting this Ermine curtain when Britain declared war against the Nazi tyrants. Sunday September 3rd. R.W.' [*see colour plates*]). In touch with her German Jewish relations, Maud had been closely watching events unfold in Germany over the previous decade. After the National Socialists came to power in 1933, her German Jewish cousin Alexander Schönberg, a rising chemist, quickly realised he could not fulfil his ambition of becoming a successful academic in Germany. Maud and Gilbert helped him and his family to England, from where he obtained a visiting professorship at Edinburgh University before going to Cairo University with a permanent position. As conditions for Jews deteriorated in Germany, another cousin living in Berlin, 13-year-old Esra Bennathan, was sent in 1936 to the United States to live with his father. In the months leading up to the outbreak of war, Maud began trying to get other Jewish relations to safety.

Fastidious by nature, Maud continued to run Mottisfont to the exacting standards of bygone days even though she knew the house and estate were too big for the times and the lifestyle 'strikingly anachronistic'.[15] An army of staff kept the house and grounds pristine and looked after Maud and her guests in the formal, old-fashioned manner. For Maud this was not only habit but a necessity if the house, her picture collection, and her many rare and beautiful possessions were to be kept in perfect condition. Part of Mottisfont's charm was the welcome and comfort it afforded her guests, and Maud was affronted when it was suggested that she might be able to save expense and bother by hiring less help.

Maud brought the same conscientiousness to her duties as 'head' of the village at Mottisfont. She chaired the school board into her eighties, oversaw church appointments, opened fetes, sponsored the cricket club and regularly called on neighbours, engaging herself in their concerns. Although she had become an atheist, she continued to go to church and supported attempts to increase attendance as numbers dropped in the 1950s and 1960s. She was also involved with running the estate, keeping a close eye on the upkeep of the rivers (including four fishing beats), the land and the numerous tenancies comprising two farms and 62 cottages. Talking to villagers who remember Maud, one gains the impression of a woman who was well-respected, natural in her dealings with her neighbours and

15. Russell, unpublished diary, May 2, 1948.

appreciated as a fair landlady. She took an interest in the village children, sometimes helping to further their education, and would go to lengths to obtain better treatment for ill neighbours.

Many people were unable to see beyond Maud's grand lifestyle to the woman within, wrongly describing her as conventional. The writer Frances Partridge, a frequent guest at Mottisfont with her husband Ralph, grasped the difference: 'Though her way of life was conventional she herself was an original character, with something a little Oriental in her appearance and her movements. She had a great sense of humour and a low gurgling laugh. Also, though she put people at their ease and talked in a relaxed way herself there was a hint of the dark horse about her, a sense of mystery never quite cleared up.'[16]

Maud's 'mysterious' character was also noted by the art critic Clive Bell. She did not have an expansive nature, disliked talking about herself and would dismiss her achievements with a chuckle and a self-depreciating remark. She preferred intelligent conversation and male company and was known to cuttingly put down anyone – often women – who she felt was interrupting the flow of highbrow talk. Of herself she wrote in 1964, 'I am an awkward, aloof, critical person. Men like me better than women do… Many people, I know and feel clearly, dislike me and these are mostly women. I am not cosy and not very like other people. And I am selfish and more self-sufficient than most.'[17]

For all her astute self-awareness, Maud was generous to family and friends alike. It's clear from reading her diaries and correspondence that she was quietly buying houses, paying for education or providing annuities to help those around her. She was her own person in that she did not seek approval for her actions or opinions. The disparate ages, tastes and callings of her many friends is evidence that she was open to diversity and change and not ruled by social convention.

As a grandmother, Maud was gently inquisitive, testing the water for further intimacy. There was great delight when small confidences were exchanged. She was always friendly but never demonstrative – as kin we were able to read this as affection. Holidays and weekends at Mottisfont were paradise. As children, we ran wild on the estate, turning up dirty and bedraggled at meal times, which we ate separately from the grown-ups. To entertain and get to know us better, she would invite us to play croquet and Scrabble, beating us at both. As we grew older we joined the adults and were

16. Partridge, *Everything to Lose*, p.286.
17. Russell, unpublished diary, July 22 1964.

initiated into the mysteries of providing good company and conversation.

Maud was aware that her diaries might be of historical interest but she did not want them made public for 30 or 40 years. She inquired whether the British Library would like them but changed her mind when she learnt it would want to look at them first. Instead she nominated the biographer James Pope-Hennessy as literary editor on her death. After Pope-Hennessy was brutally murdered in 1974 by some young men he had brought home, she appointed *The New York Times* arts correspondent John Russell, who was a close friend and relation by his first marriage to her niece Alexie Apponyi.

Despite family requests to see the diaries, John only gave them to my older brother Julian in 2004 after the death of our father Martin, Maud's son. Then for more than a decade, the diaries remained mostly unread in a cardboard box on a bookshelf. When I began reading them in March 2014 it was nominally to make a decision about what we should do with them. Were they of sufficient interest to write a biography? Did they contain horrifying family secrets that we might want to know about first before giving them to a library or institution where historians and biographers could access them?

What I found in the first surviving journal that began in the autumn of 1938 was a fascinating account of her views on the looming Second World War; her efforts to obtain visas to England for her Jewish relatives in Germany; Whistler's work on the drawing room at Mottisfont; her close friendship with Ian Fleming; a meeting in Paris with Matisse; and numerous social engagements with leading politicians, artists and writers of the day. There were also family revelations.

It became evident that her War Diaries were of interest in their own right, not just for historians but for a wider public. They encapsulate an exciting period of Maud's life, both because of the historical context and the personal tragedies, worries and challenges that she faced over those years. The loss of a husband; the fate of two young sons during wartime; her inner struggle to pluck up the courage to take a job; and her reinvention as a single woman are just some of the stories that are told within these pages. The diaries, in both their language and content, also open a window into a byegone age of privilege and class that occasionally makes uncomfortable reading today, but which was still firmly in place in the pre-war years.

Maud usually updated her diary on Sunday mornings, sitting up in bed – her refuge – with cream or a beauty mask covering her face. She wrote a day-by-day recap of the previous week, recording in detail all her social engagements and even appointments with the hairdresser, manicurist or doctor. Of the roughly 350,000 words she penned over the period that covers the Second World War, I have cut her text by about two-thirds. In doing so, I have tried to keep a sense of Maud's immensely active life and wide interests. As part of this process, the dates in this book often refer to the day and place the events took place rather than when they were written. I have also changed punctuation, corrected rare spelling mistakes and occasionally edited the text to aid understanding. Maud moved in a large social circle and I have not footnoted everyone she lists at the numerous dinners and parties she attended. These omissions, and any inconsistencies or errors in the footnotes, are purely my own.

Otherwise I have let Maud tell her war story in her own words adding explanatory text when necessary. The entries capture her capacity for observation, sense of humour, worldly outlook and critical judgement. They also reveal strong emotions that were usually concealed by her habitual reserve; a defence mechanism she may have developed as a young woman of German origins in the years leading up to and during the Great War. But behind her defences lay a woman with an insatiable curiosity about life, a lifelong interest in people, a strong intellect and unswerving sense of right and wrong. Above all she was a constant soul; loyal to her friends, true to herself and steadfast with her commitments.

The Principal Characters

FAMILY

Nelke, Maria, née Conrad (1869-1971) 'Mama'. Maud's German mother. Born in Frankfurt, she was the daughter of Carl Conrad, the master of the German mint. Married in 1891 German Jewish stockbroker Paul Nelke (born in Berlin, 1860-1925). She accompanied him to London, where he had been working for some years, to start their married life. Both naturalised British.

FAMILY – *Russells*

Gilbert Russell (1875-1942) 'G.'. Maud's husband. Served with Grenadier Guards in Sudan, Egyptian and South African campaigns, and as an intelligence officer on the front in the First World War. Established successful investment bank Cull & Co with three other partners. Committed family man and liberal. Admired for his wit and good company.

Martin Russell (1918-2003) Maud's eldest son. During the Second World War served under Duff Cooper at the Ministry of Information and then in Singapore, before being evacuated to Sri Lanka where he worked as a cypher clerk. Amassed an important collection of Sri Lankan art focused on the painter George Keyt. He later became a banker. Absent-minded and shy.

Raymond Russell (1922-64) Maud's youngest son. Studies in history and music at Cambridge interrupted by Second World War. Conscientious objector. Eventually served with the Royal Fusiliers. Studied the harpsichord. His many collections included keyboard instruments, surgical instruments, Maltese coins and antiquarian books on music. Sensitive, he fiercely guarded his privacy. Author of *The Harpsichord and Clavicord: an Introductory Study* (1959).

Conrad Russell (1878-1947) Gilbert's favourite sibling. After working in the Colonial Office and on Wall Street, withdrew to Somerset to farm in 1927.

Avid naturalist, amateur philosopher, prolific correspondent. Intimate but apparently chaste friendship with Lady Diana Cooper. Also an admirer of Katherine Asquith and Daphne Fielding.

Sir Claud Russell (1871-1959) Gilbert's brother. Diplomat. Ambassador to Portugal 1931-35. Married Athenaïs Atchley 1920. First class brains, governed by reason, self-sufficient.

Athenaïs Russell, née Atchley 'Ath'. Daughter of Shirley Clifford Atchley OBE. Married to Gilbert's brother Claud. Prolific producer of tapestry cushion covers.

Diana Russell (1874-1971) Gilbert's sister. Like her sister Flora, she never married. Her mother Lady Arthur Russell apparently scared off potential suitors. Skilled needlewoman. Unpretentious. Maud's favourite sister-in-law.

Flora Russell (1869-1967) Gilbert's sister. A talented water colourist, keen bird watcher and botanist.

FAMILY – *Apponyis*

Kate Apponyi, née Nelke (1893-1977) 'Kitty'. Maud's younger sister. At 18, married Hungarian count, Anton Apponyi, living first on the Apponyis' estates in Hungary, then Vienna and finally in Ouchy, Switzerland. Adored horse racing and everything to do with horses. Worked at Red Cross in Geneva during the Second World War. Three children: Mary, Tony and Alexie.

Count Anton Apponyi (1883-1954) 'Tony'. Maud's brother-in-law, married Kitty in 1912. Described himself as a 'sportsman' when asked his profession. Moved among central European aristocratic circles. He was unable to maintain his extravagant lifestyle and was financially supported by his wife and her family.

Alexandrine Apponyi (1919-) 'Alexie'. Maud's niece, daughter of Kitty and Tony. Aged four, sent to live in England with Maud and Gilbert who thought of her as a daughter. She stayed with them for four years and for prolonged periods thereafter until her marriage in 1939 to Julius Lanzcy, unbeknown to her a Hungarian spy. She yearned to break-out of the confines of her upbringing. Later married the art critic John Russell and finally Andreas Mayor, an ancient manuscripts expert.

Mary Irby, née Apponyi (1913-52) Maud's niece, daughter of Kitty and Tony. Lived with Maud and Gilbert while doing the 'London season'. Married Anthony Irby 1934. Three children: Paul, Peter and Charles.

Anthony Irby (1908-86) Married to Maud's niece, Mary Apponyi. Lawyer. During the Second World War, served in the London Rifle Brigade, and the Special Operations Executive. On the Allied Commission (Military Government) in Rome and Vienna. After war, became a Parliamentary Counsel.

Anton Apponyi, (1915-2003) 'Little Tony' or 'Tony'. Maud's nephew, son of Kitty and Tony. Worked at Shell for many years, then moved to Mexico where he loved to entertain visitors with tales of Austria and Hungary. Deeply interested in history, an ace at backgammon. In 1941, married Sally Brooks (died 1991), a devoted mother and grandmother.

GERMAN JEWISH RELATIONS

Agnes Mühsam, née Nelke (1866-c.1943) 'Tante Agnes'. Maud's aunt who lived in Berlin. Married Jacques Mühsam (1857-1930), a highly successful Berlin cotton fabric manufacturer. His collection of glass – considered one of the world's finest – is held in the Chicago Art Institute and the Metropolitan Museum of Art in New York. Three children: Ilse, Lieselotte and Hans Werner.

Lieselotte Margolin, née Mühsam (1896-c.1941) Maud's cousin, daughter of Agnes Mühsam. Doctor. A Communist, she worked as a medic for the Workers' Party of Marxist Unification in Barcelona during the Spanish Civil War. Separated from her husband, also a doctor, Ilya Margolin.

Ilse Namenyi, née Mühsam, (1899-1994) Maud's cousin, daughter of Agnes Mühsam. Married first an economist Nathan Bennathan, secondly in 1937 a Hungarian art historian Enrö Namenyi with whom she lived in Budapest.

Hans Werner Mühsam (1903-45) Maud's cousin, son of Agnes Mühsam. Living in Berlin, Hans Werner was a man about town who dabbled in journalism.

Friederike Franck, née Nelke (1864-1945) 'Tante Fritze'. Maud's aunt who lived in Bonn. Her husband Johannes Franck (1854-1914), also born Jewish, was Professor of Germanic Languages at Bonn University. They raised their four children, Hilde, Lisel, Otto and Lotte, as Christians.

Hildegard Lubelska, née Franck (1892-1945) 'Hilde'. Maud's cousin who lived in Bonn, daughter of Friederike Franck. Divorced from the Jewish-born Polish sculptor Mieczyslaw Lubelski, who converted to Roman Catholicism as a young man. Two children: Urla and Jan.

Elizabeth Müller, née Franck (1894-1984) 'Lisel'. Maud's cousin who lived in Berlin, daughter of Friederike Franck. Art historian. Lisel's husband was an up and coming Egyptologist, Hans Wolfgang Müller (1907-91). Owing to Lisel's Jewish background, in 1937 Hans Wolfgang was threatened with dismissal from his post at Berlin's Egyptian Museum and they came to an amicable agreement to end the marriage. They had one son, Peter.

Otto Franck (1895-c.1945) Maud's cousin, son of Friederike Franck. Professor of Serbo-Croatian. Awarded Iron Cross for bravery in the First World War. Left Germany in late 1930s to work in Skopje, Macedonia as a teacher, similar posts being barred to Jews in Germany.

Lotte Franke (1902-83) Maud's cousin who lived in Bonn, daughter of Friederike Franck. She lived at home and looked after her mother. Maud described her as a 'very kind and very good person'. Devoted to her family and garden.

Ursula Lubelska (1919-98) 'Urla'. Daughter of Maud's cousin Hilde Lubelska. Came to England as an au pair in 1937. Married Polish architect Czeslaw Podleski 1943 and they spent their honeymoon at Mottisfont. Worked as a Polish and German translator for BBC after war and later as a legal advisor for local government.

Jan Lubelski (1922-95) Son of Maud's cousin Hilde Lubelska. Sculptor and art teacher, studied at Slade. Joined the Polish airforce at aged 17, serving as a navigator and translator. Suffered persecution at the hands of the Nazis as a teenager in Bonn and post-traumatic stress disorder after the war, leading to mental health problems for much of his life.

Czeslaw Podleski (1913-97) 'Utek'. Married Maud's cousin Urla. Architect. Served in France with the Polish army in exile during the Second World War, winning the country's highest military decoration, the Virtuti Militari.

Peter Müller (1936-2014) Son of Maud's cousin Lisel. Maud funded his education at Gordonstoun School. Investment banker and corporate treasurer.

Alexander Schönberg (1892-1985) Maud's cousin, the son of Paul Nelke's third sister Dorothea. Chemist. Due to rising anti-Semitism, Alexander left Germany in the early 1930s accepting a post as Visiting Professor at Edinburgh University and then a permanent job in Cairo. He advised his mother, Dorothea, to leave Germany at the same time and she went to live in Zurich, Switzerland.

FRIENDS

Aberconways See Henry McLaren, 2nd Baron Aberconway, and his wife Christabel, née Macnaghten.

Anrep, Boris (1883-1969) 'B.'. Russian artist dedicated to mosaics. Maud's lover from the mid-1940s until his death, his expressiveness warmed up her life. The mosaics at the National Gallery, Bank of England and Westminster Cathedral were among his most important commissions.

Asquith, Margaret, née Tennant, Countess of Oxford (1864-1945) 'Margot'. Political hostess and diarist. Married H.H. Asquith as his second wife in 1894. Her direct nature and high-handedness drew criticism but she was loved by Maud.

Astor, Alice Muriel (1902-56) American heiress and socialite. Kind to her friends, a nuisance to her four husbands, eccentric and with a will of iron, according to Maud.

Beaton, Sir Cecil (1904-80) Photographer and stage designer. A 'bright, young thing' and Maud's friend from the 1930s onwards. 'Lively, bright and funny.'

Bell, Clive (1881-1964) Art critic and writer, one of the founders of the Bloomsbury Group. An early connoisseur of modern French art, Clive was an important influence on Maud's own collection. He regarded her as 'mysterious'. Married in 1907 Vanessa Stephen (Virginia Woolf's sister).

Bonham Carters See Violet and Sir Maurice 'Bongie' Bonham Carter – close friends of Maud and Gilbert's.

Bonham Carter, Sir Maurice (1880-1960) 'Bongie'. Liberal politician and civil servant. PPS to H.H. Asquith 1910-16. Married Asquith's daughter, Violet, in 1915. Maud was very attached to Bongie and admired his good nature. Loved to fish at Mottisfont.

Bonham Carter, Violet, later Baroness Asquith of Yarnbury (1887-1969) Liberal politician, created Life Peer 1964. Daughter Prime Minister H.H. Asquith. Married Maurice Bonham Carter, her father's private secretary, in 1915. Unflinching champion of her father's political legacy. Russells' friend from early married days. 'Very brilliant and swift in thought and speech,' according to Maud, but unable to hide boredom in dull company.

Campbell-Gray, Lieutenant-Colonel Sir Ian (1901-46) 'I.C.-G.'. Served Royal Engineers. Fencer, amateur painter. Maud's close friend. Married Diana Cavendish 1942.

Churchill, Randolph (1911-68) Writer and politician. Conservative MP 1940-45. Son of Winston Churchill. 'I was fond of him but a little went a long way,' Maud wrote in 1968. 'He was boisterous, argumentative, quarrelsome and a trial.'

Clark, Sir Kenneth Clark (1903-83) Art historian, museum director, author and broadcaster, best known for BBC television series *Civilization*. Made life peer in 1969. Married Elizabeth ('Jane') Martin 1927, a fellow student at Oxford.

Cochrane-Baillie, Harriette, Lady Lamington, née Neilson (1897-1968) 'Riette'. Patron of young musicians. Emotional and passionate. 'There was nothing she wouldn't do for people she liked – especially her protegées,' according to Maud.

Colefax, Lady Sibyl (1874-1950) Society hostess and interior decorator. During the Second World War she held lunches and dinners at the Dorchester known as 'Ordinaries' with each guest paying for their own meal. Maud admired her for her liberal outlook and zest for life 'in all its finest forms'.

Connolly, Cyril (1903-74) Literary critic and writer. Cofounder and editor of literary magazine *Horizon*. From 1950 until his death, chief literary critic *Sunday Times*. 'Enormously lively and amusing', according to Maud.

Coopers See Duff and Lady Diana Cooper. Maud and Gilbert loved the Coopers' company and saw them frequently in the 1930s and early 1940s.

Cooper, Duff, later 1st Viscount Norwich (1890-1954) Politician, diplomat and author. Part of Winston Churchill's inner circle in the 1930s. Outspoken opponent of Chamberlain's appeasement policy. According to Maud, Gilbert's wit sparkled in Duff's playful company. Married in 1919 Lady Diana Manners.

Cooper, Lady Diana, née Manners (1892-1986) A beauty and leading light of the Coterie, an influential group of young aristocrats and intellectuals. Intimate friend of Gilbert's brother Conrad Russell. Married Duff Cooper 1919.

Courtauld, Samuel (1876-1947) 'Sam'. Industrialist and art patron, building up Britain's finest collection of French impressionist painting in the 1920s. He was unusual and unlike a rich man with a liberal and a moral outlook, according to Maud. Founded the Courtauld Institute of Art in 1932. Trustee of Tate 1927-37 and of National Gallery 1931-47. Principal sponsor of Boris Anrep's first three mosaic pavements at the National Gallery.

Fleming, Ian (1908-64) 'I.'. Author, journalist and naval intelligence officer, best known for his James Bond series of spy novels. Maud's intimate friend and probable lover. Charismatic personality and dark good looks.

Glenconner, Christopher, 2nd Baron Glenconner (1899-1983). The son of Edward Tennant, 1st Baron Glenconner, and Pamela Wyndham, Christopher became heir to the Glenconner title after his older brother, Edward 'Bim' Tennant, died in the First World War. Actively managed family business and responsible family man. Liaised with Norwegians on behalf of Ministry of Economic Warfare 1939-40, head of the Cairo office of special operations in 1942-43. Family seat at Glen House in Scotland. Close friends with Maud.

Glenconner, Elizabeth, née Powell Married Christopher Glenconner in 1935. Elizabeth, and her sister Anne (married names Toynbee and then Wollheim), were Maud's closest female friends in her later years.

Harvey, Oliver, later first Baron Harvey of Tasburgh (1893-1968) Diplomat. Private Secretary to Lord Halifax, Secretary of State for Foreign Affairs

1938-40. Minister to Paris 1940. Assistant Undersecretary Foreign Affairs 1943-46. Ambassador to France 1948-54.

Henley, Hon. Sylvia, née Stanley (1882-1980) Daughter of Edward Stanley, 4th Baron Sheffield and Mary Bell. Childhood friend of Gilbert's. Sister to Venetia Montagu. Married in 1906 Brigadier-General Hon. Anthony Henley (d.1925).

Herbert, Lady Beatrice, née Paget (1883-1973) 'Bee'. Daughter of 6th Marquess of Anglesey, married to Reginald Herbert, 15th Earl of Pembroke, owners of Wilton House, Wiltshire. Beatrice was the aunt of Caroline Paget, Rex Whistler's beloved.

Herbert, David (1908-95) Second son of Reginald Herbert and Lady Beatrice Paget. Socialite, memoirist and interior designer. Openly gay in 1930s/40s, settling in Tangier, Morocco after the war where he is remembered for his lavish parties and flamboyant personality.

Herbert, Reginald, 15th Earl of Pembroke and 12th Earl of Montgomery (1880-1960) 'Reggie'. Married Lady Beatrice ('Bee') Paget 1904. Family seat at Wilton House, Wiltshire.

Hill, Derek (1916-2000) Portrait and landscape painter. In the late 1990s, he left a substantial modern art collection to Mottisfont as a tribute to his friendship with Maud.

Janzé, Phyllis de, née Boyd (1894-1943) Married and later divorced Vicomte Henri de Janzé. Socialite. The long-term mistress of Conservative MP Hubert Duggan. Childhood friend of Maud's.

Johnstone, Harcourt (1895-1945) 'Crinks'. Liberal politician. Secretary of Department of Overseas Trade 1940-45. Maud's friend from early married days. Extravagant, generous and old-fashioned.

Lazzerini, Adele Claudia (1894-1975) Maud's lady's maid. Born in Florence, Adele began working for Maria Nelke before Maud's marriage. At Mottisfont she was referred to as 'Mademoiselle' by estate staff and villagers alike. A child evacuee, John Clark, remembers her 'running the place' during the war when Maud was working at the Admiralty. Often visited by the family when she retired to Hazel Cottage on the estate.

Lyttelton, Oliver, later 1st Viscount Chandos (1893-1972) Businessman and Conservative politician. Brought into government in the Second World War as President Board of Trade, Minister Middle East, and Minister Production. Old friend of Maud's – she attended his mother Edith Lyttelton's school on Great College Street. Despite his gruff manner, Maud found him kind-hearted. Married to Lady Moira Osborne (1892-1976).

McLaren, Christabel, née Macnaghten (1890-1974) Hostess and art patron. Married Henry McLaren, 2nd Baron Aberconway 1910. Close friends with Samuel Courtauld. Maud was godmother to Christabel's youngest son Christopher.

McLaren, Henry, 2nd Baron Aberconway (1879-1953) 'Harry'. Industrialist and horticulturist who developed the gardens at the family estate in Bodnant, north Wales, now a National Trust property. Married to Christabel. Maud took her gardener George Buckell to Bodnant to examine the garden.

Montagu, Lionel (1883-1948) 'Cardie'.The politician Edwin Montagu's youngest brother (and through him Venetia Montagu's brother-in-law). A regular guest in Gilbert's lifetime. Enjoyed high-living.

Montagu, Venetia, née Stanley (1887-1948) Friend of Gilbert's from childhood. Much to his surprise, she converted to Judaism in 1915 to marry the politician Edwin Montagu (1879-1924). Confidante of H.H. Asquith, the Liberal prime minister 1908-15. Sylvia Henley's sister. She was very intelligent, cheated at cards and was 'harsh, direct and outspoken', according to Maud.

Mortimer, Raymond (1895-1980) British writer, art critic and literary editor of New Statesman 1935-47. According to the art historian Richard Shone, Mortimer set up the commission for Matisse to draw Maud's portrait. In 1958 Maud and Raymond spent five weeks travelling together to Beirut, Jerusalem, Tehran and Persepolis.

Nicolson, Sir Harold (1886-1968) Diplomat and writer. Married writer and gardener Vita Sackville-West 1913, with whom he had an open marriage with infidelities, often same-sex, on both sides. Together they created the famous gardens at Sissinghurst. Maud was also friends with their children, Nigel and Ben, the former asking Maud's advice in 1968 about the suitability of publishing Vita's account of her affair with Violet Trefusis.

Pembrokes See Reginald Herbert, 15th Earl of Pembroke and 12th Earl of Montgomery, his wife Lady Beatrice and their son David. Family seat at Wilton House, Wiltshire and the Russells' neighbours.

Cathleen Queensberry, Marchioness of (1896-1959) *née* Mann, Portrait painter and costume designer. Painted portrait of Gilbert in 1934. Maud admired her 'spiritedness and courage'.

Quennell, Sir Peter (1905-93) Biographer, literary historian, editor, critic. Friend from the 1940s.

Rothschild, Baron Philippe de (1902-88) Member of Rothschild banking dynasty. Grand Prix race-car driver, celebrated winegrower at Chateau Mouton Rothschild. Joined Free French forces in London.

Russell, John (1919-2008) 'New John Russell'. Highly influential art critic first at the *Sunday Times* from 1945 (thanks to an introduction from Ian Fleming) and then from 1974 at the *New York Times*. Worked in Naval Intelligence 1943-46. Married first Alexie Apponyi, Maud's niece, remaining lifelong friends with Maud and becoming her literary executor.

Sackville-West, Edward, later 5th Baron Sackville (1901-65) 'Eddy.' Influential music critic and novelist. Good friend of Maud's. From 1945, lived at Long Crichel in Dorset with Desmond Shawe-Taylor, Eardley Knollys and later Raymond Mortimer and Derek Hill, establishing in effect a male salon.

Sinclair, Archibald, later 1st Viscount Thurso (1890-1970) 'Archie'. Liberal MP 1922-45. Secretary of State for Air 1940-45. A friend from her youth, Maud much admired his good looks.

Spender, Sir Stephen (1909-95) Poet, novelist and essayist. Co-founded *Horizon* magazine with Cyril Connolly and Peter Watson (editor 1939-41). Friend from 1940s onwards, frequent guest.

Tennant, Christopher and Elizabeth (see Glenconner).

Tennyson, Clarissa, née Tennant (1896-1960). 'Clare.' Socialite. Known for her beauty, temper and succession of marriages. Daughter of Edward Tennant, 1st Baron Glenconner and Pamela Wyndham. Sister of Christopher

Glenconner, niece of Margot Asquith. Close friends with Maud until the late 1940s.

Vansittart, Robert, later 1st Baron Vansittart (1881-1957) 'Van'. Diplomat and civil servant. Permanent Under-Secretary for Foreign Affairs 1930-38, then chief diplomatic adviser to the government and adviser to Hugh Dalton, the head of the Special Operations Executive. Outspoken opponent on appeasement. Childhood friend of Maud's.

Volkova, Mariya (c.1900-56) 'Maroussia'. Boris Anrep's common law wife (or as Boris disingenuously told Maud in a 1936 letter 'my sister-in-law who lives with me'). The relationship began in 1917 when Boris chaperoned Maroussia, the sister of his brother Gleb's wife, to England from Russia. She moved in with Boris and his wife Helen Maitland and continued to live with him after Helen left Boris for Roger Fry.

Whistler, Rex (1905-44) Artist, designer and illustrator. His murals at the Tate Gallery in 1927 drew critical acclaim and launched a promising career. Maud commissioned him in 1938 to embellish the drawing room at Mottisfont in a 'modern gothic' style.

ONE

The Whistler Room at Mottisfont Abbey

NOVEMBER 1938 – NOVEMBER 1939

In which war approaches.
Maud seeks visas for German Jewish relatives;
she visits Matisse in Paris;
and Rex Whistler transforms the 'big room' at Mottisfont.

It is late 1938 and German aggression under Adolf Hitler is casting a shadow of fear over Europe. In March, Germany had taken control of Austria and at the end of September, the British prime minister, Neville Chamberlain, together with the German, French and Italian leaders, had signed the Munich Agreement under which a large area along Czechoslovakia's border, inhabited mainly by ethnic Germans, was handed over to Germany. Many people welcomed the agreement for appearing to avert war in Europe, but there were also vocal critics of the British government's policy of appeasement. Hitler is audaciously advancing across Europe without using military force and reports are increasing of persecution of Jews in Germany.

These events are particularly complex and worrying for Maud and Gilbert Russell. Quite apart from Maud's German heritage, she has two Jewish aunts and cousins on her father's side living in Germany (see family tree). To further complicate things, her sister Kitty is living in a hotel in Budapest with her Hungarian husband Tony, having fled their home in Vienna at the time of Germany's annexation of Austria. Hungary was an ally of Germany in the First World War.

Maud's diaries open with life continuing largely as normal for her and Gilbert. They divide their time between their London home in Princes Gate, Knightsbridge, and their country estate, Mottisfont Abbey, Hampshire, where they often host large house parties. Among their most frequent guests are Duff and Lady Diana Cooper. A Conservative MP and Cabinet minister, Duff opposes Chamberlain's appeasement policy and resigned from the government the day after the Munich Agreement was signed.

At 63, Gilbert suffers from increasing bad health due to asthma and only occasionally attends the offices in the City of his private banking firm Cull & Co. He is so much part of Maud's life that he is curiously absent from her diaries – it would have been stating the obvious to write that she sees him. Nonetheless, it is evident from later diary entries that he is the pivot around which her life revolves.

Sixteen years his junior, Maud is very active, running to perfection their London and country houses and keeping up a whirl of social engagements. A serious modern art collector, she regularly visits museums and galleries and meets up with artists and literary friends. She enjoys the company of younger men too and regularly sees the future novelist Ian Fleming ('Ian' or just 'I.') and Sir Ian Campbell-Gray ('I.C.-G.'), an aspiring painter.

As war approaches, Maud is overseeing the decoration of the original entrance hall to Mottisfont – or the 'big room' – by a friend, the fashionable artist Rex Whistler. In an earlier diary entry on October 27 she recorded that she went to the London Library to look at books on gothic tapestries to help him with suggestions. She envisions a 'modern Gothic' design to reflect a house which began as a medieval priory and evolved over the centuries into a contemporary home. To achieve this, she wants murals of trophies painted in grisaille, leading to tension with Rex who is inspired by colourful landscapes that she feels are too Georgian in style.

Maud and Gilbert's eldest son, Martin, is in his last year at King's, Cambridge, studying economics. Their 16-year-old son Raymond ran away from Eton in June 1938 and is being privately educated at home with the idea of entering university on an organ scholarship.

<hr />

London, Wednesday November 9, 1938

Spent the morning at 29 Fitzroy Square with Rex looking at drawings and discussing the big room and drinking slivovitz [*plum brandy from central and eastern Europe*] rather carelessly. I like any time spent with Rex.

Mottisfont, Sunday November 13

On Friday [*Remembrance Day*] I was caught by the 11 o'clock maroons[1]

---

1. Church bells ringing prior to the two-minute silence on Remembrance Day which, until 1939, was held on November 11 (when the First World War ended in 1918) and not moved to the nearest Sunday.

outside St Thomas's Hospital on a wonderful morning and sat in a taxi during the silence thinking of the millions of men who were killed in the last war and what a ghastly fate may be awaiting many millions more. Came down here. In the evening William and Lesley Jowitt,[2] Ulick and Cockie,[3] Gerry Wellesley,[4] Hutchy,[5] Guy and Cis Dawnay[6] and Venetia [Montagu] came to stay. We shot in a half gale on Saturday. Randolph [Churchill] arrived and soon there were fierce arguments and an immense amount of nonsense was talked, especially after dinner. I thought again what a mediocre man William J. really is apart from his legal brain. Guy D. talked interestingly about offence and defence and he thought that they all but cancelled each other out. Today Gerry talked slight anti-Jewish stuff after dinner and for once I saw Venetia rather angry and she took him to task. Friday saw terrible organised attacks on the Jews all over Germany.[7]

London, Thursday November 17

I went to the Aliens Department of the Home Office on Wednesday to make inquiries about how to get my aunt Agnes and her son Hans Werner into England. She'd written after the happenings of last Friday [*Kristallnacht*] and implored me to get visas for them. The Aliens Department was, of course, full of aliens. After a wait I saw a Mr Oates, polite and I am sure efficient, whose main business it is to keep as many people as possible out of England. He gave me no encouragement and no help except the address of the secretary of the German Jewish Aid Committee. Today I went to see Miss Stiebel,[8] secretary of the Germany Jewish Aid Committee, and arranged to apply for visas for

2. William Jowitt, later 1st Earl Jowitt (1885-1957), Labour politician and lawyer. Labour Attorney General in 1929 under Ramsay MacDonald, served as Solicitor General and other positions in Winston Churchill's coalition government 1940-45, Lord Chancellor 1945-51 under Clement Atlee. Married in 1913 Lesley McIntyre.
3. Sir Ulick Alexander (1889-1973), Extra Equerry and Keeper of the Privy Purse and Treasury to HM King George VI 1936-52, and his sister Jacqueline Hoogterp, known as 'Cockie' (1892-1988). Childhood friends of Maud's.
4. Gerald Wellesley, later 7th Duke of Wellington (1885-1972), diplomat and architect.
5. St John Hutchinson, 'Hutchy' (1884-1942), barrister and Liberal politician. Art collector.
6. Guy Dawnay (1878-1952), army officer and merchant banker, and his wife Cecil, *neé* Buxton.
7. *Kristallnacht*, a coordinated series of attacks against Jews across Germany and Austria on 9-10 November 1938 by Nazi paramilitary forces and civilians.
8. Joan Stiebel MBE (1911-2007), secretary of the Jewish Refugees Committee, which aided some 85,000 refugees from Germany and central Europe from 1933-45.

the relations and to guarantee their existence here. She promised to send me forms. At 4 o'clock I went to see Rex and stayed two hours discussing the big room. I enjoy seeing him scribble his ideas on paper, holding his pencil so strangely and clutched half way down between his second and third fingers. His pencil drips ideas.

Mottisfont, Monday November 21

Rex came for lunch and for two hours afterwards we stood and sat and talked in the big room, settling first one thing and then another. The colour was the chief preoccupation. R.'s first little sketch had been done in a pinkish-mauve and this colour we tried out and settled on.

London, Thursday November 24

Dined with I.C.-G. [Ian Campbell-Gray] at the Jardin des Gourmets and we went to the Ring at Blackfriars. Saw some all-in wrestling and a match between a sinister looking wrestler and an old, fat, clown-like boxer. The boxer had gloves, of course, and was allowed to box while the wrestler was only allowed to wrestle. So the wrestler waited and took some cuffs and spent a few seconds on the ground. Then he sprang up at the foolish, gaping boxer, twisted him head over heels, and tied him into a neat, painful knot and the match was over amid howls and murmurs of disapproval. The scene at the Ring is delightful and as English as possible in spite of all the foreign – chiefly Jewish and Asiatic – faces in the audience.

Mottisfont, Sunday November 27

Came down here on Friday. Sonia and Rollie Cubitt,[9] Diana and Duff [Cooper], Jasper [Ridley],[10] Crinks [Harcourt Johnstone], Alfred Beit[11] and Viola L.[12] arrived. Duff looks preoccupied. He is very fair about his ex-colleagues – no diatribes. Today everybody was sleepy and after lunch, when

9. Sonia Cubitt, *née* Keppel (1900-86), and Ronald Cubitt, later 3rd Baron Ashcombe (1899-1962). The grandparents of Camilla, Duchess of Cornwall.
10. Jasper Ridley (1887-1951), barrister and banker. Chairman of the Tate Gallery and Trustee of the National Gallery and British Museum.
11. Sir Alfred Beit (1903-94), Conservative politician, philanthropist and art collector.
12. Hon. Viola Lyttelton (1912-87). Married in 1946 Robert Grosvenor, later 5th Duke of Westminster.

Diana had finished asking the *Sunday Express* questions, almost everybody fell asleep, nicely and peacefully, in the darkening room. Duff and Diana sat next to and rather near to each other, upright on the sofa, both asleep. There was something noble and touching about them.

London, Friday December 2

Kitty [*Maud's sister*] and Alexie [*her daughter*] are staying. Kitty is talking of leaving Hungary with the family for good and settling in France or England because anti-Semitism is starting there too. She wants to get little Tony [*Kitty's son*] a job in England. G. [*Gilbert*] has been urging her to do this for years, and now that it's really difficult to get a job for a young foreigner, they are beginning to think it might be a good plan. Today I went to see Miss Stiebel of the German Jewish Aid Committee and made a visa application for my cousin Lisel Müller and her baby and gave the guarantee. Had an impression the organisation was being haphazardly and inefficiently run though Miss S. is niceness itself. Ilse Namenyi came to lunch. She is a half first cousin, Tante Agnes's daughter, and married to a Hungarian Jew. She'd just been to Berlin to see her mother. My cousin Hans Werner does not dare sleep in his own flat for fear of being carried off – or worse – in the night. He cannot sleep at his mother's because she has an 'Aryan' maid who is under 60, or whatever the age is that it's considered safe by the Nazis for a Jew to sleep in the same flat as a Christian.[13] So he spends the night with different friends, one lot being 'Aryan' women, who give him shelter.

Cologne, Saturday December 3

I flew to Cologne, leaving Croydon at 12 in a Belgian Sabena aeroplane. Only one passenger to Brussels besides myself. Stopped at Brussels for 20 minutes. Then on, this time alone, into Germany. Weather by then not good and we came down in sheets of rain and a high wind. Was helped out by a robust friendly young porter who made me think: well, after all, Germany isn't peopled with Goebbels and Hitlers. I had arrived on the day when all Jews in Germany were ordered to stay indoors between 8am and 8pm so I wondered whether my appearance might arouse comment, but it didn't.

After a quick tea I hired a car and drove out to Bonn, Hindenburg Strasse

---

13. The 1935 Nuremberg Race Laws deprived Jews of German citizenship, prohibited Jewish households from employing non-Jewish maids under the age of 45, and outlawed marriage or sexual relations between Jews and people of 'German or related blood'.

138, where my cousin Hilde Lubelska lives with her son Jan. She'd changed a great deal since last year and looked old and ill. She told me how anxious they were and that no one ever knew what was going to happen. Her mother Tante Fritze had not been bothered. No official had been to her house, nor had her pension been stopped. But they were all the time expecting something to happen. She herself had been called on by a police official who'd asked to see the passport of the 'Jewish Lubelska'. She'd retorted, with spirit, that the Nuremberg laws didn't apply to Poland, that she was Polish and her name was Lubelska, but that the words 'Jewish Lubelska' had no application to her. He said: 'Well, as a matter of fact I don't know much about the Nuremberg laws.' Whereupon she said, 'Well, you ought to. You have to carry them out and they are the alpha and omega of the National Socialist Party,' to which he answered: 'I don't bother my head much about the National Socialist Party either. You see I haven't got many children. But I have one son, so I thought it better to join the party and I did so in 1937.' Hilde says this phlegmatic attitude is characteristic of the Rhinelanders. They are good-natured but not very intelligent. Hilde's position is difficult. She has a Polish passport – which is lucky – but is divorced from a Polish sculptor who lives in Warsaw. If she leaves Germany she has to leave all her money behind. The sculptor isn't well-off and she hates the thought of depending on him.

We went on to Tante Fritze's – Endernicher Allee 14. She was perfectly alert and made one or two of her little dry jokes. I told her that she'd only to let me know and I would make arrangements for her to come to England. We looked at each other and she thanked me deeply but not with outward signs of emotion. Her two daughters [*Hilde and Lotte*] stood round and the moment was solemn. In the past during any of those many periods of crisis in Jewish history there must generally have been a relation, more fortunately placed than the others, who came forward and helped. I don't feel any more Jewish than I did – and I never do much – but I feel a duty, an obligation laid on me, to help and to leave no stone unturned.

The relations told me a story. An SS detachment went to a neighbouring small town and said to the Burgomaster, 'We have come to help you clean up your Jews.' Whereupon the Burgomaster thanked them, but said he looked forward to the pleasure of doing so himself. So they left and the Burgomaster had saved his Jews. A printed notice was glued on the swing door of my hotel saying: 'Juden Unerwünscht' [*'Jews unwelcome'*]. This seemed the stock phrase and I saw it on the door of every hotel or café my eye lit on.

Mottisfont, Monday December 12

Went to see Rex at 11.30 on Friday to settle about the painting of the door of the big room. I don't want him to cramp the decoration. I don't want narrow, pinched effects. But I daresay I shall get them. Then to Mottisfont. The Lytteltons [Oliver and Moira], Glenconners [Christopher and Elizabeth], Alexie [*niece*], Mark Howard,[14] Martin [*son*], Catherine Sinclair,[15] Ian [Fleming] and John Follett[16] arrived. Ian with a bad cold and simply wanting to have a quiet few days in the country. On Saturday we shot. Sir Joseph Ball[17] extra gun. His job is interesting. Home National govt propaganda and research into possible line of new Conservative Party legislation. He is an undistinguished sort of man but shrewd, pleasant and open-minded. At present he is investigating the possibilities of family allowances. The totalitarian states have already got them. I fancy we ought to take a good many leaves out of their book and quickly too.

Mottisfont, Wednesday December 14

Rex was expected on Tuesday morning to choose the colour for the big room by daylight but he didn't arrive till the early afternoon, so I made him stay on for the night to be able to see the colour again in the morning. He is often tiresome where appointments are concerned and rather inconsiderate. To be certain he is going to get the plan he has promised by the promised day one has to telephone, write or badger him, in fact not lose sight of him. Otherwise he doesn't do anything but takes Caroline[18] out the day he has arranged to come. If one can pin him down he works very quickly and his ideas flow all the time.

London, Saturday December 17

Kitty and Alexie lunched early and left for Hungary. They are thinking of

14. Mark Howard (1918-44), killed in action in the Second World War. Son of Maud and Gilbert's friend Geoffrey Howard of Castle Howard and his second wife Ethel Methuen.
15. Catherine Sinclair (1919-2007), daughter of Maud and Gilbert's friend Archibald ('Archie') Sinclair, 1st Viscount Thurso (1890-1970).
16. John Robert Follett (1906-53), racehorse owner who married the painter Cathleen Mann in 1946.
17. Sir Joseph Ball (1885-1961), intelligence officer and political administrator. Served in MI5 from 1915-27, then ran sometimes shady propaganda operations for the Conservative Party. A Chamberlain ally.
18. Lady Caroline Paget (1913-73), socialite and minor actress. Rex's love for Caroline was unrequited, causing him much unhappiness during the period he worked on the room at Mottisfont.

leaving that country, certainly temporarily, perhaps for good, because it's becoming anti-Jewish and has come within the Nazi orbit.

London, Tuesday December 20

Went to the Antique Art Galleries with I.C.-G., who helped me buy a Xmas present for Cecil Beaton to whom I felt I had behaved badly and wanted to placate. It took the form of a bare china leg, perhaps Dresden, with a cameo as a finish to the thigh – eighteenth century surrealism.

London, Thursday December 22

This morning I had a letter from Van [Robert Vansittart]. I telephoned him 10 days ago and asked his kind offices in putting pressure on the Home Office for granting visas to Tante Agnes, Hans Werner, and Lisel Müller and her child, for whom I had made applications and given guarantees a fortnight earlier. This letter said that he'd had an interview with the person concerned and was assured that the visas had been granted. I am now going to make further applications for Tante Fritze and Lotte as Tante F. is determined they must leave. I don't believe she will ever get here. She is too fragile.

Mottisfont, Sunday December 25

There was snow on the ground and the nursery-garden was frozen. After tea yesterday we had a small Xmas tree for Mary's little boy [*her niece Mary Irby and son Paul*] and there was present giving. I had plenty of records – flamenco, Beethoven's 8th Symphony and the whole of Don Giovanni. Today, Christmas Day, missed church, through muddling the hour. We talked and tried – and failed mostly – to do *The Times* Xmas general knowledge questions.

London, Wednesday December 28

I filled the morning industriously with a manicure, a pedicure, a hair-wash, and a trying on of hats before lunch. Then lunched with I. [Ian Fleming] at Boulestin's and he told me about his dallying flirtation with Loelia Westminster[19] and again about Muriel [Wright][20] and from there on to

19. Loelia Grosvenor, *née* Ponsonby (1902-93), in 1930 married Hugh Grosvenor, 2nd Duke of Westminster. A 'Bright Young Thing', needlewoman and magazine editor.
20. Muriel Wright (1909-44), with whom Ian Fleming had a long-term relationship.

odder topics.[21] Van and Sarita [*Van's wife Sarah Ward*] dined. I hadn't seen him since the spring and thought he looked older and heavier. He is very bitter, disgruntled and in despair about the PM's [*prime minister Neville Chamberlain*] past and present policy. He feels very unhappy about England's position in the world and that we are behaving as if we were a second-rate power. He can't get over the loss of such a valuable ally as Czecho. He was <u>very</u> pessimistic. 1939 he thought would be an anxious year but 1940 the critical year.

On December 30, Maud and Gilbert boarded the P&O liner Stratheden *at Marseilles, bound for Sri Lanka, or Ceylon as it was then called, stopping off at Port Sudan and Bombay. Maud's lady's maid Adele Lazzerini travelled with them. They spent six weeks in Sri Lanka. 'We are both very happy on this journey and have plenty of jokes and fun,'[22] Maud wrote. Gilbert's health improved 'beyond all recognition' and he walked 'more easily than he had in five or six years.'*

During the trip Maud kept a close eye on progress to bring her Jewish relatives to England, noting that Lisel Müller and her son Peter left Germany in the third week of February. She was also in touch with Dr Ilya Margolin, the separated husband of Lieselotte, another German Jewish first cousin, who was in prison in Barcelona for taking part in Trotskyist activities while working as a doctor there.

Colombo Sunday February 19

I had a wire from Dr Margolin to whom I had telegraphed for news of Lieselotte M., who has been in prison or in a concentration camp, saying that there was no news of her since the fall of Barcelona.[23] I am afraid she may have been shot. She was imprisoned nearly two years ago by the Spanish government for being a Trotskyist. She was a doctor, working in a hospital in Barcelona. The staff, mostly Trotskyists, were arrested and several of them shot. No charge was preferred against her but she was told she would be kept under supervision till she could leave the country. As her German passport had meanwhile expired and she was 'non Aryan' there was no possibility of her leaving; and she remained on miserably in prison or in a concentration

21. I think the 'odder topics' are likely to refer to sex and possibly their own relationship.
22. Russell, unpublished diaries, January 31, 1939.
23. The Spanish Nationalist army captured Republican-held Barcelona on January 26, 1939 in the Spanish Civil War.

camp. I first heard of all this, *en passant*, in October. In December, I think, her mother Tante Agnes first wrote to me about her. I was not able to do anything then as I was trying to get visas for six German relations through Van and couldn't bother him further at that moment. As well as that, though one or two of the relations wrote to me and talked to me about her, they never told me the whole truth, for fear perhaps, of antagonising me. The night before I left, having collected more facts, I told the solicitor Mr Pollock what I knew and asked him to act for me. Very quickly, all in one breath, he said he couldn't do anything and talked about the standing of his firm, that they were solicitors of the Bank of England and that he did not feel justified in mixing them up in any political matters. His attitude was dreadfully orthodox and not very edifying. The next day we left. On the ship I wracked my brains about who to turn to and finally decided on Hutchy to whom I wrote at length. Eventually his answer came. He had consulted Sir Stafford Cripps[24] who had recommended a solicitor – Thompson – as the right man. But in the meantime Barcelona had fallen. She may be alive but the chances seem slender. She and Dr Margolin were divorced 12 or 14 years ago but he seems to have been doing all he can to rescue her. I think these months are enormously significant and interesting but I wish I was living on another planet.

On March 1, Maud and Gilbert left Sri Lanka for home via Egypt where Maud met with another German Jewish cousin Alexander Schönberg, a chemist working at the University of Cairo, and talked about their relations.

On March 15, Germany marched into Czechoslovakia, meeting little resistance.

Assouan, Sunday March 19

Czecho-Slovakia no longer exists. The Germans carried out their plans without a hitch. They have committed a crime. I suppose the rest of Europe knows now exactly where it stands vis-a-vis Germany – and Mussolini too. We listened in one night to Mr Chamberlain's Birmingham speech. It had a new note in it. The days are very anxious. I feel miserable because I now think war a certainty – this year or next. The massacring of

---

24. Sir Richard Stafford Cripps (1889-1952), lawyer and Labour MP. Ambassador to Soviet Union and Minister of Aircraft Production in Churchill's coalition government. President of Board of Trade and Chancellor of Exchequer in Clement Attlee's post-war government, laying foundation of Britain's economic prosperity.

each other by blameless, ordinary common people makes me ill to think of. But German predominance in the world makes me ill to think of too. The issues seem clear: pacifism and subservience to Germany, or war, its horrors and risks.

London, Wednesday March 29

We arrived home today. Diana R. [Russell, *Gilbert's sister*] came to tea and told us that Herbrand[25] and Tavistock[26] [*Duke of Bedford and his son*] broke the family entail four years ago because they disliked the way Ian H.[27] [*Tavistock's son*] was shaping up. I said I thought it monstrous to judge a boy so severely at 18. Trustees have been appointed and can give – for life, I imagine – Woburn and the vast income to any member of the family, including Ian. Ian is now engaged to a woman of 35 called Mrs Hollway.[28] She is said to be very ordinary in every way. The family are appalled and are, of course, overdoing the conventional attitude and prudish aversion.

London, Friday March 31

Just before lunch I went to see Archie Sinclair to ask his help and influence for my cousin Lieselotte who is still in Barcelona. He listened attentively, showed complete indifference to her political complexion and couldn't have been nicer. The European situation is very black. I just don't see how we can escape war. Although I view it with horror, and look on it as a limitless calamity, I feel almost resigned; or perhaps this is simply fatalism.

Mottisfont, Saturday April 1

Today Rex came to tea. His two workmen, after 13 weeks' constant work, haven't done more than half the big room and Rex has hardly touched it. He complains of the slowness but is partly to blame because if he was on the spot

---

25. Herbrand Arthur Russell (1858-1940), 11th Duke of Bedford and Gilbert's first cousin. Agriculturist and philanthropist.
26. Hastings William Sackville Russell (1888-1953), Herbrand's heir and future 12th Duke of Bedford. Evangelical Christian and pacifist.
27. Ian Russell (1917-2002), Hastings' eldest son and future 13th Duke of Bedford. Styled Lord Howland. Landowner and writer. Opened Woburn Abbey to the public. In later life Maud became good friends with Ian and his third wife, the French film producer Nicole Milinaire.
28. Clare Hollway, *née* Bridgeman (1903-45). She tragically died of a drug overdose.

and working himself he could supervise, criticise and speed up his painters. As it is, he hasn't been here more than four or five times since we left.

On April 7, Italy occupied Albania.

Mottisfont, Friday April 7

I don't remember which day it was we listened to the BBC's résumé of Hitler's speech – perhaps the 1st – but when we heard Hitler had mentioned the next Nuremberg Congress [*the annual Nazi rally*] as a 'Peace Congress', we had a moment's delirious joy. The reports in the next morning's papers brought us to earth again. Kitty, Tony, Alexie, little Tony, Mary, Anthony [Irby], Paul and Mama are staying. We listened in to all the broadcasts on the landing of Italian troops in Albania. They have broken the Anglo Italian treaty. Who can pretend they haven't? Little Tony, thanks to Gilbert, has got a job here with Shell, and I have received a charming letter from Archie about Lieselotte. He is approaching Sir Samuel Hoare.[29]

Mottisfont, Tuesday April 11

Kitty and I drove to Stewart's nursery garden on Sunday where I bought a cedar. I tried to discuss with her plans in case of war, and whether she'd made any financial arrangements in Hungary for some friend to lend her money in case Eng. and Hung. were enemies, and she couldn't get her income from England. I couldn't get her to talk seriously about it. She became obstinate and angry and talked like a child. Today the Lindleys[30] came to tea. Frank L. would leave Eastern Europe and the Balkans to anybody who wanted them. I suggested it might be unwise to disassociate ourselves from an interest in the fate of Greece and Turkey. Tony and I couldn't resist asking him about the Japanese menace. He was ambassador in Tokyo and is said to have encouraged Japanese aggression.

Following Hitler's occupation of Czechoslovakia, Britain and France had pledged military support to Poland should its independence be threatened. After Mussolini's invasion of Albania, the British government provided similar guarantees to Greece and Romania.

29. Sir Samuel Hoare, later 1st Viscount Templewood (1880-1959), Conservative politician, Home Secretary 1937-39. An ally of Chamberlain.
30. Sir Francis Oswald Lindley (1872-1950), diplomat. Ambassador to Japan 1931-34.

Mottisfont, Sunday April 16

On Thursday news of the PM's guarantees to Greece and Romania was on the streets by 4. I motored down here on Friday and arranged for the ARP [*Air Raid Precautions*] room to be made ready and water and food put in it. On Saturday the BBC gave a résumé of Roosevelt's message to Germany and Italy, calling on them to declare they have no intention of aggression during the next 10 years. The longing for peace is like a religion. At night, going to bed, I thought suddenly and acutely of Anthony Irby, who has been sitting quieter than usual thinking, I suppose, of what the next weeks will bring; of Mary who must be sick with fright for him; of Martin who seemed nervous and emotional once or twice tonight and must be wondering what is in store for him and us; of little Tony just starting a new job in London and who may be called up in Hungary any time and parted from peace. And so I groaned.

Mottisfont, Sunday April 23

Last Wednesday I motored to Oxford to see my cousin Lisel Müller and her little boy who are staying with her friends the Bülbrings.[31] She is sad, shy, drooping and plain. The little boy is charming. We four discussed her future and where she might live. I told her I would make her an allowance of £300 a year. Little Tony came to dine with us at Claridges Grill on Thursday to discuss – secretly – what he should do if he were called up, an appalling prospect for someone who is quarter Jewish, who would have to fight on the same side and partially for Germany, and who would cut himself off for good from England. All the pros and cons were discussed. We could only advise him to wait and see how things shaped up and, if the worst happened, not get his mobilisation order by changing addresses or by going to America at the last moment. We thought we might be able to arrange this for him. His position would be hateful and one hardly knew what advice to give him that didn't seem vile. Lunched with I. at Boulestin's on Friday. He'd just come back from doing *The Times* Special Correspondent in Russia and was wholly and completely anti-Bolshevik.

London, Wednesday April 26

I dined with Oliver Harvey at the Ritz where we talked from 9 till 12. He said the PM loved to surround himself with mediocrities – look at [Leslie]

31. Edith Bülbring (1903-90), pharmacologist at Oxford University, who lived with her sister Maud.

Burgin.[32] He would not include Winston [Churchill] in the Cabinet. He was arrogant and he thought he could do everything best himself. Oliver thought it was obvious that at this juncture he should form a National Govt. The Labour Party would certainly join and have a number of portfolios. But the PM wouldn't consider it. Oliver said the PM had been well and sprightly when he accompanied him and Lord Halifax[33] to Rome in January, but since Czecho he'd aged and shrunk. Said Halifax only outstanding person in the Cabinet, that he was high-minded and respected by all. Nevile Henderson,[34] in Berlin, cut no ice. Phipps,[35] in Paris, had been a great failure, spineless and slippery. During Eden's time in the Foreign Office, Phipps had been ardently pro-Eden but when Eden went he became equally ardently pro-Chamberlain (powers that be). O. thought the course of events of the last six months might have been different if we'd had a strong Ambassador in Paris.

We talked about Van's persistent refusal of the Paris Embassy. O. said if Van had been there things might have been very different. He might have spurred and put spirit into the French and roused the Cabinet at home. We talked long about Van's character – how simple he is in many ways. O. said, 'If there is a big hole in the middle of the room Van will walk into it.' That he was excitable and alarmist politically, courageous and honest in his dealings, but inclined to hammer away and hadn't much instinct for the suitable moment to press his point, or the suitable method of approach. His expositions were too violent and injured his case, whereas quieter ones would have had more chance of gaining an ear. Oliver said Van <u>would not</u> leave the Foreign Office. It was suggested again and again in various ways that he should go to Paris or Washington, the traditional step for most Permanent Undersecretaries, but he would not do so. The answer was always that Sarita would hate to go abroad. I said Van seemed very embittered. O. said he'd no reason to be so. He said Sarita was a dangerous and horrible woman. She leads unsuspecting men on by stories of Van's neglect – marital neglect – and then goes and tells Van.

32. Edward Leslie Burgin (1887-1945), Liberal politician, Minister of Supply in 1939. Chamberlain ally.
33. Edward Wood, 1st Earl Halifax (1881-1959), Conservative politician and diplomat. Viceroy India 1926-31, Foreign Secretary 1938-40 and associated with Chamberlain's appeasement policy. Churchill's main rival for premiership after Chamberlain's resignation. British Ambassador to Washington 1941-46.
34. Sir Nevile Henderson (1882-1942), diplomat. Ambassador to Germany 1937-39. Author of *Failure of a Mission: Berlin 1937-1940* (1940). His great-niece Sarah Sutherland married Maud's great-nephew Charles Irby in 1971.
35. Sir Eric Phipps (1875-1945), diplomat. Ambassador to Germany 1933-37 and to France 1937-39.

Mottisfont, Sunday April 30

I lunched with Sibyl Colefax on Friday and sat between Segonzac,[36] the painter, and David Keir, Lobby Correspondent of *The News Chronicle*. David Keir, a dark intelligent young man, talked about the PM whom he sees from time to time. The PM once said to him that he had two great advantages in life: (1) that a subject only worried him till he'd taken measures to deal with it, when it passed from his mind and (2) that he slept well. Keir saw him only three days ago. He seemed very tired and worn, his eyes dry, his body drooping, his voice dull. K. thinks he is a poor psychologist, a man with little human warmth or understanding of human nature. Hence what looks like high-handed treatment of opponents and his errors of non-consultation. Keir tips Winston as PM if war comes, says he has been right in his warnings for two years or more, has a big following in the country, and is at the height of his power.

From David Keir, I turned to Segonzac and had quite a different sort of talk. He is short, grey-haired and bourgeois in appearance and has shrewd bluish eyes. He said Matisse was intolerant of criticism even 30 years ago. Segonzac noted that he had no plastic sense and his objects had no weight. A French painter or critic had said that it needed four men to move a piano, but if Matisse had a piano in the corner of one of his pictures, one felt that if someone were to open the door and a gust of wind washed in, the piano would be blown clean out of the window. Seg. said of Matisse and his painting: 'His painting is like this,' spreading his arms and hands wide, 'but the man himself is like this,' and he brought his hands close together. He said Matisse had always been afraid of Picasso. When they were in the same room together Matisse was uneasy and silent. He never dared criticise him. Seg. said Picasso was 'demoniacal'.

[*Another guest*] Paul Maze[37] I have met several times before. I never like him much. He does not seem very sincere. Talking of Hitler, he said there was nothing so very remarkable about him. He was just like a man going down an uninhabited street not knowing that the houses were empty and could easily be broken in to. Then, half by accident, he successfully breaks into one. Encouraged by this, he breaks into another and then another. But he won't be able to go on like that for ever. Maze drew this picture to illustrate that Hitler wasn't really a clever man, as several people were saying, following bit by bit a pre-arranged plan, but a man who by accident had stumbled on a success which he hadn't expected, but had had the wits

36. André Dunoyer de Segonzac (1884-1974), French painter.
37. Paul Maze (1887-1979), Anglo-French painter. Artistic mentor for his friend Winston Churchill.

to follow up. He thought he'd made bad mistakes and would finish himself in time with a last stupidity.

Mottisfont, Sunday May 7

I lunched with I.C.-G. on Wednesday. He took me to see the Segonzac's at Wildenstein's and all but forced me into buying one and then dragged me to the Academy which we tore around.

G. and I went to see Van at the Foreign Office on Thursday to ask him about the Apponyis and what their position here would be in case of war. He seemed to think there would be no difficulty about Kitty and Alexie and that Old Tony would be alright if he were under someone's protection (probably his own) and lived quietly in the country.

Motored here Friday. Rex was working. Ian, Clare [Tennyson], the Glenconners, Jimmy Coats,[38] the Coopers and Conrad [Russell, *Gilbert's brother*] came to stay. I. started well but turned moody. Poor I. On Saturday I spent the afternoon with Rex. The point had been reached when I had to make up my mind what I wanted to have in the panels – whether romantic scenes or trophies or what. Rex had chalked in some delicious scenes – ruins, stages, bowed trees to tempt me and I was tempted. But I returned again to trophies. He left that evening.

Cecil Beaton, bringing his mother, sister and brother-in-law, came for drinks. He wanted badly to see Rex's room and asked for the drawings the moment he arrived. I had foreseen this and taken the precaution of hiding them just before because I felt certain Rex wouldn't want them poured over and criticised before they were finally settled on. Diana [Cooper] too called out for them but my lie was ready. Cecil said nothing at all – not even the conventional things. I. said he was dumb with envy and rage.

London, Tuesday May 9

I lunched with Sibyl [Colefax] finding myself between Duff [Cooper] and Bruce Lockhart,[39] who had just come back from a lecture tour in America.

---

38. Sir James Coats, 3rd Baronet Coats (1894-1966). Obtained rank of Lieutenant-Colonel in the Coldstream Guards and headed up the Coats Mission, a special British unit to evacuate the Royal Family in case of invasion during the Second World War.
39. Sir Robert Bruce Lockhart (1887-1970), diplomat, journalist and author. In 1941 appointed Director-General of the Political Warfare Executive, which was responsible for propaganda in enemy and occupied territories.

His audiences were pro-English but anti-govt and anti-Chamberlain, but still more anti-dictator. Duff was rather silent as he often is in the middle of the day. At Mottisfont talking to me about the PM and Munich he said: 'Between you and me, the PM was ready to concede everything Hitler asked for at Godesberg. Seven of us would have resigned if he had and we threatened to do so. So the PM gave in to us. Then came Munich and it all came to the same in the end.' Duff said Chamberlain had the mind and outlook of a small businessman and, till late in life, only the experience of a small businessman. Van and Sarita dined. Van's line always is that he told them so, that if only they had listened etc. He must have made mistakes too but I don't think he can remember them.

London, Wednesday May 10

We dined with Sylvia [Henley] and I sat between Edward Stanley[40] and Lionel Cohen, the King's Counsel, who was most charming and said he would help me find out how to deal with Lieselotte Margolin's case. My attack on Sir Samuel Hoare through Archie Sinclair has as good as failed. Sir S.H. wrote to A. and said he could do nothing and suggested I should begin from the beginning in the normal way. The normal way, even if successful, might take months and I had hoped to cut out preliminaries.

London, Friday May 12

Sibyl Colefax took me to a Toscanini[41] rehearsal at Queen's Hall, Beethoven's 6th & 7th Symphonies. A great treat. I thought the empty hall made the music sound better than ever. I hardly know whether there is anything I would rather do than go to a Toscanini rehearsal. In the morning light T. looked a small, rather stiff, shabby little figure in his black coat buttoned right up. The orchestra didn't stand up; they called out 'good morning' and he did too making a movement of greeting with his hand. He didn't stop them even once; but at the end called one or two of the leader players to him and gave some instruction. The orchestra itself looked much more interesting in their varied, coloured day suits.

Caught the 2.10 to Birmingham where Dr Margolin met me and took me

---

40. Edward Stanley, 6th Baron Sheffield (1907-71). Sylvia Henley and Venetia Montagu were his great-aunts.
41. Arturo Toscanini (1867-1957), Italian, one of the most acclaimed conductors of the twentieth century.

to his house where my aunt [*Tante Agnes*] is going to live when she arrives from Germany. He showed me the prospective room and opened a cupboard which was full of hers and Han Werner's clothes, sent on by them in advance. There were several trunks of theirs too, which he hadn't unpacked but which we peeped into. There seemed to be quite a lot of silver in them – put into the boxes, I believe, by the packers after they had been passed by the police. Dr M. tells me they are getting surreptitiously both money and objects out of Germany. The other day he received a cheque for £100 from the Hungarian branch of a Bulgarian bank and he still does not know whose it is, though probably Hans Werner's. Clients of his who have been to Germany bring back things with them. He showed me a gold snuff-box, very heavy and consisting of £40 worth of gold. It looked alright outside but was quite roughly finished inside and he told me these boxes were made for the purpose of getting gold out of the country. We talked about Lieselotte and he told me a little about her highly-strung neurotic character and how she'd tried to commit suicide in 1933. He'd just been able to save her life. She is fond of women. He still seems devoted to her. He made a good impression on me and seems to be building up a medical practice.

Woburn, Sunday May 14

Yesterday G. and I and Alexie motored down to Woburn for a night. Raymond followed in the afternoon and Martin came over today for a few hours. The house and the occupant belong so much to the past that everything connected with them has a special interest. Herbrand [*Duke of Bedford*] is now alone, or as much alone as his relations will let him be. Diana [*Gilbert's sister*] took us over the house. The pictures are nearly all in a very bad state, dark and the varnish dried in. Only a few have been cleaned. The Van Dycks are nothing like as good as those at Wilton, or the Canalettos as good as those at Castle Howard. Everything else looks in good order. The rooms have a comfortable, intimate Victorian-Georgian charm. None of them are big. There are a crowd of footmen and under-butlers who rush like a herd of bullocks when H. rings the bell and career round the table. Woburn is the only house I have ever known in which the servants knock at the living room doors before coming in. This must be a Russell idiosyncrasy. After tea we all went out driving in three old Fords which had chains tied around their wheels so they could be driven across grass. Footmen mounted the box of each car and off we clanked feeling something between Royal and ludicrous. We made for Woburn church. This visit was to enable H. to hear Raymond play the organ. He'd already talked once or twice about 'our young organist'. I had warned

R. what to expect. We all settled ourselves in a pew at the back of the church like birds on a telegraph pole. I then suddenly became shy for my son, fearing he might play too loud or too long or too badly! But except for a few rolling and creaking peals, all was well.

G. and I, certain there wouldn't be any sherry or drinks before dinner, were prudent enough to bring a thermos full of Martini cocktails, and were more than thankful we had done so. It lasted well for three meals. After dinner we sat again in the Canaletto room which had been thoughtfully provided with many copies of the *Evening Standard*, and gradually we all sank back behind them or took shelter behind the *Tatler* or the *Field*. It isn't easy to talk to H. for long. He is too old and lives too secluded a life to catch onto general conversation. At 10.15 sharp H. suggested bed and we retired. Alexie and Raymond came to my bedroom where we had a nice half hour laughing, remembering and recapitulating. As they left to go to their rooms, the entire house was plunged into darkness. We stood laughing and hesitating in the passage till we were discovered, and made to feel almost guilty, by the night watchman who took A. to her room. He said there were always four night watchmen on duty and that his Grace gave orders that all the lights were to be turned out as soon as the guests had retired. This rather precludes chattering in bedrooms or even a visit to the lavatory.

Mottisfont, Monday May 15

Rex came and we discussed trophies and Gothic armour. He chalked a Queen Anne vase on the wall which refused to look anything but Queen Anne, no matter how many Gothic twiddles he added, or how many scrolls he placed against it.

Mottisfont, Sunday May 28

Had a drink with I. at Ebury St in his big room on Tuesday. He has just bought the first 20 or 30 copies of *Iskra*, Lenin's organ. He is making an interesting collection of the first book, broadsheet, pamphlet or paper on a particular subject. I think he would like to do secret service work, or journalism, or both. He wrote a report about Russia and another about Germany after he'd been there this spring to show to his friends. G. read one of them and had the idea of introducing him to M.I., which he did. [*M.I. probably refers to Military Intelligence, indicating that Gilbert may have played a part in getting Ian his job in the Naval Intelligence Division which came about at around this time*].

London, Sunday June 4

Mr Schilizzi, our local ARP warden, came and fitted our gas masks on us on Thursday. Mine was too small and he changed it. Then dined with Glenconners. John[42] there. Went to 'Nine O'clock Revue', very funny. After that, supper at Quaglino's and, because the Glens had never been and seemed to long to be taken to a lowish haunt, we went on to the Nest where John ordered a bottle of gin. It was crowded with blacks and whites, debutantes and prostitutes and some of Mary Lygon's wedding party of the afternoon.[43] Poor G. in bed with asthma – or more properly – a germ caught in Ceylon which has flared up and given him general malaise.

Mottisfont, Sunday June 18

Martin was 21 on Monday. He went to the opera with Mama and afterwards joined us at the Savoy and we had a family supper – Mama, Martin, Alexie, little Tony, Kitty, Tony, Raymond, Mary and Anthony and G. and I. There were no special celebrations or presentations. I don't think they would have done in these times. And we have only been here four years so country celebrations would have been absurd.

London, Wednesday June 21

Dined with John Follett in his maisonette. Victor Rothschild's sister [*Kathleen*] and her husband Baron Jules de Koenigswarter were there. We talked about the world situation and Koenigswarter said that one of the dangers of the situation was that England now wanted war! Before leaving Tony Apponyi said that it alarmed him that England was becoming so bellicose. I am glad if that is the impression foreigners now get.

Mottisfont, Sunday June 25

Went out with Derek [Hill] on Thursday and we looked at pictures at the Courtauld Institute. Reid and Lefevre [*Gallery*] have asked him to have a show which is flattering for him. After I left him I remembered the King and

---

42. Sir John Wriothesley Russell (1914-84), son of Gilbert's cousin, Sir Thomas Russell ('Pasha Russell'), the head of Cairo police. Diplomat. At British Embassy in Moscow in 1941. Ambassador to Ethiopia 1962-66, Brazil 1966-69 and Spain 1969-74.
43. Lady Mary Lygon (1910-82) married Prince Vsevolod Ivanovich of Russia on May 31, 1939.

Queen were due to return from Canada so I hurried to the Mall, stood in a big crowd and just saw the tops of their heads. Later from between the trees of Green Park, I saw them and the children come out on the balcony. The crowds were immense.

Camilla and Christopher [Sykes],[44] Jo and Laura Grimond,[45] Michael D.,[46] Catherine Sinclair, Viola Lyttelton, Alexie, Brendan Bracken[47] and Martin came for the weekend. Rain came down all the time and the party was dull. Poor Brendan had no one to button-hole politically and was lost. Rex was here till Saturday and everybody trooped into the room and admired, or not, according to their tastes and temperaments.

London, Monday June 26

G. and I dined with Sibyl Colefax. I was between Somerset Maugham[48] and [Henry Bogey] Harris[49] and had a most agreeable long talk with Maugham, whom I got on with from the first. I have often found him rather dry and difficult and alarming. Our two main subjects were incest and happiness. I told him I had lately heard of two cases of incest between brother and sister among the educated classes. I didn't give the names as I had no idea whether the stories were true. Maugham told me he'd written a story around the subject of incest between brother and sister. It followed closely a real story that he'd known of in the East, and that after the brother had returned to England and became engaged, the sister had shot herself the day he married. We agreed that if incest was only the result of lust it was not very interesting. But that if it happened because of love between a brother and sister then it was something most extraordinary, most terrific, most terrible. On the subject of happiness and unhappiness, Maugham asked me which I thought

---

44. Christopher Sykes (1907-86), writer. Married in 1936 Camilla Russell (1912-83), daughter of Gilbert's cousin Sir Thomas Russell ('Pasha Russell'), the head of Cairo police.
45. Joseph ('Jo') Grimond, later Baron Grimond (1913-93), politician. Liberal Party leader 1956-67. Married in 1938 Laura Bonham Carter (1918-94), the daughter of Violet and Maurice Bonham Carter.
46. Sir Michael Duff, 3rd Baronet (1907-80), statesman and socialite. His second wife was Caroline Paget, with whom Rex Whistler had an unrequited love affair.
47. Brendan Bracken, later 1st Viscount Bracken (1901-58), Conservative politician, Winston Churchill's private parliamentary secretary 1940-41, Minister for Information 1941-45.
48. W. Somerset Maugham (1874-1965), novelist, playwright and short story writer.
49. Henry 'Bogey' Harris (d.1950), art collector and dealer.

most people were. When I said unhappy he looked as if he hadn't expected that answer, and said, 'Do you realise (or know) what you are saying?'

London, Tuesday June 27

Ian Howland [*Ian Russell, future Duke of Bedford*] brought his wife [*Clare Hollway*] to lunch and Claud and Athenaïs [*Gilbert's brother and his wife*] were there to help. I had heard too many unpleasant things about her to like her though I tried to free myself from prejudice. She is 37 and Ian 22. She doesn't look more than 32. She has a markedly oriental face – Jewish, Armenian or Syrian. There is a lot of scabrous talk about her and Andrew Scott[50] told G. that a part of her body was trimmed in the shape of a love heart. I felt annoyed with myself for not being able to forget the things I had heard about her.

Paris, Sunday July 2

On Friday flew to Paris, one hour and five mins in air. Today went to see Matisse at the Hotel Lutetia, where he is staying, his wife having turned him out of his flat. I had a drawing of his, a nude, which I wanted to change and had brought with me to Paris. Found him sitting spruce and formidable in the hall. We went to his bedroom, a melancholy drab room, with his bed and an additional one in it for the nurse, he said, who looks after him, as he is still far from well and has been having insomnia for a long time. He seemed older, no more amicable than before, and I felt he was somehow in a bad way, through health or insomnia or domestic troubles. I found it difficult to explain that I wanted to change his drawing and he didn't help me. But I persisted, though he wasn't very gracious. He said he couldn't see much wrong with it and that it was a good drawing. I answered that I wouldn't presume to criticise but, with someone as ignorant of art as I, everything depended on how much one liked the picture, in a personal way, and that I found it hard to explain. He said that at the moment he couldn't get at his pictures in the studio, but that I should come and see him at Nice after September, or in Paris before September. I left my drawing with him.

This is likely to be the drawing that Maud bought from the Leicester Galleries

50. Brigadier Andrew Montagu Douglas Scott DSO (1906-71). Irish Guards and 1st Guards Brigade. 'An immensely funny man, quick witted, comic,' according to Maud. Married first Lady Victoria (Doria) Haig 1929.

on February 21, 1936. She never received a replacement or a refund. Maud first met Matisse in 1937 when she sat for him in Paris.

Paris, Tuesday July 4

Today I lunched with Derek [Hill] near the Bourse at Marins and then we went to Vollard's[51] close by. I asked first to see his books as I know he is very proud of them. There were two magnificent volumes, *Cirque*, and another with illustrations done by Rouault. Expensive: £40 for *Cirque*. In this room there was a portrait of V. by Cézanne and some Maillol statuettes. V. came in and out of the room, not very forthcoming. We were shown into a rich heavy Empire dining room – but not used as such – where there was a wonderful, brilliant, pink, blue and gold portrait by Renoir, a big nude by R., a dull Courbet, a Cézanne and a statue by Renoir. Derek then had to leave. V. returned and started talking, and I found him charming, agreeable and attractive. He is a very handsome old man with beautiful, dark eyes and a weathered, ornamental face. He looked like a bust that has stood out of doors for centuries, and has been beaten and ravaged by years of storms and rains. His expression is melancholy but his face and eyes light up suddenly, and then suddenly the light goes out. He talked a good deal and treated me to little anecdotes of all kinds, from the traditional little jokes about women to stories about painters. He lamented that 120 Van Goghs had passed through his hands in early days – and even later ones – and he'd never foreseen what prices they were going to command, and had missed tremendous profits. He said, 'The painters I saw didn't think much of Van Gogh. Cézanne didn't care for him and Degas and Renoir didn't either. How could I foresee the admiration now felt for him?' But I daresay he is an old liar and he did pretty well out of his Goghs.

Mottisfont, Sunday July 9

On Thursday I went to see Mr Butler, the Windsor Herald, at the College of Arms to make certain Rex was doing nothing extravagant with G.'s arms in the big room. Went to ball at Blenheim on Friday. Blenheim was a wonderful sight, a sort of landmark of beauty, something lovely to store in one's memory. The floodlit front was staggering. A great buffet ran all along the hall and

---

51. Ambroise Vollard (1866-1939), influential French art dealer and collector, credited for providing exposure to many great artists of the time, such as Paul Cezanne, Aristide Maillol, André Derain and Vincent Van Gogh, among others.

88.   Matisse   Paris   1939.

Friday flew to Paris 4.45.. One hour & 5 mins in air. Ritz. Dinner in bed

Saturday morning, two maddening hours at the hairdressers". Lunched with Henri de Jongh at the Ralli Plaza? if a place with such a name really exists. Also there a Baronne Thénard & a Comte — ? Derek came to tea. Dined Ritz Grill with Glenconner, Veronica Tennant & a nameless young man & went to the "Première Legion" an excellent & enthralling play by an American. Jesuits & an all man cast. Moving. Supper at Maxim's.

July Sunday 2nd. Went to see Matisse at the hôtel Lutétia where he is staying still, his wife having turned him out of his flat. I had a drawing of his, a nude, which I wanted to change & had brought with me to Paris. Found him sitting spruce & formidable in the hall. We went to his bedroom, a melancholy drab room with his own bed & an additional one in it for the nurse, he said, who looks after him, as he is still far from well & has been having insomnia for a long time. He seemed older, no more amiable than before & I felt he was somehow in a bad way, through health or insomnia or domestic troubles. I found it difficult to explain that I wanted to change his drawing & he did not help me. But I persisted though he wasn't very gracious. He said he could not see much wrong with it & that it was a good drawing.

Maud's diary covering the visit to Matisse in Paris in July 1939 (*for the text of the entry see page 59*).

there was always a crowd standing or sitting and talking in it. Ian saw me as I arrived and took me at once to see the garden. The cedars, obelisks and lake were floodlit and the scene was magically beautiful. I was glad I saw it with Ian who is so starred with romance and whose romantic needs are so seldom satisfied. I got here from Blenheim at six on Saturday, wide awake and not wanting to go to bed. But it was a rainy morning so to bed I went.

Mottisfont, Sunday July 16

We went to a charity ball at Osterley on Thursday, some in fancy-dress. The house looked extremely pretty. I was tired and, after noticing first the weight of my crinoline and then the weight of the bag in my hand, I lived up to the period of my clothes, and felt dreadfully faint, and had to lie on a banquette in a stone passage where, no doubt, the people who saw me said: 'There is Mrs Russell, drunk as usual.' On Friday lunched I. at Boulestin's where he propounded to me the partitioning of Poland. My Liberal blood revolted and I turned on him.

Mottisfont, Sunday July 23

Last week Raymond went up for his organ exam at the Royal College of Organists and he has heard that he has failed. Dr Pritchard, his master, complained to me a month ago that he was working badly. Opening *The Sunday Times* today I see that Vollard has been killed in a car smash.

London, Friday July 28

I went to tea with my cousin Hilde Lubelska on Monday, now installed with her children Urla and Jan in a small flat near Regent's Park. Dined with I. on Wednesday after picking him up at Ebury St where we had a rabid political talk before going to dine at Quaglino's. Q.'s was empty so we went to the Jardin and partly walked, partly bussed home. Today I went to the German Jewish Aid Committee at Woburn House to try and find out about Lieselotte, and managed to get in without an appointment. There I saw Mr Michelson, who I thought was in charge of the case, but it turned out that a Mrs Scott, working in the same small room, was doing it. The files of the case were sent for and it took 50 minutes for them to be brought. I imagine this is symptomatic of the running of the whole organisation. I got them to promise to let me know as soon as their application on L.'s behalf is sent up to the Home Office so that I can then get Van to use his influence. I had made this request several times in writing and had never been given an answer.

Mottisfont, Sunday July 30

Alexie, Mary, Paul and Raymond are here. Martin is still abroad, probably in Marseille. Rex is working steadily and his two assistants [Victor] Bowen and [Percy] Willets are still here. He pays them each over £9 a week. So the slowness of the work is unfortunate for him. Some of it is his own fault. He ought to have come here much more in earlier days and hurried them on and told them not to fiddle about. And then he should have been here a lot more himself in the summer to finish the trophies. Only one has so far been finished. And I suppose he should have made more careful calculations last year when he gave me his estimate of £1100 for all the work. He didn't go carefully enough into how long the job would take. I shall have to give him a present at the end.

Maud and Gilbert used to spend most of August at Mottisfont, essentially retiring from London for the month, inviting the wider family to stay.

Mottisfont, Sunday August 6

Days much the same. Garden, house, papers, bills, photograph albums, hanging pictures, moving ornaments and visiting the village. There was rain every day and the weather made everybody feel relaxed and depressed. I listened to the whole of *Zauberflöte* [Mozart's *Magic Flute*] one day and a good part of it again another. I had a talk with Alexie on Friday afternoon. She said she wanted to leave her parents and work in London. She's got a job with the Hungarian Military Attaché [Julius] Lánczy and she was going to London to start a short secretarial course in a fortnight's time before going to work with him in the autumn. I was rather appalled as I know what a ghastly family row there would be. A. is dull and unhappy at home. She has talked to me about working for some time and I think it will be good for her. But I don't think the present is a good moment to break away from her family, with the accompanying rows. They are homeless and countryless and it would seem very hard-hearted of her. I tried to dissuade her from doing anything now. On Saturday evening she came to my room and said she'd decided against breaking away for the present. Her character is very fine and sweet.

I talked to Raymond about autumn plans for him, namely to send him to Geneva to learn some German and improve his French. Of course, he didn't like the idea at all, and I daresay we shall have trouble with him about it.

Mottisfont, Monday August 14

Adele [Lazzerini, *lady's maid*] told me that Raymond was planning to run away again, this time the day before we start for the south of France, so as to force us to let him stay in England instead of going to Geneva. Adele had only got this indirectly through Alexie who had said she was going to tell me. Alexie left today to motor across France to join Kitty and Tony at Ouchy [*Switzerland, where they have moved to from Hungary*].

Mottisfont, Wednesday August 16 [52]

Randolph [Churchill] came to tea and stayed for dinner. During dinner and afterwards he talked and harangued unceasingly. We all enjoyed this – except perhaps Gilbert – as we have been living quietly in the country for some time and have had few occasions for political argument and very little news. Randolph, having had a good deal to drink, roared and bellowed, sprang to his feet like some fair gorilla, clenched his fists and shook them in the air, pranced, cursed Chamberlain and Baldwin, Munich, all opponents of his father's, the doddering Cabinet – except Hore-Belisha.[53] It was real and yet unreal. I think he felt he was on a political platform, and though his sentiments were sincere, they were made to seem insincere by his demagogic platform manner. He said – but in a great many more words and not once but several times – 'What have you all and the people of England been doing all these years? How have you let things get to such a pass? Now Martin and I are going to get killed all because of these Germans, who have been allowed to arm, and should no more be allowed to possess arms than young children. It was madness, madness. When Martin and I are dead you must make the right peace terms. Treat them well, give them food, finance them, let them trade. But never let them have arms, see they never have arms again.' Finally, about 2, he started back to Tidworth after one final, immensely loud harangue. The evening had certainly been animated and we were woken up out of our country sleep and made to roar mildly too.

---

52. Maud stopped writing her diary on August 14 when war seemed inevitable. She started writing it again on October 22 when she also wrote up the missing entries with the help of her engagement diary.
53. Leslie Hore-Belisha, 1st Baron Hore-Belisha (1893-1957). Liberal MP. As Minister of Transport 1934-37 introduced a number of road safety measures including Belisha beacons. Replaced Duff Cooper as Secretary of State for War, introducing conscription in 1939.

Above The south front of Mottisfont Abbey.
Maud and Gilbert bought the house in 1934,
prior to which it had been empty for many
years. In 1957 Maud donated the house and
its 2000 acre estate to the National Trust.
(© National Trust Images / Robert Morris).

Right Maud commissioned the garden
designer Norah Lindsay to design the parterre
at the front of the house. Boris Anrep's
Guardian Angel mosaic hides under the
wisteria growing by the steps in the far corner.
(© National Trust Images / Robert Morris).

Below The five notebooks that make up
Maud's diaries for the years covered by this
book. In full, they run to 350,000 words and
were written weekly on Sunday mornings in
bed. (© Emily Russell).

Above left Maud as a young woman by Ambrose McEvoy. (© Emily Russell).

Above right Charcoal drawing of Maud by Henri Matisse, 1937. Maud was never comfortable with the 'mournful' expression. This is one of two portraits of Maud by Matisse, which were sold after her death. (Succession H. Matisse/DACS 2016).

This lovely pencil and watercolour portrait of Gilbert, looking gentle and thoughtful, was done by Sir William Orpen in Paris in 1924. (© National Trust Images).

A very modern-looking Maud by Sir William Nicholson in 1914.
(© Desmond Banks / Ferens Art Gallery, Hull Museums, UK / Bridgeman Images).

Two of Rex Whistler's sketches for what is now known as the Whistler Room at Mottisfont Abbey, the 'big room' which Maud commissioned Whistler to decorate in 1938. (© National Trust Images / John Hammond).

Trompe l'oeil of a little paint pot with a brush in it on top of one of the pilasters in the Whistler Room. Hidden from ground level, Rex's inscription next to the paint pot was only discovered in 1950 and marks his whereabouts when Britain declared war on Germany. (© National Trust Images / Anna Pizzey).

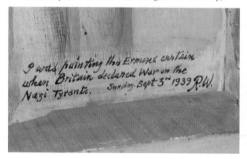

Rex Whistler's 'smoking urn' *trompe l'oeil* at Mottisfont, representing Maud's dislike of bonfires but also her love of art, music and literature.

The letters tied up in pink ribbon on the books resemble bundles of letters from Gilbert. (© National Trust Images / Andreas von Einsiedel).

The Whistler Room at Mottisfont as it looked in Maud's day. (© National Trust Images / Andreas von Einsiedel).

Above Boris Anrep by Leonidas Inglesis in 1948. A Russian artist, Inglesis was in charge of Boris's studio in Paris and did the cartoon in the background of an angel flanking Christ for Anrep's mosaic in St Patrick's Chapel in Mullingar Cathedral, Ireland. (Private Collection).

Left The Guardian Angel of Mottisfont by Boris Anrep in 1946 bears a strong likeness to Maud. (© National Trust Images / Sue Laws).

Below Boris Anrep's Holy Trinity mosaic in the Red Room at Mottisfont. The 'hand of God' is Boris's hand. (© National Trust Images / Andreas von Einsiedel).

Mrs Gilbert Russell sitting in Bed by Boris Anrep in c.1935. This was probably done shortly after they first met. Maud was unwell at the time. She was attracted by his vitality and amusing bedside chatter, he by her 'great capacity for response to anything warm and alive.' (© Victoria and Albert Museum, London).

Nude among the Ruins by Boris Anrep in 1944. A gift to Maud, and probably painted as a tribute to her. The figure brings to mind Maud hovering over the ruins of the former Chapter House at Mottisfont. (© Tate, London 2016).

Maud as *Folly* in Boris Anrep's mosaic floor for the National Gallery in London, based on a snapshot of Maud at San Remo in 1914. Maud thought of the 'strange Russian fairy-tale head' peering over her shoulder as Boris, and she especially liked his treatment of her hair and neck. (© The National Gallery, London).

Defiance by Boris Anrep for the National Gallery mosaic floor. It was Maud who suggested that Boris depict Winston Churchill giving the victory salute. (© The National Gallery, London).

Both mosaics are part of Boris's fourth mosaic pavement for the National Gallery, called *The Modern Virtues*. The project was proposed to the National Gallery board in 1945 by Sir Kenneth Clark, who was director at the time. Maud paid for the work.

London, Wednesday August 23

Tante Fritze and Lotte accompanied by a nurse arrived in London from Cologne by air yesterday and went to a nursing home I had found in Hampstead. Saw them today. Journey went off beautifully. They hadn't waited till their luggage had been sent off. They had decided not to delay longer. Lotte said how wonderful it was to be able to go to a swimming-bath again, meaning by this that she was free of the restrictions that prevented Jews from going to public places. She looked very pleased.

London, Friday August 25

I lunched with I. at the Carlton yesterday. It was crowded with uniforms and I thought of the last war when, too, it was full and crowded with uniforms. We have no more thoughts of going to France and have decided to move all the servants from London to Mottisfont. Dined this evening with Raymond at Hyde Park Grill and went to the *Importance of Being Ernest*, a wonderfully chosen play for the times, so unlike them, so frivolous, so superficial, so gay. Audience very appreciative. Packed. We found Claud and Ath and Eddie Marsh[54] in the crowd. We all went on to supper at the Savoy. Venetia [Montagu] was sitting alone and came to us. We talked, everyone eager for news.

Mottisfont, Sunday August 27

Motored to Mottisfont yesterday, the car stacked with fragile things among which poor Jason [*family dog*] staggered and rolled. Raymond lost his cat at the last moment and stayed behind, hanging out of windows, looking for it. All the household moved to Mottisfont except Wright, whose sons are working in London and so it was arranged for them all to live at Princes Gate. Claud and Ath came to stay for the war.[55] Randolph came to dinner. Rex here. Today Claud, Ath and I motored to Bognor [*Bognor Regis, Duff and Diana Cooper's Sussex home*] for tea. Kätchen[56] was there and Conrad.

---

54. Sir Edward Marsh (1872-1953), distinguished civil servant, scholar and discerning patron of arts. Private secretary to Winston Churchill 1905-1915.

55. Claud and Ath were invited 'to stay for the war' as they did not have a country home and people were advised to leave London. They later took a long lease on Trematon Castle in Cornwall.

56. Dr Rudolf Kommer (d.1943), former secretary to Max Reinhardt and close friend of Lady Diana Cooper.

Diana was <u>very</u> depressed, Duff very nervous and deeply depressed. I think he was afraid the PM was going to back out of obligations and let honour and the continuance of democracy go to the wall. He hardly spoke. We listened to the news at 6, sitting in the garden, and Duff seemed almost in tears.

Mottisfont, Thursday August 31

Monday to Winchester. Tuesday to Romsey. These and other expeditions of the sort were shopping expeditions to buy black ARP stuff for curtains, candles, candlesticks, torches, oil-lamps, crockery and cutlery, pots and baths, towels and lockers for the evacuated school children we are expecting.

Mottisfont, Friday September 1

News came from the stationmaster at Dunbridge that a train of 700 evacuated children were to arrive at 10.20. Mr Kirkham [*the Mottisfont Rector*] and I drove down to the station. We found the children collected together in the yard of the Dunbridge Arms. They each were carrying a small suitcase or bundle, some rations, a gas mask, and their names were written on labels sewn to their clothes. They looked serious but not at all depressed. The reception officer let them through the gate of the yard in batches and they were settled in the motor buses, with a teacher and a helper or two in charge, and off they went to an unknown destination. Our children were the last. We found to our surprise that there were only 39 instead of about 80 or 90 and that of the 39, 31 were boys. Most of the villagers – and I too – had said they would rather take in girls. The children came up to the school in a bus, sat down at the desks and most opened their ration parcels and had some food. The writing of their names and the apportioning of them to the different villagers was efficiently done by Bundy [Alfred, *the Mottisfont estate foreman and billeting officer*]. Finally I was given six, three pairs of brothers as well as two school teachers and their wives as helpers.

We got to the house just before 1 and an Irish stew was produced for them within a short time. The couples are Nellthorpe and Clark; the children Miller, Fletcher and Heighow. I have arranged a long room over the stables as a dormitory with 10 beds in it – camp beds, army blankets, eiderdowns, lockers. The harness room is a sitting room; and the gun room a scullery and bathroom for the boys. The grown-ups are in a flat over the garage. The children looked clean and as if they belonged to decent families. The school teachers looked bewildered but pleasant and pleasant they have been ever since.

When I got back to the house after the children arrived, I heard that the Germans had invaded Poland.

Mottisfont, Saturday September 2

All these last days have been days of great strain and dull tension. We listen in to the wireless news several times a day from Martin's bedroom as the morning room wireless had gone to be repaired. We do little else but listen in, go away and do some small job and then hurry back to the wireless. The thought of war once again fills me with horror and loathing. I remember the clichés, clap-trap, jokes, soldiers' farewells and misery of the last war. But what alternative there is I can't imagine except total pacifism.

Mottisfont, Sunday September 3

Adele told me when she called that the PM was going to speak at 11.15. That could mean one thing only. At 11.15 we listened to his short broadcast and knew where we were.

Ian Fleming is now working in Room 39 at the Admiralty as the personal assistant to Admiral John Godfrey, the director of Naval Intelligence. His gift for running things, speedy drafting of documents and abilities as a 'skilled fixer and a vigorous showman' were to play a vital role in the Naval Intelligence Division's wartime work .[57]

London, Wednesday September 6

On Tuesday dined with I. at the Berkeley. Packed with uniforms. I. was in a sub-lieutenant uniform and looked as if he'd always worn those clothes. We had one of our usual shouting matches and both rather enjoyed it. There was an air raid warning at 6.45 this morning at Claridges. I was already awake. The eerie wailing Martian War of the Worlds sound was unmistakable. I thought, shall I get up? Yes, better, it will be curious to see how this works, the other people at Claridges, how they behave and the ARP arrangements. I went to the WC, powdered my face, combed my hair, got into a coat and skirt, took my bag and gas mask, and clattered down five or six flights of backstairs to the basement. We sat in a converted store room shored up and strengthened with a steel door. Various kinds of night-attired ladies with fuzzy

57. McLachlan, *Room 39*, p.8

grey hair, smart foreigners in super-gigolo dressing gowns who appeared to be the hotel staff. I read the evening paper through several times. At the end of two hours coffee was served. By then we were very hungry, rather tired and pretty bored. All clear sounded after two hours and twenty minutes. Lessons learned: to have a book, brandy, biscuits. Probably a torch and perhaps a pickaxe too! I never like being underground and shut in.

Mottisfont, Thursday September 14

On Wednesday lunched with I. at the Carlton. He asked me to give him his identification disc[58] when eventually they are issued. Today lunched Boulestin's with Raymond Mortimer and Elizabeth [Glenconner] and had bad oysters but pleasant talk. Raymond said he had it on good authority that Lord Halifax thought the war would be over by Xmas. Balls. Motored to Mottisfont with a car-load of four. Martin's last night at home.

Mottisfont, Friday September 15

I was called late and Martin, who had thought he wasn't wanted till later in the day, had looked at his card when he was called and found he was to report early. So he'd gone. Perhaps he meant to do it that way. I daresay I might have. Derek [Hill] lunched. He is worried because he cannot bear to kill. He doesn't mind hard work. He doesn't know what to do about it. The evening was cold, wet, windy and melancholy and I felt very depressed. Went to talk to Rex. I was afraid of crying but the room was dark and I managed not to. I was glad to reach my room and cry.

On September 17, the Soviet Union invaded Poland from the east and occupied territory assigned to it under the secret protocols of a non-aggression pact signed with Germany on August 23.

London, Wednesday September 20

Duff and Diana on their way to Cranborne came to tea on Monday. Diana said she'd a feeling there would be a big peace movement in the autumn sponsored by the neutrals and headed by Roosevelt. Duff said nothing. He is dreadfully depressed and the only thing to do is to gossip with him, or to

---

58. All British military personnel wore identity tags to help identify soldiers, especially if wounded.

talk about some book, or somebody's love affair, and take his mind off the war. Dined with I. at the Berkeley this evening. He loves his NID [*Naval Intelligence Division*] better than anything he has ever done, I think, except skiing. I don't ask him about it so as not to tempt him to be indiscreet.

Mottisfont, Thursday September 21

Martin is at the Rifle Brigade Depot at Winchester. It appears that he got mixed up with the Hampshire Regt at Winchester Station by mistake and before he knew what had happened he found himself on the train for Southampton. He spent two or three days on the Isle of Wight and was then returned to Winchester. He wrote describing barrack life and that he minded the discomforts less than most. Tonight G. scolded Raymond, who was rude, and tapped his shoulder. R. sprang up from the piano and hit G. hard on the back of the head. Mama was present and caught hold of his hands. He called her a silly old woman. G. was very upset by it and I was horrified and alarmed at his mentality. We decided to send him away with a tutor.

London, Thursday September 28

Lunch with I. at the Carlton. Told me unsolicited that he and another man had taken two German submarine officers, captured lately, out to lunch the day before at a club. There was only one exit and that was watched. They could not be made to give anything away. Food and wine made no difference. The other man, who had experience of this sort of thing in the last war, said the prisoners were quite different now. They could be got to talk much more easily then. I. is fascinated by his work.

Mottisfont, Sunday October 1

Came down here on Friday with Rex, Ath and John Follett. Diana, Duff and Edward Stanley came later. Randolph brought his girl Pamela Digby[59] on Saturday (*see photo in black and white plate section*). He'd telephoned me

---

59. Pamela Digby (1920-97), socialite. Daughter of Edward Digby, 11th Baron Digby, and Constance Digby. She apparently accepted the proposal from Randolph Churchill on the first evening they met. Married Churchill in 1939, Broadway producer Leland Hayward in 1960 and US railroad millionaire and Democrat politician W. Averell Harriman in 1971.

on Monday to say he was engaged. Had known her for 10 days. Said: It's Hitler's fault. Sounded pleased. She is pretty in a common way and supposed generally to be very silly. But I didn't think her so bad. Manner silly but not really at all silly. Rex drew her as a present for Randolph. We shot the partridges. Lovely day.

London, Wednesday October 4

Went to Randolph's wedding in Smith Sq. Winston was cheered when he arrived and everybody stood up in the church thinking that the bride had arrived. He cried a lot during the service. Randolph was correct, self-confident and pleased. I haven't the slightest doubt he is marrying because he thinks it's time and right that Winston must have a grandson. He has proposed to four or five women in the last few months. I know for certain of two: Claire Luce, the actress, and Caroline Paget. From the church we went to Admiralty House and had a stand-up lunch. About 60 people there. None of the Cabinet and few MPs. Winston was called to make a speech but got out of it by calling on Randolph. What could he have said? You are my only son, I love you dearly, I know why you are marrying, you are now a soldier, soon you will be in France and before the year is out you may be dead. Or else banalities. So R. said a few words of thanks and that he'd enjoyed his wedding.

Dined with Puffin[60] at Claridges. He had to leave early so I sat down with Lesley and William Jowitt. Lesley was the same as usual but William a most miserable sight, dejected, nervous, terrified at the taxation announced in the new budget, craven-hearted, craven-spirited, wanting assurances. I think I always knew he was like that. But I was astonished and rather disgusted. He said it really wasn't worth him taking briefs now if he only got a shilling or two in the pound out of them. This struck me as a singular remark for a Socialist.

Mottisfont, Saturday October 7

Found Raymond's new tutor Mr MacDonald here yesterday. He has lately left Japan where he taught for three years in the Imperial Naval College. Has taught in Italy and lived a lot abroad. Good for Ray. Today they left for Gloucester where they are going to spend two months.

60. Hon. Anthony Asquith, 'Puffin' (1902-68), film director. Son of Margot and H.H. Asquith.

London, Wednesday October 11

Lunch with Christabel [McLaren] at Jardin. She was at her nicest. One story amused me. She told me that the village at Bodnant had been told they were going to be sent mothers and babies under the evacuation scheme. She understood they would bring their own bedding with them. It was only two or three days before they were due that she made inquiries and heard they were bringing nothing. So C. and the villagers set to work to do what? Not to scour the neighbourhood and the shops for beds or mattresses or even lilos, but to make palliasses which they filled with hay (that is wrong too because fleas like hay but not straw). Well, the mothers and babies arrived and were shown into the barn, or wherever it was, and found palliasses. Two or three days later they said they'd like to go, and when asked why, said they preferred being at home. When asked whether they hadn't been comfortable they were polite and said no, they had been quite. C. told this story so as to illustrate how unaccountable such people are. 'It wasn't as if they had been uncomfortable,' she said. She is quite rich enough to have bought a 1,000 beds and mattresses.

Mottisfont, Sunday October 15

We heard the news of the sinking of the *Royal Oak*[61] yesterday and were all rather depressed. Today Derek [Hill] came after lunch and he, I, Elizabeth [Glenconner] and Rex spent a delicious afternoon. It was a dull wet day so we quietly left the others and spent the afternoon and after tea in the big room. Rex high on a ladder painting; Elizabeth, who had been allowed by Rex in the morning to do the shading on the ecclesiastical trophy, painting too; and Derek at first doing some shading on the hunting trophy and then, not pleased with his work, drawing Elizabeth. I read aloud to them, Max Beerbohm's Essay *No 2. The Pines*. I was very happy and wished every day could be spent like that. Derek's drawing of Elizabeth is exact and charming. I shall miss that day. There is no good writing about it.

London, Tuesday October 17

Went to Princes Gate to sort out and label as we are closing and emptying the house for good. It was chaotic with luggage, packing-cases, hampers, disgorged contents of drawers, dismantled curtains etc. There were three sets

---

61. HMS *Royal Oak*, torpedoed by German submarine at the Scapa Flow naval base in Scotland, with the loss of 833 lives.

of labelling done, one for things to go to Mottisfont; another for things to go into store at Partridges at Bath; and yet another for things to be temporarily stored at Bath to furnish a flat for Tante Fritze and Lotte. When some of this was over, I went back to Claridges where I stay now when I come to London and, exhausted, had dinner in bed.

London, Wednesday October 18

Princes Gate. Sorting and interviewing packers. Dr Margolin came from Birmingham to see me and stayed for the afternoon. The war stopped all consideration of the grant of a visa to Lieselotte and she is still in Spain. And the Mühsams [*Maud's aunt Tante Agnes and cousin Hans Werner*], their visas cancelled, are still in Berlin. We discussed what could be done. I dined with I. at the Berkeley. He is in Naval Intelligence and so absorbed in and fascinated by his work that he can barely detach his mind from it.

Bournemouth, Branksome Tower Hotel, Saturday October 21

Motored to Bournemouth with G. and Adele. Felt as if I was starting on a voyage. Indeed the change here was as great as if we had moved to another part of the world, or back into the past. No uniforms, no sign of war, elderly invalids of means with nurses, some weekending couples, the bustle of a hotel but the placidity of pre-war life.

Bournemouth, Tuesday October 24

Today I was amazed to get a letter from Alexie saying she'd been in England for five weeks and that she'd married a Hungarian, called Lánczy, in Edinburgh on the 20th. She left Ouchy on September 16th, spent a night in Paris, another in Calais, a week in London, and the rest of the time in Edinburgh. My first feeling was one of pleasure that she was in England again and the marriage didn't appal me at once. Then gradually it dawned on me what a cruel trick she'd played on her parents and what a rash thing she'd done. I sent her a telegram and she rang me up at lunchtime. She told me he was 46. She is 20. She said she hadn't mentioned him to her parents as they dislike him and 'would have refused'. That was wrong. They were given no chance. G. says he must be a scoundrel to take away a young girl of 20 and he 46.

London, Wednesday October 25

Alexie came to see me at 6 at Claridges. She looked pretty and rather changed. At first she seemed on the defensive. Later when we had talked more her eyes filled with tears. I didn't scold her but I told her I thought she'd behaved badly to her parents. They had not heard one word from her for five weeks and didn't know where she was and had been horribly worried. I said too that I knew she'd been in a very difficult position but I couldn't approve of Lánczy's behaviour. He had experience of life and was 46. I didn't say what I thought, namely that he is an adventurer and a scoundrel. I said they should have at least <u>asked</u> her parents' permission. If it had been refused, as it would have been, that would have placed them in a different position. She answered that it was her fault. He'd wanted to talk to Tony but she'd dissuaded him saying it would be no good. I answered that at his age he should know that it had to be done even if a refusal was a certainty. When she left, she said from the door, in a trembling voice: Thank you for seeing me. I said I would always want to see her whatever she'd done. Ah well, she was like our daughter.

Due to financial and marital difficulties at home in Hungary, in 1924 Kitty thought it would be in Alexie's best interests to live with Maud and Gilbert, and her cousins of a similar age, in England. Alexie lived with Maud and Gilbert for extended periods from the age of four, calling them Muzzer (mama in German) and Papa.

London, Thursday October 26

Lotte Franck came to see me and we talked flats. At 12 I was at the Foreign Office to see Van about Tante Agnes who writes to say that she and her son have got their passports and permission to leave if I can get their English visas renewed which were revoked at the outbreak of war. Van must be bored with these requests by now but I have to make them. He listened patiently. I told him too about Alexie and asked if it were possible to have a slant on Lánczy who is military correspondent for a Hungarian newspaper and writes occasional articles for the *Gazette de Genève* and, I believe, the *Evening Standard*. I expected Alexie and Lánczy at Claridges at 1 for a drink, and a short not too embarrassing meeting, but they arrived late, at 1.30. It was a bad start. I was prejudiced no doubt but I took a strong dislike to him. He is short, spare, dapper, repellent and reptilian. His manner was rather lofty, but the sort of loftiness one never meets with in the really lofty. We only had five minutes talk as I told them I was lunching at once, which they knew beforehand and which was true. I daresay the meeting was an ordeal for him too. I said goodbye to him first and then kissed Alexie. He shot out of the hall without waiting for her and she followed like a child. These manners didn't endear him to me but perhaps he was very nervous. I am horrified at the marriage.

Clive Bell and Tony [Apponyi junior] lunched with me. Clive was much the same as ever and hasn't veered away from pacifism. He says it has nothing to do with a dislike of killing and if he were ordered to go and fight he would do so at once. But he thinks war a far greater disaster, entailing far greater misery, setbacks and destruction than any arrogant and loathsome dictatorship, no matter how repugnant or how disastrous it may be to a small minority of rich or intelligent people. I can understand that, taking a long view, he may be right. But it goes against all one's instincts, feelings and ideals to stick to this, no doubt, logical view.

Mottisfont, Sunday October 29

Today Reggie Pembroke and David [Herbert] lunched. David told Rex and me about a song Beatrice Lillie[62] had sung a night or two before to the troops at Wilton and what laughter and what roars there had been. The song had been about Hitler's 'secret weapon' which he'd threatened his enemies with a few weeks ago and was, of course, indecent and very funny.

Mottisfont, Tuesday October 31

Conrad [Russell], Daphne Weymouth[63] and Derek [Hill] lunched yesterday. Derek is working on a farm. I think he will make up his mind to go before a Conscientious Objector's Tribunal. It needs courage. Later went to see Clare [Tennyson] who is staying at Wilsford [Manor] while Stephen [Tennant,[64] *Clare's brother*] is away. He has spent an enormous amount of money on it and indulged in every whim and fancy. The house appalled me. I couldn't see anything personal or individual about the decoration. It's simply super Syrie

---

62. Beatrice Lillie (1894-1989), comic performer and actress.
63. Daphne Fielding (1904-97), writer and socialite. Married 1926 Henry Thynne (then Viscount Weymouth), who became 6th Marquess of Bath, who she helped to run Longleat. After a divorce, married Xan Fielding. Another of Conrad Russell's close female friends and executor of his will.
64. Stephen Tennant, socialite, known at the time for his decadent lifestyle. Friends with Cecil Beaton and Rex Whistler, Tennant was referred to as the 'brightest' of the 'Bright Young Things' set.

Maugham,[65] screeching colours, bad pickled furniture, dull plaster masks of a young man repeated all over the house – the same mask – dull ornaments. So much effort, such blankness and dreariness.

London, Wednesday November 1

Lunched with Sibyl Colefax. The Duchess of Devonshire, Lady Berkeley, Victor Cazalet,[66] Kenneth Clark and Harold Nicolson there. Sat next to H.N. who had just been to the Maginot Line with a party of MPs. Gave a fascinating account, telling his story so well that I don't think he can have told it often before. They arrived in Paris by air and were taken straight off to meet the new Polish govt, then rather unwillingly to a concert in aid of the Poles. Then train to Nancy or Metz or Thionville. Conducted by generals they got into cars and drove till they arrived at a big gate 'like Wandsworth, exactly like a prison gate,' he said. That was the entrance, or one of them, to the Maginot Line. I asked where it was. 'In a wood,' he said. After various formalities they went in and were taken in a lift to the deepest part, the firing chamber. Galleries and tunnels stretched away. There was a kind of funfair train. They saw, too, a big 75 – how it was hidden in the ground, and how it rose up out of it, noiselessly except for a slow humming sound, 20 or perhaps 40 men in the turret. Through a slide worked on the *camera obscura* principle they saw three miles into Germany. The British pilots were highly praised but said to be too daring and some general said to H.N: 'You people at home must be told that,' meaning the young men must be stopped from throwing away their lives.

London, Thursday November 2

Lánczy came to see me at 4. We sat in a corner of the inner-hall at Claridges and I let him talk only asking an occasional question. As he spoke in a low voice I only heard part of what he said. He gave me an outline of the story of his life, he owned to having got through all the money left him by his father and said it was mostly due to folly. He said he knew it was difficult to defend his run-away marriage with Alexie and indeed he had the wisdom not to try to do so. He told his story quite well and I tried to listen without prejudice. This wasn't easy as I kept on remembering that he was an adventurer and

65. Syrie Maugham, *née* Barnardo (1879-1955), interior decorator. Married Somerset Maugham 1917. First British woman to pursue interior decoration as a career.
66. Victor Cazalet (1896-1943), Conservative MP.

must be an old hand at telling his story, leaving in this, leaving out that, and presenting as acceptable a picture as experience had taught him it was wise to present. I liked him rather better but not very much.

Mottisfont, Sunday November 5

Sat. morning Rex finished the room and left. He left quickly and I felt as if a loved person had gone for ever or as if part of the house I was living in had been suddenly pulled down. When I was in London this week I wrote to R. and said that as he'd done so much more in the room than originally contemplated – painting pelmets, designing of wall-lights, helping with furniture and so on – and as I knew it had taken months more than he thought it would, I would like to add £300 to the sum originally fixed. I knew that he'd been dissatisfied in some way in August. He wrote as much to Gilbert once when G. urged him to hurry on with the work and fix a date for its completion and stick to it. I think he was disgruntled then because he thought he wasn't making as much out of it as he should have and because he saw it was taking months more to complete than he'd bargained for. This was partly due to wrong calculation on his part, partly to his own idleness and partly to my indecision in May when it came to settling on trophies versus landscapes and some minor details. Anyhow I had the feeling that he felt sore about it, at any rate in Aug. I naturally didn't say all this to him in my letter. I put it in the way I thought would be easiest for him to accept.

On Friday night when I went to talk to him after dinner he said quickly and directly, in his quick direct way, that he was most moved by the offer and my generosity but that he couldn't possibly accept it. If he did, it would mean that he could never see me again, and he preferred to see me again. I tried awkwardly to make him change his mind but couldn't. He said he thought it would be fair to give him £100 more than the original sum for the extra work done but that he couldn't take more. I, in my room, was moved, and strange to say dumbfounded because, sad to say, I don't remember anybody I know in the whole course of my life ever refusing money. I don't know why I say 'sad to say'. It's so natural to accept money if one is in need of it or if it's going to make possible some holiday or pleasure. Rex's refusal made a deep impression and I loved him for it.

TWO

Invasion Fears

In which Germany invades Denmark, Norway,
the Low Countries and France.
The Battle of Britain begins.
Officers are billeted at Mottisfont; and the
Russian artist Boris Anrep arrives in London.

Britain and France, together with Australia, Canada, New Zealand and South Africa, have declared war on Germany following its invasion of Poland on September 1, 1939. The Soviet Union has attacked Poland from the east and is preparing to invade Finland in accordance with the secret protocols of a non-aggression pact that it signed with Germany in August 1939. However, in a period known as the 'Phoney War', the Allies have responded with limited military opposition to these developments. The United States remains neutral. A blackout is in force and food rationing is set to commence in January 1940.

Some of Maud's German Jewish relatives are safe now in England but Tante Agnes Mühsam and her son Hans Werner have had their UK visas rescinded and are still in Germany, and Tante Agnes's daughter Lieselotte is still stuck in Spain. Maud and Gilbert are living at Mottisfont, often staying in hotels on the south coast to improve Gilbert's ailing health. Maud also goes up to London for a couple of nights most weeks to see friends, staying at Claridges.

As part of the war effort, Maud is holding weekly 'knitting parties' for the troops, attending a St John Ambulance first aid course at Broadlands, collecting money for the fund to build Spitfire airplanes and occasionally working at the Food Office in Romsey. She also regularly visits the local Searchlight unit, a night bombing defence system in which sound detectors, searchlights and anti-aircraft artillery seek out and shoot down enemy airplanes.

Mottisfont, Friday November 10

Yesterday David [Herbert], Cecil [Beaton] and Michael [Duff] fetched me at Claridges and we had a gay, pleasant evening together. David took us to a bar frequented by homosexuals. We groped down a dark alley and up narrow stairs. The room was full of men drinking and talking. I was the only woman there. There was no dancing as I had hoped and no caressing. In fact it was DULL. Then we went to the Nest, David's spiritual home. Here a terrifying altercation started between a black man and some young, insolent tipsy white. The black man had my sympathy though I was afraid of a fight. He roared angry abuse. The tension was extreme but after more roaring and hurling of insults he pulled himself together or was coaxed away. He came and sat with us and complained of the manners of some white people. And there he is right. I got to bed at 5.

Mottisfont, Sunday November 12

Crinks, Fred,[1] Jasper [Ridley] and Nevile Henderson staying. N.H. is a friend of Claud's [Russell]. I had never seen him before. He has a handsome face but rather a narrow forehead. He is small and very much bent. He struck me as rather a simple sort of man, honourable, sincere, direct but I should never have thought him equal to the immensely important post of ambassador to Berlin. Today he talked about the Germans. I asked him which of the leading people he would have been most struck by if he'd met them casually without knowing anything about them. He said: Goering. He had much the most personality. Hitler hadn't ever impressed him. He never felt his charm or magnetism. He thought him ordinary and commonplace. He said Goebbels was cultivated and could be most pleasant and charming to talk to. Ribbentrop he hated and could hardly talk about. Hess he had hardly met. He said Hitler's eyes were brown. I had imagined them, from photographs, to be very light blue. I asked him whether he thought Hitler's rages and screaming fits were genuine. He hesitated and then told me this story. He said that Hitler, in the last days before Henderson left, had stormed and raged at him. At his next interview Henderson had something he wanted to say and made up his mind to feign anger and rage at Hitler. He started violently but

---

1. Lt.-Cdr. Frederick Heyworth Cripps, later 3rd Baron Parmoor (1885-1977). Decorated with a DSO in the First World War. Served in the Royal Navy Volunteer Reserve and 13th Lancashire Parachute Battalion in the Second World War.

not in genuine anger. He forced himself. But after two or three minutes he found himself infected by this assumed rage and his rage became genuine. He seems to think Hitler's rages were of the same order.

Mottisfont, Sunday November 19

On Tuesday I started a knitting party for the troops in the housekeeper's room.[2] Some of the villagers came and we were about 26. Mama, Mary [Irby] and Ath, wearing a lilac turban, were there too. On Wednesday Mary and I went to the Searchlight at Mount Farm to find out whether the detachment was in need of anything. Yes, they said, some wood to complete their washing and cookery huts, and some books and papers. Raymond and Mr Macdonald came for the weekend. R. is delighted with Gloucester, the cathedral, the organist, the choir but not so pleased with the work he has to do [*to get into university*]!

London, Thursday November 23

Took Tante Fritze and Lotte to the Police Court at Rosslyn Hill as a preliminary to the tribunal. Didn't care for the atmosphere. Manners rough. Aliens timid, patient and pale. No German interpreter as far as I could see. Some of them knew no English and other aliens had to translate to them as best they could. Must lead to unnecessary delay and confusion. The inspectors and police are no doubt quite well-intentioned but their manners are rough: you people there; this old woman; these women etc. It made an unpleasant impression.

Mottisfont, Monday November 27

Rex came to lunch yesterday. He hadn't yet seen the curtains up and the room more or less finished. The 10 wall lights had arrived and R. fixed the position and Burden put one up while he was there. R. looked pale and ill, he has just had laryngitis. He is going to finish a picture of somebody's house which he started months ago and then he may do a memorial for Lord Lytton in memory of his son. Today we shot. Extra guns Bishop and Alcock. Colonel

---

2. These knitting parties were eventually held in the Whistler Room, according to a later diary entry. Thanks to the efforts of Mottisfont, the War Comforts Fund at Serle House was able to send 2,250 items to each overseas battalion of the Royal Hampshire Regiment, according to a letter to Maud on October 18, 1944 from the chairman of the fund (Hampshire Records Office, ref 13M63/428).

Bishop,[3] who is an Australian, on being shown Rex's room said, 'Gosh, what would the old monks think? It looks like the back room of a brothel.' This is a new light on the room.

On November 30, the Soviet Union invaded Finland.

London, Thursday November 30

A Mr Hermann Ringel came to see me. I had paid money into his father's a/c for Lieselotte in Spain. The first sum she seems to have had. He didn't know much about it but promised to make inquiries. He was in Spain a year or two ago and met L.'s friend, Betti Josephson,[4] whom he disliked intensely. He said she was an evil influence and had a bad reputation. He wouldn't say more. I gathered the bad reputation applied to morals as well as politics. He has a brother-in-law in Spain and is going to find out what he can and help L. if it's possible.

Bournemouth, Thursday December 7

I am 48. I like the company of young people but not much of my contemporaries among women or older women. I don't like their staleness. There are plenty of exceptions, Diana [Cooper], Goonie,[5] Nathalie [Ridley, *née* von Benckendorf], Lady Horner[6] and anybody wide-awake. I don't think I am spoilt or difficult to please or blasé. I enjoy an enormous amount of things, some not so simple. I like high life and snatches of low life. I like queer, difficult people but I like simple people too, like George[7] or Randolph [Churchill]. The more I see of life, the more I hate cruelty and the more struck I am by fine, generous, noble behaviour. My heart and thoughts are often

3. Lieutenant Colonel Gibson Bishop (1893-1979), born New Zealand, served with the New Zealand Expeditionary Force in Gallipoli, awarded Military Cross. Settled in Hampshire.
4. I haven't been able to confirm Betti Josephson's identity. However, like Lieselotte, she was probably gay and a Trotskyist.
5. Lady Gwendoline Churchill, 'Goonie', *née* Bertie (1885-1941), daughter of Montagu Bertie, 7th Earl of Abingdon, and Gwendoline Dormer. Married in 1908 Winston Churchill's brother, Major John 'Jack' Churchill, who worked for a time in Paul Nelke's stockbroking company.
6. Frances Jane Horner, *née* Graham (d.1940), hostess and art patron. Married in 1883 Sir John Francis Horner.
7. Probably George Josselyn Howard, 11th Earl of Carlisle (1895-1963) who Maud and Gilbert saw a lot of in their early married life.

rather sad but I suppose I have a good deal of vitality in a feeblish frame, a great capacity for enjoyment, a love of beauty in all forms, the power of still looking forward to things and am still excited about life.

London, Wednesday December 13

Took Lotte to the Aliens Tribunal at Moreland Hall. Had permission from Osbert Peake,[8] now Under-Secretary at Home Office, for Tante Fritze not to attend on account of age and health. Whole affair well conducted. Personnel civil, pleasant and efficient from door-keeper to judge. Waited for about an hour in a large hall with an immense coal fire roaring up the chimney – didn't quite warm the room though the good intention was plain to all. About 80 people there. Atmosphere so easy that they were quite gay unlike at the Police Court. Slight mirth when a serious young inspector came in from time to time and read from a list the names of the refugees whose cases were ready to be considered. Many of the names were unpronounceable – Czech or Polish.

After waiting about an hour Lotte was called to Tribunal II and I went with her. The judge sat at a desk in a small, well-heated, apricot-pink room, flanked by a man and two women, one an Austrian, I think, who did any translating that was necessary. We sat on two small wooden chairs in front of him. The proceedings can't have lasted more than seven minutes. He had all the relevant papers. He asked Lotte her name and what relation she was to Tante Fritze whose passport lay in front of him. Then he asked L. why she and her mother had decided to leave Germany. She answered, 'Because it isn't a place that Jews can live in.' He then said, 'Are you prepared to be loyal to the British Empire?' To which she said, 'Yes.' Then he said words to this effect: 'Do you hate Hitler and all he stands for?' Answer: 'Yes.' He asked her whether she'd ever had employment in Germany and whether she intended taking up employment here, to which she said, 'No.' He asked her how much money she had and how she intended to live. I said I was their guarantor and was making them an allowance. He said, 'Is it correct that you are going to make them an allowance of £450 a year?' 'Yes,' I said. He said everything was in order, cracked some little joke I didn't quite catch and wished us good morning and we left.

8. Osbert Peake, later 1st Viscount Ingleby (1897-1966), Conservative politician. Parliamentary undersecretary of state for the Home Office 1939-44, Minister of Pensions and National Insurance 1951-55. Maud consulted Peake regularly during the war on the status of her foreign relations.

London, Thursday December 14

I had a cold, tiring morning looking at a prospective flat for Lotte, with Lotte. Dined with I.C.-G. at Jardin, he in uniform. Saddened me to see this unmilitary person in uniform. And sad at thought it might be our last meeting at Jardin. There was a railway station farewell feeling.

Mottisfont, Wednesday December 20

Took G. to Bournemouth on Monday. Returned to Mottisfont yesterday for the village knitting party. I.C.-G., now at Salisbury with a band of 15 artists learning camouflage, came for the night. He thought Rex's room lovely having rather scoffed at it when I used to tell him about it, and not having liked it very much when he saw it in the summer. He gave a sort of gasp of surprise when he saw it and said Rex was a genius.

Mottisfont, Monday December 25

On Friday visited people in the village I thought might be badly off. Presents for Xmas. Whites, Ingwoods, Watermans, Rogers. School children's tea-party at 4 on Saturday. Twelve evacuated children there out of only 19 left [*some evacuees returned home in the absence of air raids but six children from Portsmouth are still staying in the house*]. About 65 children in all. Yesterday, Xmas Eve, tea in Rex's room for Paul [Irby] and two small friends. Owen Lancaster's children and Mrs Kirkham brought her two children. Today Xmas Day. Gave the servants presents and Xmas boxes. Church 3. Chorals. Raymond played organ.

Mottisfont, Friday December 29

Lunched at Wilton where they were preparing a Xmas Pantomime for the troops. All the cast were dressed up for the dress rehearsal that afternoon. Cecil B. looked wonderfully funny, wearing a lace negligée of a previous Lady Pembroke's. Rehearsal in Herbert Memorial Hall. Cinderella, Bee [Pembroke]; the Queen, Lady Margaret Drummond-Hay; Prince Charming and very good indeed, David [Herbert]; Buttons, Oggie,[9] Ugly Sister, Cecil. David danced professionally and quite prettily. But Cecil was outstanding, so fantastic, so comic, such a strange figure and superbly grotesque when he danced.

---

9. Olga Lynn, 'Oggie' (1882-1961), a professional singer and singing teacher.

Mottisfont, Monday January 1 1940

We didn't sit up to see the New Year in. There may be very little to welcome. Shot on Saturday. Guns, self, Claud, Generals Cuthberston and Chaplin, Admiral Brand and Sir Joseph Ball. The latter read something out of a letter he'd just received from the PM, words to the effect that things will no doubt get busy in the spring. We all guess that much. I.C.-G. came for dinner and the night. Ath perked up. She likes company. I wish she could have one or two admirers.

Bournemouth, Friday January 5

Mama, Claud, Ath and Raymond left on Tuesday. I remained for the sewing party. G. and I had dinner alone together and were grateful for absences. Wednesday morning we came here. Massage for rigid shoulders. Finished Harold Nicolson's Penguin book *Why we are at War*. Agree pretty well with all he says. Felt appalled when I read the brief account of the dismemberment and then engulfment of Czecho-Slovakia and our complete inability to deal with the situation as it should have been dealt with. Ghastly mess.

London, Tuesday January 9

Dined with the Glenconners at the Berkeley. Christopher told me about some of his difficulties with the Norwegian Delegation over here. Before Xmas he'd exploded at one of the meetings and caused consternation. He complained of their timidity and their desire to be allowed by us to trade as much with Germany as Germany desires so as to give Germany no excuse for an invasion. I couldn't help sympathising with them but Christopher said they and Sweden were craven. They had always taken a high line in the League of Nation meetings, spoke in the voice of Democracy, condemned oppression, urged sanctions and now was the moment for them to decide whether Democracy and their high ideals were worth defending. They couldn't have the best of both worlds. It would be greatly to our advantage, he said, to have them in with us and be able to use their ports, police and coasts and prevent the Germans getting the Swedish iron ore. If Germany made a move against Sweden it would be a good thing for us. We could come in and defend them and seize their ports. Strategically no doubt he is right but the intrigue is unpleasant.

London, Wednesday January 10

Lunch with I. at Carlton. Complained he hadn't seen me for three months. Couldn't tell poor I. he'd talked so much war-nonsense the last two times I saw him that I hadn't enjoyed his company. Went on to a second lunch at Alice's [Astor]. H.G. Wells[10] was there. Wells talked at length and with extreme cynicism about Russia, their incompetence, their futility, their disregard for all we consider the Rights of Man. He talks slowly, clearly, rather nasally. I thought the subject a little tedious because we've all said the same ourselves.

London, Friday January 12

G., Martin and I lunched with Van at the Carlton. Van told G. that, from information he had, there was nothing wrong with Lánczy in a political sense. Among things we've heard about him from Kitty and Tony is that he has hypnotic powers! That he is a blackmailer; 'sold' his first wife when someone came along who wanted to marry her; constantly appeared in central Europe with young foreign girls and palmed them off; and is a homosexual. I am prepared to believe one or two of these things but not all. Martin and I saw *Swan Lake* at Sadler's Wells. Then went to Hanover Lodge [*home of Alice Astor*] where we had supper. Freddie Ashton[11] and Bobbie Helpmann[12] joined us. Helpmann had a very funny imitation of how a swan <u>really</u> walks on land compared with the exquisite steps and movements invented for the swan-princess. He gets into a semi-squatting position with knees turned out and waddles, bumps and flops along, hissing.

Torquay, Wednesday January 17

G. and I came here, Hotel Imperial, on Monday. Difficulty in getting G., breathless, along a packed platform and a long train. He has a slightly inflamed ear and is frightfully deaf. Saw a local doctor today who told me privately he thought G.'s Eustachian tubes were collapsed. They could be blown up which would improve his deafness temporarily but he thought he would become increasingly deaf. Oddly enough I began to feel very faint and had to go and lie down. I don't know whether it was the shock of the warning that made me so, or whether it was too much smoking in the morning. The

10. Herbert George Wells (1866-1946), novelist, best remembered for science fiction.
11. Sir Frederick Ashton (1904-88), ballet choreographer and director.
12. Sir Robert Helpmann (1909-86), Australian dancer, actor, theatre director and choreographer.

news has depressed me. It would be hard for G. not to take part in general conversation any more and make our talks alone quite different.

Torquay, Sunday January 28

Quiet week. The intense cold wore off. Appears to have been coldest winter since 1894. G. and I went for drives most days. Hotel car appears to have unlimited petrol. Country charming. G. had his ears blown out. Since then gradual improvement. Ian Howland had a son, born at the Ritz! Sounds a suitable place for his son to be born! I should hate to have been born in it. Though I don't know that it's much worse than Mrs Langtry's bed in Pont Street which is where I was born, Mama and Papa having no house and having taken Lillie Langtry's for some months.

Torquay, Sunday February 25

Most days same routine. Get up very lâte, five minute walk, if fine, with G. before lunch. Pleasures: coffee after lunch, arrival of letters at three, drive, news at six, cocktails before dinner, coffee after dinner. Reading: *Horizon*, a new monthly review edited by Cyril Connolly. Good and readable. Stephen Spender's *September Journal,* simple, well-written and moving. Another review is *Abinger Chronicle,* contributors Max Beerbohm, Oliver Lodge, E.M. Foster. Otherwise mostly newspaper reading – *The Times, New Statesman* – and letter-writing.

London, Wednesday February 28

London with G. We both dined with Violet Bonham Carter. Bongie [*Violet's husband Maurice*], Archie Sinclair, Harold Nicolson there. Jan Masaryk[13] came in at the end of dinner. Masaryk told a story which is nothing when written but was oddly impressive in the telling. During the last war the division he was in was attached to a Prussian Army Corps. It was autumn and on an exceptionally beautiful evening M. went out into the forest to breathe the air and look at the loveliness. A little way off he saw a German taking the air too and, he imagined, enjoying the evening in the same way. But to his amazement he saw the German draw himself up and perform the goose step – or perhaps practice it – like that, alone in the forest.

13. Jan Masaryk (1886-1948), Czech diplomat and politician. Ambassador to UK 1925-38. Foreign Minister of Czech government in exile 1940-48. Probably murdered by Russians.

London, Friday March 1

Dined alone with Alice [Astor]. She talked a lot about herself. Said she was going to marry Philip Harding, political correspondent of the *Financial News*. Said he was an intellectual type. I wonder why she must marry. Last year she wanted to marry Jamie Hamilton.

London, Saturday March 2

Lunch at the Ritz with G., Cockie and Rex. Went up to see Howland baby. Reddish hair, small, nice like all tiny babies. Howland sitting room bleak, no newspapers or books lying about, not even a wireless. Only a few orchids on the mantelpiece. Felt they must be leading a dull life.

Bournemouth, Thursday March 7

Knitting party in afternoon. The villagers complained that owing to the confusion from evacuation their children only go to school half the day, whereas the few remaining evacuees go both morning and afternoon. Shortage of desks is said to be the reason but that can't be the case. I must do something about it. *[She discusses the situation with the school teacher Mrs Pitts the following week].* We still have six evacuated school children in the house. In the evening we came here. G. very far from well – nervous, tired, depressed. He stayed in bed. I am always very sad when he isn't well. I dread the inevitable. And for 23 years I have thought about it. Where most women panic about their children, I panic, and always have, about G.

Bournemouth, Monday March 11

G. is better. Doing nothing, hardly even reading. Finland, as good as abandoned by her neighbours, negotiating.

On March 13, Finland signed a peace treaty with the Soviet Union, ceding border territory and economic benefits, after a conflict that lasted a little over three months. Denmark, Norway and Sweden had not allowed Allied troops to cross their territories to aid Finland, believing that it was a pretext for the Allies to gain a foothold in Norwegian ports and Swedish iron ore mines.

London, Wednesday March 13

The Glenconners, Eddy Sackville-West, Alice [Astor] and Angus [Menzies, *actor*] came to dinner. We went to see Edith Evans, Peggy Ashcroft and Alec Guinness in *Cousin Muriel*. This is the second time I have seen Alec Guinness. He is a very good actor. He has some special quality that makes him stand away, apart and above his fellow actors.

London, Thursday March 14

G. and I lunched Carlton with Van and Sarita. Van was as violent and bitter as ever. He hasn't a word of praise for anyone, not even Lord Halifax. I gather he thinks him as fish-like as the rest. When talking about who the next prime minister could possibly be he put forward Sir Samuel Hoare. I exclaimed in surprise. Van said, 'None of the others will take any jump but Sam Hoare will, if you lead him up carefully to a small one.' Talking about Lord Halifax, Van said, 'He is the sort of man who has to put on his spectacles to see whether we have been hit below the belt.' Sarita said that he always seemed to talk to one as if he were still seated on an elephant. Van said he'd written a memorandum in 1933 drawing attention to Germany's rearmament and saying they would be ready for military action by January 1938. I daresay a great many other people wrote memos to the same effect. Van seems to have got himself into an extraordinary position. No one of any importance comes near him or consults him. And he cuts, or won't speak to, any number of people. He is very bitter and critical. I have been puzzled at this *cul-de-sac*. He stands four-square face to face with nothing. His opponents are all busy with something else to do. Somehow he has got himself clumsily into this impasse. I dined with Ian. He still persuades himself the war will be over, somehow, in a few months. His job absorbs him. Said War Loan has been much undersubscribed as I guessed from the absence of headlines and trumpetings.

Mottisfont, Easter Sunday March 24

I started the week with racking rheumatism. Saw a Dr on Monday who said: influenza. On Tuesday a rash started and spread, at first timidly and delicately. By Wednesday there was no timidity and I was an ugly sight with German measles. Am quite happy in bed, indeed I always am. Raymond went to Cambridge and did his entrance exam for King's last Saturday. On Friday G. had a long letter from Beves[14] saying he'd failed, work superficial, appeared to have a dislike for learning and for authority, although showed

---

14. Donald Beves (1896-1961), Vice-Provost of King's College, Cambridge.

some originality. It's too disappointing. R. thought he'd passed. Martin came on five days' leave yesterday. He was up to be vetted for a commission with five others. All the others – two of them Communist friends of his – passed and he was rejected. He was seen by a Brigadier General Lumley for whom he took a violent dislike. It may have been mutual. So that is how we stand at Easter 1940. One in bed, one rejected for a Commission, one rejected by King's, but the other, praise God, rather better than he has been.

London, Wednesday March 27

Went to lunch with Alice [Astor]. Asked to be there at 1.15. No one there when I arrived. Sat down, started reading. After 25 minutes Victor Cazalet and Jimmy Smith[15] arrived. We started talking about Philip Harding, Alice's young man, who is in their AA Battery and they said, 'Well I suppose it's all over by now.' That was the first hint that Alice was married that morning and that I'd been asked to a wedding breakfast. She'd told me about Philip H. but I had no idea the wedding was so imminent. A few minutes later they arrived. He is dark, rather good-looking, in a moody rather morose way. At lunch were only Alice and Philip, his mother and his brother, Jimmy Smith, Victor and myself. After lunch a few people came in who had just had telegraphs or telephone messages and were surprised and excited.

London, Thursday March 28

Lunch with Rex at Jardin. He has a room in Raimund's[16] house which he likes. After Xmas he painted two portraits of Christabel's little girl Anne and now he is starting to do the décor for a ballet of Freddie Ashton's. G. came to London. Dined with I. at the Savoy Grill and we talked and talked.

London, Monday April 1

We came to see Beves, King's admissions tutor, who was passing through London, to consult him about Raymond – whether it's worth him having another try for King's or whether he could help us get him into another college. Beves was charming. I thought him very wise and shrewd. He had

15. James Frederick A. Smith (b.1906), son of Lord and Lady Hambleden of W.H. Smith, the newsagents and booksellers.
16. Raimund von Hofmannsthal (1906-74). Of Austrian parentage, Raimund married first Alice Astor in 1933 and then Elizabeth Paget (the sister of Caroline and Beatrice Paget) in 1939.

Raymond taped. Beves would not actually say that there was no point in him trying for King's again though I begged him to say so if that was his view. He said he would like to think it over. Alexie and Lánczy dined and we went to a film. G. hadn't seen L. before.

On April 9, Germany invaded Denmark and Norway. Denmark surrendered almost immediately while, despite Norwegian resistance, German troops were able to land and occupy Norway over the next two months.

London, Tuesday April 9

Today news of the invasion of Norway and Denmark. Duff, who came to have a drink with G. at 12, gave us the news about Denmark. Seemed to think we were too late again. I was overcome with depression.

London, Friday April 19

Went to bed [*at Claridges*] on the 10th with a rainbow-coloured throat and influenza. I have been in bed these 10 days, devouring the newspapers and listening to the wireless, plunged, most of the time, in gloom except for some hours of elation when the Skagerrak[17] naval victory was announced. There is something unexplained. How did the Germans get unmolested into all the ports? What about our secret service? I listened to Ian broadcasting to the Germans in German. He wasn't bad. His voice is higher than I thought. I had never noticed the pitch of Ian's voice before. He says the stuff given him to broadcast is dreadful, dull stuff and he tries to improve it.

It appears from a letter of Colonel Ireland's to G. that Martin was rejected for a commission because when interviewed by Brig. Lumley he made a 'deplorable impression'. He was 'dreamy' and seemed not to care whether he got one or not. Ireland who likes him says he 'put up a poor show'. He added he was really unfit to become an officer in a fighting unit and should never have been recommended. He paid tribute to his niceness but said his recommendation was a mistake. The trouble about Martin is that he's very

17. On April 12, 1940, *The Times* reported that 'a heavy toll had been taken by our submarines on German transport and store ships crossing to Scandinavia in the Skagerrak'. However, although the Royal Navy enjoyed partial successes against the Kriegsmarine in the battle for Norway, this was only after the German navy had managed to land troops in Narvik and Trondheim in the north, and also Bergen in the south.

untidy, careless, unpunctual, 'unsmart' and inclined to be very dirty unless washing is made easy for him by having a well-equipped bathroom close at hand. Today Martin telephoned to say he was being sent back to Swindon because of slight asthma and was not considered fit to go abroad yet.

Mottisfont, Wednesday April 24

I came here after lunch on Saturday morning still weak. G. in much better health. Mama and Conrad here. Conrad too very depressed about the German invasion of Norway, unlike G. who saw it as a real blunder. Laughingly, Conrad said G.'s optimism had really irritated him, as it had me. Yesterday, St George's Day, Duff made a magnificent, inspiring, heroic kind of oratorical speech which was broadcast.[18] It was admirably delivered and must have been passionately felt.

Mottisfont, Tuesday April 30

One day has been much like another. All would have been pleasant if it hadn't been for the war which forms the background, when it isn't in the foreground, of all one's thoughts. We have been alone, G.'s health is much better, the weather has been warm, spring is gaining ground. This past week I have been nursing my mind. I found that listening to wireless news several times a day, devouring the newspapers and brooding over the war were making me uselessly nervous and depressed. So I only glance at the newspapers and don't listen to the wireless and I am much better. I have been arranging books, seeing villagers etc. [*The agent*] Woolley came on Friday morning and explained a ghastly project for bringing the grid with its towering steel pylons right through the heart of our land. Martin came on Sunday. He has now been marked B1 e.g., not good enough health for frontline fighting but up to garrison work at home or abroad, or lines of communication. Asthma did it.

Mottisfont, Friday May 3

Lunched with Archie Sinclair at the Log d'Or. He was looking young, well and alert. He talked about Norway. There were stories of much muddle and confusion – the code for the north being given to those in the south

---

18. Duff Cooper gave a patriotic speech at the Royal Society of the Order of St George on behalf of Churchill, who could not attend, which was broadcast on the BBC.

and vice versa. There was bad liaison work between French and English. Said Winston was a tired man, unpopular with the Conservatives. I said I longed for a change of govt. He said he thought it hardly mattered who was the next PM, the important thing was to change. I congratulated Archie on his Scotch speech the other day (Edinburgh), the speech that has been criticised as recklessly attacking the PM. Archie said he did not regret one word but it was possible this speech was premature and might only result in reuniting the restless members in the Conservative Party. He didn't think the debate next week would cause the PM's fall but it might shake him rather severely.

The Norwegian fiasco led to a debate in the House of Commons and calls for Neville Chamberlain to step down as prime minister.

London, Wednesday May 8

Lunch with Sylvia [Henley]. Phyllis [de Janzé] and Hubert [Duggan][19] there. All excited about the debate that started yesterday and is going on today. The PM's long statement was insufficient to explain the position we now find ourselves in in Norway. Hubert is one of the Conservative rebels who has never yet voted against the govt. He has merely abstained. At lunch he hadn't quite made up his mind what he would do. He thought there might be quite a big vote, he thought the PM might be shaken but he didn't think he would fall. I suppose that is the general view. I dined with Phyllis. Hubert was at the House and came in for a hurried dinner, left and came back about 11.30 with the news of a small majority of 80 votes [*from a notional majority of 213*], of the tone, temper and feeling of the House, of Duff's good speech, and of the lamentable impression caused by the PM when he said, turning half round, 'Anyhow I have still some friends left,' as if personal loyalty were the main issue. No one quite knew what the next move would be – Cabinet reconstruction – or disappearance of the PM?

Mottisfont, Thursday May 9

Rumours that the PM is to see the King. I thought it looked like resignation. G. thought not, just a visit to give first-hand information.

---

19. Hubert Duggan (1904-43), Conservative MP. Broke the whip, voting to bring down Neville Chamberlain in 1940. The lover of Maud's friend Phyllis de Janzé.

On May 10, Germany invaded France, Belgium, Luxembourg and the Netherlands, hastening the resignation of Neville Chamberlain and appointment of Winston Churchill as prime minister and the formation of a National Coalition Government.

Mottisfont, Friday May 10

Adele came in and told me that the Low Countries had been invaded. I was appalled. My heart sank at the thought of the coming slaughter. In the evening on the 9 o'clock news we heard that Chamberlain had gone and Winston become prime minister. Jubilation. Violet[20] and Fred [Cripps], Doria Scott[21] and Cecil Beaton are staying.

Mottisfont, Tuesday May 14

Conrad arrived Sat. The Coopers were expected but didn't come and we guessed Duff was being considered for a Cabinet post. Fred is a lieutenant in the Royal Navy, stationed on shore at Scapa and has 10 days leave. He has been living in a caravan in Arctic cold. Sunday we lay about. Fred fished all day with a burnt face and slight sunstroke, his head tied up. Doria very depressed. Andrew [Scott, *her husband*] is in Norway. Cecil drew, and painted a nice picture of the strange contorted oak near the Chapel Porch.[22]

Duff Cooper was made Minister of Information among other Cabinet appointments, including Labour MPs, in the National Coalition government.

London, Wednesday May 15

Dined with Alice, bringing with me Christopher and Elizabeth [Glenconner], and Michael D. [Duff]. Freddie Ashton sat next to me. He was caught at The Hague with the Sadler's Wells ballet and got back two days ago – 700 people on straw in the hold of a cargo boat. Said the roar of aeroplanes over The Hague was shattering. Constant machine-gun fire but bombs only dropped on the outskirts. Said he couldn't laugh or joke as some of the others could. At one meal

---

20. Violet Cripps, later Baroness Parmoor, *née* Nelson (1891-1983).
21. Victoria Doris 'Doria' Scott, *née* Haig (1908-93), daughter of Field Marshal Douglas Haig and Dorothy Maud Vivian. Married to Col. Andrew Scott DSO (1906-71).
22. Beaton provides a wonderful description of this weekend in *The Years Between: Diaries 1939-44* (Weidenfeld and Nicolson, 1965).

he couldn't eat, at the next he gorged. One night he couldn't sleep, the next he lay like a log and he slept all the way across to Harwich. They lost their music, clothes, scenery etc. From having thought that nothing was as important to him as his art, he now felt that there was something more important.

London, Thursday May 16

Dined with I. at the Ivy. We were very gloomy and depressed and filled with forebodings about north France and Flanders.

Mottisfont, Tuesday May 21

Eddie Marsh, Guy Charteris,[23] A.E.W. Mason,[24] Violet and Bongie spent the weekend. The weather was flawlessly beautiful. We lay in the garden all day and talked and talked. Violet always talks well. Her political memory is vast and her stories and anecdotes always good. But I can remember none with the exception of a very amusing story about Winston looking round the dining room table at Venetia's on his 60th birthday, his eye lighting first on Lady Castlerosse [*Doris (1890-1942), notorious for her affairs with rich men*], then on Phyllis [de Janzé] and then on some other beauties and saying, 'Shtained perhaps, but poshitive.' All these last few days I have been deeply anxious and depressed. I am afraid of the encirclement of the northern armies. People seem slow at seeing what may happen. G. says I am defeatist. I am <u>not</u>. But I look ahead and watch the map.

London, Wednesday May 22

Lunched with Violet B.-C. Van and Sarita there. He was dreadfully depressed and sad to see. He can't pull himself together and get away from his accusations and lamentations. We asked him who the Quislings [*collaborators*] were, hinted darkly at in the Whitehall Letter which G. and I take in. He said Maule Ramsay, an [*Scottish Unionist*] MP. He'd collected information about him weeks or months ago, sent it to the appropriate quarters but nothing had been

---

23. Guy Charteris (1886-1967). The father of the society hostess Ann Charteris, the future wife of Ian Fleming. Apparently Ian and Ann met each other at the Charterises' family home, Stanway in Gloucestershire, while the Russells were leasing it in 1934 (Lycett, *Ian Fleming*).
24. Alfred Edward Mason (1865-1948), novelist, best known for *The Four Feathers* (1902) about courage and cowardice in wartime.

done. Dined with Sam Courtauld. Sat next to [Gladwyn] Jebb.[25] Discussed Sir John Anderson[26] and the Home Office. I then said, 'Do you know a man called Maule Ramsay?' He gave me a surprised look and asked, 'Why do you jump to Maule Ramsay?' I answered, 'Because we were talking about the Home Office.' He said, 'Why do you connect the two?' I: 'Home Defence.' He: 'Do you mean the Fifth Column?' I: 'Yes.' I saw he knew something.

London, Thursday May 23

After lunch I saw on the posters that Maule Ramsay has been arrested. Mosley and the Fascists are being rounded up. Went to see the Francks [*Tante Fritz and Lotte*]. They are in Category C [*enemy aliens considered no security risk*] and haven't been bothered.

London, Friday May 24

Alexie lunched with me. Said Home Office had asked her and Lánczy to leave by June 20th. Would probably go to Hungary for a few days and then to Switzerland. I urged Portugal. Cheap to live in and pleasant. Poor Alexie. She was anxious. I can't see what their future can be.

On May 26, the evacuation of Allied troops from the beaches and port of Dunkirk begins after German forces encircle and trap Belgium, British and French troops. Some 338,000 Allied troops were evacuated.

Mottisfont, Tuesday May 28

Today came the news of King Leopold's [*of Belgium*] surrender. One's capacity for being astonished by anything is almost exhausted. Have felt

---

25. Gladwyn Jebb, later 1st Baron Gladwyn (1900-96), civil servant, diplomat and politician. Private secretary to head of diplomatic service at Foreign Office. Assistant undersecretary Ministry of Economic Warfare 1940-42, where he was put in charge of the Special Operations Executive. In 1942, he was appointed head of the Foreign Office's Reconstruction Department.
26. John Anderson, later 1st Viscount Waverley (1882-1958), civil servant and politician. Home Secretary 1939-40 overseeing the mass internment of 'enemy aliens', Lord President of the Council 1940-3, responsible for the Home Front, Chancellor of the Exchequer 1943-5. Initiated the development of an air-raid shelter, known as the 'Anderson Shelter', which people could put up in their garden. Churchill advised the King in January 1945 that in the event of his and Anthony Eden's death, Anderson should be made prime minister.

horribly anxious about Germany's encircling movement. Now it's moving fast. Such anxiety.

London, Wednesday May 29

Lunched with Clare [Tennyson]. Cardie [Lionel Montagu], Ulick [Alexander] and Montie Abingdon[27] there, loathsome now. He talked extremely defeatist stuff, might have been Haw-Haw's mouth-piece.[28] I became incensed. Lunch was disagreeable. Everyone left at once afterwards. Dined at the Savoy with Christopher and Camilla Sykes and Ian. Christopher much upset because his pioneer battalion [*the Green Howard's newly formed 7th Battalion*] which naturally was all but unarmed, had been wiped out in France. They had found themselves fighting with little more than their bare fists.

London, Thursday May 30

Lunched with Elizabeth [Glenconner] at the Mirabelle in the garden after which we went and looked at pictures and to Sotheby's, snatching some moments of oblivion from the terrible anxieties of the hour. Agonised about fate of BEF [*British Expeditionary Forces*]. Alexie came to tea, in better spirits. L. has managed to join the LDV [*Local Defence Volunteers*] at Chelsea Barracks. Fancy anyone taking a Hungarian military correspondent! I hid my dislike of the idea. Dined with Cardie at the Savoy. As we were leaving, Rex came in in uniform. Welsh Guards. Very neat and smart and obviously very pleased with his nice new uniform. Poor Rex.

Mottisfont, Friday May 31

Martin has been released from the army for six months and is going to the MOI [*Ministry of Information*]. Duff telephoned and proposed it to G. on his second day in office. We were very touched at his thinking of such a thing, of such a kindness during the confusion of his first days at a new ministry. G. was so emotional that he could hardly speak to Duff for tears. Martin arrived an hour late for lunch, his train held up because of the great number of trains

27. Montagu Bertie, 8th Earl of Abingdon and 13th Earl of Lindsey (1887-1963). Capt. Grenadier Guards.
28. Haw-Haw was the nickname given to the English-language broadcaster William Joyce of the German propaganda radio programme *Germany Calling*, broadcast to audiences in the UK.

containing the BEF back from France. They are getting back. It seems almost like a victory.

Mottisfont, Monday June 3

Made ARP arrangements at the school in the morning. In the afternoon, made new arrangements about the evacuees, two big boys getting out of hand. So settled for them to sleep in the house under Hanson's[29] eye. Weather continues supremely beautiful. This has been so for more than a month as if to tease us with the beauty of the world.

London, Wednesday June 5

Dined with I. at the Ivy. I was low-spirited of which I was ashamed of later. I. gave me a rough talking to and shook me out of my blues. A man talked noisily, drunkenly and stupidly at a nearby table. I. got up quickly and stopped him. Though one reads of people turning white I don't think I have ever seen it happen before. But Ian's lovely face was white, or rather, turned white. Martin was at Claridges when I got back, looking not B1 but C3 ['*fit for home service only*'] with the excitements and long hours of his work at the Ministry of Information. He works in a room next to Duff's with Lord Hood[30] who is private secretary. Last Sunday was a nightmare, he said, Lord Hood away, Duff in Paris and he, Martin, a new boy of two days' standing, trying to understand his work.

London, Friday June 7

Alexie came round early to Claridges to say goodbye to G. Alexie and Lánczy are supposed to be leaving England on the 15th for Portugal and Spain. Sad outlook. The great battle Somme-Aisne-Chiens started on Wednesday. We must hold them or only give way slowly, and after causing them great losses, for two or three months. After that I think we can look forward.

Mottisfont, Monday June 10

Evacuees bathed on the lawn on Saturday and Adele and I sat over them.

---

29. Richard Hanson (1883-1944), chauffeur. With the Russells for over 20 years.
30. Samuel Hood, 6th Viscount Hood (1910-81). Private Secretary Minister of Information 1939-41, with Foreign Office 1942-69.

I've been busy seeing the farmers and finding out what help they might need at harvest time, then canvassing the village for offers of help – paid help of course. Whole village employed and those working at Dean and Wallop on dumps and aerodromes get home late after a busy day.

London, Wednesday June 12

Alexie came to lunch. She cannot get her exit permit. Joined Moira Lyttelton and her children Rosemary and Anthony at Sadler's Wells and somehow sat through *Don Giovanni*. It was a bad performance but I don't think I should have been able to pay attention even if it had been very good. Music doesn't seems to help the present or belong to it. We all went on to supper at the Savoy and Clare [Tennyson], Harold and Mark [Tennyson, *her children*] joined us. Mark went through the whole Dunkirk evacuation on his destroyer. Said his men fell asleep where they stood with fatigue. His sleep averaged two hours in 24 hours. The French came on board with all the equipment they could bring and anything else useful they could lay their hands on. He became very constipated because he could never leave the bridge.

London, Thursday June 13

I was to have dined with I. tonight but had a message in the morning to say he'd gone to France. I don't know what his job is. Lunched with I.C.-G. Jardin. Pleasant to spend an hour or two in the same place and in the same way as before the war. News disastrous all the time, France collapsing.

On June 14, the Germans enter Paris. On June 16, the French prime minister, Paul Reynaud, who was under pressure from his military commanders to make peace with Germany, resigns and is replaced by the vice-premier, Philippe Pétain, who seeks an Armistice. Reynaud's undersecretary of war, Brigadier General Charles de Gaulle, flies to England to continue the resistance. Britain recognises de Gaulle as the Free French leader on June 28.

Mottisfont, Monday June 17

Christabel [McLaren] and Sam [Courtauld], Xandra Haig,[31] Eddie M. [Marsh]

---

31. Lady Alexandra Haig (1907-97), daughter of the First World War commander Field Marshal Douglas Haig, 1st Earl Haig (1861-1928). Married first in 1941 Rear Admiral Clarence Howard-Johnston, secondly in 1954 the historian Hugh Trevor-Roper.

and Raymond M. [Mortimer] are staying. Raymond very depressed, hand shaking and pessimistic. France has asked for an armistice. Reynaud gone. New French Cabinet. We sat in the garden and Eddie read his translation of Horace's *Odes*. Lovely escape from the bad present. We sat about yesterday and I played backgammon with the children in the stables.

Following the French collapse, Churchill delivers his 'This was their finest hour' speech in the House of Commons in which he puts the case for Britain's 'inflexible resolve' to continue the war and warns the country that the next step will be the 'Battle of Britain'.

London, Tuesday June 18

Knitting party. Then London 5.10. Dined with Clare [Tennyson] at the flat and listened to Winston's broadcast, more or less a repetition of what he'd said in the House in the afternoon. His voice was tired but the broadcast was excellent all the same and courage-giving. The last few minutes of it were inspiring.

London, Thursday June 20

Cocktails at the Ritz at 1. Violet [Cripps] and Diana C. [Cooper] talked of sending their children to America. Syrie Maugham is sailing almost at once with Liza, her daughter, and Liza's baby and Syrie had rung up Diana and offered to take John Julius.[32] I think Duff's child should stay in Canada not the USA. Saw Ed Stanley for a moment at the Ritz. He said – I hope it's true – that the two big new French battleships now nearing completion have been got away and towed across the sea to safety. Perhaps I. has been working on a job such as this.

Mottisfont, Friday June 21

The curious thing is how much better people's spirits seem – certainly mine are – now that we stand alone and all depends on us. I find comfort in the thought that we are all compact and each person must play his part and must not fail. The strain of the last weeks of daily and hourly retreats is over. Each day was and is misery. The end of this disastrous phrase has, paradoxically,

---

32. John Julius Norwich, 2nd Viscount Norwich (1929-), Duff and Lady Diana Cooper's son. A historian, writer and broadcaster. Maud considered asking John Julius to be her literary executor.

brought with it a sense of relief, at any rate to me. There is no sense in this, though it may be the relief of getting rid of a gangrenous limb. The longest day is almost over. I can see, on us, an endless winter.

On June 22, France signs an Armistice with Germany that establishes a German occupation zone in north and west France, leaving the rest to be governed by a puppet-French government based first at Bordeaux and then at Vichy.

Mottisfont, Tuesday June 25

France has signed armistices with Germany and Italy. One doesn't know what pressure was brought to bear but the terms seem shameful. I wait and wait to hear news of the French fleet joining us or going to guard their colonial possessions. There are rumours they have but I fear we may get surprises there too. Last night some of the French Air Force were said to be arriving here and we were warned that we might hear some making for Andover. I only heard five or six in the night and they may have been our own. They were flying very high. Last night Alexie telephoned in tears to say Lánczy had been arrested, taken off to Bow St, the flat searched and that he was going to be interned. I had half expected it. He may be harmless but he is the sort of man who might be up to anything. Poor A. She is 20 and her troubles are starting.

London, Wednesday June 26

Martin and I lunched at the Ivy. Said there were rumours of Cabinet wobblers. Tea Violet Bonham Carter. Talked about wobblers. This was news to her. But as we were talking a friend rang up and gave her version saying Lloyd George was the nucleus of whatever movement there was, that he was holding his hand and been heard to say, 'I am not going to speak yet.' Violet said that a young Frenchman talking to Sylvia H. had said, 'Who is de Gaulle?' in that snobbish manner foreigners have of talking about someone who does not belong to their social world or political party. If many French continue to do this, then goodbye to France. V. said that Mme de Margerie, when talking about the collapse of France and the formation of the Bordeaux govt, said, 'C'est tout à cause de cette femme.' V. asked (privately amused) who she had in mind and Mme de M. said 'Reynaud's friend, Mme de Portes,'[33] with whom he is having an affair.

33. Hélène de Portes (1902-40), mistress of the French premier Paul Reynaud (1878-1966). Known for her shrill voice and clamouring manner. Churchill nicknamed her 'the parrot'.

Mottisfont, Thursday June 27

To St John's Lecture Broadlands 7. After late dinner took blankets and lilos to several people in the village for the new evacuees. 35 girls arrived this morning.

Mottisfont, Saturday June 29

Billeting officer arrived this afternoon to arrange for six officers in the house. There have been one or two air raid warnings for Romsey this week. A bomb dropped in the park at Broadlands Thursday night, a couple at the Wallops another night and we heard undisturbed German aeroplanes on two nights flying around, on reconnaissance work, I suppose.

Mottisfont, Monday July 1

Went to tea with the Pembrokes at Wilton yesterday. The Southern Command are taking possession of the house and the vans were arriving as we drove up. The Pembrokes are left with their two bedrooms, two spare rooms, the servants' rooms, her sitting room and the long room they always sit in to serve as dining and living room. The furniture from the rest of the house has been stacked in the riding school. The Van Dycks have been left in the Double Cube. Reggie looked thin and seemed agitated at all these happenings, Bee much less disturbed. David was there, hot from Southampton where he is learning wireless operating. Hurried back for a service on the Rectory Lawn, the Bishop of Southampton preaching. Watched distant air battle from my window last night. Much too distant to see the aeroplanes but saw searchlights come together and shells burst. Today nothing. Feeling listless. Took papers, vegetables and socks to Searchlight at Mount Farm. Listless and restless.

London, Tuesday July 2

Alice [Astor] dined with me at the Ivy and Raymond M. [Mortimer] and Malcolm Bullock.[34] Raymond was exhausted by his new work at the Ministry of Information and was very despondent. He and Malcolm talked mostly about the French, de Gaulle, the difficulties of forming a Nat. Committee, the lack of spirit of the French, the political and religious tangles and the lamentable position we'd been forced to take up vis-à-vis the French over here – that we were doing our best to get rid of them as being too half-hearted

---

34. Captain Malcolm Bullock, later 1st Baronet (1890-1966), Conservative MP.

to be anything but a hindrance and a danger and that this was, perhaps inevitably, being done clumsily.

Mottisfont, Monday July 8

Drive with G. yesterday. Got out and sat on the hill beyond the Deans. Lovely view, blue sky and high, occasional white clouds. Peaceful scene. I felt rested. Today busy going through the roofs and attics settling places for stirrup pumps and ARP devices, seeing the local builder about how to protect the walls of Rex's room in case it should be used by the military or as a hospital, talks about the evacuees and to them. Then St John's Lecture at Broadlands.

London, Tuesday July 9

Dined with Violet B.-C. Bongie there and a Frenchman, Georges Boris,[35] once private secretary to Léon Blum,[36] about 40, left, intelligent, agreeable, shrewd and speaking excellent English. Said Blum was in France and would stay there. Said he was a man who would not leave his country in the hour of defeat. He would think his place was there. Boris was moved when he spoke of Blum and seemed deeply devoted. Said the complete collapse of France was most difficult to understand and it would be for the historians to trace the causes. Thought the death of religion had been a contributory cause. There was this void and there had been nothing to fill it. He said this remarking that he himself was an atheist. Then the rottenness of the right, the ossification of the General Staff, the disrupting forces of Communism. Net result: the French did not want to fight. The evening was sad.

On July 10, the Battle of Britain begins with the start of heavy air raids by the Germans.

Mottisfont, Sunday July 14

On Friday we did the annual fire drill. It strikes me that most of the girls of the servant girl class are very hysterical, goosy, spoilt and silly. They seem

---

35. Georges Boris (1888-1960), French politician, journalist and economist. Evacuated from Dunkirk in 1940, worked for Free French in England.
36. Léon Blum (1872-1950), French Jewish politician, identified with moderate left. Prime Minister three times. When Germany defeated France in 1940, he became a staunch opponent of Vichy France. He survived imprisonment in Buchenwald concentration camp.

to have some of the characteristics and the excessive femininity of young women of the Victorian era. They were very timid and didn't want to go down the chute. Then I said I would go first and gradually half a dozen followed. Two or three made a fuss, couldn't get started, cried, called out, begged to be pulled out again. Women of the upper classes are never like that now. They are mostly anxious to do anything their brothers or husbands do; ski, fly, explore. These working class girls seem far behind their epoch. And what a nuisance they would be in an emergency.

London, Tuesday July 16

Lunched with Cecil Beaton in his new pretty boudoir-like house.[37] Cecil talked about America, their excitement and hysteria about the war, their gloom and despondency, the strong pro-ally leanings of the people he'd met, and the critical attitude to our war efforts past and present. He was amazed at finding people in such good spirits here. He'd expected deep depression.

London, Wednesday July 17.

Lunched with Duff and Diana at the Dorchester. Martin and Conrad there. Duff was quiet as he always is at lunch. Diana was tiresome with him, rather nagging, saying he never told her anything. If she wanted anything done she went to other Ministries. Told us of a letter she'd written – an amusing idea – to the War Office. As the Germans would probably dress their parachutists in English battle-dress, why not paint the faces of our soldiers a different colour each day so as to distinguish them from the Germans? The order would go out each morning: blue today, or brick today. She apologised to the War Office for what they might consider the eccentricity of her suggestion. They answered politely, thanked her and said there was no need to apologise, they received many far sillier letters. Boris Anrep gave me tea at the Café Royal. He has just got back from France. Said his escape was due to 'these miracles and the direct intervention of St Nicholas'. It took him 12 days to get from Paris to London, exhausting, exciting, despairing, horribly uncomfortable.

London, Friday July 19

Tea with the Francks. Found them pale and depressed, fearing they may be

---

37. Ashcombe House, Cranborne Chase, which Beaton leased from 1930-45, and wrote about in *Ashcombe, The Story of a 15 Year Lease,* republished by Dovecote Press 1999.

interned any moment.[38] Many of their friends have been. Tried to reassure them. Brendan [Bracken] and Violet [Bonham Carter] dined with us at the Savoy. Talked about internment camps. Violet said they should be inspected. Brendan agreed. Tried to think who suitable. Brendan suggested Cis Asquith.[39] I didn't like to disagree as Violet was there but it strikes me that a woman with organisation experience would be worth twice Cis, whose gifts are of a different order. Brendan defended Winston having made Kingsley Wood[40] Chancellor of the Exchequer. Said he was put there because he wouldn't obstruct, he was pliable and would give way and do anything he was told to do. This should mean that [John Maynard] Keynes[41] and Winston direct him. But what a queer state of affairs – a Chancellor who isn't in the Cabinet and who takes orders.

Mottisfont, Tuesday July 23

Today five immensely smart, youngish officers arrived and asked to see the house with a view to billeting a corps headquarters here. I was aghast when they said they might want almost the whole house, possibly even the whole house. The terrors of packing and storing loomed monstrously. But we are all now so unsettled that, after they had left, G. and I talked about it and soon found ourselves discussing where we would try and find a house and were quite resigned to this horrible move. G. was asthmatic today so I put off London. Knitting party.

London, Thursday July 25

Martin came to breakfast and we talked of the violent and scurrilous press attacks on Duff. Alexie came later. Lánczy sleeps on the floor at Liverpool camp. The internees aren't given any green vegetables.

38. Between May and July 1944, some 22,000 German and Austrian aliens were interned, and 4,000 Italians.
39. The Hon. Cyril 'Cis' Asquith (1890-1954), barrister and high court judge. Fourth son of former prime minister H.H. Asquith. Appointed chairman of the advisory committee on aliens in 1940.
40. Sir Kingsley Wood (1881-1943), solicitor and Conservative MP. As Air Minister, Wood successfully oversaw the build-up of Britain's air fleet in 1938 and 1939. Churchill appointed him as Chancellor in 1940 but he was not included in the War Cabinet. The economist John Maynard Keynes was on an advisory committee to the Exchequer.
41. John Maynard Keynes, 1st Baron Keynes (1883-1946), brilliant economist. His revolutionary *The General Theory on Unemployment, Interest and Money* (1936) laid the foundations of modern macroeconomics. Member of Bloomsbury Group.

Mottisfont, Monday July 29

Cis Asquith <u>has</u> been appointed Commissioner for the Internees. But someone should be sent to report on the feeding, medical, sanitary and comfort side of the camps at once. I wrote to Brendan and suggested a woman would be best for that job – Dame Rachel Crowdy,[42] Lady Reading[43] or Miss Florence Horsbrugh.[44] The internee scandal is very great, everything done in a mad hurry, no organisation, no foresight, dreadful and unnecessary hardships and injustices perpetuated, not intentionally but through muddle and unpreparedness.

Bournemouth, Thursday August 1

Came here Tuesday morning. Hotel almost deserted. Delicious quiet here yesterday. Sea alluring and the beach animated. There is hardly anything better than bathing and lying on the beach.

Mottisfont, Monday August 5

We came back here on Thursday. Alexie came for a few days, looking thin and worn. We were all rather silent. G. and I went for a drive to Farley Mount on Saturday. Lovely, the roads empty, the country beautiful. Alexie fished. Raymond arrived that evening from Gloucester, well pleased with himself and wearing a Peace Pledge Union Badge. G. asked him, as a favour to us, not to wear it. No result. Today I asked R. as a great favour to take of his PPU badge. It was a personal appeal and succeeded. He was nice and amiable and I saw clearly for the first time what I had seen signs of over the last year. His character is softening and expanding.

Mottisfont, Thursday August 8

Clemmie Churchill[45] and Clare [Tennyson] arrived. Clemmie aged, hair very

---

42. Dame Rachel Crowdy (1884-1964), nurse and social reformer, who made her name in the First World War running the Voluntary Aid Detachments (VADs).
43. Stella Isaacs, Marchioness of Reading, later Baroness Swanborough, *née* Charnaud (1894-1971). Founded Women's Voluntary Service (WVS) in 1938.
44. Florence Horsbrugh, later Baroness Horsbrugh (1889-1969), Scottish Unionist Party and Conservative Party politician. Parliamentary secretary Ministry of Health 1939-45 and Ministry of Food 1945.
45. Clementine Churchill, *née* Hozier (1885-1977), married Winston Churchill in 1908. Childhood friend of Gilbert's. Created life peer in 1965 after Churchill's death.

white, face tired. She talks even more than ever. But she is nice and quite funny. Clemmie's account of Winston's last visit to France was roughly this. He received a telegram from the French govt asking if he could come over to Tours. The telegram didn't come in code as usual and so the Germans might easily have known of its contents. Some thought it a trap, others an oversight. The military authorities didn't want Winston to go, thinking it too risky, but he decided he would, but he would get there one and a half hours early to evade German aircraft which might be waiting to intercept him at the correct hour. He arrived at Tours aerodrome which was deserted – not even a taxi driver. Messages were sent into Tours and finally they were picked up. The French officer in charge of their party asked if they'd had lunch. Winston hungrily said no, they would very much like some. There seemed nowhere to take them. Finally they were taken to a restaurant which was packed with people – no room at all. The officer with them sent word round that the English prime minister and his staff were there and would like lunch; could people move out or make room? This was done at once and Winston had lunch inside, a number of people moving into the street. There was general confusion at his early arrival. When 2.30 came he went to the *Mairie* [*City Hall*], I think, and was all but attacked by Mme de Portes who seemed to want to scratch his face. He passed in. Mme de Portes tried to get in but was prevented by a French naval officer. She screamed and was hysterical and demanded to be admitted. He said an important meeting was being held and no one could be let in. She said, 'You don't know who I am. I am Mme de Portes.' He: 'Then I shall most certainly not allow you in.'

London, Wednesday August 14

G., Raymond and I took 3.20 train from Southampton to Brighton yesterday. Air raid as we were travelling. Saw a building near the coast rising in dark smoke, anti-aircraft guns streaking flame and a distant German aeroplane, leaving a trail of black smoke behind it, sink over the sea. Spitfires came from distant quarters. We darted from window to window. Today I came to London. Boris and Raymond M. lunched with me at the Mirabelle. R. said he'd met de Gaulle. I asked, 'Do you ask his advice about suitable broadcasts to the French and does he give you hints?' [*Raymond is in the French Section of the Ministry of Information*]. Raymond said in a very self-satisfied manner, 'There is nothing they can teach us.' So I scolded him for his conceit. Dined with I. at Jardin. He spoilt part of the evening by saying, partly as a joke, that there had been a bad air raid on Brighton so I rushed to the telephone, gave the wrong number in my haste and, of course, got no reply. This happened several times, till I thought it must have been blotted out.

Mottisfont, Thursday August 15

To Mottisfont. Arrived in time for a big air battle. There was a great, heavy roar of high, approaching bombers as I started my tea in bed. I was very tired and at first I couldn't bother to move. Then the heavy noise, distant machine-gun fire and explosions roused me. I thought I would be safer on the ground floor. So I spent the next three-quarters of an hour running from the dining room windows to the morning room windows, north to south, south to north, to watch the fight high overhead. After a burst of machine-gun fire, I saw one German aeroplane hit and grey smoke trail out as it sunk to fall and crash some miles away. Reeve[46] [*the butler*] and the hall-boy stood in the middle of the lawn and saw four hit and start losing height. Reeve was enormously excited and laughed a great deal. His face was pink and 15 years younger. He is usually rather sour and ill-tempered.

At 7 I went to Broadlands by taxi. At the Lodge Gate we were stopped by hot, rather flustered-looking soldiers and told we couldn't drive in. I explained about my first aid lecture and eventually we were allowed to pass. It then transpired that a German fighter was lying wrecked a few hundred yards away in the park. For one painful moment it looked silver from the distance and like one of our own fighters. But it was German, blueish grey and fearfully smashed and scattered. It was still smouldering and we weren't allowed near. Not a soul turned up for the lecture so the taxi driver and I decided to try and find the other crashed aeroplanes. Near Wellow we saw a great deal of smoke but we weren't allowed near the scene because there were still unexploded bombs in the aeroplane. We made for Braishfield and beyond it came across a wrecked bomber, burnt out and deeply embedded. Part of it lay in the road. This we examined closely with a small number of people who had come for the same purpose. Among the wreckage lay chunks of human flesh, unidentifiable. My primitive glee was checked. The wreckage was complete. Except for a moment's hesitation at Broadlands it never struck any of us onlookers that the aeroplanes we saw being destroyed in the air or lying on the ground could be anything but German.

46. Arthur Reeve (d. 1943), butler who worked for the Russells on and off for more than 15 years.

Brighton, Saturday August 17

Yesterday I left for Brighton by the 3.20. An air raid warning started as I got in, the blinds were pulled down and we sat in the station for 20 minutes or so, worried we shouldn't be allowed to start. But we were. There was nothing till near Selsey. Then we saw a big building hanger which had just been hit and a couple of minutes later three German bombers came over the train. One couldn't tell whether they mightn't bomb or machine-gun it. I chiefly remember feeling rather stupid. We ought to have crouched down on the floor but it seemed a ludicrous thing to do. I daresay if I had ever been in a bombed or machine-gunned train I should have done so at once. But nothing happened. The bombers wheeled round in a great-circle and returned to their original target.

Brighton, Monday August 19

Yesterday G. and I went to see Maurice Baring[47] at Rottingdean. He was in a bare little bedroom on the ground floor. It had Morris wallpaper and there was a crucifix on the mantelpiece. A pet love-bird crawled round his neck and pecked at his face. I was made sad by his state and the change in his appearance. His purple colouring had gone and his face was thin, long and pale. He shook agonisingly at moments. Both hands moved upwards together in a slow, claw-like movement towards his face two or three times and remained shaking and claw-like at the level of his eyes for a second or two. He looked so tired and I thought how short a time he must have left to live. At present he is rather worried by the air raid warnings and nervous. The house is unpretentious, comfortable but not beautiful, and stacked with books. In the drawing room I saw a pile of scrapbooks, handsomely bound and dated. Maurice's bedroom was rather like a bedroom in a convent.

Brighton, Sunday August 25

Today G. and I lunched with Clive Bell at Firle.[48] He'd said 'we' when telling me what time they lunched. I didn't know what 'we' meant but it turned out to be, to my pleasure, Vanessa Bell,[49] Duncan Grant[50] and Clive's son.

---

47. Maurice Baring (1874-1945), poet, journalist and author. The godfather of Gilbert and Maud's son, Raymond.
48. Almost certainly Charleston, the country home of the Bloomsbury Group, near Firle in East Sussex.
49. Vanessa Bell, *née* Stephen (1879-1961), painter and member of Bloomsbury Group. Married Clive Bell in 1907. Duncan Grant's long-term partner. Sister to Virginia Woolf.
50. Duncan Grant (1885-1978), painter and Bloomsbury Group member.

Strange to say I had never met any of them before. I was very attracted to Vanessa B., her dignity, her shy manner, her voice and the ruin-like remains of her beauty. I felt as if I could have got on very well with her if I had known her better. As it was I felt drawn by her enormous shyness and her diffidence. Clive introduced Duncan Grant without mentioning his name but by saying something like: 'You know most of the great painters and yet I don't believe you have met this one.' I found him delightful and a charmer whose charm was so natural to him that it operated whenever he moved a hand or uttered a monosyllable. When he talked to me at lunch it was as if we were alone and there was no one anywhere near. As if neither food, nor the clattering of plates, nor Clive's emphatic, mannered voice, nor his massive son, nor aloof Vanessa belonged to the scene.

Mottisfont, Tuesday August 27

Did my First Aid Exam at Broadlands yesterday and made one hideous mistake. This little exam became a nightmare to me the last two days and I couldn't remember a thing I had learnt!

Today Raymond, who has been staying with the aunts, came back with his clavichord which we had travelled with to Brighton a fortnight ago. It then seemed a very unusual piece of luggage to be travelling with in wartime and in an air raid. But we have always travelled with strange luggage – crocodiles, salamanders, snakes, giant tortoises, armadillos, dogs and cats, accordions etc.

London, Thursday August 29

Alexie and I dined at Claridges yesterday. Started to go to a film but found there was an alarm and we couldn't get in. There was nothing to do but go to bed early. I was already in bed when Martin turned up wanting dinner, which he hadn't been able to get on his way home as all the restaurants refuse to admit newcomers during a raid. This raid lasted seven hours. I watched some of it from my balcony. Lunched with Oliver Harvey at the Ritz today. He talked about Duff – for Oliver is now head of the French Section of the MOI – and said he admired him. But he said he sometimes seemed remote and absent when he was talking to him. I laughed to myself a little at this because Martin had told me that Oliver, once started, finds it hard to stop talking, winding on and on, and that Duff doesn't know how to put an end to it.

Mottisfont, Sunday September 1

On Friday I bought a black scarf and dark stockings with difficulty because when I got to the shop the Air Raid Warning sounded and no one would serve me. Herbrand died on Tuesday. He'd been ill and failing, half-blind and miserable for some time. Claud, Ath, Martin and I lunched at Claridges and drove down to the funeral at Chenies. Most of the female members of the family were there and some of the older men. Martin and Ian [Howland] were the only young men. The service was very short and simple. Herbrand had been cremated. The urn was on a table on the chancel steps. A German bomber flew over during the service. After the service we stood about outside in the sun. Today Rex came to put the inscriptions right. He is sunburnt and has grown a moustache which hides too much of his lovely face. He was docile and nice. He doesn't like being in the army. He altered the inscriptions. *Praevalebit* had been misspelt and he'd originally put in the wrong years for the beginning and finishing of the room.

London, Wednesday September 4

Lunched with Boris at the Mirabelle in the garden. An air raid warning went off as I was on my way there. I was afraid they might not serve lunch but they did, in the garden as well as indoors. So 60 people remained eating in the garden under a blue sky and an aeroplane or two. Boris talked about Vanessa [Bell], Duncan [Grant], Roger Fry[51] and the others. He'd known them all many years ago. The Bloomsbury circle started with Roger Fry, Lytton Strachey[52] and Keynes. Duncan, a much younger man, came into it through Roger F. who loved him. Vanessa and Virginia [Woolf] were the only two women who really belonged; no theories or views had any value for them unless they were held by this small circle of men. They were all very arrogant, brilliant, inquiring, charming and gifted. Then Keynes took Duncan away from Fry. Then Duncan began to look out for young men himself. Then Fry fell in love with Vanessa and she loved him. But after a little time Duncan left his boys for Vanessa, cutting out poor Fry. Vanessa and he have remained together ever since and her youngest child is his. But though they remained together, there were storms and Vanessa was often unhappy. Then in 1928

51. Roger Fry (1866-1934), Bloomsbury Group member, painter and influential critic, raising awareness in England of modern art with his advocacy of French post-impressionism (a term he coined).
52. Lytton Strachey (1880-1932), Bloomsbury Group member, writer and critic. Author *Eminent Victorians*.

Boris's wife Helen [Maitland] and Fry fell in love and lived together till he died. Keynes married [Lydia] Lopokova [*Russian ballerina*] and drifted away a little, spending his money not on the circle but on financing plays and building an Art Theatre in Cambridge. This was almost treachery! Boris says that Vanessa and Duncan are not quite indifferent to money and the comfort it provides. But few people are. At the time Vanessa and Fry fell in love, Clive [Bell] and Mary [Hutchinson] did the same, so no one felt lonely or unhappy. But neither Clive nor Mary belonged to the inner circle though Clive was constantly with them and knew them intimately. Now they are all oldish or dead and these intricate, intimate and confusing relationships long past. They fascinate me. One day letters and journals will come to light and some fortunate person will be able to write freely about them, their theories, influence and loves. Boris himself is an interesting man. His mind is curious and out of the ordinary, his critical faculties alert and untrammelled. I like his company and his originality. Lent my Pryde[53] to the National Gallery for an autumn exhibition. The Matthew Smith[54] is there too.

Mottisfont, Friday September 6

Went with a box and collected for the Spitfire Fund at Carter's Clay. People generous, but don't like doing it. One very dirty cottage, an idiot daughter, a filthy mother, eighteenth century dirt and squalor, but very pleasant and generous.

London, Thursday September 12

To London 8.47 yesterday. Train no further than Clapham Junction as Waterloo was damaged three or four days ago. Took electric train to Victoria. Porter there said, 'Bond St and Piccadilly have been bombed: pity to think all those beautiful shops spoilt.' Actually very little damage done. But my hairdresser's floor in Old Bond St had been damaged and an unexploded bomb lay nearby. So I had my hair done at Douglas's. The moment it had been washed the sirens went and, as the hairdresser didn't want to continue in the shop, we went, I with a dripping head, to a shelter round the corner where she proceeded to set it to the amusement of the other people there. Struck me there should be tiers of bunks in all the bigger shelters and hammocks in the others. Martin came and had dinner in my room. Siren went off soon after

53. James Pryde (1866-1941), painter. *The Unknown Corner*, 35'x 28', oil on canvas.
54. Matthew Smith (1879-1959), painter. *Reclining Nude*, 24'x 20', oil on canvas.

8 and from then till 12 there was constant and heavy anti-aircraft fire which half-deadened the heavy dropping of bombs. Noise very considerable. An AA gun in a mews or on a house close to the hotel broke in violently from time to time. No searchlights playing. Just grim sound. Martin said it was the loudest night so far chiefly due to the many new guns brought into London during the last 24 hours. The raid continued till 5.30. I stayed in bed and, as sleep didn't seem possible, put wax in my ears and took a sleeping draught at 1, and managed to sleep reasonably well, only waking for a few moments during the louder bursts.

Mottisfont, Tuesday September 17

I went out collecting for the Spitfire Fund on Friday. Villagers very generous. Buckingham Palace bombed again. On Sunday went on walk with Claud and Ath. Saw the bridge over the Test being mined. Guards are there ready to blow it up. Yesterday collected again. 185 German machines brought down.

On September 27, Germany, Italy and Japan sign the Tripartite Pact forming an Axis against the Allies.

London, Friday September 27

Lunched with I. at the Coq d'Or. Has been touring the coastal defences. The house he was in at Dover was blown up and everyone killed soon after he'd left it. We discussed how either would know if the other was killed. Not knowing at once gives an empty blank feeling. Later went to a film with Boris and had coffee and talked at Lyons. He told me about his 'fate', Maroussia [*Boris's common law wife*], and why they had lived together for such a number of years.

Mottisfont, Sunday October 6

G. in bed all these days as the result, I suppose, of an anti-catarrhal injection that induced all the symptoms of cold and quick breathing. Lunched with Boris at the Mirabelle on Thursday. Two nights before, his studio [4 *Pond Street, Hampstead*] was all but destroyed by a landmine. He was reading in bed at 4 in the morning. There was a mild thud. He turned over a leaf – there was time – and then he was conscious of a weight on his chest, of the lights being out, and of people with torches groping and calling out. He must have lost consciousness for some minutes because they couldn't have been on the spot immediately. There was a heavy table with iron legs upside-down on him. Whenever he tried to extricate himself, there were showers of glass. Being a studio, almost everything was glass but his very heavy curtains had somehow caught themselves up and formed a tent over him and he was uncut. Glass fell and tinkled at his slightest movement and the floor crunched under him when he finally dragged himself up. Maroussia was sleeping in a sort of cubby-hole and had fallen through the floor but, beyond a cut, was uninjured. When I asked him how he'd spent the remainder of the night, he said he'd been given tea by a beautiful girl and then walked about the streets. He had the studio built for M. as a kind of investment. She is entirely dependent on him. Poor Boris. We talked a great deal. He told me he is in love with me. I am now nearly 49. The last time anyone said this to me was three years ago.

Mottisfont, Monday October 7

Raymond came to my room early having discovered late last night that he was due at Cambridge [*to study history and music at Downing*] today instead of Tuesday. I told him that he mustn't ask for privileges and I think that struck him. I told him too how deeply most people feel about this war, that they are ready to make almost any sacrifice and to suffer every loss and misery. I don't think this had ever struck him before. He'd only thought of them as blood-thirsty, selfish, imperialistic and jingoish. Then I told him that he was a person of passion and impulse, not a person of logic and reasoning, and that he mustn't allow himself to be carried away, bolstering up his impulses with false reasoning. I saw his astonishment. But I think he saw there was something in what I said. Poor R., how he is going to bump about. Anyway he went off to Cambridge in high spirits.

Bournemouth, Monday October 21

G. and I came here to Branksome Towers Hotel last Wednesday. The dining room, which last year was packed with over-dressed, richish, unattractive people, presented a different spectacle: 80 officers and about four women. The scene somehow moved me. They all looked incredibly English – angular, not very handsome, not very intelligent, but decent people. Not perhaps imaginative enough to dread fear, or think about it till the moment came. Cool, brought up in the tradition of a race of conquerors, ready to do, as a matter of course, what their forefathers had done before them. Not proud but confident – hardly even confident, but certain of themselves without giving certainty a thought. I felt like either laughing or crying.

London, Wednesday October 23

Went to London 8.47. Lunched with Boris at a Chinese restaurant. Food delicious. Afterwards went to his bombed studio on Hampstead Heath. The little village is desolate with its piles of ruins. All the studios near his are demolished. His hasn't fallen but the roof has shifted, the walls have great cracks running across them and the place is uninhabitable. It's a long ground floor building consisting of seven or eight small rooms opening out of each other. The windows look out onto a passage. There is no prospect. But a few steps away there is Hampstead Heath, wild, countrified and charming. Hired a car and went to the Van's at Denham [*in Buckinghamshire*], giving lifts to people standing at the bus stops. Van was more like his usual self and talked a great deal. Agrees with me that the overrunning of Europe is not weakening Germany – a dispersal of her strength, as Martin and G. say, but an addition to her already enormous strength.

Mottisfont, Thursday October 24

Alexie met me at Claridges. Told me Lánczy had been re-interned. He was free for four weeks. She looks very thin and ill. She went to see Brendan about him taking every relevant and, I dare say, irrelevant paper. Of course she firmly believes in his innocence. She walked into No. 10 without the slightest difficulty. Brendan was wonderfully nice to her, she said. Met Boris at 3 and we sat in a teashop and talked till my train left. He is a very extraordinary man. The more I see of him the more I think so. Anything less like an Englishman one couldn't imagine. He talks richly, volubly and intelligently. Sometimes there are a few flowery artificialities about my beauty or youthful appearance or charm but I take those very lightly as, no doubt, they are meant to be taken. All an Englishman would say under the circumstances is: You're looking well today.

Mottisfont, Friday October 25

Someone reading this diary one day will wonder why I say so little about the war. The comments I might make, buried here in the country, would be dull. I seldom hear anything worth recording. The war itself is never out of one's mind. It's in the background, always, of all one's thoughts and actions, sometimes the foreground. It colours everything from the food or materials one can or cannot get, the trains that do or do not run, the planting of the kitchen garden, to the thought of the tremendous hazard, the things at stake, ideal and material, the loss of deeply-loved people and life itself. At times we talk of it a great deal, at other times not at all. But it's never out of one's mind. It's as much there as art is to the artist or love to the lover. Sometimes these thoughts are too dreadful to put into words. One's mind reels; horror invades one; a despair at the greed, pride and lust for conquest of human nature or the systems or individuals it tolerates. But these moments of complete realisation pass. If they didn't one would take means to die.

London, Friday November 1

Yesterday Alexie came to Claridges at 12. She says L. is in darkness at Pentonville from 6.30pm to 7.30am – total darkness. The prison isn't blacked out so the cells can't have lights. The nights are endless, terrifying and horrible. This sounds very wrong. Today lunched I. Coq d'Or. He has been on some dangerous job again. He cannot ever tell me what they are. A house in which he was dining was blown from under him. He and his friends were left marooned on the third floor, the staircase and most of the floors below were blown away. Eventually there was a tap on the window, a fireman's head appeared and they left the house by the fireman's ladder. The story was told as if there hadn't been any danger.

London, Thursday November 7

Lunched with Boris at Mirabelle and sat there till 3.30 talking. I wish I could remember the many good things he says. We talked of the sect of flagellants in south Russia and from that to the act of intimacy between man and woman. He said it had for him something like a religious significance, the losing by man of himself in the universe. Without that it would be nothing else but 'the goat'. This was an allusion to the customs of some of the Caucasian peoples who offer their wives and daughters to the visiting stranger but warn him not to touch the goat. This talk continued, and ended in a profound and complete silence. We sat like two figures in a temple.

On November 20 and 23, Hungary and Romania respectively join the Axis powers.

London, Wednesday November 20

I went to the Home Office before lunch. Lánczy had written a pathetic-sounding letter to me saying he was dying, had angina pectoris, begged me to look after Alexie. Thought if he had angina HO might move him to a country prison-hospital. Angina in Pentonville and bombs falling sounded dreadful to me. Saw Osbert Peake's woman secretary who said there was no mention by the prison doctor of angina. I asked whether we could be told, roughly, the nature of the charge against Lánczy. She said they had to make a rule not to give this information.

Brighton, Saturday November 23

Dr Bánczky – a Hungarian asthma specialist – came down to see Gilbert. Seemed intelligent. Wants to try his gold and tuberculosis cure. Says emphysema cannot be cured by him but the asthma can. Depends on how much emphysema there is. G. discovered he knew Lánczy. Says he is a complete scoundrel. Say money is all he cares about. Says he has Nazi sympathies.

London, Monday November 25

Had lunch with Tony [Apponyi] and Sally, the woman he lives with. She looks after him well and seems practical and quite nice. He wanted to talk about a scheme of going to Peru. Hungary's adhesion to the Axis has made him nervous about what his position may one day be here and he thinks he isn't getting on sufficiently well at Shell. Told me one or two things I didn't like about Lánczy. Said he didn't conceal his Nazi bias.

London, Thursday November 28

Lunched with I. at Coq d'Or. He had a narrow escape at the Carlton a week or two ago sleeping on the third floor. The night was hellish, bombs dropping all round. Then one on the hotel. The place swayed, masonry started falling, the wall to the passage disappeared and I. was covered with cement, plaster and bricks but miraculously not hurt. Heard cries and moans. Rescued a waiter and a maid pinned down by debris. Finished the night in the hotel grill-room where other people were sleeping.

Mottisfont, Sunday December 1

Duff, Diana, Andrew Scott, Martin, Clare [Tennyson] staying. Talk and laughter and gaiety. Duff told a very funny story about the Duke of Connaught [Prince Arthur (1850-1942), *Queen Victoria's third son*) attending the Grenadier Guards and proposing General Higginson's (aged 99) health. 'His name – the name that is well known to all of us – this name which has for so long been associated with the Grenadier Guards, this name revered by all of us here etc. etc. – the name of the General... er, er, er, er.' Forgotten of course. The Duke turns his head to be prompted, a whisper 'er, er, General Higginson.' Suppressed guffaws all round. Diana looked beautiful and untired though she goes to a canteen every morning at 7 and lives at the gin-palace, the Dorchester, where cocktail parties and dinners are nightly affairs.

Mottisfont, Saturday December 7

49 today. Don't feel old – but people seldom do except in their joints, as I do! I enjoy life and find more and more to interest me in it.

Mottisfont, Wednesday December 11

There are now six officers in the house and seven evacuees, six soldier-servants in the stables, three more evacuees and two helpers. On Monday Clare and I worked from 10-4 at the Food Office in Romsey and yesterday started a free midday meal in the Parish Hall. Food cooked in house and carried across. About 16 there, mostly seamen and dockworkers. Nearly all had lost house and everything they possessed. Spent the afternoon visiting them in their billets, finding out their wants and the complaints – if any – of the householders. Busy again today. Went to see people at dinnertime to see whether there was anything I could do for them. Then to the Food Office Romsey where I got them emergency ration cards and worked for an hour. On return found more refugees in the Parish Hall. Put them in the Club to wait till Bundy [*billeting officer*] came. My two evacuees, an 87-year-old West Indian negro and an old white friend of his, went at once to the house. Ended by putting up three more evacuees for the night.

London, Friday December 13

Alexie came to see me at Claridges at 12. I talked to her about Lánczy and what he is said to be like. The family have been urging me to do this for months but I have always hesitated as the thought of shattering her illusions or her faith in him seemed dreadful. But as things are now I suppose it's best she knows what he's said to be like because if he were released and told to leave the country, she ought to know what she may be in for. I tried to be as gentle as possible and I think she saw I wasn't activated by spite and that I hated doing what I had to do.

Lunch with I. at Coq d'Or – his favourite for the moment. Saw Diana [Cooper] and Conrad [Russell] lunching there again. Their favourite place I suppose.

Maud's mother Maria, Raymond, Martin and Clare, Harold and Mark Tennyson come to stay for Christmas and over the New Year.

Mottisfont, Christmas Day, Wednesday December 25

Yesterday G. went to bed with a slight cold or some reaction against the gold inoculation Bánczky gave him on Friday. Two Canadians arrived at lunchtime sent by the Dominions Hospitality Centre at Aldershot. They talked a lot about Christmas and things at home. I felt we ought to have had a huge, bulging tree for them and hung stockings up at the end of their beds and sung hymns and carols. Today G. was still in bed, nervous and upset.

Mottisfont, Saturday December 28

Clare, Mark and I went to lunch with Stephen Tennant at Wilsford. From what I had seen of his house last year and from what I'd heard about his extravagances and aberrations, I was afraid I wouldn't like him. But his makeup wasn't too glaring and I found him easy to talk to and gay. The extraordinary house had gained a great deal from his presence and care, beautiful arrangement of flowers, spread of ornaments and the electric light on in every room, but gracefully shaded. The curtains weren't drawn but the windows were draped with chiffon and muslin so that only a very unreal light came through. This time the house felt lived in and that is all that really matters in a house. His hands are very beautiful, small and delicate and he wore yellow gloves all through lunch except when he was actually eating.

Mottisfont, Sunday December 29

Bánczky came last night and gave G. another injection after dinner and G. went straight to bed. When I came up I found him in a heavy sleep and with the light on. I woke him and said I would turn his light out. Two hours later he came into my room in great fear and bewilderment. He remembered nothing after the doctor left his room. He was dazed and frightened. Made him get into my bed to comfort him. His right arm and leg moved slightly, as if convulsively, from time to time. Gradually this stopped. I reassured him and he went back to bed but wanted to see Bánczky this morning. B. tried to reassure him but didn't stay long. All he did was stop both medicines, one containing a sedative and caffeine, which together with the small quantities of Adalin he'd been taking, seems to have doped him to start with and overwrought him when the narcotic was wearing off. Whether from fatigue or shock, I felt first faint then sick but continued to do neither. Today G. stayed in bed with a fast and poor pulse. His whole system seems to have been upset by the injections and the medicines. Sickening.

THREE

Family Anxieties

JANUARY 1941 – MAY 1942

In which Germany invades Russia;
Martin goes missing in Singapore;
Raymond becomes a conscientious objector; and
Gilbert's health worsens.

Germany, Italy and Japan have signed the Tripartite Pact that formed the Axis alliance, joined shortly afterwards by Hungary and Romania. The Axis powers now control most of continental Europe but Britain has managed to stall German invasion plans after fending off the major air offensive known as the Battle of Britain. In North Africa, British Commonwealth forces have launched a successful counter-offensive against Italy's invasion of Egypt and driven the Italians back into Libya.

Gilbert is increasingly ill with asthma and nerves, staying mainly at Mottisfont or in a hotel on the coast. Maud continues to go up to London most weeks for a much-needed dose of social life and distraction but, as Gilbert's health worsens, often only for the day. At Mottisfont, she continues to busy herself with the evacuees and refugees, collecting Rural Pennies for the Red Cross and visiting the Searchlights. The Rural Pennies fund for relief work in the Second World War aimed to seek small donations from the many, rather than large donations from the few. Maud noted in her diary that in 1944 Mottisfont raised £81 (the equivalent of approximately £3,330 in 2016).

Mottisfont, Wednesday January 1, 1941

Corporal Buchanan, a Canadian lumberjack sent by the Dominions Hospitality Centre, arrived for dinner yesterday and was only just not drunk. He'd left his companion somewhere between Aldershot and here because, as he said, 'He had another job on!' Public house, gutter, brothel? About 48 and the toughest type imaginable. During the night he tried to get into Mama's room which was next to his. Called through the door, 'I'll be in in a minute and a half.' Ate no breakfast, went out, bought whisky and drank in his room. He then asked to be taken to the kitchen, which completely puzzled us. It transpired he wanted to see the maids with a view to selection. Next move: invitations through the butler to the maids to come and drink whisky with him in his room. Lunch started and by then he was blind – whistled, muttered and occasionally roared. Every now and then he had a moment of lucidity. Agony for all of us. I had already settled with the butler to get him out of the house after lunch and during that interminable meal, I sat paralysed and dazed dreading the interview. It went off to perfection, the butler posted within ear shot and I saving his face by saying Flora and Diana were arriving suddenly to stay because G. was ill and there was no room they could have but his. He understood and behaved well. A taxi was there and he was gone within 10 minutes. Relief, what relief.

Mottisfont, Monday January 6

Diana, Duff and Conrad arrived on Friday. On Saturday we shot. Very cold. Played 'Definitions' after dinner. Clare adores it and it's quite amusing with people of the same intelligence. But Duff found it boring and our definitions – which seldom were definitions but lights and clues – too haphazard and harum-scarum for his logical mind to follow. Also he passionately wanted his side to win and was inclined to dispute his opponents' claims. So there was wrangling and not enough fun; and I was tired. We sat indoors yesterday, read Nathaniel Gubbins and did several crosswords. Duff seemed tired all weekend. After dinner I avoided Definitions. He started reading Pierre de Ronsard aloud but badly so that it was difficult to hear. After considerable argument between Clare, who wanted one thing, and Duff another, D. got his way and read Tennyson's *Vision of Sin* but again so badly and so indistinctly that it was grotesque and embarrassing. His eyes are suddenly going back on him as they do around 50. Diana tried to get him to see an oculist but hasn't yet succeeded and he was wearing spectacles bought by her for him at Selfridges. He had to guess at half the words and perhaps he was slightly tight. Poor sweet Duff. He ended better, standing in front of the fire with my spectacles on his nose reading the *Death of King Arthur* clearly and poetically. What a funny evening. Yes, and rather sad. G. is still ill but came down to lunch.

London, Wednesday January 8

Alexie told me she wants to divorce Lánczy. This would mean an annulment. I don't quite understand how this change in her feelings has occurred but I think it's primarily due to the marriage having been only in name. This has affected her nerves and altered her opinion of him. It's a miserable state of affairs for her.

Maud organises legal representation for Alexie and over the next year accompanies her on visits to the solicitor, Mr Harden, and to Dr Eardley Holland (1880-1967), one of foremost obstetricians of the day, who provides the necessary medical report for the annulment case.

London, Wednesday January 29

I dined with Violet B.-C. who told me an amusing story of a scene between Clemmie and Capt. [David] Margesson[1] which took place last summer after the French collapse. He was lunching at Downing St with Winston, Clemmie and another person. Margesson made some criticism about the French; that their fall was partly due to their always putting party before national interests and an inability to combine in the face of danger – a remark that was quite harmless and would have been unexceptional in anyone else. But coming from him, who rightly or wrongly always put Party above the country, it infuriated Clemmie, who has always disliked him. She took him violently to task and was so outspoken that Winston kept on intervening saying, 'Clemmie you really can't say that.' But Clemmie wasn't going to be stopped. Finally Margesson said, 'I'm so sorry; I'm sure you'd prefer me to go. Let me go.' Winston quickly said, 'Of course not.' But Clemmie said, 'No, no <u>you</u> shall stay but we [*Clemmie and the other person*] will have lunch elsewhere.' Winston, terribly uncomfortable, said, 'My dear, finish your lunch next door in the small dining room; that will be best.' But Clemmie got up magnificently

---

1. David Margesson, 1st Viscount Margesson (1890-1965), Conservative MP. From 1931-40 government chief whip. Gained reputation as strict disciplinarian.

and said, 'In the small dining room? Certainly not. We are going to the Ritz,' and swept from the room, head in the air.

Brighton, Friday February 7

Fall of Benghazi [*in Libya*] announced at 1 – days before we expected it. Very pleased. This [*Western Desert*] campaign has put a different complexion on the war and given us something to be proud of. The people of England have shown such great courage and patience with so little to point the way to ultimate victory. Dunkirk was a triumph – but a triumph of disentanglement only – a negative triumph. The defeat of the big August air raids were real defeats and left us confident. Then came the terrible night-bombings. But the people stood and didn't flinch. Now the tide has turned and at last we are securing victories – positive and tangible.

Maud's hopes for a complete victory in North Africa were to be short-lived. Allied forces were diverted to Greece in expectation of an imminent German invasion there, while the Italians in North Africa were reinforced by the arrival in Libya of German troops under General Erwin Rommel.

London, Friday February 14

Lunched with Sylvia who told me a curious story. It seems that Mr Harry Hopkins,[2] the President's Investigator over here, either had a letter with joint signatures or else several letters from influential people – I don't remember which – saying words to this effect: 'Don't believe what you have no doubt been told that everyone in this country is united in believing in a complete victory and a smashing of the German might. We (or I) don't believe this possible. We think the war will result in a stalemate, and that the sooner a negotiated peace is made the better.' One of these lily-livered people, so Sylvia told me, is Lord Kemsley. Mr Hopkins is reported to have said that he is looking forward to the day when he can publish these letters.

---

2. Harry Hopkins (1890-1946), President Roosevelt's intimate advisor and unofficial emissary to Churchill and Stalin. Key policy maker in the Lend-Lease programme that sent aid to Allies.

Mottisfont, Monday February 24

G. and I went to see General Oldfield [Sir Louis Oldfield, 1872-1949]to talk about the Home Guard and whether Mottisfont was keeping up to the mark. Lady Oldfield bored me about her spaniel when I wanted to hear what General Oldfield had to say. What a number of women do that. At Mottisfont the butler stopped me in the passage and said, 'Hitler's been making a terrible noise on the wireless again; took him about an hour.' That's all the impression Hitler made on him.

London, Thursday February 27

The solicitor Harden telephoned yesterday to say he'd arranged for me to go to Pentonville to identify Lánczy before a copy of the Petition was handed to him. Today Mr Brown, the solicitor's clerk, called for me at Claridges and we drove to Pentonville. My heart sank at the thought of this dreadful meeting. Vile scoundrel though Lánczy is, he is at the lowest ebb of his fortunes and the thought of inflicting this blow seemed horrible to me. The sight of the prison filled me with gloom. It's a particularly forbidding pile of masonry. We were let in through the little door of the big outer gate and waited for some minutes under the archway. The rain was pouring down and an alert had just been sounded. Two convicts came in with a warden having perhaps been clearing gutters or engaged in some outdoor task. Their faces were red and shiny but they looked cheerful. I was struck by the barbarity of having a prison in a town and not in the country, where every prisoner could have an allotment and grow vegetables or flowers, breathe the fresh air, use his muscles and have the satisfaction of seeing the result of his labours.

After a bit, the warder unlocked the inner gates and we were taken to a small room where clerks were working. We gave our names and stated our errand. We waited sitting side by side, close together on a bench in a cubicle. Finally a warder came and took us across the passage into a small room with a big fire, a solid table in the middle and several chairs. Lánczy was brought in and stopped at the other side of the table. I was too horrified by his appearance and the misery of his condition to greet him or say some lame sentence. We looked dully at each other. The clerk got up, turned to me and said, 'Is this Captain Lánczy?' I bowed and he handed the Petition across the table to Lánczy. We all seemed to wait for something. Lánczy put his hands on the table and leant over the document but didn't seem to read it. I felt he didn't know what was happening. I wondered whether he was going to have a heart attack – or feign one – but he remained bent over the document saying nothing. The warder called him, saying, 'That's all. Come along,' but he didn't move. I was paralysed. The warder called again. Then Lánczy said, 'I must sign.' The clerk bent forward saying loudly, 'No, no, there isn't anything to sign; you can take it away.' The warder called out again, 'Come along now,' rather peremptorily and roughly. L. turned on his heels, taking the paper and walked stiffly out. We hadn't said a word to each other. I hadn't managed to utter a syllable. The Governor said there was to be no conversation or discussion but I wanted, if the opportunity presented itself, to ask after his health or say some little human thing. I couldn't manage it. Afterwards I felt shame and the deepest pity. I hardly remember leaving the building. I felt tears creeping into my eyes. Lánczy's appearance seemed dreadful to me. He was always almost terrifyingly ugly and unpleasant looking. Now he has a rough beard, is fatter, his face red and shiny and his expression, or rather lack of it, tells of a man half-dead with misery. I shall never forget this morning, the horror aroused in me by the prison or the horror and shame of the interview. Something must be done about prisons and punishment.

I met B. for tea at Shanghai and showed him photographs of my Matisse drawings. He too was staggered when he saw them and seemed inclined to treat them as a joke. But that only lasted a moment. Then he began to see their merits – the grace of one, the vigour of the other. In the second one he thought every feature, taken individually, correct but the whole not like me. I saw him getting interested in them. I was still so overcome by the Pentonville visit that I told him all about it though I had meant not to. He was immensely sympathetic. He has this wonderful gift of understanding and sympathy. He is very quick, sensitive and intuitive. His nature is rich, full and human. And warm.

Cambridge, Thursday March 6

Yesterday I went to Cambridge to visit Raymond, staying at the Master's Lodge with the Richmonds.[3] R. and I went out, had a snack and then to *Measure for Measure* which I have never read or seen. We laughed a great deal. I enjoyed the undergraduates' healthy, unrestrained laughter at the more ludicrous twists of the complicated plot. Afterwards R. and I had supper and very pleasant it all was. Today I hurried off to see R.'s tutor Whalley-Tooker,[4] young, easy and sympathetic. I found R. had discussed his pacifism with him.

3. Admiral Sir Herbert William Richmond (1871-1946), naval officer and Master of Downing College 1936-47. Married, in 1907, Florence Elsa Bell (c.1880-1971).
4. Hyde Charnock Whalley-Tooker (1900-92), Senior Tutor Downing College 1931-47, University Lecturer in Law 1931-67.

W.T. took a wise and liberal-minded view. Advised R. to register as a CO [*conscientious objector*] at Cambridge where the Tribunal was understood to be fair. Afterwards I sat in R.'s rooms till lunch and talked.

Brighton, Saturday March 8

G. and I had tea with Clive Bell. Vanessa B. was there and Duncan Grant, she with the remains of all that beauty, dignified and soft-voiced but most bedraggled looking. Duncan trim, spry and lovely-voiced too. Clive had news of people in France. Maillol at Nice or Perpignan, Matisse there too with his Russian and a new addition – a 'Chinese Princess' – Mme M. tucked away in the country. Gide alright somewhere, Picasso in Paris. The Mexicans have offered him asylum and a passport but it isn't known whether the Germans would let him go or whether he wants to. Charleston has all the atmosphere of the Bloomsbury group – walls decorated by Duncan, tables painted by some or all of them, comfortable sofas, lovely pottery, charming but unobtrusive curtains and chair-covers, and everywhere pictures, statuettes, pots etc. The feeling in the house is one of beauty, comfort and refinement.

London, Thursday March 13

Dined with Sylvia. Came home alone by Tube to see the sleeping crowds [*who were using the Tube as an air raid shelter*]. They lay under blankets neatly and at first glance they all seemed asleep (11.30), but soon one saw that many were awake, here an arm stretched, there a leg, or the whole body turned around in its wrapping or blanket. Bunks against the wall but the whole floor-space covered with swaddled forms. Wherever there was an arch or doorway the draught was terrible. There was complete silence and the few travellers on the platform walked carefully and talked in low tones. Sad but not tragic scene.

London, Friday March 14

I lunched with I. at the Carlton Grill. He is just back from Spain and Portugal where he was attached to the American observer, Colonel Donovan [*President Roosevelt's special envoy on intelligence cooperation between the US and Britain*]. Lovely for him. Been away a month. Says that on Wednesday night, when there were many and widespread raids over the country, we had for the first time on a big night, more planes over Germany than they had over this country. Good. He is afraid we may be going to have a second Norway fiasco in Greece.

Brighton, Saturday March 15

To Flora's [Russell, *Gilbert's sister*] with G. for lunch where Martin is staying. He says Expeditionary Force is on its way to Greece but no word of it is allowed to be mentioned by express wish of General Wavell,[5] though the Germans, Italians and all the near east must know of it. Said that when Duff was cogitating about the chances for and against the Expeditionary Force, said, 'Better another Norway than another Munich.'

London, Wednesday March 19

I dined with I. at the Coq d'Or and we talked as fast and as violently as we usually do. He tells me Cathleen Queensberry has been sent to Spain to paint the portraits of any distinguished Spaniard who will sit for her. Great fun for her. What else is she meant to do I wonder? Interest them in England? Walked back with the guns booming and a fairly heavy raid on.

On March 25, Yugoslavia formally joined the Axis powers and signed the Tripartite Pact.

Mottisfont, Tuesday March 25

Yugoslavia has bowed to Germany in spite of the dismay and abhorrence of many of her people. I wonder whether there is still a chance of a coup d'état by the army.

London, Wednesday March 26

Lunched at the Ritz with Crinks, Diana and Duff, Violet B.-C. and Maynard Keynes. I asked Duff what chance he thought there was of a military coup d'état in Yugoslavia. He said an 8 to 1 chance. Duff said kind things about Martin. I said I feared he might be slow. Duff said he had been but was much better now and added with a laugh, 'One can't expect speed from a Russell.' 'All Russells are slow,' said Diana and Keynes together, laughing. 'Slow,' said Duff, 'in movement and speech and their reactions are slow.'

---

5. Field Marshal Archibald Wavell, 1st Earl Wavell (1883-1950), Commander-in-Chief Middle East until July 1941, then Commander-in-Chief India.

London, Thursday March 27

Lunch with B. who was moody. In Leicester Sq. we bought a newspaper and saw the Yugoslav news – a coup d'état, the young king acclaimed, a new anti-pact Cabinet, and the country and the church standing rock-firm. I felt that the news was tremendous. Heroic and glorious it certainly is.

London, Thursday April 3

Lunch with B. at a Turkish restaurant. We talked about Virginia Woolf who is missing and is thought to have drowned herself. Boris thought it un-aesthetic of her to have chosen cold water. She was very beautiful. I only met her once, lunching with Clive. I spent the afternoon talking with Boris. He'd been listening to the great roar of traffic passing unendingly and he thought of life passing so quickly, and then of his work and whether it had been much good.

On April 6, Germany invades Yugoslavia and Greece. Meanwhile in North Africa, the Axis forces are pushing the Allies back to the Libyan border.

London, Wednesday April 9

Yesterday lunch I. at Carlton Grill. He said, 'Be prepared for bad news.' I said I was. News or rather lack of news except from German or neutral sources is disgraceful. With very little trouble and without giving away military secrets it must be possible to issue communiques. I was in a rage all day and mad to think we have so miscalculated the German forces as to be in danger of losing Egypt. The safety of Egypt should have been our first consideration, and what we could spare to send to Greece only the second, however heart-rending the appeals from Greece and however poor a figure we had to cut in our response. I roared myself hoarse.

Mottisfont, Thursday April 17

Raymond was home for Easter and went back to Cambridge. We got on well on the whole. He is still, alas, unable to work seriously and his Cambridge reports are poor even in music. He has a passion for the harpsichord now. I can't help thinking he sees he will never become a very good organist and is consoling himself with the harpsichord. News of a very severe raid on London last night. Thought in a rush of friends and relations there.

Mottisfont, Friday April 18

News consistently bad in Greece. Slow, continuous, bloody retreat. Germans arrested on the borders of Egypt. Communiques still miserably scanty, tardy and evasive. A scandal. This must be put right. They make a horrible impression and at best are nothing better than idiotic.

Mottisfont, Monday April 21

News of another serious raid on London yesterday. Anxious, very anxious about friends. Retreat continuing. Greek prime minister dies suddenly and mysteriously. I daresay he couldn't bear any more. G. not well, tired and nervous. First cuckoo this morning. Spring mocks. No that is not right. It seems wholly disassociated with the thoughts that cram into and scramble in one's mind. It's a backcloth that doesn't suit the scene. Yesterday as I walked along the Pigeon Walk I thought I must look carefully at all this rare beauty and not miss any of its quick stages. And then I thought, in a disconnected way, I shan't see another spring.

London, Thursday April 24

Took Martin to dinner at Alice's [Astor]. Kenneth Clark there, very supercilious about the Air Ministry booklet 'Battle of Britain' which has had such a huge public success. I said I thought it was good, not meaning the writing was fastidious but the story riveting and well put together. He said, superciliously, how surprised he was I should think it good, that Jane and he had been horrified when they saw the manuscript.

Mottisfont, Monday April 28

On Friday I lunched with I. at the Carlton Grill and had a riveting retrospective talk. To Mottisfont 3.30. Violet, Bongie and their little boy Raymond arrived. Claud came after lunch on Saturday and I. for dinner, looking thin and rather worn. G., who hadn't seen him for two years, says he looks like a man of 40. Lazy day on Sunday. Plenty of talk, crosswords etc. Little Raymond is a brilliant child, uninhibited, very talkative, passionately interested in everything said by the grown-ups. He certainly talks too much at present and bored G. dreadfully but I think Violet is right not to check him. He is very remarkable. I. talked too, it must be said. Athens has been taken by the Germans and Greece lost. Our communiques have been disgraceful, always a day or two behind the enemies. Much better to be the first to announce our military disasters not a bad second.

Mottisfont, Tuesday May 13

Yesterday hoed flower beds working too fast like all amateurs do at anything easy. Astonishing news in an announcement from Germany that Hess, Hitler's deputy, had disappeared in an aeroplane. Amazed to hear today that Hess is in England. A thousand speculations. Imagine flight due to fear. Perhaps there is a split in the Nazi Party and this is the first crack. Our spirits soared. But one has to be sober. This is only the beginning. The end is far off.

London, Wednesday May 21

Dined with Sibyl at the Dorchester where every Wednesday she has a dinner at which each one pays his share – 15/6 I think it is. I hadn't been at so big a dinner since the war. [Gladwyn] Jebb teased Oliver [Harvey] incessantly about the MOI but there is a story behind that. Oliver blinked through his thick glasses and turned an impassive face to his persecutor. The MOI is abused night and day often for reasons over which it has no control. It's the whipping horse for the other ministries. Dinner was pleasant, I thought Sibyl's idea a good one.

Mottisfont, Sunday May 25

On returning to Mottisfont on Friday I found G. most strange, nervous, repressed and eyes odd. Had been nervous all day. Dr Wainwright came. Said sort of nervous breakdown. Put G. to bed and Wainwright gave him morphine. G. said he couldn't explain his nervousness but almost felt like throwing himself out of a window. At 2 he rang, I fell dazed out of bed and hurried to his room. He complained of nerves, misery and sickness. Was eventually sick. I dragged my mattress into his room and slept on the floor till he woke. I was dreadfully alarmed but then a strange calm came over me. I felt as if I could face anything. G.'s eyes and expression normal again though he still feels nervous. What are these strange unknown bogies coming to the surface? War strain, health strain, obscure fight against life of inaction and what else?

Mottisfont, Sunday June 1

Roosevelt's Fireside Chat[6] very satisfactory. America is slow but seems sure. Today news of evacuation of Crete. Yesterday I gardened. Homeless and distracted refugee – Freemantle – came to see whether I could fix his wife and son up in village. Drove round late but village all but full up. Took them into the house over Whitsun with dog, parrot and belongings.

Mottisfont, Wednesday June 4

Lunch with B. at Istanbul. He was nervous and depressed and said he'd been sleeping badly. He badly wants an occupation. He has been active for so many years and now all his mosaic work is finished and he finds himself in wartime with nothing to do and straightened finances. Returned here at 9 o'clock. G. so pleased to see me I felt I mustn't be away from him for too long. Two nights a week – that means three days – is too much in his now permanent semi-invalid state.

Mottisfont, Monday June 9

Martin here for the weekend. The MOI is in a turmoil. They are in revolt against the anomalies of their position – restrictions imposed on them by the Foreign Office, scanty and belated news grudgingly given out to them by the Defence Ministries, appointment unbeknown to them of a successor to Lord Lloyd at the British Council, and Sir Gerald Campbell's [*appointed British Consul General to US in 1941*] new powers at Washington. The press is almost wholly pro-MOI; Lord Beaverbrook a dark horse and probably scheming to sack Duff; the PM preoccupied and indifferent; and the public ill-informed.[7]

6. President Franklin D. Roosevelt gave a series of evening radio addresses known as 'fireside chats' between 1933 and 1944. On 27 May 1941, Roosevelt clearly stated the threat to the world presented by Hitler.

7. The Ministry of Information's ability to provide timely relevant news was hampered by the three service ministries – the War Office, the Admiralty and the Air Ministry – which were reluctant to give up their hold on news of what was happening in the war. The reference to the press baron Lord Beaverbrook, the owner of the Express group of newspapers and a member of the war Cabinet, probably refers to Beaverbrook's advice to Churchill not to issue a statement about Hess's flight to Britain which prevailed over Duff's own view that a declaration should be made.

Mottisfont, Sunday June 15

Sibyl Colefax, Osbert Peake, the Toynbees,[8] Freddie Ashton and Alice [Astor] staying. Freddie is gay and has a nice laugh (*see photo in black and white plate section*). I laugh easily when he is there. Wonderful weather today and we lay in the garden. I made the mistake of asking Sibyl to read aloud forgetting one can never hear what she says when she talks. There is much rattle and babble and she seems to try and say 100 things at the same time. So we didn't hear much of the Beerbohm story and the reading died out. For the amusement of later years I note the number of people in the house last night: G.R., M.R., Sibyl, Osbert, Alice, Freddie, Philip and Anne Toynbee, Adele, three housemaids, a cook and three kitchen-maids, a butler, two footmen, an odd-man, a negro refugee from Southampton, five evacuee children and eight officers. In the stables there are eight batmen,[9] two evacuee children and Mr and Mrs Gould – she as a helper – as well as the butler's wife and a young man, another Southampton refugee.

Mottisfont, Sunday June 22

G. rang through at 10 to say Germany had invaded Russia. We talked constantly about it all day and the extraordinary situation arising out of this new alignment. I pity Russia. Colonel Meinertzhagen,[10] Doria [Scott] and Sam C. [Courtauld] are staying. Meinertzhagen is a strange fish. He loves being here. He was born in the house and tells me a lot about it as it was in the 1880s. The mock wall on the top floor on the north side was taken down by his father, bringing to view again the sloping roof and dormer windows. This mock wall is shown in the 1822 British Museum drawing and must have been put up to make the house look more important or to prevent the servants from seeing out onto the lawns. Violent raid ostensibly on Southampton but

8. Philip Toynbee (1916-81), writer, and his wife Anne, *née* Powell, the sister of Elizabeth Glenconner. Philip was very intelligent, a good talker and 'ugly, tough and virile', according to Maud. After the Toynbees separated, Anne married the philosopher Richard Wollheim. Anne and Elizabeth remained among Maud's closest female friends into old age.

9. *Batman,* a soldier or airman assigned to a commissioned officer as a personal servant. Batmen were abolished after the Second World War.

10. Colonel Richard Meinertzhagen, CBE, DSO (1878-1967), soldier, intelligence officer and ornithologist. His parents leased Mottisfont in 1884 from the then owner Mrs Marianne Vaudrey, and Richard grew up at Mottisfont where his interest in the study of birds developed. Maud and Richard went on to share a great-nephew, James Mayor, Alexie Apponyi's son by her third marriage to Andreas Mayor.

a strong wind blew the landmines away and they fell in the country. Six inch naval guns made the night disagreeable. The house – walls and floor – shook.

Mottisfont, Sunday June 29

Drink with Boris at Café Royal on Friday. He was telephoned by someone at MOI and asked to listen to Russian news at Reuters. He all but went mad the first two days trying to take notes – he can't do shorthand or type – and remember the connecting links between his chain of notes. Reception is often bad, new expressions used and proper names mumbled by the Russian broadcaster. I think now he rather enjoys the experience and the contretemps as well as the excited atmosphere of a news agency. The Russian business goes slowly, oh, so slowly. It feels as if they have been at war with Germany for weeks not just seven days. They are retreating as expected and it all seems terrible. I hate Communism but I like Russia.

Mottisfont, Monday June 30

I went to a meeting of the Parish Representatives of the WVS [*Women's Voluntary Service*] in Romsey. We are being asked to make plans for the communal feeding of the civil population in case of invasion. In my case this means about 500 people. The Mill Arms and probably the Mottisfont Club will be commandeered and the parish fed in them.

Hove, Sunday July 6

Motored over to tea at Bognor with G. and Martin who had arrived the night before. Duff, Diana, Phyllis and Hubert there. The little white house and garden masked with climbing roses, very bright on the white walls, looked like a stage-set. Diana showed me proudly the cow, pigs and chickens she looks after. To reach the cow we clambered along a rough path behind and close against the beach defences. Here and there among the concrete blocks and barbed wire were posts with soldiers in them. The debate on the MOI took place last week and was very unsatisfactory. There are no changes worth mentioning in its makeup and the Minister is as powerless as before vis-à-vis the Foreign Office and the Service Ministries. Duff was placed in the extraordinary position of winding up the debate as government spokesman and having to defend a position he must find nearly intolerable. He'd wanted to open the debate and leave the House to criticise to their heart's content.

London, Thursday July 10

Dined with I.C-G. at Jardin like old times. He is a major now and stationed at Chester. He thinks an invasion may come even while the Germans are occupied in Russia. We walked along the empty, hot Soho streets and hearing an accordion walked into a house and found ourselves in France. It was a plebeian French dancing place and all the people – sailors and civilians – French, square and stocky. I was glad to see a crowd of them together again, drinking, singing and having a nice evening, but at the same time I felt sad. And we felt like intruders not only because of Ian's uniform.

London, Friday July 11

Saw Victor Russell in the Temple at 4.30 about Alexie's case and finding someone to give evidence as to Lánczy's domicile. Victor gave me confidence. He was very alert and clear-minded and didn't waste time and words unnecessarily. Thinks I may do for evidence of domicile. The Temple is an extraordinary sight now. Cars can't drive in owing to the number of wrecked houses and workmen clearing up the mess. Crown Office Row, where I thought I would find Victor, doesn't exist anymore. I stopped at the corner, not knowing where I was, and asked some workmen the way. In front of us lay the jagged remains of houses. A workman said, 'This is Crown Office Row.' And so it had been but there was nothing left. The church gutted and shattered looked very romantic and so did all the little streets and squares, romantic and fantastic to a degree.

Mottisfont, Wednesday July 16

Yesterday lunched with Diana at Bognor. Norah Lindsay[11] there. Same delicious whimsical humour and mock-serious face as usual. Diana says that Duff – never given to optimism – is beginning to think the war won't be such a long affair after all. Diana had collected some hens for me from neighbouring farmers and Adele took them on by train. Diana said she would like to go to Washington. Lord Halifax hasn't been a success and there are constant rumours that Duff is being removed from the MOI. Today immersed in village and garden.

---

11. Norah Lindsay (1873-1948), garden designer. 'Irreparable, unique Norah, witty, fantastical, poetical, lover of beauty... sly and funny,' wrote Maud in 1948. Designed the box-edged parterre at Mottisfont.

Mottisfont, Saturday July 19

Martin, the Glenconners, Cardie and Diana Cavendish[12] are staying. Talk is animated and Christopher very funny. MOI in a turmoil. The press tips Brendan – he was to have come here this weekend but sent a wire to say he couldn't come, so I suppose he is in the running or has passed the post. Martin confided to G. that Duff is being sent on a mission to the Far East and that he has asked Martin to go with him.

Mottisfont, Monday July 21

The new appointments were in the papers: Brendan MOI, Duff Chancellor of the Duchy of Lancaster and destined for a mission to the East, base probably Singapore. Lovely journey and experiences for Martin but he may never see G. again.

Mottisfont, Sunday July 27

Alexie and Boris came from London. Showed B. round. He said about the flower bed – Norah's bed – on the front of the house, 'This is terrible, it couldn't be worse, it doesn't correspond with anything. This thing is much too large and everything is wrong about it.' He thought the tunnel lime-walk a mistake and the scale too small. He liked the wild, rough lawns and clumps of trees. His presence is always warm and stimulating. I think G. and Conrad liked him. He is as Russian as can be. No cosmopolitan stuff. After lunch he and I taxied to Biddesden to look at the mosaics he did some years ago for Bryan Guinness[13] in a gazebo. They are very gay, bright, beautiful and rustic – if one can use such a word about such a sophisticated art. Dropped him at Andover Station. Raymond has been here since Wednesday. He is having ARP lectures at Cambridge with a view to being a warden. He registered as a conscientious objector a week or two ago.

---

12. Diana Cavendish (1909-92), daughter of Rt. Hon. Lord Richard Frederick Cavendish and Lady Moyra de Vere Beauclerk. Married first Conservative politician Robert Boothby in 1935, then after a divorce Ian Campbell-Gray in 1942 and thirdly Henry Gage, 6th Viscount Gage, in 1971.
13. Bryan Guinness, later second Baron Moyne (1905-92), lawyer, poet and novelist. Part of the Guinness brewing family. Married Diana Mitford in 1929, later divorced. Boris's mosaic was fixed in the gazebo in 1931.

London, Wednesday July 30

Lunch with and to newsreel with Freddie Ashton. Saw signing of Anglo Soviet Pact with John Russell [Wriothesley], pale, serious and correct, in the background. Stalin looking a wily villain and as if not belonging to the picture. Russia still holding up to the Germans, to everybody's intense surprise. The result is a wave of optimism as regards the war and its duration which has infected high and low alike. A garrulous old porter who carried my bags at the station said, 'I don't hold with Communism but it's come in handy this time.'

London, Sunday August 3

Came to London yesterday with G. in a taxi. Martin dined. Duff's staff consists only of Martin as private secretary, a Major Robertson as military adviser and they hope to pick up Mr Tony Keswick[14] in Washington. Duff hasn't a seat in the War Cabinet as he should. Today drove round the City with G. in the morning to see the devastation. It's very extensive and, if one could still be horrified by devastation, horrifying. G. was staggered. Martin lunched and dined. I think he feels leaving Gilbert very much. Both feel they may never see each other again. I do my best not to think about it. The Cooper party leaves Tuesday for Lisbon.

London, Monday August 4

Alexie and Martin dined. Duff, Diana and Venetia [Montagu], who were dining at Claridges too, came upstairs afterwards. Diana said she'd rather be going in a bomber. It's death with luxury, like the *Lusitania*[15] going down, that she hates the idea of most. In a bomber there's no incongruity. Duff was heavy, silent and depressed.

Hove, Tuesday August 5

Adele went early to the Cumberland [*where Martin is staying*] to wash Martin's linen, run errands and pack his 100 lbs of luggage. G. and I lunched at Claridges. Martin didn't turn up. He was sitting at the Foreign Office trying to arrange for Paul Kruger to be wangled a seat in their plane at Diana's urgent request and

14. Sir William 'Tony' Keswick (1903–90), a specialist in Far Eastern affairs who went to Singapore as Duff's chief advisor.
15. *RMS Lusitania*, British ocean liner torpedoed and sunk by a German U-boat on 7 May 1915, causing the deaths of 1,198 passengers and crew.

Duff's too. In the end Kruger stayed behind. Their train was leaving at 4.15. At 3.15 Martin telephoned, still at the FO. G. and I went to the Cumberland. A suit was missing, medicines hadn't arrived. Finally Martin came, papers and oddments were flung in clumsy confusion into a bigger suitcase, the suit appeared and was crammed in among the papers. Martin and G. said goodbye on the pavement among a jostling crowd. It was no place for emotion. Both must have been thinking the same. We went off in a taxi and Martin leant forward twice to catch the last glimpses of G. At the station there were two crowded trains going to Bristol and a doubt about which was the right one. Finally the compartment was found, reserved in Martin's name. Three minutes before the train started Duff and Diana arrived with their luggage. I gave Diana a St Christopher and slipped a St George into Duff's pocket. Short goodbyes. The train started, Diana at the window, her face long and dismal. It was only when the three of them were in the compartment that it occurred to me how strange it was that Martin, so young and still so untidy, like a schoolboy in appearance, should be going off alone with them, they more in his charge than he in theirs. Returned to Claridges where I found G. reading quite happily, the feared moment behind him. That fortunately is how he is. After tea came down here by car. I was exhausted.

Hove, Wednesday August 6

Woke up at 3 and lay awake for some hours thinking of them in the air, in the dark. When the first grey streaks of dawn came I was relieved, thinking Diana too must be seeing it and the others. G. woke up several times in the night but told me that he never once thought of them. I felt ill today.

Hove, Monday August 11

Newspapers report safe arrival [*of Coopers and Martin in US en route to Singapore*]. Relief. Russia fighting stubbornly on. Seven weeks at war yesterday. The war must be appalling. One can hardly realise the horrors of it. I try to. One must know. Deafness and blindness to these cries and agonies seem like betrayal.

London, Tuesday August 12

Tea at Dorchester with Sibyl. Duke of Devonshire and Lord Tyrrell[16] there.

16. William Tyrrell, 1st Baron Tyrrell (1866-1947), British civil servant and diplomat.

Latter looking older than ever, a fragile little monkey. But his mind is as clear as ever and I thought him delightful. I used to see him in my early married days but didn't appreciate him, his malice, shrewdness and paradoxical humour. I remember being revolted one night when he sat next to me at dinner at Cavendish Square because he pulled a tooth-pick out of his pocket, stuck it in his ear and proceeded to clean out his ear. His talk is difficult to repeat because of its twists and turns. He said that Winston was a bad judge of character but an excellent judge of situations. Maudie and Oliver Harvey and Bongie dined with me at Boulestin's where we talked till late. Oliver was very optimistic – like everybody else now – about the course of the war. He said the German attack on Russia was a major error and couldn't imagine why they'd launched it.

Mottisfont, Sunday August 24.

Had a talk with Raymond who went before the CO Tribunal a week ago. He described the Judge, Campbell,[17] as fair and a King's College don on the Tribunal called Claydon[18] as trying to catch the COs out, sarcastic and disagreeable. I gather the COs as a crowd surprised even R. by their eccentric appearance and behaviour. R. was posted for non-combatant duty which he resents and is going to appeal against. He says he stated he was willing to do Civil Defence duties. He objects to any form of duty in the army, he says, as he considers all armies an evil. His reasons were wholly illogical and I ended by getting, for once, very irritated with him. What bunk COs talk. No wonder the King's don was impertinent and sarcastic.

Mottisfont, Monday August 25

Heavy rain all day Saturday. There will be a bad harvest just when a good one is needed. Yesterday Conrad showed me how to make a cheese. I enjoyed the business and Conrad's slow instruction. The morning was taken up measuring, stirring, heating and cutting. Adele and I had milking lessons from Mrs Pitman. I was a failure, Adele much better. I was nervous for the cow and thought I might hurt it.

17. Most likely His Honour William Campbell (1890-1970), a county court circuit judge 1937-62, and chair of East Anglia Conscientious Objector Tribunal.
18. Probably not Claydon, but Professor Sir John Harold Clapham CBE (1873-1946), an economic historian at King's College, Cambridge and member of the East Anglia Conscientious Objector Tribunal.

Maud became a dab hand at making cheese which she used to complement the rations and give as presents to people in the village and friends in London.

Mottisfont, Sunday September 7

On Friday a pretty, alert, nimble little cow arrived. She was tethered. Two hours later she was loose and being pursued by a disorderly but well-meaning army of evacuee children and servants. This time she was roped to a poplar. Yesterday I was up at 6.30 and out to unrope the cow in torrents of heavy rain and take her to be milked. I sat in the hot shed, wet but steaming and pouring with heat and tried to coax the cow into generous speed. She was gentle but insufferably slow. Milked again at tea-time. I get so hot each time that I have to change my clothes.

Mottisfont, Sunday September 14

Cardie and John Follett are staying. Yesterday shot partridges. Cardie would insist on trying to see me milk the cow. I milk the cow every afternoon, Adele in the morning. Russia fights desperately on but the Germans have advanced steadily from the first day. These terrible battles weigh heavily on one's mind.

London, Thursday September 18

Lunch with B. He talked plainly about the war. He has little or no feeling about it. He doesn't want Hitler to win but if he did, B. said he would do nothing against him. He said that his attitude was perhaps egotistical – and so indeed it is – but he wanted only to be left alone to lead his life as he wants to. He says he has had enough of wars and revolutions. He said, 'Again I have to decide on whose side I am to be.' This I think is reprehensible. He has taken shelter here, spent many years here before 1927, and had the benefits, peace and comfort of the orderly and pretty free life this country has to offer. His attitude is not unlike Raymond's, though with the big difference that Raymond has never till now had wars in his life let alone a root-destroying revolution. I can make allowances for B. but I cannot approve.

London, Thursday September 25

Saw Sickert[19] exhibition at the National Gallery. I can see why the French aren't very interested in him. Matisse never looked at him when he, Clive [Bell], Mary[20] and I went to Monty Shearman's[21] house to look at his collection and show Sickert to Matisse whom he pretended never to have seen. Matisse went straight from the doorway, leaving the Sickerts on his left, and made for a Steer which he looked at attentively. He only glanced – and hardly that – at the Sickerts. There was a picture of his own which he pretended to have forgotten. Monty Shearman wasn't there to show Matisse around. There were some good pictures but they were crowded together and badly hung. The only picture I remember Matisse admiring was a Jongkind,[22] probably because Jongkind is dead. Later, 18 months ago, Monty Shearman's pictures were exhibited and sold – he had died during the winter – apart from one or two pictures he left to the National Gallery. He left Mary and Hutchy [St John Hutchinson] one picture to be chosen by themselves. The owner of the Redfern Gallery told me they hesitated a long time between a Matisse – a pink woman I think – and the snow-bound Monet they finally settled on. He thought the long hesitation wasn't quite genuine. It would have been more fashionable to have taken the Matisse and certainly more in their line. But the Monet was priced higher and a more solid investment.

The day we all went to Monty Shearman's house, Matisse had been lunching with me at Princes Gate. Clive and Mary were there to meet him, Phyllis de Janzé for her looks and her French and Hubert Duggan because I couldn't find anyone else. Matisse looked as smart and polished and as like a successful doctor as ever. He ate very slowly and talked a great deal and, I think, enjoyed himself because he stayed talking till 4. He talked very well, amusingly, maliciously. He castigated Derain mercilessly and made fun of him personally – his person, habits, decisions and indecisions. From this I imagine he sees a possible rival in Derain. He wouldn't speak of Picasso when I sat for him and didn't on this occasion. He knows he can't criticise much there and cannot bear to praise. He only praises the dead. He spoke warmly of Renoir and told a moving story of Renoir on his death-bed, crippled as

19. Walter Sickert (1860-1940), painter. As an artist and teacher, Sickert was an important influence on British painters.
20. Mary Hutchinson, *née* Barnes (1889-1977), married to the barrister and art collector St John Hutchinson ('Hutchy'), drawn by Matisse in 1935 and long-term lover of Clive Bell.
21. Montague Shearman (1857-1940), foreign office official and art collector. First owner of Matisse in England according to *Burlington Magazine* Vol. 135, No. 1084 (July 1993) p480.
22. Johan Jongkind (1819-1891), Dutch seascape painter, considered forerunner of impressionism.

he'd been for years, by arthritis, I think, and how the day of his death he got up and walked alone. It seemed miraculous. He talked about Augustus John[23] pleasantly – in whatever way that might be interpreted! As a painter I never know what to make of Matisse. I think he is over-rated – though it is precisely for his painting he is so much admired. Good of course, but so good? Many of his drawings are very good. Picasso seems to me a much bigger figure. Almost everything I see of his moves me. The next time I saw Matisse was a month or two before the war. He was ill and miserable. He has a drawing of mine by him which I wanted to change.

London, Monday September 29

Lunched with B. in Italian restaurant. He was in bad spirits, tired by the nervous strain of work at Reuters. I think these moods are not uncommon with him but they are sad to see. He looks out at the world with suspicion. A worm seems to gnaw. When he is in good spirits he is delightful, gay, amusing, buoyant, festive, all the fountains playing. He said he didn't feel satisfied with the work he's done. It hasn't been what he would have liked it to be. He alluded to the calm, serenity and strength of Picasso's and Maillol's work. I asked him when he started being dissatisfied. He said: always. He said he'd only had 20 years in which to work. He started mosaics late, the last war interrupted him almost before he started, and now this war.

London, Tuesday September 30

G. and I lunched at the Ritz with Crinks and Oliver Lyttelton. Oliver is thinner but otherwise unaltered. I was afraid he might have become Minister-conscious or spoilt by his rapid rise and success but he was just the same: nice, genial, jolly, commonish, raconteurish, shrewd and joke-loving. Talking about de Gaulle, Oliver said he was an extraordinary person, one day quiet, correct and normal, the next day talking about the Syrians as 'mes fiefs', saying he should be made *Connétable de France*[24] and when someone was trying to explain what France was saying, or thinking, he brushed the arguments aside with 'La France – C'est Moi'. The trouble is that no one can guess which of these two people he is going to be. Oliver has a high opinion of him. He thinks him very unusual.

23. Augustus John (1878-1961), painter. Leading portrait painter by 1920s.
24. The 'Constable of France', one of the original five great offices of the French Crown, abolished in 1627

Hove, Thursday October 2

Quiet day. Read Orwell's *Lion and the Unicorn*. Yes, we are on the way to big changes. One mustn't work against the <u>progressive</u> movement of one's times, only against the retrogressive ones. These changes won't be very agreeable for us, the rich, but I know in my heart they are right. Don't let me forget this.

Hove, Saturday October 18

G. was in bed and asleep almost all day on Tuesday in a rather alarming doped state. Very fast pulse. Strange fixed eyes. Doctor rather mystified. G. had an idea he might have, by accident, taken two sleeping draughts being rather muddled due to taking bromide for nervous 'jam-jams' for the last three weeks. Then he and Adele discovered that a newish bottle of whisky had been drunk right down and it looks as if, stupefied by his drugs, when he got up during the night he had long swigs at the bottle. Better on Thursday. Think his illness must have been due to an accumulation of bromide, double sleeping draught plus half a bottle of whisky. I laugh about it now.

London, Friday October 24

Raymond came before the Appeal Tribunal on October 8. His appeal was dismissed and he was ordered to do <u>any</u> duties in the Army so his position is worse than it was. Today I went to see Robert Pollard, the Quaker solicitor, to seek advice. He said there was nothing to be done now. R. should have been legally represented at the Tribunal and Appellate Tribunal. If, as he intends, R. disregards call-up papers, he will get 3-12 months hard labour, probably sharing a cell with two or three others as prisons are so crowded. He might get on the land quick but even then it's unlikely he would be left there. After a term of imprisonment, COs are generally left alone although sometimes reimprisoned. Afterwards I went to Claridges where Raymond met me. I tried to tell him he wouldn't do any good either to himself or anyone else. He made one or two preposterous statements showing a mind of childlike inconsequence. But we didn't have a row. I dreaded the meeting. I was afraid I mightn't be able to keep my temper, or that I might say something needlessly sharp, or make him entrench himself still deeper. Poor R. what an outlook.

London, Wednesday October 29

Lunch with Violet B.-C., Cis Asquith, Neville Lytton[25] and Russell Page there. N.L. left France, where he made his home for some years, in August. De Gaulle to the de Gaullists, and many others, represents the purest flame of patriotism and of honour. He is their Pole Star. They know nothing about him or what he looks like, fortunately perhaps. He is their inspiration. He is listened to, his advice taken and his orders obeyed. Lytton said he prayed that he wouldn't be superseded or pushed out no matter how difficult or tiresome his dealings with us may be. His value is immense.

Dined with Alice at Claridges. Others there, Cecil [Beaton], Osbert P. [Peake] and Dr Weizmann,[26] head of the Zionist organisation and his tedious wife. I met him years ago in Paris. His appearance is extraordinary and arresting. He is a dark Lenin with a Jewish cast to the Slav or Tartar features. His eyes are fanatical. The head is magnificent because of his dark colour, burning eyes and look of power. He appeared depressed and seemed to think that his efforts were being blocked, as no doubt they are. Wants to get to Palestine but thinks the authorities want to keep him out of it. Said the Jews offered to raise an army of 50,000 at the beginning of the war. This was turned down. One can see why. Arab question. Then it was agreed Palestine might raise that number, half to be Jews, half Arabs. The Jews agreed. But the project fell through as the Arabs never came forward. Now there are 8,000 Palestinian Jews in the Armies of the Middle East.

London, Thursday November 13

Yesterday Violet [Cripps] and Ann O'Neill[27] lunched with me at Claridges. Ann pretty, anxious to please, gay, nice and frivolous. Esmond Rothermere[28] wants to marry her. I don't know what the difficulties are. They have known each other well for several years. I think she has other lovers though not Ian as some people think. Alexie came to dinner and we talked about her horrible

---

25. Neville Bulwer-Lytton, 3rd Earl of Lytton OBE (1879-1951), artist. Active service in the First World War, an experience he represented in frescos in Balcombe village's Victory Hall.

26. Dr Chaim Weizmann (1874-1952), Zionist leader and first President of Israel 1949-52. President of the World Zionist Organisation 1935-46.

27. Ann Charteris (1913-81), society hostess. Married first, in 1932, Shane O'Neill, 3rd Baron O'Neill (killed in action 1944); second, in 1945, the newspaper magnate Esmond Harmsworth, 2nd Viscount Rothermere; third, after a divorce, Ian Fleming in 1952.

28. Esmond Harmsworth, 2nd Viscount Rothermere (1898-1978), British Conservative politician and newspaper proprietor.

divorce. I wish it were over – one way or another. It's an added burden to other burdens: Raymond and G.'s health. The war colours and permeates all other troubles. Today Cecil B. fetched me and took me to Vogue Studios where he photographed me for an article on 'how to use one's coupons' in *Vogue*. Detest being photographed though less so by Cecil than anyone else. I really like him very much.

London, Thursday November 20

Today lunch with Alice. Freddie [Ashton] on leave and Kenneth Clark there. How agreeable K.C. can be and how clever he is. If only one could like him instead of detesting him which I do every other time I meet him. I was talking today about Christabel [McLaren] and the elaborate and flawless stories she invents to conceal something she doesn't want known and K.C. compared her amusingly to the alabaster figures shown one by a sacristan, perhaps in Rome, who points at the solid figure and then says, 'but wait a moment, ladies and gentlemen' and lights a match behind the figure and lo the whole pretty thing is transparent.

London, Thursday November 27

Dined with I. at the Ivy. He is beginning to want a more active life than he gets at DNI though he is lucky enough to move about quite a lot. He wanted to know what I thought about him resigning and going to King Alfred's Training Ship and getting an MTB [*Motor Torpedo Boat used by the Royal Navy during the Second World War*]. I said I didn't think he would get much excitement there from what Mark Tennyson tells me. I daresay he is more useful where he is.

London, Friday December 5

Lunch with Raymond M. at Pastoria. He told me that Vanessa Bell and Duncan Grant are outraged at their daughter Angelica[29] going to live with David Garnett[30] because the latter and Duncan had had an amorous passage themselves in the past. Certainly the situation is unusual. A man doesn't often

29. Angelica Bell (1918-2012), writer and painter. Daughter of Vanessa Bell and Duncan Grant, but recognized by Clive Bell as his daughter. Married David Garnett in 1942.
30. David Garnett (1892-1981), writer and publisher, associated with the Bloomsbury Group.

have a love affair with the father and then after a number of years with the daughter. When David Garnett looks into Angelica's eyes he must often see reflected his past with Duncan. The similarities and differences between father and daughter may have a strange piquancy.

Hove, Sunday December 7

50 today, half a century old. How very strange. I enjoy life very much, very richly, very fully, in spite of this nightmare war, poor Gilbert's health, Raymond's troubles and Alexie's approaching annulment case. I hope this capacity will go on, this constant interest and participation in life and all the wonders to be found in sight, hearing, smell, touch and thought. Then let old age come but don't let me lose interest in life. That is death before death. The difficulty will be to strike the balance between interest in life and a calm attitude to death.

At the end of the day we heard Japan had attacked us [*in Malaya, Singapore and Hong Kong*] and the USA [*at Pearl Harbour*] and at midnight, on the wireless, that she [*Japan*] had declared war. The world is now at war. Poor human race.

On December 8, the US entered the Second World War with its declaration of war on Japan.

London, Wednesday December 10

On Monday I read with astonishment of Japan's attacks on American bases in the Pacific where the Americans appear to have been dozing complacently. Astounding. Yesterday motored to London with G. and Adele. Alexie and Anne Toynbee came to dinner. A. has to fill in a large buff form to apply for permission to come to Mottisfont for Xmas. Among the questions are whether she possesses an aircraft or a yacht! How could anyone in these times, let alone a miserable foreigner? This morning horrible news of sinking of *Prince of Wales* and *Repulse [off Singapore]*.[31] Gloom. English people feel naval losses very severely. G. was more upset by the loss of these two ships than by the retreat from Flanders and the evacuation of Dunkirk.

31. The battleship HMS *Prince of Wales* and battlecruiser HMS *Repulse* were sunk by the Japanese navy as they were returning to Singapore after unsuccessfully seeking to intercept the Japanese invasion of Malaya. Following the Pearl Harbour attack, the loss of these two ships left the Allies extremely vulnerable in Southeast Asia.

London, Thursday December 11

News of the picking up of a great part of the crews of the two battleships. This is a relief. To see I., ill in bed, in his room at Athenaeum Court. Not looking at all ill but having a nice rest, reading a long novel and looking very handsome and splendid or 'dazzling' as Ian Campbell-Gray says. I. said he laughed a good deal (in spite of the gravity of the occasion) when he heard of the US Pacific losses. I think everyone laughed because the Americans have been telling us for years how to run the war, how dull and slow and stupid we are, though heroic, and we had to be polite about it all. Now we've had our laugh.

Raymond agreed to accept the Appeal Tribunal's ruling and take part in active service after Gilbert wrote to him in November and asked him to show Maud, his mother, some consideration.

Hove, Sunday December 14

The Senior Tutor, Whalley-Tooker, wrote a week ago to say Raymond had his medical exam and been passed Grade II. That means, I gather, non-combatant duties. It's an immense relief he has been up for his medical. He is applying for a postponement of calling-up until June so as to be able to take his wartime degree.

London, Thursday December 18

Dined with Ian at Jardin yesterday. I was pleased when he said he felt comfortable with me. Lots of people don't. They think me frightening and I hate that.

Mottisfont, Saturday December 20

Fourth pheasant shoot. Wonderful day. Warm and beautiful. Shot about 100 pheasants. None fed or reared, of course, for two years. There have been plenty all the same. They fetch high prices. 13/- a bird is the most we have got and a great deal it is. Conrad came in time for lunch. He is always a pleasure. We talked about cheeses, cows and chickens for hours.

Mottisfont, Thursday December 25, Christmas Day

Yesterday I made a cheese, walked, talked, wrote letters, and sent off Xmas cards which have great fascination for me now that they are almost unprocurable. Raymond in good spirits. Decorated small Xmas tree. Thought of Martin. Today Church 3.30 with Clare [Tennyson]. Mama never supports. Alexie, Tony and Sally couldn't get permission to stay here for Xmas as planned because they have just become enemy aliens. News bad from the Far East. Hong Kong surrendered on the 24th, Japanese advancing in Malaya, invading Philippines in large numbers, invading Sarawak and N.E. Sumatra.

Mottisfont, Friday January 2

General Cuthbertson came to see me about feeding the Home Guard in case of invasion. Said I may feed them in the village and from the house. Talked of feeding of civilian population. Each village in this area is supposed to have emergency rations for two or three days hidden in some houses. I haven't been told where they are in the village.

London, Thursday January 8

To Zwemmer's where I bought a Picasso etching of three women for I think 11 gns or thereabouts.

Hove, Saturday January 10

Letter from Sibyl Colefax saying Coopers or rather 'Mr M. Russell and Party' were on their way home. It was announced on the 1 o'clock news. Delighted but wonder why Duff is returning. Has he been a failure again or is he the victim of intrigue?[32]

Hove, Tuesday January 13

Lord Hood writes to Gilbert that the Coopers and Martin are coming back via Cairo. What's the explanation of their return? Australian barracking or Malayan intrigue? Conrad had a letter from Diana written on Dec. 18th and posted in London on Jan. 6th saying what a dreadful muddle everything was and that she was distressed and worried.

---

32. Duff's mission was to report on the situation in the Far East, especially on defence. Following Japan's bombing of Pearl Harbour and its rapid advance he was ordered back home. At the time the public unfairly associated him with these defeats although he had had neither the power nor the time to prevent them.

Hove, Wednesday January 14

The papers say Coopers left Singapore yesterday during an air raid and while bombs were actually dropping on the aerodrome.

Hove, Saturday January 17

Today telegram from Martin saying not returning with Coopers but staying on in Singapore. Doesn't say with whom or as what. There seems to have been an alternative choice – to go to Russia with Sir Archibald Clark Kerr who has just been appointed Ambassador there. I feel Martin has done right – that he can be useful in Singapore in a most difficult moment. Naturally I would like to have seen him again soon but those things take second place now. Poor G. was dreadfully disappointed. I know he thinks that he won't see Martin again. The Japanese are 100 miles from Singapore.

Hove, Tuesday January 20

Heavyish snowfall. Dry and beautiful. G. very short of breath and craving to get back to Mottisfont. Intended returning there with him today but the roads were like glass. All Malayan news bad.

London, Thursday January 22

Oliver and Maudie Harvey and Eddy Sackville-West came and dined at Claridges. Oliver went to Russia with Mr Eden. He only saw Stalin once: at the banquet given for Mr Eden. It was given in the Empress Catherine's throne room in the Kremlin, a vast room with malachite columns or pilasters. There was no pomp, extravagance or show about it. There was plenty of food and drink, including Russian champagne and vodka and brandy. There were a great many speeches and toasts. None of the Russians spoke English or, indeed, any other language, or if they could they didn't. Stalin's entrance to the room was almost unnoticed he came in so quietly. Everybody was assembled and waiting. Suddenly Stalin was there without any fuss, flinging open of doors or flunkeys. He was wearing his usual greyish tunic. Oliver said his manner was very gentle and quiet and his voice was quiet and pleasant. He looked very benign. Oliver thought him much smaller than he expected and said there was nothing remarkable about his face. If one had seen him in the street, one would have passed him without thought. Oliver wasn't sitting very far away from him and watched him carefully. He reminded him of a kindly old uncle or grandfather giving a party for the children and coming to it rather late himself, not taking part in it, but looking on in a benign rather distant manner.

London, Wednesday January 28

Marigold and Archie [Sinclair], Violet [B.-C.], Crinks and Raymond Mortimer came to lunch at the Ritz. Archie looked handsome as usual. He and Crinks had been in the House and heard Winston open the debate on the War Effort. Winston spoke slowly, seriously, consulted notes, peered through his spectacles and treated the whole affair in the most serious manner, dropping for this special occasion, so they said, all his usual exuberance and buoyancy, tricks and arts. He showed he understood the temper of the house and the importance of the situation. The speech read very well, I thought. Went and bought beehives after lunch.

Mottisfont, Monday February 2

On Saturday I took the estate foreman Bundy and the cook Mrs Bennett to see how field-ovens are built and work at Bushfield Camp near Winchester. I had got in touch with a Captain Miller who showed us round. The idea was to see what we could build here to cook for the Home Guard or the civil population of the parish – numbering about 500 – in case of invasion.

Malay troops all withdrawn now from mainland on to Singapore island. Singapore is beleaguered. No news from Martin. Today G. wrote to Brendan to ask whether he can find out where Martin is and what he is doing. It's impossible not to feel anxious.

London, Thursday February 5

Lunched with B. at Istanbul and spent afternoon with him. He says all the old Russians in London want the Germans to beat New Russia. Only some of them would then like us to beat Germany. Boris says he is a man of no country and only wants to be left alone. He doesn't care for the Germans much, thinks them unpleasant, but he hasn't really any feeling against anybody or anything. He simply wants to be left alone.

Mottisfont, Sunday February 8

Lord Hood wrote in answer to G.'s letter to Brendan about Martin that he was making inquiries. It appears that Martin had telegraphed to the Foreign

Office for cyphers two days before Hood wrote. That's all we know. On Saturday I took Clare, Buckell the gardener and Miss Bishop, the woman-gardener, to a lecture on beekeeping in Romsey – a fascinating subject but much too advanced as it turned out for us.

Mottisfont, Tuesday February 10

Today knitting party, then visits to both Searchlights. Singapore was invaded late Sunday night. Cable from Martin dated 9th saying he is a sergeant, well, and that life is stimulating and not unpleasant so far. G. and I depressed at prospect of Martin being in army again, having ignobly hoped he might be evacuated from Singapore as a civilian.

Mottisfont, Wednesday February 11

I telephoned Lord Hood to give him news of Martin's telegram. He said Brendan had just written to G. and that Martin was attached to Army Headquarters Singapore as a cypher clerk. He suggested Martin had been put into uniform to regularise his position.

London, Thursday February 12

Lunch with I. at Boulestin's. He thinks we are in for a bad six months. This tune is unusual with him. I saw he was rather appalled when on him asking about Martin, I said he was still in Singapore. Met I.C-G. afterwards at Leicester Galleries. Quick look at Epstein's new monsters, *Joseph and the Angel,* carved out of a beautiful block of pink alabaster. It goes without saying that it's powerful and impressive.

Mottisfont, Sunday February 15

Yesterday made a cheese. Thoughts of Martin. Today, first no news from Singapore. I knew what that meant. Then, at 9pm, the PM spoke and during the course of a long, most serious statement on our situation, announced the fall of Singapore. Day and evening passed heavily, thoughts busy. Our prospects look so black, one must face it. For the first time I thought there was an absence of confidence in Winston's voice. He has always had confidence to such a remarkable degree even on the most desperate occasions. This time there was a hollow sound and the absence of conviction in the phrases dealing with a successful outcome of our present trials and disasters.

London, Wednesday February 18

Lunch with Violet Cripps at Claridges. Ann O'Neill and the Duke of Marlborough joined us. Ann talked frivolous nonsense about us being unable to sink enemy ships and that they always sank ours – forgetting the many misses and occasions, fairly numerous I daresay, when our ships are hit but not sunk and manage to limp and hobble into harbour to undergo repairs. I hate that sort of ill-considered talk just because we are going through a bad patch. Manicure and face massage. As I lay there, thought of Martin. Idea struck me of telegraphing to Tony Apponyi in Switzerland to personally approach Japanese Minister and ask, as a favour, whether he could find out where and how Martin is.

Cambridge, Thursday February 19

G. telephoned early to say a telegram had been received from Whalley-Tooker saying Raymond was in hospital, critically ill, and would I hurry to Cambridge. I telephoned Addenbrooke's hospital and found he was conscious and out of danger. I hurried off to Cambridge by car arriving at 12.30 and went first to see Richmond, the Master, as I couldn't remember the name of the hospital. There I heard the beginning of the miserable story which was added to by other people during the day. R. was picked up unconscious in the gutter with a black eye. Mrs Prior, a middle-aged friend, happened to be passing and identified him and accompanied him to Addenbrooke's. Owing to the state he'd been in for some days, she suggested to the doctors that they use a stomach-pump. They did so and found opium remains.

Last Saturday night the University Lecturer on psychology, Dr MacCurdy,[33] had put R. in Evelyn's nursing home for the night as he'd taken half a bottle of Adalin. Whalley Tooker and Richmond decided after talking things over not to inform us, thinking it was a folly that mightn't occur again. It did, in a more squalid way, yesterday. The surgeon in charge, Mr Pennell,[34] knew about the two overdoses but thought there wasn't a serious intention to commit suicide as otherwise why only take half a bottle and why go out to dinner after taking it?

Peter Hey, R.'s very pansyish friend, said R. had complained of depression

33. John Thompson MacCurdy (1886-1947), Canadian psychiatrist. Lecturer Cambridge University.
34. Vernon Charles Pennell (1889-1976), surgeon Addenbrooke's Hospital, director of medical studies at Pembroke College, Cambridge.

and said he'd taken morphine on one occasion. On Saturday night R. had mentioned *en passant* that he'd had a notice to report to the Royal Army Service Corps [RASC] at Matlock today. Mrs Prior said R. came to her house last Wednesday talking oddly and wildly, complaining of depression. He said he sometimes thought of putting his head in a gas oven. Mrs P. said Hey was a homosexual, thought R. might be too, and that R. and Julian Huxley's son were rivals, both having an 'emotional attachment' for a Greek called Dimitris Capitanaikis [sic], an older man working in London.

I saw R. three times. He was a little hazy but not badly so, didn't seem to remember anything of the accident and was quite pleased to see me though he said he'd told them not to send for me. I didn't ask any questions.

Cambridge, Friday February 20

I saw Dr MacCurdy at 11.30. A big, bluff, outspoken Canadian, pleasant to talk to for me but hopeless for someone so divorced from reality as Raymond. He seems to have told R. half a dozen home truths which were unpalatable and, at such a moment, unsuitable as treatment. That's the difference between a man with academic knowledge and a man with practical knowledge. MacCurdy talked outspokenly and perhaps impatiently to R. as I might do in a moment of irritation. That's not what one hopes for in an experienced psychologist. I saw R. at 1.15. Collected some clothes from his lodgings after lunch. Found notice from RASC telling R. to report on the 19th which has to be dealt with immediately. I saw Whalley-Tooker at 3.30, showed him the notice and got him to telegraph the Commanding Officer at Matlock.

Mottisfont, Saturday February 21

Went to see Peter Hey at his lodgings at 10. Hey told me R. had never talked about the possibility of being called-up at any moment. Even after the notice arrived, R. talked about a couple of concerts he was going to give and various details in connection with them. It sounds lunatic. Caught 1 o'clock train home. Plunged straight from my strained world and anxious, agonised thoughts into a warm Mottisfont house party – Clare, Conrad, Duff, Diana, Sylvia, Crinks and Mark [Tennyson]. I poured whisky down my throat and shook off as best I could my extreme worries. G. mercifully well and enjoying the company. Diana looks beautiful, rested and much younger than before she left. Very pleased to see dearest Duff again.

Mottisfont, Sunday February 22

Strange. Found it almost impossible to talk about Martin or ask what life in Singapore had been like before the Coopers left. In fact I don't think I did. It seemed such dusty ancient history. Duff has some very amusing imitations of Sir Shenton Thomas[35] and Brooke-Popham,[36] both of them always having some excellent reason why something new shouldn't be done. Terrible, of course, though we laughed. Sylvia asked about R. – as usual 1,000 indiscreet questions; where were his bruises, why none on the body etc. etc. Crinks put away great glasses of port. Duff read, talked, played bridge and was nicer than ever. Yesterday, strangely enough, a long letter came from Martin giving his reasons for staying in Singapore. It was a formal letter and had a farewell sound about it. He thought Singapore would hold out for one to two months only. In fact it held out for one month from the date of his letter, Jan. 15. He expressed affection for Duff. G. has telegraphed to Tony Apponyi to try and get information of his whereabouts from the Japanese Ambassador in Switzerland.

Maud returns to Cambridge on February 24 to see Raymond, still in hospital, and determine what should be done next. After discussions with the doctors, it's agreed that Raymond should go to Mottisfont to rest but Raymond opposes this plan. He insists on staying in Cambridge to pack his books and store his harpsichord and piano. Exhausted and feeling she can do nothing more for Raymond, Maud acquiesces.

London, Friday February 27

To London [*from Cambridge*]. Exhaustion and depression continued. Lunch with B. He embarked on criticisms of the English as fighters and said their lives were so comfortable and easy that they didn't want to fight and didn't feel there was anything to fight for. This seemed a strange argument. They might surely think it worthwhile fighting to preserve their privileges and their comforts, if nothing more. Thinking as I am a lot about Martin, this kind

---

35. Sir Shenton Thomas (1879-1962), colonial governor of Straits Settlement 1934-42. Interned by the Japanese on the fall of Singapore. The Straits Settlement were a group of British territories, including Singapore, in south-east Asia which was dissolved in 1946. Historians tend to agree that Britain's defeat in south-east Asia was primarily due to failures in the armed forces and lack of air cover, not of the civil authorities.
36. Sir Robert Brooke-Popham (1878-1953), air force officer. Commander-in-Chief of the British Far East Command 1940-41. Replaced shortly before Singapore fell to the Japanese.

of talk was unpleasant. I feel deeply depressed about everything and like a person distraught. Meant to go to Mottisfont but felt too concussed and got into bed.

Mottisfont, Wednesday March 4

Driven out of bedroom last night by half-gassed bats who squeezed through any and every crack in their efforts to escape doom. Inspector for National Society of Prevention of Cruelty to Animals arrived out of the blue thinking to find Lánczy's bull-terrier here – which of course it wasn't – in order to collect it and send it to him or a friend. Indoors with cold, still very depressed, overwrought and impatient. Everything comes at the same time.

Mottisfont, Friday March 6

Wonderful news. Telegram from Tony Apponyi saying 'Reliable source informs Martin prisoner official confirmation will take weeks should I try to have him transferred to officers' camp?' G. and I overjoyed – as if being a prisoner were desirable and delightful. It was the relief of knowing him alive after having such dark and dreadful thoughts. I know we may not see him for many years, perhaps never again. But he is alive. For him that is everything, for us a hope. I feel up to taking on life again.

London, Tuesday March 10

Dined with I. at Boulestin's. Talked about my personal griefs and told him all about Raymond. Poor I. had a very troubled youth himself and understands this dreadful tangle better than anyone I know and better than I do. He understands it from R.'s point of view and from mine. He groaned as I told him. His heart is so good.

The case to annul Alexie's marriage to Lánczy finally came before the courts on March 11. Maud accompanied her niece to the hearing which took place over two days. Alexie and Lánczy gave evidence on the first day.

London, Thursday March 12

Alexie came to Claridges at 10 and we were at the Law Courts before 11. I gave my evidence about domicile and about the occasion in January 1940 when I asked A. whether she'd slept properly with L. and she told me:

no. I suppose I wasn't in the box more than three or four minutes. The feeling was strange. I felt lost, at sea, not very nervous, but as if I were in a strange element in which the reality I knew didn't count as reality, in which wood wasn't wood or people, people. I felt vague and doubtful and yet the only person alive, everyone else non-existent. Then Marshall Reynold, Lánczy's counsel, and Victor Russell [*Alexie's counsel*] made their speeches to the judge. The judge then made a short summing up and pronounced the annulment.[37] Relief, astonishment, delight. The whole thing seemed a dream. I saw Alexie peering at me from between the glass doors of the court. Her face was wreathed in smiles, she looked transformed and radiant, thanked everyone warmly and then threw her arms round me. The nightmare is over. Came here in the highest spirits by the 5.30 train. Arrived to find G. with very bad asthma which he seems to have had on and off the last days. Jerky breathing. Gave an injection, my spirits began to fail and nervous exhaustion set in.

Mottisfont, Saturday March 14

G. and I have been married 25 years today. It feels like 25 or 50 or 100 years – not because we haven't been happy together but because we have lived through such restless and violent times. We were married during the last war and except for three or four years immediately following, we felt oppressed and saw the cloud we were living under grow larger and larger. But the tremendous news is a telegram which arrived yesterday evening from Martin, sent off from Colombo. It said remarkably little except that he was in Colombo and well. It was a jaunty young man's telegram. He said something about Army biscuits and tea being delicious so I guess they were short of food on the journey, which must have lasted 24 days if they left Singapore the day it fell. Normally it wouldn't take more than six or seven. Enormous relief. G. could hardly speak and seemed to want to cry whenever he mentioned Martin's great luck and ours. I feel astonished at this change in the sum of luck.

---

37. This is the last reference to Lánczy in the diaries. He was arrested under Article 12(5)a of the Aliens Order, 1920, which allowed aliens to be detained on security grounds. He was still being held by the British authorities in 1945 with no immediate expectation of release. The family believes he was a spy but I have not been able to confirm the nature of the charges against him, nor could I find him listed in the public records of alien internees at the National Archives, suggesting he may have been in a more serious category.

Mottisfont, Tuesday March 17

Cheese-making Sunday and yesterday. Drove with G. both days. G.'s asthma is much better and this is such a load off my mind. I become a nervous virago when it's bad and there seems nothing to be done. G. is a patient saint and martyr, loving, freakish, most good to me and sweet to live with.

London, Wednesday March 18

Dined with I. at Prunier's. We talked till it closed. He said he'd heard a record of a woman being interrogated by the Gestapo. They make these records, he said. He didn't say how it had been got hold off. A woman at a nearby table had a seizure or fit during dinner and her cries and moans rang out. I saw Ian was paralysed by them, rooted to his seat and his head averted. I said, 'Hadn't I better go and help' two or three times, but he never answered and kept his head averted. I knew he was filled with horror and couldn't speak.

Mottisfont Sunday March 22

Violet B.-C. and Bongie staying. Today an icy wind blew and we hardly moved from the house. Talk: politics, politicians. I can see that Violet's interest is moving from Winston to [Stafford] Cripps. She has an excellent memory and chooses her words easily and happily. Her description or accounts are often very graphic, her feelings ardent, for she is a woman of very strong feeling: but I think her judgement is occasionally at fault. She is carried away, often a little ludicrously, by the intensity of her feeling and at those moments she is naïve.

Mottisfont, Tuesday March 24

I made a cheese. In the afternoon we went for a drive through Lockerley Woods. The spring is very late. No camellias yet, nothing but great quantities of snowdrops, just over, and a few aconites. Today a telegram arrived from Martin saying he was 'taken off' from Singapore on the 13th [*February*]. He arrived Colombo 11th [*March*] and was at sea all the time. Says journey was 'relaxing and sometimes grim' meaning perhaps a shipwreck or going in a small boat and perhaps deaths. Seems to be doing cypher work. Great relief to hear from Martin again. The first telegram was so unexpected I felt it was hardly authentic. This evening our second cow arrived with her calf.

London, Wednesday March 25

Lunch with B. at Istanbul. He talked a lot. Among other things he said I was 'a harmless thing after all,' which amused me a great deal. I always suspected him of thinking I was an over-sophisticated woman, tricky, fickle, dangerous, unprincipled and quite unreliable: and so it seems he did. I can't help laughing. What brought him round to seeing me as harmless?

Mottisfont, Thursday March 26

A clergyman, Mr Lambert, came to see me at Claridges at 12 [*with a view to replacing the Mottisfont Rector Mr Kirkham*]. A curate, a possibility. Caught 5.30 down here. Found G. saying 'Well the blow has fallen.' This meant a telegram from Whalley-Tooker saying Raymond had refused to go to Matlock and the army that day, as arranged, and would I come to Cambridge and take all responsibility. I couldn't feel surprised, dismayed or excited anymore. G. said, 'You can't go. It's no good and you've only just come back.'

Cambridge, Friday March 27

I rang up Ian, who had such a stormy childhood himself, and lunched with him at the Carlton Grill. I told him the latest Raymond developments, asked his advice and was prepared to follow it. It boiled down to this in the end: 'Go on, make more sacrifices. You won't forgive yourself unless you do, unless you do your utmost. If you can, be emotional. Cry if you can.' My heart was heavy and I felt sorry for myself.

I caught the 3.45 to Cambridge, went to the University Arms and waited, reading on my bed, for the hour when I was to go and see Whalley-Tooker. Just before the arranged time there was a knock on my door and Raymond's voice asking to come in. I had a moment's amazement because he didn't know I was coming. I was still further astonished when he explained that it was all a misunderstanding, that he'd told several people that he wouldn't join up but hadn't meant it, must have talked like that because he'd 'taken things' again. As he was talking so freely, I ought to have asked him quickly what he was taking and I am sure he would have told me. But I hate asking him direct questions, and he usually resents them, so I missed seizing this opportunity.

He said he was prepared to go the next morning, had done half his packing and had tried to stop me coming when he heard I'd been sent for. Said the Master had written him a very severe letter and that Lady

Richmond[38] had been frightfully kind and seen him several times. He seemed moved by her kindness and grateful for it so I gather he must have been pretty miserable. Whalley-Tooker came to see me afterwards. Said responsibility had become too much and the strain and worry great. He was immensely surprised by the *volte face* but said he never believed in the suicide act. I gathered R. has been half-insensible on and off the last week – or at any rate on one or two occasions. R. joined us and soon after Whalley said goodbye, saying quite naturally to R. that he must come back after the war, if he felt like it, and take his degree. In fact he behaved admirably and wisely as he has all along. R. sat on with me in my bedroom and I kissed him as affectionately as I could when we said goodnight.

Mottisfont, Sunday March 29

I wondered as I dressed yesterday whether I would really be able to get R. off – or rather, whether he would go. But he came round, quite ready, soon after 10 and sat talking till it was time to fetch Dr Noble's certificate and catch the 11.20 train to Kettering. Dr Noble gave R. some sort of excusing certificate to explain why he hadn't reported at Matlock on Thursday as told to. Not knowing I'd arrived, Lady Richmond most angelically went to the station to see R. off. I saw him into the small cross-country train. His face was human and natural as he looked out to say goodbye and off he went, remaining at the window, waving once or twice. What a business. I said I was amazed when he knocked on the door on Friday night but really I was only slightly so because for many years I have been prepared for anything and everything and have lost the sharp sense of surprise.

I left Cambridge at 3.30 and went to I.'s flat to tell him how things had turned out. I think he felt he'd contributed nothing to the outcome and as things turned out he hadn't. But he'd fortified and strengthened me and, if it'd been necessary, I should have acted on his advice. Arrived here exhausted. G. thought I'd achieved a miracle but I told him to praise Elsa Richmond. I know I had less than nothing to do with the *dénouement*.

Mottisfont, Wednesday April 1

On Monday the prospective clergyman Mr Lambert, his wife and four-

---

38. Florence Elsa Richmond, *née* Bell (c.1880-1971), married in 1907 Admiral Sir Herbert William Richmond, Master of Downing College.

month-old baby came to lunch. They both made quite a good impression. She is dull but nice no doubt. He is alert and a gentleman – rare nowadays among young clergyman. Later I collected for the Red Cross. Yesterday made butter for the first time, whisking cream non-stop for 25 minutes till my arm all but refused to function. Two billeting officers came at 3. We have 20 privates in the stables at the moment and they'd like to get in 10 more. Kitchen at 7.15, trying to learn to cook in anticipation of the day when I shall have to. It amuses and interests me. Raymond has written to me – a long, descriptive letter and uncomplaining. It's the friendliest letter he has written me for years.

Mottisfont, Saturday April 4

Bishop of Southampton[39] came to dinner. I warned G. and Mama about grace but both forgot, Mama sitting down to dinner talking busily, as usual, and G. also talking. During the mumbled grace I heard him say that somebody, or something, was indecent. Comico.

London, Wednesday April 8

Yesterday Alice came to dinner [*at Claridges*] and was very melancholy because her strange, uncouth husband neglects her, doesn't write much and doesn't seem to want her to live near him. He is a marine, in Cornwall, and may go abroad soon. Poor Alice was dirge-like and a tear escaped her eye. Today lunched B. at Istanbul. B. teased me about being law-abiding and said he was a gangster. And so he is. Most certainly I am law-abiding. The law is too useful, nay, essential a thing, to flaunt. I pin my sail to it.

London, Thursday April 16

Fitted at Strassner. They can't promise any fittings for new clothes for three months. They have so few work-people and so much to do. The excellent Czech tailor works till late in the night trying to get through the work and looks at death's door. Lunched with B. at Istanbul. He'd been on night-duty at Reuters and was only just awake. Helped him to buy a shirt at Selfridges for a wedding. I was privately amused because really men's shirts don't show enough to bother about. But he made the purchase very seriously.

39. The Right Reverend Arthur Karney (1874-1963), Bishop of Southampton 1933-1943, formerly first Bishop of Johannesburg.

Mottisfont, Saturday April 18

At tea time without telephoning or ceremony Lord Strabolgi[40] (who said I should pronounce his name Strab<u>og</u>ey) blew in without apology. He sat down, drank a good many cups of tea with sugar and milk, ate everything put before him and helped himself freely without comment, cutting cakes etc. In short he made a lamentable peace or wartime impression. The reason he honoured us so was that he wanted some fishing. He offered to take a piece here or there, or a rod, and inquired bluntly about the shooting. He said he would like to have a gun in it though it isn't a syndicate. He did all the talking, treating us rather like impoverished applicants whom he was going to dismiss. Need I say that I took a strong dislike to him?

London, Wednesday April 22

Yesterday Hillier gardeners planted fuchsias, hydrangeas and yuccas along the retaining wall. The beds look much too small but that's how Norah [Lindsay] planned them. She ought to know. Today London 8.47. Staying Savoy. Dined with I. at Savoy Grill. He is optimistic as usual. He thinks the Navy the most remarkable organisation in the world and the level of efficiency and intelligence very high. This is pleasant to hear from someone who isn't a sailor by profession and at all times rather critical.

Mottisfont, Tuesday May 5

Marjorie and Alick Russell[41] arrived for a few days on Friday. Their son Stephen is a prisoner-of-war in Germany and Roddie, the elder boy, is in Burma in charge of some border tribesmen. With Burma invaded and falling to the Japanese, M. and A. are going through horrible agonies of suspense. Dawnays came on Saturday. Guy argumentative, pretentious, dissatisfied, rather Fascist, anti-Winston, anti-Labour, anti most things and tiresome generally. Cis nice and cosy. Lovely weather continued on Sunday and we sat out.

40. Joseph Kenworth, 10th Baron Strabolgi (1886-1953), Liberal and then Labour MP, opposition Chief Whip House of Lords 1938-42.
41. Hon. Alexander Villiers Russell (1874-1965), first cousin of Gilbert's, and his wife Marjorie, *née* Guinness. Both sons survived the Second World War.

Mottisfont, Wednesday May 6

Said goodbye to Marjorie and Alick. Marjorie said, 'You have saved our lives,' meaning the strain and worry of Burma had been almost too much for them at home and these days had been a rest. I understand all those things now. Martin doesn't cable or answer our cables. Either something has happened to him or else he is very unimaginative. His second and last cable was sent on March 24th.

Mottisfont, Wednesday May 13

A series of quiet days. G. rather asthmatic. I made cheeses twice and spent time in the kitchen peering fascinated into saucepans. There were army exercises in the district but little noise at night. On Monday I drove into Bournemouth for a permanent wave. I got back in time for Adele who was with me to milk the cow.

London, Thursday May 14

Lunched with B. at Istanbul. He fears he and the five or six other Russians at Reuters may be turned out to make room for Bolshevik Russians. There are complaints of the present team being White and unsuited to selecting the Russian news. I gather there are complaints too about the tone of their talk – which doesn't surprise me if B.'s political talk is a sample of it. It's tactless talk, not harmful.

Bournemouth, Wednesday May 20

Came here to Branksome Towers on Saturday with G., who is asthmatic again. It's very depressing. G. is dying of asthma, that's the dreadful truth. If he had cancer that's what one would say. But he has asthma and no one ever talks of dying of asthma. It's a most horrible illness and dreadful to see.

Gilbert, Raymond and Martin visiting Mottisfont for the first time in 1934.

Family photo taken outside the Whistler Room at Mottisfont in April 1939. *From left standing*: Raymond, 'little' Tony, Mary, Anthony Irby, Martin and Alexie. *From left sitting*: Maud, Tony Apponyi, Paul Irby, Maria Nelke, Gilbert and Kitty.

Above: Maud (left) with her mother and Kitty at the turn of the twentieth century.

Above: Maud's closest childhood friend, Iris Tree, at Wood Lea in the early 1900s.

Below: Paul Nelke with his grandchildren at the family's Berkshire estate, Wood Lea, c.1921. *From the left:* Mary, Paul, Alexie, Martin and Tony. Raymond hadn't yet been born.

Maud caught by the camera in the bath c.1917.

Gilbert looks the most relaxed of his Russell siblings in this 1890s photo. *From the left:* Conrad, Gilbert, Diana, Claud, Flora and Harold (from youngest to oldest).

Maud wore an Italian gown of silver and white floral brocade with a silver gauze train trimmed with lace and orange blossom for her wedding to Gilbert on 14 March 1917.

4

Gilbert and Martin c.1920.   Maud with Martin and Raymond as a baby in 1922.

Maud, Gilbert, Martin and Raymond on holiday in Oslo 1932.

Cecil Beaton was a close friend of Maud's and photographed her many times. This was one of her favourites and was taken at Kammer in Austria in 1937.

Clarissa Churchill, Margot Asquith, Martin and Gilbert at Mottisfont in about 1938.

Siegfried Ruben, Gilbert, Robert Vansittart (Van) and Maud at Heveningham Hall, Suffolk in 1929. Maud said it was thanks to Van, a childhood friend, that she was able to help her Jewish relations flee Germany in 1939.

Staying with the Russells at Blickling Hall in Norfolk in 1931. *From the left:* Siegfried Rubens, Noel Blakiston, Pauline Rubens, Clemmie Churchill, Jasper Ridley, Simon Lovat, Eddie Marsh and Maud.

Rex's Whistler's assistants, Victor Bowen and Percy Willetts, working on the Whistler Room in 1939.

Rex Whistler on the terrace at Mottisfont while decorating the Whistler Room in 1939.

The finished Whistler Room, photographed in the early 1950s. (©National Trust Images).

Maud and Gilbert in the 1930s.

Duff and Diana Cooper at Mottisfont in about 1939.

Opposite page:
Top: The grass grew high at Mottisfont during the war due to petrol rationing. Some family members say it was the pollen from the uncut grass that brought on Gilbert's final and fatal asthma attack.

Centre: Mottisfont was requisitioned in February 1944 as a small hospital for the military.

Bottom: Mottisfont village school during the war.

Above right: Maud's aunt Agnes Mühsam with her son Hans Werner in Berlin in the 1930s.

Below: Maud's cousin Lisel Muller and her son Peter in Germany c.1935.

Below right: Maud 'gave away' the Polish architect Utek Podleski to her cousin Urla Lubelska at their wedding in 1943. The couple spent their honeymoon at Mottisfont.

Shortly before they married in 1939, Randolph Churchill (right) bought his first wife Pamela Digby (middle) to Mottisfont to meet Maud. Edward Stanley is on the left.

The ballet dancer and choreographer Frederick Ashton at Mottisfont in 1941.

The actor Angus Menzies, Maud and Ian Fleming pour over photographs at Mottisfont.

This previously unpublished wartime photo of Ian in Naval uniform takes up almost an entire page of Maud's photo album.

Above: Raymond playing the harpsichord in the late 1940s.

Left: Martin joined the army in 1939 before being found unfit for active service due to asthma.

Below: Alexie looking radiant on her marriage to John Russell in November 1945.

Above: Boris being gregarious while William Jowitt reads the paper at Mottisfont. June 1942.

Above: left to right; Martin, Diana Abdy, Cressida Ridley, Lys Lubbock, Eddy Sackville-West, Peter Quennell and Cyril Connolly spending the weekend at Mottisfont soon after the war.

Below: *standing left to right*; Clive Bell, Maud, Martin, Raymond, Michael Stratton and Violet Bonham Carter: *sitting left to right*; Raymond Mortimer, Cressida Ridley and Eddy Sackville-West, right.

Above: Maud's mother Maria and sister Kitty sit under the great plane at Mottisfont, Easter 1949.

Above right: In old age Maud regarded Elizabeth Tennant (above) and her sister Anne Toynbee as her dearest female friends.

Below: Maud in the kitchen garden at Mottisfont with Cathleen Mann's mother, Dollie, on the left and Clare Tennyson on the right in July 1942.

FOUR

Gilbert

MAY 1942

Maud wrote the following entries in August 1942 when she was staying with the Glenconners in Scotland.

The last entry is where I stopped writing my diary in May. Nine days later Gilbert died. He died on May 28. He was dying when I wrote the last entry, he'd been dying for at least 18 months. His death had been my horror and dread since I married. When I was young I bought myself a revolver to shoot myself when he died and when I was middle-aged I had a *verde antico*[1] urn made large enough to hold his ashes and mine. I started my diary again in another book a fortnight or so after he died. I shall now write about Gilbert's last days. The main, the fullest, the richest and the most feeling part of life ended with him. I gave him all the tenderness I possessed. There was little over.

Wednesday, May 20

We returned by taxi to Mottisfont. G. was longing to get back. His breathing was very bad.

Friday, May 22

I decided to get a nurse in. G. dressed with my help in the late morning. Raymond Mortimer arrived at 5.15. This was the Whitsuntide weekend and he and Sibyl Colefax were due. I didn't know what to do about them. I didn't like to put them off. I didn't know that G. wouldn't be better in a day or two as

---

1. 'Antique green' stone

had happened before. Nurse George, red-haired, timid and not very attractive, arrived at 7. G. had great difficulty in coming upstairs to bed. He said, 'Don't leave me.' I rubbed G.'s chest with ointment at bedtime. He was pleased and said to the nurse that I was a magician and could do this better than anyone else.

Saturday May 23

Rose[2] [Soward, *housemaid*] called me before 8 saying G. wanted me and had 'nerves' again. I was tired and irritated. It was difficult to know with G. what was nerves and what was illness and he knew this himself. I went to his room and talked to him. Dr Wainwright came later. I made a cheese, went up and down to see G., who was often dozing because of his drugs, and talked to Raymond M. Sibyl arrived for dinner. During the day I felt a growing oppression and a necessity to keep going, be occupied, not to think. I think from this day on I was pessimistic. I don't quite know why because G. had been alarmingly ill twice before – in April or May last year and at the end of December 1940.

Sunday, May 24

Either this day or the next there was something new about Gilbert, a sort of capriciousness about taking his medicines – refusing one and saying he would try another – in a manner that was somehow childish. This frightened me. He seemed a little less the person I knew. His oxygen apparatus and cylinder stood in a corner of his room and he would <u>not</u> have it moved to beside his bed. He got up every few minutes when he was awake, generally unaided, to take some. This restlessness was distressing to see.

Monday, May 25

I took Sibyl and Raymond to lunch with the Mountbattens at Broadlands. Lord Louis whom I had never met before was there. He is handsome and attractive but rather cold and formidable. At lunch there was his nephew Prince Philip of Greece, a nice looking man, who speaks perfect English and is in the Navy. It struck me afterwards that he would do for Princess Elizabeth

---

2. Rose Soward began working for the Russells in the early 1920s, rising to the position of house keeper and retiring in 1958.

but Sibyl said Lord Euston[3] had been selected. I saw little of Gilbert this day. I was out in the afternoon collecting Rural Pennies for the Red Cross and when I went into his room he was mostly asleep.

Tuesday, May 26

Dr W. came and suggested getting a more sympathetic nurse, someone a little prettier and more attractive to talk to. He wasn't suggesting her as a second nurse but to take Nurse George's place. I decided to have her as a second nurse and telephoned to Dr Rossdale telling him there was no immediate hurry, we could wait a day or two, till a nice one turned up. That's how things looked on Tuesday morning. Gilbert's breathing was almost always bad these days – high, uncomfortable breathing, asthmatic of course, done with great effort. In the afternoon I made a cheese. I tried to keep myself occupied and not think.

Wednesday, May 27

Dr W. came in the morning. G.'s pulse, which had often in the past gone up to 120 when he had a spell of asthma, was doing so again. His face had a strained look and his eyes too. I was anxious, miserable and agonised. I had difficulty in preventing myself from crying whenever I wasn't talking or occupied. I felt it was all up. In the early afternoon I drove into Winchester to a meeting of the Hampshire County Nursing Association. I forced myself to stick to this date but I don't think I should have and I wish now I hadn't. G. said to me when I was going, 'But I thought you weren't on the committee anymore.' I said this was a special meeting and I ought to go.

The drive there and back and the meeting were a torment. When I got back I telephoned to Wainwright to come again and he did, about 7. I told him how anxious I was. He said that Gilbert was very ill but stood quite a chance of pulling through. I asked him not to let G. suffer unnecessarily if he saw G. couldn't live; to give him something and save him misery. He said of course. When I came up after dinner, G.'s breathing was dreadfully distressed and he looked very ill. I see him sitting in front of the oxygen cylinder, hunched, breathing laboriously and saying to me, 'I am not going to die am I?' I held

3. Hugh Denis Charles FitzRoy, later 11th Duke of Grafton (1919-2011). Devoted much of his life to the preservation of historic buildings. Prince Philip was not considered as a contender for Princess Elizabeth's hand until after the war – the engagement was announced on 9 July 1947.

his head against me and said, 'Of course not.'

Just before going to bed for the night, G. got up wanting to go to the lavatory. He complained of feeling very weak and I took his arm and led him in. It was now about midnight. I must have seen him settled in bed and said goodnight. I daresay I kissed him and asked him to send for me if he felt wretched but I don't remember anything about it or the last sight of him conscious. When I look back I wish I'd had a camp bed put up in his room and slept there. It's very painful to me to think he only had a nurse with him that last night.

Thursday May 28

The nurse came in soon after 7 and said G. had had a collapse and that she'd given him the injection to stimulate his heart. I went in in my dressing gown. He was propped up on his pillows and had on the oxygen mask. He looked better in colour than the day before. I sat down. I had some of the tea that had been brought for him and breakfast on a tray. Occasionally I got up and arranged the mask and it was not for some time that I realised he was unconscious – I think not till the nurse said something about it. From then on I was in his room almost all the time, sitting by the bed and occasionally readjusting the slipping mask. Sometimes I felt his pulse. Once, just once, he opened his eyes wide and I saw their blue for the last time but he was unconscious and they were unseeing. I was quite calm; I too was doped. These were the most dreadful moments of my life. There is nothing more dire than the cutting of the strands that bind husband and wife. The relationship of husband and wife is the most complete and the most entire. The survivor half dies too. I don't believe remarriage would alter this.

About 11.15 I felt his pulse again. There was no perceptible beat. I called to the nurse to give another injection and she gave it. I stood by and watched, looking into Gilbert's face. As I watched I saw death come into it, into him, without a movement without a struggle. His face changed colour that is all; that was everything. After some minutes and there was no chance of a mistake I left the room.

From time to time I came back but mostly I was very occupied sitting in bed, sending off messages and telephoning. This I did for six or seven hours, doing everything that had to be done, making all the arrangements. The night before I'd wired to his brothers and sisters saying G. was having a bad asthma attack and that I would telegraph daily. I telegraphed to them at once and to Raymond, Martin and Alexie; and to some of our closest friends. In my telegrams to Claud and Conrad I asked them to stay with me till the funeral. Claud arrived at Salisbury at 8, Conrad at Winchester at 9. I remained in bed. I felt supported by the presence in the house of my two Russell brothers-in-law and they were, all the time, exactly what I most wished them to be – calm, quiet, natural and practical.

Friday, May 29

At 12.30 the undertakers from Garstin arrived with the hearse. I saw the man and arranged Gilbert should not be disturbed till the hearse was ready to start the next morning. At 2.30 Claud drove into Romsey with me to the Registrar's to register death. I had to take with me Gilbert's Ration Book and Clothing Card and hand them over as he was no longer alive and didn't count anymore for food and clothes. This seemed to me a ghastly task. Late at night I said goodbye to my dear love, my darling husband. I was glad I had no fear at all of him dead. I had dreaded I might. But I felt quiet and calm and in some strange way intimate and tender with him. He looked very ill but he had a sweet, tender, half-smiling look on his face which I remember well and connect closely with the early days of our marriage.

Saturday, May 30

I dressed early. I asked Adele if she would see G. put in his coffin. I could not do so. She said – I use her words – she would love to. I stood at the door of my bedroom as the coffin came out of Gilbert's bedroom and was carried downstairs. Claud and Conrad stood in the gallery as it passed. The hearse started at 8; Claud, Conrad and I in a car of Garstin's 10 minutes later. Hanson [*the chauffeur*] in tears stood at the lodge gate. We drove to London. Claud and Conrad dropped me at Claridges and I went straight to bed. They went on to Golders Green where the cremation started at 10.30. Mama too was there. Raymond arrived from Bakewell on a week's compassionate leave looking terrible, poor boy, in his unbecoming khaki, his hair shaved so that the scalp showed through, his face yellow and wearing spectacles. I was <u>very</u> pleased to see him and his presence was a source of comfort to me. We discussed music for the service and rang up Dr Smith, the organist at Chenies, and settled on the music. Gilbert wanted a small, quiet, private funeral but a Christian one. The service was at 3 at Chenies and lasted, R. thought, not more than 15 or 20 minutes. The big green urn I'd had made many years before at Spink from a Roman model, and which is big enough to hold both Gilbert's and my ashes, was placed in the side-chapel among the other Russell urns. During this time, I rested in the dark. R. was back by 4.30. Claud came and told me about the funeral at 6. Mama, Alexie and R. dined; they in the sitting room, I in bed. Mama and Alexie looked like mourners when we first met. I don't want that. The people I like best to be with are calm, natural, unsentimental people, especially the people who talk quite naturally about G. as if he were still there and don't avoid his name. That is one of the painful things that happen. Some people out of a mistaken sense of delicacy avoid mentioning G.'s name and every time that happens, the sad fact of his death is brought home cruelly to me. I want to go on talking about him as if he were still in my life and in everyone else's. Some friends go on talking just as before and that is lovely and healing.

Monday, June 1

Gilbert would have been 67. Dined with I. at Frascati. His solid friendship helped me these days. He understood how I felt about G. I think he was very distressed about Gilbert himself.

These first days I was haunted and tormented by several things: that there had been no farewell between me and Gilbert – that he'd disappeared without a word or a message; that there were things I wanted to ask him and could never ask him now; that he may have known he was dying but kept the knowledge to himself, that he purposely didn't send for me to spare me; that I should have spent more time during the last days with him; and that I hadn't been as sweet and kind to him these last years as I should have been. I was stupefied and tormented when I began to think these things. I was appalled when I realised I could no longer ask him questions. I tried to be reasonable but was appalled.

Saturday, June 6

Took the 9 o'clock train to Mottisfont. This was a moment – the arrival and first hours at Mottisfont – that I'd been dreading so much. Poor Hanson was stationed again at the lodge-gates as I drove in. It was his way of showing his sympathy. I understood it very well and appreciated it. All this week in London I found myself talking a great deal and laughing whenever there was anything even only faintly funny to laugh at. I couldn't bear silence because silence became thought. This talk was automatic and a defence. I still do it, but less now. I was stunned, half dazed. I felt I didn't belong to the living or the dead. I lived in a sort of No Man's Land. My friends and relations were most good and kind and their love helped me enormously.

FIVE

Standing Alone

JUNE 1942 – MAY 1943

In which the Axis advance stalls in North Africa, Russia and the Pacific;
Maud's Jewish relatives in Germany go missing;
She faces loneliness and lack of purpose;
Italian POWs work in the woods near Mottisfont.

The Axis powers have continental Europe largely under their control, now including Greece, and are edging ahead in the military campaigns for command of North Africa, Russia and the Pacific. However, the Allies have held ground in the Battle for the Atlantic and prevented an attempted blockade of food and materials to the United Kingdom. Most importantly, the United States (US) and its much-needed military strength has entered the war against the Axis powers, following Japan's surprise attack against the US naval base at Pearl Harbour in December 1941.

After Gilbert's death, Maud seeks to keep busy. She resumed writing her diary on June 16. She feels lonely and useless at Mottisfont with her husband no longer alive to look after and her sons in the army. She spends most of the week at Claridges, returning to Mottisfont at weekends, and begins to learn to type and practice her German in preparation for a possible job at the Admiralty arranged by Ian Fleming. She picks up the reins of handling the family's financial affairs and running the Mottisfont estate, and continues to collect Rural Pennies for the Red Cross relief work fund and visit the local night bombing defence units, known as the Searchlights.

London, Thursday June 18

Yesterday I visited Ian ill in bed at his flat. He is very good to me and has been my standby since G. died. He died. This is the first time I have written these words for myself. The pain is very great. Today I lunched with Alice. Gerald Berners[1] and Chips Channon[2] there. His talk was rather pro the men who attack the PM. I know he, Channon, is the sort of man who would 'collaborate' without a pang. He is the lounge-lizard type. B. came to Claridges at 4.30. His friendship is a help too. I am fortunate to have such kind and warming friends. They make life possible.

Mottisfont, Monday June 22

Mr Knight, valuer for probate, came to value G.'s personal belongings, his poor clothes, his cigarette case. It's difficult to face these horrors, the dotting of I's and crossing of T's of death. I get through the days. There is nothing much I want. The war is going badly.

London, Wednesday June 24

Today Margot [Asquith] came to lunch wearing a black astrakhan hat, a faintly figured grey silk blouse of a pretty tone, a blue chiffon scarf tied round her neck, a short black coat and a long black skirt. She was tired and difficult to hear at first but after eating and drinking she became much more like her usual self. She told me about Peter Flower,[3] her seven-year love and said she'd lived with him – been intimate with him – not exactly in the conventional man and woman way. But in other ways. I could not bring myself to ask in which ways. She said she'd written out this story. It was rather indecent, she said. Duff had read it. She talked about Mrs Harrison[4] and Lord Oxford [H.H. Asquith]. She behaved admirably, understandingly and generously over

1. Gerald Tyrwhitt-Wilson, 14th Baron Berners (1883-1950), composer, novelist, painter, eccentric. His most enduring ballet *A Wedding Bouquet* (1937) was choreographed by Frederick Ashton and the cast included Robert Helpmann and Margot Fonteyn.
2. Sir Henry 'Chips' Channon (1897-1958), American-born British Conservative politician, author and diarist.
3. Margot Asquith was only 19 when she fell passionately in love with Peter Flower (the younger brother of Lord Battersea), an unreliable, penniless, heart-breaker who was 20 years her senior. The affair lasted until 1891. She became H.H. Asquith's second wife in 1894.
4. Mrs Hilda Harrison, widow of Major Roland Harrison, killed in action in 1917. H.H.A. *Letters from Lord Oxford to a Friend*, ed. by Desmond MacCarthy, 1933/1934.

that old-man and young-woman friendship. I know that from many sources. Today, when she talked to me about it I saw her face alter and understood that she'd suffered over it. Talking about Lord Oxford's letters to Mrs Harrison, she said that at the time she couldn't make up her mind whether she wanted them to be beautiful and admirable – for his sake – or dull and prosaic as a sign the friendship wasn't a deep or important one – for her own sake. She added with a laugh: 'They were rather dull, darling, weren't they?' I agreed, quite honestly, they were. At 3, Mr Marx[5] came and Mr Yates, the solicitor, and we sat talking about trustees and investments. Marx would like me to sell Mottisfont. I can't, even if it's an extravagance to keep. I should feel too homeless and rootless and without responsibility. Perhaps later on.

Mottisfont, Friday June 26

The new clergyman Mr Lambert was inducted and instituted at 6.30, the Bishop of Southampton officiating. I presented him as I had Mr Kirkham, stepping into the aisle and saying my short presentation sentence. The church wasn't more than half full. Afterwards had coffee with the clergyman and some of the neighbouring clergy and the bishop, then hurried back to the house. The Aberconways, Jowitts and Eddy Sackville-West had arrived. I changed, the bishop drove up and we had a curiously successful dinner, the bishop and William [Jowitt] arguing about education, the church and the state, and the bishop scoring rather neatly.

Mottisfont, Monday June 29

Boris arrived in time for lunch on Saturday, large, spruce and composed (*see photo in black and white plate section*). Mr Lambert and his wife came to lunch bringing their baby in its perambulator which was wheeled, baby and all, into Gilbert's study. Yesterday William and I went to morning service and heard Lambert read those extraordinary 39 Articles. They aren't easy to read but he read them very well, correctly punctuated and almost intelligibly. They all left this morning except for Boris. The weather was flawlessly beautiful and we walked down to the river and sat under the trees until he left. Saw some strange geese on the river. I think they were Egyptian but I couldn't get very near. I put B. into a train crowded with troops at Andover and off he went, waving in his shirt sleeves. Then to the

5. Hermann Marx (1881-1947), one of Gilbert's partners at Cull & Co, and previously a partner of Maud's father Paul Nelke. A relation of Karl Marx and brilliant stockbroker.

Searchlights and Mr White, beekeeping neighbour, came and helped with the bees. Everything to do with them is fascinating and well worth a sting or two.

Mottisfont, Tuesday June 30

Made a cheese. Long cable arrived from Martin. He's only just heard of G.'s death. My cable had been held up and taken a month to reach him. He is recovering from pneumonia, got how I wonder in that warm climate? Poor M. recovering from pneumonia and hearing of G.'s death.

Martin is now working in the Intelligence Corps' headquarters in Sri Lanka as a cypher clerk.

London, Friday July 3

Lunch with B. at the Shanghai yesterday with heaped plates of shoots, roots, buds and leaves. Sometimes he says things that make me laugh a lot to myself, like this last weekend when he heard me describing someone as 'slippery' and turned to Lesley [Jowitt], next to him on the sofa, and said, 'Would you say I was slippery, Lesley?' He is a huge, broad, fat man and weighs over 17 stone.

London, Monday July 6

Alice came to Claridges at 6 and together we went to I.C.-G.'s eve-of-wedding cocktail party. Diana [Cavendish] looked happy and so did Ian though he has been so hesitant about his marriage since Diana first mooted it. Honey Harris who is – or was – one of his flames was there looking rather like a bedraggled bird. I gave Ian a cheque and Diana a George III set of mother-of-pearl dessert knives and forks. Back to Claridges, met Alexie and went to the ballet *Giselle*. Margot Fonteyn danced well, especially the mad scene. Helpmann good too. Saw them afterwards and helped Bobbie H. to search for the top of his hair oil bottle on the ground among 20 small pairs of dancing shoes.

London, Thursday July 9

Went and looked at flats, or rather I tried to because there is hardly anything empty in Mayfair. Only succeeded in finding a room and bathroom in Athenaeum Court. I was overcome with melancholy when I looked at it; small, bare, modern and lonely. Remembered Cavendish Square; dignified, warm and dingy, ample and civilised, and the rich full years of life I spent in it. I feel lonelier and more depressed every day. Now comes the longer struggle to take up the burden of life again.

Mottisfont, Friday July 17

Paid a visit to Vita[6] at the Ridgeway. This visit to the Ridgeway was very painful. G. and I spent many days during the first four or five years of our marriage at the Ridgeway and I connect it with calm, the closest companionship and happy love. G. and I used to go there when it was still a house owned by the six brothers and sisters and we were often quite alone. It was difficult to see it again without G. All the relations – mine as well as Russells – had come to lean much on him.

Mottisfont, Saturday July 18

Saw Mr Jennings, the only officer now billeted in the house, and talked about ways and means of keeping the 60-odd soldiers living in the village from boredom. He said they hardly know anything about the war. They haven't got a wireless and they hardly ever see a newspaper because of their scarcity. Only subscribers get them in country villages. Mr J. said, 'They never hear about the war and yet they are expected to fight.'

London, Friday July 24

To Oxford 9.45. Lotte met me and I found old Tante Fritze waiting in a taxi outside looking spry but when the taxi moved off she slipped down in her seat and wasn't strong enough to right herself. She lay almost flat on the seat and I felt horrified. She didn't ask to be lifted up and Lotte paid very little attention to the small, mummified body for several minutes. We went straight to Lisel Müller's house, 5 Raleigh Park Road. She looked well. Peter, the little boy, is tremendously active and healthy and very intelligent. He drew a good picture in the manner of Utrillo. We talked, had lunch. Tante F.'s sister-in-law, whom they call Tante Johanna, has been transported at the age of 72 to Poland from Bonn by the Germans. Her son and daughter-in-law are thought to have committed suicide. That is Germany.

---

6. Lady Victoria Leveson-Gower (1867-1953), married in 1896 Harold Russell, Gilbert's oldest brother, who died in 1926. The Ridgeway, in Surrey, was bought by Lord Arthur Russell, Gilbert's father, and initially shared by the children on his death.

London, Monday July 27

Dined with I. at Prunier's and walked across St James's Park afterwards. I gathered he sometimes goes on dangerous jobs though he gave no details. I asked him to make some arrangement to let me know if he didn't come back and he said he'd already done so. It's all dreadful and I have a feeling of nervousness and dread. Perhaps I am so pessimistic and apprehensive because my nerves are out of order. I hope I didn't make Ian nervous and apprehensive.

Maud and Gilbert usually invited family and friends to Mottisfont in August. This year, Maud travelled around the country staying with various friends and relations, starting with her brother-in-law Claud Russell and his wife Ath at Trematon Castle, Cornwall.

Trematon Castle, Tuesday August 4

The days pass deliciously and I rest and eat and don't think much. I lie in bed late and have now almost finished answering the 200 or so letters I had of sympathy. Many of these were a sad pleasure for me to get, nearly all of them detestable to answer. I have read through and just finished the letters of Gilbert's father, Lord Arthur, to his wife, and the few there are of her to him. They loved each other too. I think G. had much more spirit and initiative than his father, though he was less clever and cultivated. They both had sweet natures and tempers but G. had much more wit and humour. Lord A. seems to have been slow at making up his mind and rather inclined to hesitate. G. never did. He was off at once and sometimes had to be steadied. He was tender, loving, soft-hearted and affectionate, and so was his father. Read letters from Diana Cooper when unmarried to Gilbert. They are vigorous, original and admirably expressed. (Note. I destroyed them at G.'s request).[7]

Claud has a charming story told him by the late Prince Arthur of Connaught who was sent to represent King Edward VII at the funeral of the murdered King of Portugal. One of the Emperor William's sons was there too. He had a revolver in his pocket fearing further outrages and assassinations. When he saw Prince Arthur he said, 'I have in my pocket my Browning.' 'Oh, have you, what a good idea,' said Prince Arthur thinking the German Prince was afraid the service might be tedious and had put a volume of poetry in his pocket. A comment on the outlook of Continental and English Royalty.

The war in Russia goes from bad to worse [*following the Axis powers*

---

7. Written in a different pen and added at a later, undetermined, date.

successful summer offensive on Stalingrad]. The Russians retreat and retreat; it's the same story all the time. I wonder whether we know what we are in for.

Bodnant House, Tal-y-Cafn, Sunday August 9
[home of Henry and Christabel McLaren]

Only other guest Sam Courtauld. Also here [*McLarens' children*] Charles[8] and his wife Deidre; Elizabeth[9] and her three children; Anne,[10] the 15-year-old daughter; and Christopher,[11] my godson, aged 8. Sam C. is Christopher's other godparent and I think must be his father too. Their profiles are so much alike. Sam and Christabel are more constantly together than any attached couple I know and, here too, are always sitting, walking and talking together. Christabel talks to him and draws him out more than he does her. She is the more active partner.

Yesterday afternoon, in a storm and downpour of a supernatural kind, Christabel, Sam, Anne and I piled into a small taxi and drove to the centre of the slate-quarry district. Curving round and up across gated fields on a road that till lately was only a track, we reached the caves that house almost the entire National Gallery collection. The narrow newly-metalled road stops abruptly at a large door set flat in the face of the rock. Seen in mist and rain, it looked odd and mysterious but not half as odd as it really is. For who would have guessed that one of the biggest picture collections in the world is housed in that mountain with 300 feet of slate over it and galleries and caves deep below? The great door was opened and we drove into a high and dripping tunnel, the water pouring down in places. We walked up the tunnel and reached a brick wall with a door in it; through this we went and found dotted about in the big caves long, brick, slate-roofed buildings, ventilated and heated to a special temperature between 65 and 70 degrees all year round. In these huts the pictures were hung or stacked against the wall. A long wooden screen ran down the centre of the huts and on both sides pictures were hung as well. Any picture you want to see can be shown to you at once. They are all easily accessible if not actually on show. It was an odd emotion seeing them

---

8. Charles McLaren, 3rd Baron Aberconway (1913-2003). Industrialist and horticulturist. In 1941 married Deirdre Knewstub.
9. Hon. Elizabeth McLaren (1890-1974), eldest child of Henry and Christabel McLaren.
10. Dr Hon. Anne McLaren (1927-2007), geneticist, second daughter of Henry and Christabel McLaren.
11. Hon. Christopher McLaren (1934-), third son of Henry and Christabel McLaren. Maud's godson. Married in 1973, Jane Elizabeth Barrie.

so intimately. There was no stepping back to see them from a distance. There they were in all their grandeur, very close, sometimes on their sides, occasionally upside down. The Titians, Veroneses, Rubens, Rembrandts, Tintorettos etc. lost none of their majesty. I saw the two Rubens of the old woman – one being a new acquisition from Lord Crawford for £20,000 and Kenneth Clark criticised for paying so much for a picture not so very different from one they already possess. Then I saw three Chardins, the El Greco and Botticelli I had seen in London, and hundreds and hundreds of pictures. I should have liked to have had a bed and slept in the caves and picnicked there and gone on looking at the pictures under these informal conditions.

Bodnant, Tuesday August 11

I get up late after writing letters. Yesterday I walked about the garden again with Harry who looks lonely. Christabel spends all her time with or fussing around Sam. This afternoon I read a number of Russell letters written in the 1890s. G. seems to have kept almost all the letters written to him by the brothers and sisters and parents. I want to read them all. I feel very lonely here. I daren't think. If I do, I cry and what does that help and what good does that do? I would like to think of G. all day long and remember our joint lives and his sweet gay nature, his jokes and witticisms and our devotion. But if I do I am invaded by black despair and I know life for what it is.

Glen House, Innerleithen, Wednesday August 19
[Home of Christopher and Elizabeth Glenconner in Scotland]

Yesterday and today I got up late, wrote letters, went for short walks, recovering health and sleep. The atmosphere of this house is charming and Elizabeth so nice at home and so graceful and pretty. There is quite a big library. The dining room, hall and billiard room – now the sitting room – have been done up since Christopher and Elizabeth married and are white and modern. The Reynolds, Gainsboroughs etc. look well on the white walls. Eliz. is a big and varied reader.

Glen House, Innerleithen, Wednesday August 26

The days pass without incident. I get up late every day, read in a desultory way, picking out books in the excellent library. I wrote and finished the account of Gilbert's death in the diary I was writing at the time of his death [*she started writing her diary in a new notebook after he died*]. I wrote and felt very sad. There were things that were puzzling and tormenting me and I felt I wouldn't get better and calmer till I had written about them. There are only three servants in this biggish house. I brought Adele from London and she does my rooms and bathroom. One day I washed my own hair – the first time I'd ever done so – and Elizabeth set it. My stay here has done me immense good and I have slept without a sleeping draught for a fortnight. The country is beautiful and calm and remote from war. I should be happy to stay on here indefinitely, doing nothing and without responsibility.

London, Friday August 28

Dined with I. at Prunier's yesterday. After dinner we walked across Green Park, mysterious and full of rustling shadows. I talked about getting a job and he said would I like the Admiralty – NID [*Naval Intelligence Division*] section. I said yes. He said he would get me fixed up four days a week, unpaid, to start early Oct. He was in the Dieppe raid on a destroyer and said it was thrilling and pretty dangerous. The attack failed at most points except Lord Lovat's section. But I think I. thought it'd been useful. I felt certain he'd been on that raid as soon as I heard of it because of something I felt in his manner the last time I saw him in early August. At dinner he asked me to get him an identity disc or a bracelet. At the beginning of the war he asked me to get him one but later said he didn't want one. This time he gave me his number and specified he would like it in gun-metal, if possible, with a heavy flat bracelet. Today I went round trying to get a gun-metal bracelet and disc but they've never existed and can't be made now. I got a plain silver one and put my initial on as he wanted.

London, Wednesday September 2

Hermann Marx sent me a typist from Cull & Co – Miss Marks – to teach me how to use a typewriter. I was extraordinarily stupid and the reverse of machine-minded but I enjoyed trying it as I enjoy everything I try and learn.

Mottisfont, Friday September 4

To Mottisfont yesterday. Blueie Baker[12] was waiting at Winchester Station

---

12. The Rt. Hon. Harold Baker (1877-1960), known as Bluetooth or Blueie, Liberal MP. Contemporary of Gilbert's at Balliol. Financial secretary to War Office 1912-15. Maud enjoyed his 'dry, erudite, malicious talk.'

and we drove here. Norah [Lindsay] had already arrived. Busied myself after five weeks' absence. I connect Mottisfont closely with G. It seems strange and lonely without him but I love it for him and for its own sake. Margot [Asquith] arrived after dinner. The visit was her own idea and the party built round her. She suggested a fortnight's visit and said she'd nowhere to go. I pitied her loneliness and hoped when I was 79 someone would take pity on me. Claud, Ath, Raymond Mortimer and Eddy Sackville-West arrived. A few months before he died, G. bought a book of photographs privately printed of the invitees to the Devonshire House fancy dress ball in 1897. It's extremely amusing and everybody laughs immediately partly at the stiff photographs, partly at the odd choice of fancy dress. Raymond and Eddy got Margot to look at it and she was convulsed.

Mottisfont, Tuesday September 8

During the day on Saturday we listened to Shostakovich's 5th Symphony. I think it was at lunch this day or Sunday that Margot had a telegram telling her of the death of her brother Frank.[13] She got up and I took her out of the room – not knowing what had happened. Outside in the passage she told me and cried and said how cruel her sister-in-law Annie had been not only in not letting her go to see Frank, who was dying of cancer, but in writing brutally to her and saying Frank hated her. She repeated several times: 'Women are more brutal than men' and her voice quavered and wobbled. I took her to her room and she stayed there till tea sending off numerous telegrams.

On Sunday there was more music in the big room, Eddy, Raymond and me sitting there. I wish I could remember one-eighth of the good things said by Norah and Margot, each brilliant and extraordinary in her own way. Margot's memory fails her at moments, or she telescopes the years and brings separated happenings together, but this happens most when she's tired. After she'd been here a day or two her talk became much more coherent. It's said that she drinks a lot but here she most certainly does not. She has a thimbleful of gin before lunch, sometimes a minute quantity of neat whisky at lunch, and the same repeated in the evening, sometimes followed by a small liqueur. She tells me she often takes sleeping draughts and her dope is the same as mine, namely allonal. This is quite a strong drug and often makes me sleepy in the daytime. If it doesn't wear off it might easily make her, at

---

13. Francis 'Frank' Tennant (1861-1942). According to Margot's autobiography, Frank was 'artistic, sweet and humble' but his development was 'retarded' by the violent treatment of a tutor. Perhaps this description is what he held against her?

her age, muddle-headed. She gets up just in time for lunch and is nearly always dressed as for London and very smartly. She wears smart little hats and sometimes her Cossack suit – astrakhan coat and hat. She nearly always wears high pull-on boots lined with wool such as I wear in the winter. She wears a hat for dinner too and cuts a fantastic spider or wasp-like figure. She looks very extraordinary with her big bent nose and fine dark eyes, her low forehead, neat grey hair, minute erect figure and her fanciful clothes. One night she wore a sort of tricorne with a little veil fluttering from it, a pale satin bodice embroidered with pearls cut like an eighteenth century woman's riding coat, and a long dark skirt.

London, Thursday September 10

I have come to London for a rest – to be away from the house and Margot for 24 hours.

Mottisfont, Friday September 11

To Mottisfont with Riette Cochrane-Baillie at 3.25. Cardie, John Follett and Charles McLaren came after tea. Margot and Norah had been alone. When I came into the room Margot, looking slightly guilty, waved a telegram and said, 'I thought you wouldn't mind, darling, I have asked Dr Lothar[14] and he is coming tomorrow.' I read the telegram in which he said how kind it was of me to ask him and how pleased he would be to come. I gasped that the house was going to be full – true because Margot and Norah each have a maid and Cardie brought a servant. She said he could sleep anywhere. It flashed through my mind that Dr Lothar, of whom I had never heard till that moment, might not fit in happily with Cardie and shooting neighbours. Indeed, not knowing anything about him myself, I felt reluctant to have an enemy alien, in any case a complete stranger, to stay. I then remembered that Mottisfont is a Defence Area and that permits to enter are refused to enemy aliens. Even Alexie and Tony have been refused permission to come. I told Margot this and she began to look appalled because she realised how difficult it would be to explain all this to Dr Lothar without hurting his feelings. Later we drafted a telegram and Margot begged me to write a letter explaining more fully and suggesting meeting in London later on. It appears that Dr

14. Dr Hans Lothar (1900-1944), formerly leading editor of *Frankfurter Zeitung*. Left Germany 1936. Editor-in-chief of anti-Nazi German-language weekly newspaper *Die Zeitung*, published in London 1941-1945.

Lothar is a distinguished refugee and that he was editor of the *Frankfurter Zeitung*. The imbroglio is typical of Margot. She's done this sort of thing all her life and made a 100 difficulties for herself and friends. It would be laughable if it weren't so awkward.

Mottisfont, Sunday September 13

Yesterday shot. Guns: Self, Cardie, John Follett, Charles McLaren, Sir Austin Harris and Colonel Bishop. I thought of Gilbert and of him always being the central figure even when he no longer shot. A description of the St Leger was broadcast during the running of the race and, as Cardie was interested, we listened to it during lunch. The broadcaster must have been a bookie, at any rate his voice was wonderfully common, his words swallowed and unfinished. Margot was convulsed. Margot had a small, smart hat tipped over the nose and under it she sat laughing, her eyes sparkling and twinkling. Finally she rapped out, 'Is he a Pole?' as some particularly unintelligible sounds emerged.

Mottisfont, Tuesday September 15

This morning Norah left. What a pleasure she was all the time. Margot had a story I liked about a young priest about to hear his first confession. He felt anxious and, to have guidance for future occasions, asked another priest, a friend of his and an old man, to stand close to the confessional to hear the admonition and advice he gave. Afterwards he said, 'How did I get through it? Did I manage alright?' 'Another time, my son,' said the old priest, 'when a young woman tells you every detail of her adultery, don't say: "Whewewewew," (and here Margot made a whistling sound like a rocket coming down from a great height), 'just say "Tut, Tut."'

The day Margot came to stay she put a little notice in the Court Circulars in *The Times* to say she'd left London to stay at Mottisfont Abbey with Mrs Gilbert Russell for 10 days. I rather wished she'd spared me but it was great fun for all my friends who had a long laugh. After she'd been here two or three days Reeve [*the butler*] came and said he thought I ought to know that Lady Oxford had been sending off a lot of telegrams, which were telephoned from the pantry, saying that the party was delightful and – dangerous praise in wartime – the food was DELICIOUS. After that I fully expected the police to look in. Again, poor darling, naïve as she is, she hadn't any idea she might be putting me in a difficult position – not that there are irregularities in my food supplies – but the police might have thought there must be after such eulogistic telegrams.

One way Maud supplemented food shortages during the war was by eating the plentiful rabbits on the estate, served at least twice a week according to a note in a later diary.

When Violet Bonham Carter heard Margot was coming for a fortnight she said, 'Why are you doing it, darling; out of Christianity?' The fact is that I love Margot – trying and exhausting though she is. And G. and I had many happy weekends at the Wharf [*the Asquith's home*] in the early 1920s.

London, Wednesday September 16

To London with Margot 10.31. She talked without drawing breath during the half an hour drive in the taxi to Winchester. Her young Scotch maid, who Margot thinks the world of, was sitting in front. Margot started on a long story about the excellence and egalitarian outlook of her doctor and said in a ringing voice, 'He would take as much trouble with that (great emphasis and pointing at her maid) as with the Queen.' Margot spoils her maid and the maid sounds unreliable and untrustworthy – from what Norah's maid told us. She wears Margot's jewellery and reads her letters. I don't know whether I oughtn't to tell Puff [*Anthony Asquith, Margot's son*].

London, Thursday September 17

Diana Cooper came for a drink before lunch bringing with her Conrad [Russell], whom I hadn't seen since the day we left Mottisfont together following Gilbert [*in the hearse*]. Diana has been living at Bognor all these months looking after her farm. She is fatter and looks much younger. She told me that she'd been discovered by Lord Woolton's[15] snoopers picking up rather fresh loaves at the bakers for her pigs and was going to be prosecuted. I dined with I. at Boulestin's. He's off to America almost at once. He says he doesn't want me to start NID work till he's back so it's put off for which I am sorry. I don't know whether there isn't a hitch somewhere.

Mottisfont, Sunday September 27

Duff, Crinks, John Follett, Cathleen Queensberry, Violet Cripps, Andrew and Dorie [Scott] here. This party is more of an ordeal than the others because

15. Frederick Marquis, 1st Earl of Woolton (1883-1964), businessman and politician, wartime Food Minister.

it was Gilbert's favourite kind. In this sort of company he was happiest and funniest. Today I was called away from lunch to see Inspector Dance from Romsey about a gown and hood stolen by Raymond from someone at Cambridge and which, when questioned, he owned to having taken and said were at Mottisfont. I told them I had unpacked his things myself and couldn't remember the robes and could they come back on Monday. They were very considerate and agreed. I don't feel very surprised because nothing surprises me in connection with Raymond. He has a penchant for gowns and hoods and he didn't know very clearly what he was doing those last weeks at Cambridge.

Duff went to Harvest Festival with me at 6 o'clock and read the lessons. The news had got around the village before and there was excitement about it. Diana arrived for dinner, fresh and beautiful, and straight from the farm.

Mottisfont, Friday October 2

Inspector Dance came on Monday. This time he described the colours of the gown – cream with a cherry lining. On Tuesday morning Adele and I searched the big cupboard in Martin's room where most of their things are stored. No result. I then tried R.'s room and found the hood and gown in a suitcase full of letters and papers in his cupboard. I had a long letter from R. telling me of the whole affair and saying he remembers little of it as he did it when he was doped with Adalin. He was under close arrest. He was being kindly treated and was going to see the Command Psychologist. I telephoned Inspector Dance and he sent a man to fetch the gown. In the afternoon, I made a cheese, typed, read German, listened to our broadcasts in German to the German submarines in the Atlantic – as I. had suggested. Today Mrs Miles, the village hairdresser, came and set my hair admirably after I washed it. Made a cheese, typed, listened to the radio.

London, Thursday October 8

Boris came and picked me up at Claridges at 5. He is immensely fat. He asked me whether he ever bored me. I said yes, when he criticised England, the Army and the soldiers over-severely – in which he seems to take pleasure and often talks nonsense when doing so. Faults there are – who doesn't know that by now? – but I am conventional or loyal enough not to care to hear a foreigner attacking my country with such gusto. Besides it seems to me in poor taste and always surprises me in Boris who is so sensitive in other ways.

London, Friday October 9

Shopping. Every sort and kind of thing is disappearing from the shops. If you want a certain kind of ribbon you have to hunt for it.

Bognor, Sunday October 11

Came here yesterday afternoon with Cecil Beaton. The dear little house, pretty as ever, surrounded by Diana's animals: pigs, goats, cow, ducks, chickens, geese, bees and rabbits. Duff read aloud a description of the German entry into Paris. Today the sun shone and we sat in the garden. Mr [Leo] Amery, Secretary of State for India, and his son Julian came to tea. I took a fancy – well, perhaps that is too strong a word – to Amery and so did Cecil. He is a cosy little man and as clever as a monkey. I forget how many languages he talks. After dinner we started talking about accents and then how English was pronounced in Elizabethan times. Duff recited *Shall I compare thee to a summer's day?* in Somerset dialect, Cockney and genteel-don accent. The first two didn't sound bad but the genteel don was appalling. He continued with Keats' odes in Cockney and they didn't distress.

Mottisfont, Wednesday October 14

On Monday I found a letter from Captain Wigg telling me Raymond was in hospital because of his nervous condition and could I write and tell him about R., his boyhood and health. He said there was nothing to worry about. I wonder though. I wrote yesterday and gave a kind of picture of R. and ended by saying I thought R. had taken well to army life. I cannot worry. I worried myself to death at one time and now I cannot worry anymore.

Mottisfont, Sunday October 18

On Thursday morning Goulding's manager, Mr Riggs, came and we looked at a place for the tablet Gilbert had engraved in 1939 commemorating his descent from the founder of the Abbey, William de Bruyére. This stone was never put up. It stood on the terrace outside Rex's room. Once or twice I said something about putting it up but G. never pursued the question and I didn't press it. I don't think he wanted it up in his lifetime from some superstitious feeling that his death would follow close on its erection. Have had another letter from Captain Wigg telling me there is nothing wrong with Raymond and that as Dr Hedley, who owns the gown, doesn't want to press charges, it has been dropped by the police as R.'s army character is good. Relief.

Mottisfont, Tuesday October 20

Yesterday afternoon a Goulding's mason came and started chipping away the stucco in the East Wall close to the chapel porch to prepare the place for the tablet. Today stood in pouring rain watching the stonemason hammer into the wall. After two and a half inches of stucco, flints interspersed with Isle of Wight stone came into view, the beginnings of the stone arch – apparently much like the arch of the chapel porch – and between the stone and the flint, a lot of bricks of a much later date. I had meant to photograph the uncovered wall but the rain was too violent. So I made a very rough sketch and took the measurements.

There are Italian prisoners working in the woods near here, at Pittleworth, and every day they pass in a lorry on their way to and from work. They make a good deal of noise shouting and singing and to my ear – for I haven't seen them – the noise isn't so much singing as truculent shouting. I had a feeling they weren't singing arias from Italian operas but bawling out the Giovinezza [*official hymn of the Italian National Fascist Party*] and Fascist songs! Adele said she heard the word Giovinezza the other day. But the villagers don't know this and think the prisoners are well, happy and amiable. Mrs Lawrence said she hadn't known what nice-looking men Italians were and she supposed they hadn't wanted the war. I saw she would have liked to make friends with them. She then told me that the other day, when they passed, she put up a V sign. Somebody seems to have told her she shouldn't have done that, but clearly she couldn't understand why, and I saw it was useless to try and explain it to her. She seems to have thought that as she enjoyed seeing the V sign they must too and she wanted to give them that pleasure. The postmistress next door, Mrs Coleman, is a very different type. She said, 'They look happy and well and always seem to be singing. They wave to me as they pass but I don't wave back. I remember they are our enemies. But it's right they should be well fed and well looked after. That's our religion isn't it?'

The other evening, towards dusk, motoring home from Winchester, on a deserted stretch of country road, I saw a smart figure in a most unfamiliar uniform coming towards us. The uniform was bluish and trimmed copiously with scarlet. Marc, the taxi driver, told me he was an Italian officer; they are allowed out on parole and go shopping in Romsey. They look like gay parrots in that sober town.

Boris and Alice Astor spend the weekend at Mottisfont.

Mottisfont, Monday October 26

Yesterday I taught Alice to make my famous cheese and Boris helped from time to time, the sleeves of his pullover rolled back. This sight – a great Russian with his sleeves rolled back and his arms in a bath of milk – made the kitchen maid giggle a good deal to herself. The rain came down and we didn't go out. I asked Boris to do a neat drawing for me of the bit of wall exposed for the tablet and which I had drawn roughly. The tablet is now in place. I shall paste the drawing in the Mottisfont Record Book which I keep so lovingly. There was a great argument about marriage – which state B. hates – after lunch. B. screamed and I think Alice took a dislike to him. He attacked my 'bourgeois outlook' which I didn't mind. I did my best to defend marriage on two grounds: the greater helplessness of woman than of men and the necessity to give them security; and the great usefulness to the state of stable, settled families. I too want the divorce laws made less archaic – no guilty party and so on – but I don't want marriage abolished or the divorce laws made so easy that, after a short quarrel, a quick-tempered person could run to the registrar and get divorced. On the other hand, I don't see why people shouldn't live together openly without blame if they want to and have families.

London, Wednesday October 28

Went to see Margaret Ampthill at the Red Cross prisoners-of-war headquarters to see whether I could have a job there for two or three weeks till I know whether my Admiralty job is coming off or not. It was settled and I start next Tuesday.

Mottisfont, Thursday October 29

Lunched with Raymond M. at the Ivy. Desmond MacCarthy[16] and Princess Polignac (Winnie)[17] were there. Desmond MacCarthy looked smaller and older but his charm is very great and I loved his reddish beak-nosed face. He is going through a cure for asthma. We talked about the Russells. He knew Bertie[18] well and Conrad and Claud a bit. He says the Russells love lecturing

16. Sir Desmond MacCarthy (1877-1952), influential literary and dramatic critic. Member of Bloomsbury Group, literary editor of the *New Statesman* 1920-27, from 1928 senior literary critic on *Sunday Times*.

17. Winnaretta Singer, Princesse Edmond de Polignac (1865-1943), musical patron and heir to the Singer sewing machine fortune.

18. Bertrand Russell, 3rd Earl Russell, 'Bertie' (1872-1970), philosopher, mathematician, writer and political activist. Gilbert's second cousin.

England on the smallest provocation and telling her how to behave. Do they more than most clever political-minded people? I don't know. I don't think so.

London, Tuesday November 3

I have taken a room at Claridges for one month so as to have a settled place to come to and no packing and unpacking. Today went to the Red Cross at 8 Belgrave Sq. and worked in the Missing Department of the Air Force from 9.30 till 5.30. Lunched in the canteen in the basement having an excellent lunch for 1/3 [*one shilling three pence*] and finished the hour off by reading *The Times*. Work very monotonous – copying out endless lists of missing airmen – but I don't mind drudgery. It's an opiate.

The Allies, under the command of Lieutenant-General Bernard Montgomery, began a counter-offensive in El Alamein, Egypt towards the end of October 1942, leading to the retreat over the border into Libya of the Axis powers and marking a turning point in the North African campaign.

London, Thursday November 5

Limited victory in Libya in progress. Montgomery has been attacking for 10 days – infantry opening up the way, tanks following. Now there has been a break through and 6,000 prisoners taken. Went off to Red Cross. Same drudgery. I hear strange snatches of conversation from people around me 'his body was washed ashore', 'the other bodies couldn't be identified', 'his legs were shattered', 'they held him up for two hours then they had to let go'. I look at the names of the young men I am writing down and when some number or name specially draws my attention, I think almost always along the same lines: his parents' pleasure when he was born, the excitement surrounding the birth, his schooldays, the efforts made by his parents to give him as good an education as possible, their hopes for him, his holidays at home and then, at the end, his name copied by me from a RAF casualty list.

Mottisfont, Friday November 6

Worked Red Cross 9.30-1. Then hurried to Coq d'Or where I had Margot, Bob Dixon and Dr Lothar, Margot's refugee friend, to lunch. He looks pathetically like a refugee. I knew him from afar. I think he must be a Jew though Margot says no. He is a quiet, sad, agreeable man. Told me a nice story illustrative of the English character. He said Gen. Sir Alan Brooke[19] was living at the Connaught Hotel. He said, 'It's so extraordinary, there are no guards or sentries there, he is just like any other visitor and goes in and out.' I said, 'Naturally.' He went on: 'I said all this to somebody on his staff and the officer said, "No the General doesn't like fuss." I said, "But the General probably has offices there – some typist and so on?" The young officer said, "No, nothing." I said, "But what happens if the General wakes up in the night and has an idea?" The officer said, evenly, "The General <u>never</u> wakes up during the night."'

Under the command of General Dwight Eisenhower, the Allies followed up successes in Egypt on November 8 with the US landings in Algiers and Oran in Algeria and Casablanca in Morocco, all controlled by Vichy France. The Allies recognised the French admiral Francois Darlan, who had collaborated with the Nazis and was in Algiers at the time, as head of French North Africa. In return he ordered a ceasefire on November 10.

Mottisfont, Sunday November 8

Adele came in this morning with the news Americans have landed in North Africa. Very exciting. In Libya there are 20,000 prisoners but the remaining German forces seem to have got away and are now on the frontier. Today we listened a great deal to the staggering news and heard Hitler's very indifferent speech at Munich, General de Gaulle's call, a recording of Roosevelt's broadcast message to the French, and finally Mrs Roosevelt who broadcasts well. The Libyan news is wonderful. It's a victory – a real victory after all.

London, Monday November 9

Dined with I. at Prunier's. He has been in the US and Canada for the last five weeks. Brought me back hairpins and nail varnish and looked well, fat and handsome. He said the job was waiting for me but there were doubts or reservations in his voice. I don't know why. When I challenged him he said he'd none. He was perfectly confident I could do it. Does he think this four-day week business is going to make a joke of the job? Or else that I'm not strong enough even to do four days a week or that there are going to be heavy

19. Field Marshal Alan Brooke, later 1st Viscount Alanbrooke (1883-1963), Chief of the Imperial General Staff (head of the army) and foremost military advisor to Winston Churchill in the Second World War. Promoted to Field Marshal in 1944.

air raids and, as I'm such a bad sleeper, I shan't be able to stand them? Or is it, after all, difficult for him to put me into this job, though it was he who suggested and repeated the offer, without prompting, a second time? Even tonight I didn't broach the question but let him do so. I don't know what to think but the nervous tension is doing me in, coupled with all the agonies and self-control necessary during the year, and into such stiff Red Cross work.

London, Wednesday November 11

Yesterday Red Cross, same grinding attention to detail, copying and same exhaustion and terrible doubts about myself. I don't want to take on the [Admiralty] job and fail or have a nervous breakdown. I have looked forward to it for so long and pegged myself to it because I have to peg myself to something. And I have tried to prepare myself for it. Today Red Cross. Exhausted but can't sleep when I get home. I don't know what to do. I believe I shall have to give up this Red Cross work and probably put off or refuse the other. I wrote to I. last night about it but didn't post it. I will keep it a day or two and see. I am dreadfully depressed. I want to work like other people. I want regular work. I am sick of life like this. I cry for G. all the time.

London, Thursday November 12

Red Cross. B. came to see me. Pleasant talk and chatter. I felt better for his company and strength. After he'd gone I thought about work and my health. I felt I should go mad if I couldn't rest and mad too if I couldn't work. I have cruel doubts about myself, a dreadful terror of breaking down. The desirable thing for me to take my mind off myself is steady work but I know I can't do it as I am now. It's a bitter blow. I wanted to do my war-work like everybody else and not lie in bed, or have much leisure, or live too sheltered a life. I cry and cry but have to decide myself.

Mottisfont, Friday November 13

Rang up I. early and said I couldn't take his job for the present – too tired, sleeping too badly. This decision is taken now. Went to the Red Cross. Said I wouldn't be coming in again for the present. Came here 3.25. Dinner in bed.

Unhappy about not working, Maud keeps herself busy with 'picture gazing' and seeing friends to fill the time and stop depression.

London, Monday November 16

Dined at 20 Chester St at invitation of Eddy S.W. before his concert. The concert was at Cheyne Walk and the chief draw the performance of Britten's *Seven Sonnets of Michelangelo* with Britten himself accompanying Peter Pears.[20] The last three pieces for two pianos were played by Eddy and Britten, whose technique and playing are very good and virile. Britten is a strange-looking man. One would never say: that young man must be a musician or a poet or an artist. One might easily say: that young man looks as if he would be at home on a racecourse with a grey billycock tipped over one eye. In fact he looks like a tout or tipster – receding forehead and chin, rather sallow, crinkly dark hair and only eyes that give him a distinctive look. They are grey and penetrating. The evening was a delight. Pears, the tenor, has a good well-trained voice and sings very intelligently.

Mottisfont, Sunday November 22

Sir Austen Harris brought over four Americans to tea. Like most Americans one sees over here they were short and very foreign in appearance – I mean swarthy. It turned out the four of them were of Polish descent. They were very nice and easy to talk to. I only made one bloomer when one of them asked, 'How may rooms have you got in this house?' I said vaguely, without reflecting, 'Oh, 30 or 40, I can't quite remember.' 'Whaaaht!' said the American. 'That tickles me, you can't remember how many rooms you've got in the house.' I was on the point of saying, 'Well it all depends what you mean, do you want me to include flower-room, serving-room, boot-room etc?' but decided that I should never be able to put things right.

London, Sunday December 13

Dined with I. who came to Claridges. I tried to explain why I'd had a sort of breakdown, that my health and nerves are poor and that I didn't think I could possibly ever do a whole-time job – which is what he thinks it ought to be. I found it difficult to talk. My voice was thin, words were scarce and I felt as if I weren't telling the truth – or as if I were leaving out the main objection. I walked out with him on his way home, thinking the dark would help me but it didn't. I didn't say a quarter of the things I had to say.

---

20. Benjamin Britten (1913-76), composer, conductor and pianist. He composed the Italian *Seven Sonnets of Michelangelo* in 1940 for himself and his life-partner, the English tenor Peter Pears (1910-86).

London, Tuesday December 15

Today dined with Sylvia to meet Pierre Comert, editor of *La France*, a little short-sighted Frenchman, a Protestant. Neville Lytton, his gay hair making his head wilder and stranger than ever, was there. We talked France and Darlan.[21] When asked what he felt, Comert said, 'Don't misinterpret me, I condemn Darlan, he is a scoundrel, crafty and clever, but I think it is right to have made use of him in North Africa. Thousands of lives were saved.' Neville Lytton had a story about the American Chargé d'affaires at Vichy who'd argued with Darlan about his collaboration with Germany asking, 'Why do you do this?' Darlan answered, 'Bring me 5,000 tanks and 10,000 airplanes and I won't.' After the successful landings in N. Africa, the American – who happened to be there in a political or diplomatic capacity – found himself face to face with Darlan who had just successfully turned his coat. There was a moment of slight embarrassment on both sides and then Darlan said with a smile, 'Well you have turned up with those 5,000 tanks and 10,000 airplanes and here I am.'

Following numerous reports from Europe that the German authorities were carrying out the mass killing of Jews, on December 17 the Allies issued a Joint Declaration condemning this 'bestial policy of cold-blooded extermination', and promised retribution.

London, Thursday December 17

I remember now another story connected with Comert. There was a discussion and during it Comert made some excuse for someone, or a country – it may have been France – not fighting because they didn't think they could win. Neville Lytton pounced, swooped like an eagle, saying that expectation of winning was not what made a country fight. And I thought how right he was when I remembered England in June 1940 with such a poor chance of victory but unanimous determination to fight and die, if need be – not rat away like France. This chance remark of Comert showed up one of the contributory causes to the defeat of France – the lack of guts in the French and the curse inherent in their logic.

21. Francois Darlan (1881-1942), French Admiral and political figure. After France capitulated to Nazi Germany in 1940, Darlan served in the pro-German Vichy regime at one point as deputy leader. When Allies invaded French North Africa in 1942, Darlan happened to be there. The Allies recognized Darlan as head of French North Africa and in return he ordered French troops to stop resisting the Allies.

Mottisfont, Wednesday December 23

Stopped at the wood opposite Curtis's farm on Wednesday to see the Italian prisoners who are clean-felling the wood. When I arrived, dead silence fell and all work stopped. There were 20 of them and one guard, a kindly man who has guarded the prisoners for two and a half years. He said they were little trouble on the whole. The troublesome prisoners were always removed and sent back to the main camp and sometimes to Canada. If they behaved, they had quite a passable time and a fair amount of freedom. They only thing he felt was hard was that they are only allowed one letter and, I think, one postcard a month. He thought this depressingly little. He said his own mother wrote to him every single day.

Through Osbert Peake at the Home Office, Maud manages to get permission for Alexie to register as a 'friendly alien' meaning that she is allowed to stay at Mottisfont for Christmas. Riette Cochrane-Baillie and Maud's mother, Maria, are the other guests.

Mottisfont, Saturday December 26

Yesterday Xmas Day. Church with Mama at 3.30. News of Darlan's assassination in the morning. Everybody elated though an assassination is a horrible thing. Rose [*housemaid*] came in to call Riette in the morning saying, 'Good news. Admiral Darlan has been assassinated,' adding 'and on Xmas Eve too.' Darlan's assassin has been executed.

London, Tuesday December 29

I have taken Virginia Cowles'[22] flat at 10 Berkeley St for seven weeks while she is away reporting in Algeria. Urla [Lubelska] came to dinner and brought her Polish fiancé Utek Podleski, a nice, gentle, young man. I don't think she appreciates him enough yet. His mother and sisters are or were in Warsaw and he hasn't heard from them for years.

Mottisfont, Saturday January 2, 1943

New Year's Party – to Cathleen Q.'s aristocratic flat in South Audley St. On arrival we were given tumblers of rum and from then on till after 2 I had an

---

22. Virginia Cowles OBE (1910-83), US journalist and writer who covered the Spanish Civil War and Second World War.

occasional tumbler and once champagne. I don't remember thinking I was getting drunk. At the back of my mind was the thought of Gilbert; that I was alone here, dancing, in a dazed way, the Paul Jones [*a dance involving changing partners*], sitting talking to whoever was next to me but with no plan and no one to go home to. At 2 I decided to go, got out into the street and found I couldn't walk straight. I pulled myself together to make a conventional entrance into Claridges and went to bed. I lay in a drunken stupor all morning, tried tea and toast at 1, was violently ill, then sank back into a drunken sleep till 5 when I began to come round. I mustn't get drunk again like that. It's very unattractive, especially in someone of my age.

Today Alexie came to lunch at the Akropolis and we went to Urla Lubelska's wedding at the Polish Catholic Church near the Angel (*see photo in black and white plate section*). While Alexie and I were sitting waiting for the service to begin Jan Lubelski asked me to give Utek away. I protested: hadn't he got a man friend who could do that? Surely a woman wasn't the right person? Jan said no, in the Polish church the bridegroom is given away, or accompanied to the altar, by a woman, usually a near-relation. As Utek's were in Poland would I lead him up to the altar? And that is what I did, most confused, given no time to reflect or ask questions about speed, right or left side, to smooth my coat or compose my face. I tried to force Utek into the wrong *prie-dieu* and got caught and almost tripped up the bride and her brother who followed tight on our heels. Well, I've now been best man and given away a Pole I'd only set eyes on once before. Two new experiences this week – 1. Walking home very drunk through the pitch black streets 2. Giving away a Pole in a Catholic church.

Mottisfont, Sunday January 3

Today I wrote, arranged, tidied up and went through my sweet Gilbert's clothes with a view to keeping some for the boys and giving the rest away. I had been dreading this for seven months. Whenever I thought of it, I felt ill with pain and misery and put off doing this miserable, distasteful, abominable thing. His clothes, his spectacles, the odds and ends in his room, most of them things I know so well. As I tidy up and give away his intimate belongings, I separate myself further and further from him.

London, Tuesday January 5

Dined with I. at Claridges. Talked about the job and whether I could do it. He says I mustn't stay at one of the big rich hotels but go to a smaller hotel or a flat so as to live more like the other people with whom I shall work. He doesn't understand what it feels like to be my age and he doesn't understand about insomnia, being delicate, or how, when one is very lonely, one clings to familiar places – even Claridges – and gets comfort from the faces of servants one knows. I couldn't explain because I felt I should cry if I tried to. I think I shall try this job but I wish I could start sleeping naturally again before I take it up. I should have a better chance of lasting out if I did. I. looked tired, worried and worn-out himself.

London, Friday January 8

Left Claridges with remaining bags, parcels, bottles, wireless and some flowers and came to Virginia Cowles' flat, gay, comfortable and original looking. Dined in bed and didn't feel unhappy at the move. I was afraid of feeling even lonelier. Today woke in my tiny room, got up lazily, shaking off the sleeping draught and opened the door to Mrs Martin, a maid of Virginia Cowles', who comes in once or twice a week. Dined at Glenconners. Christopher back on a few weeks' leave, looking very well. His job is in Cairo where he lives in great comfort. He says General Montgomery is so respected in Egypt that no one criticises his self-advertisement or his bombastic utterances. He behaved with exaggerated gallantry to the captured German General [Wilhelm Ritter von] Thoma and no one seemed to mind except a Pole who was horrified at this war-being-a-game mentality, remembering as he did the fate of his country.

London, Monday January 11

Kitty has been given permission to come here from Switzerland. It seems astonishing as she is technically an enemy alien. She asked Van to sponsor her application and Van did, with all his usual warmth and ardour. Van wrote and told me and enclosed the letter from the Home Office saying she would be allowed to come here but it was extremely unlikely that the Germans would let her pass through France or Italy. There have been a lot of arrests in Hungary and I fancy the Hungarians aren't so popular anymore with the Germans, or vice versa. The Hungarians are beginning to think we might win after all.

The Russian winter-offensive continues. They have pushed on far beyond Stalingrad leaving the German 6th Army ensconced in and round it. They are astonishing.

London, Wednesday January 13

Yesterday I dined with the Glenconners. The Deputy Greek prime minister, Kanellopoulos, whose headquarters are in Cairo, was there. He looks 26 but he must be 46. He talks a little too fluently on any subject. He thinks Winston one of the great men of our period. He described the first time he saw him in Egypt last summer coming up a flight of steps. '*Ce n'était pas un homme,*' he said. '*C'était au fait naturel.*'

Today Oliver Lyttelton and the Glenconners lunched with me at the Ritz. Oliver talked a lot about America and we laughed a good deal. He said a phrase with a special meaning was now in use in government and diplomatic circles: 'Give him an evasive answer'. It started in this way. A well-known film actor was in bed on the loggia of his house after a late party the night before. A producer came walking along, caught sight of him and wanting to talk with him, knocked at the door. The maid acting under orders said the actor had gone out. The producer said, 'Nonsense, I've just seen him lying in bed on the loggia. Tell him and say I want to talk to him.' The maid went off and gave the actor the message. He snapped back, 'Give him an evasive answer. Tell him to go fuck himself.' So now the phrase 'give him an evasive answer' carries this meaning. Oliver's first visit to the White House was for supper which, I think he said, started at 7 – or some early hour – and was over with great speed. As soon as supper was over the President said 'Well now we will all retire, we've got to do some work' and carried Oliver and Harry Hopkins away with him. In fact no work was done and they sat talking on every subject till 2. Oliver felt the President did this to get away from Mrs R.

London, Thursday January 14

I went to an Ordinary and sat next to Kenneth Clark. He said he'd decided not to speak on the Brains Trust broadcasts[23] anymore. He said he could never collect his wits quickly enough to say exactly what he meant to and sometimes found he said things he didn't mean. He said he'd never once had a letter from the public on any of his broadcasts showing, he thought, how little the English are interested in art. Joad and Huxley got hundreds.

---

23. *The Brains Trust* was a popular BBC radio and later television programme on which a panel of experts tried to answer questions sent in by the audience. The philosopher and psychologist C.E.M. Joad and biologist Julian Huxley were two of the original panel members.

On January 14-24, Churchill and Roosevelt meet in Casablanca, Morocco, to plan Allied strategy for the next phase of the war. One outcome of the conference was the Allied declaration that only an unconditional German surrender would end hostilities. Meanwhile the Allied armies continue to advance: in North Africa, they are approaching the Libyan capital Tripoli; in Russia, the Soviets are close to regaining full control of Stalingrad.

London, Friday January 22

The prime minister is away again. Where? North Africa perhaps? Great events are happening – the Russians advance all the time and we are almost in Tripoli. The sky is much lighter.

London, Saturday January 23

Tripoli entered this morning. Wonderful speed since El Alamein. Met I. at Studio One where we saw *Derrière la Façade* and *Quiet Wedding*. He came back to tea and I told him I wanted to start work and was making preparations to hand over little jobs and simplify my life so as to conserve health and energy for the job. I hope I succeed. He said: alright, papers will be sent. I told him I was conscientious but not to expect brainwaves from me.

Mottisfont, Monday January 25

Yesterday Mama and I went to the little house Tony and Sally have got in Hampton Court Road for the baby's christening. I was chief godmother, Queen Geraldine of Albania (Apponyi by birth) the other. The baby was christened in the dining room and I held it. It cawed once or twice but was good on the whole. Names: Anthony, Stephen, Michael. It wore the christening robe we have all been christened in and which comes from Mama's family. My other godchildren are – let me think: Pamela Hornsby, Julian Cory-Wright, Jane Asquith, Katherine Howard, Christopher McLaren and now great-nephew Apponyi.[24] Mama quite pleased. She'd wanted to escape going to the christening party. But I told her it would be unkind and families must stick together. The Russells get 1st prize for close sticking and it's a very great source of strength even in these times.

24. Later Maud added an undated note: 'Later there was Rev. Lambert's son Patrick?, Christopher Serpell's girl Camilla and Rupert Wollheim [Anne Toynbee's son by her second marriage to Richard Wollheim].'

Mottisfont, Tuesday February 2

Caught train here on Saturday. A gale was getting up. Walked round to the men's club after dinner to a concert. It was music hall entertainment and not too bad. I enjoyed the atmosphere and scene. All Saturday night, Sunday and Sunday night there was a tremendous gale with violent and terrifying gusts accompanied by torrential rain. I thought of the night before G. died. The noise that night was very disturbing and dreadful. I stayed in all Sunday and practically all yesterday, writing, reading, sticking photographs in a book, going through stores and so on. It's strange being alone. I can't get used to it. Mottisfont is very lonely.

London, Tuesday February 9

Maroussia Volkova, Boris's wife in all but name, came to lunch with me at Claridges. This was Boris's idea. He wanted us to meet and he thought she would enjoy the hats, sights and the crowd. She is an older-looking woman and not beautiful, as I had expected, but at first sight ugly, clumsy and rather repellent, with the blackest tartar face, coarse yellow skin and heavy ears. She was dreadfully shy at first and her hands trembled. She leads a very secluded life, hardly goes out and has been very nervous and frightened since the blitz two years ago. Gradually she settled down and we talked easily but I felt I hadn't much rapport with her. This may simply have been because she was physically rather repulsive to me and I kept on catching sight of an ear, heavy and red. But her face is very extraordinary and I can believe Boris who says that she was beautiful when she was young.

London, Friday February 12

Yesterday I lunched with Cecil [Beaton] in his charming crowded house with red, plush wallpaper. There: Winnie de P. [Polignac], Chips Channon, Loelia Westminster and Colonel Gaston Palewski,[25] a Free French and political adviser to de Gaulle. We were squeezed round a small table exquisitely arranged, ate delicious food off exquisite china and talked a lot. Love was talked about and I said that there came a moment when one should put thoughts of love behind one. No one agreed and all cried out except Princess

---

25. Gaston Palewski (1901-84), French politician. In French air force, joined Charles de Gaulle's Free French forces in London in 1940 becoming de Gaulle's right-hand man. An Anglophile, his diplomatic skills were invaluable in de Gaulle's negotiations with the British.

de P., who kept mum being 77. Chips Channon defended the elaborately affable treatment of the German General Thoma, the handshakes, the jokes and going over old campaigns. I said it was out of date and would look odd to our allies the Poles and others. Treat the German General decently but don't joke and make friends. It didn't suit the times. He continued to argue repeating: why not? Until exasperated, I said 'It looks silly,' which I saw infuriated him.

Today dined with Alice. Colonel Palewski there. He is devoted to de Gaulle and thinks him very remarkable. Palewski is anxious about the Russian successes and prays we may soon land in Europe and have great successes too so as to have a say in the settlement of Europe. The poor Colonel complained of being tired, drank several glasses of Kummel and told a rather indelicate story about himself. He sings snatches from time to time in a comic way. It must be a nervous habit. I thought only people in Russian plays did so.

Mottisfont, Monday February 15

Today made a cheese. Rose, the housemaid, is cooking as the cook has gone. She has two young girls to help in the kitchen and two in the house. The atmosphere in the kitchen is quite altered. There is a feeling of improvisation in the air and a breeziness characteristic of Rose. When Alexie asked her a little time ago whether she often went into Romsey she gave a laugh and said: no, she never got further than the 'Bear'. The Bear and Ragged Staff is a pub one and a half miles from here on the Romsey road. She hasn't any of the usual reticence of servants. On the other hand, she has a good deal of tact. She is Cockney. And she has been with us about 20 years.

London, Wednesday February 17

I. rang up telling me to come to the Admiralty for an interview. I hurried to the Admiralty main entrance where I waited in that small, elegant Georgian hall with a statue of Nelson in a niche in the centre of it. Oddly enough the Admiralty isn't barricaded like the other govt ministries I've been in. Eventually I was conducted to a dark, little interviewing room. Saw I. for half a second and then Commander McLachlan,[26] who talked agreeably about nothing much to me for quarter of an hour, said I might join them around

---

26. Donald Harvey McLachlan, OBE (1908-71), Scottish journalist. Head of Naval Propaganda sub-section NID 17Z 1941-45. Editor *Times Educational Supplement* 1938-40, editor *Sunday Telegraph* 1961-66.

March 5, and then escorted me, talking about Hampshire and the River Test, to the Mall entrance. Walking and thinking, I went to see a flat at 39 Upper Grosvenor St suggested to me by I. and belonging to a missing friend of his. Suits. Shall try and take it.

London, Friday February 19

Today lunched with B. at the Shanghai. We talked about Gandhi who is doing a 21-day fast and will probably die before he pulls it off. B. said he'd once fasted 20 days in Paris. His doctor told him it would cure the arthritis which was starting in a hand or foot. He started as a tremendously fat man – he had that advantage. He led an almost normal life throughout except that he didn't eat. He worked in the morning and when his assistants went to lunch he went to bed and slept for one and half hours. Then he worked till 6. When they went off to have their evening meal, he took a bath. And he went to bed very early. He drank water with a few drops of orange or lemon essence from a bottle but no food at all for 20 days. He said he felt deliciously light and gay – wonderful. But it was dreadfully boring not having the distraction and break of meals. We were talking about lullabies and he began to sing gently. His voice is a pure Russian voice; a tenor, measured, Russian and lovely.

London, Wednesday February 24

Yesterday I. fetched me and we dined at Prunier's. I thanked him for finding the flat at 39 Upper Gros. St – I signed the agreement that morning – and told him <u>not</u> to get me the Admiralty job if there were any difficulties. Today lunched at the Ivy with Raymond M., Harold Nicolson, a French writer called Joseph Kessel,[27] with an extraordinary violent head like a head of Epstein's, and another writer Maurice Druon.[28] They both escaped from France in December. They spent a week in the 'Patriotic School' when they got here and Kessel added that they were 'very thoroughly interrogated indeed'. They said conditions in France are appalling. They asked Harold N. eagerly whether the war had produced any good new writers or any good books. Both he and Raymond could only say no. Kessel then asked tentatively about how Charles Morgan[29] was regarded in England, adding that in France he was

---

27. Joseph Kessel (1898-1979), French journalist and novelist.
28. Maurice Druon (1918-2009), French novelist. Joseph Kessel's nephew.
29. Charles Morgan (1894-1958), novelist and journalist. Awarded French Legion of Honour in 1936 and elected member of Institut de France in 1949. Awarded James Tait

enormously admired. Harold N. said he had begun one of his books and only read a few pages before putting it down. R. had read one of them and so had I. Both Raymond and Harold confessed he wasn't thought much of in a serious sense. Kessel said: How strange, in France he is considered the best English writer, he is enormously admired.

Packed up after lunch at Cowles' flat as she is supposed to be coming back today from North Africa. Came with luggage to Claridges and went to bed in a state of exhaustion.

London, Friday February 26

I imagined there was little to pack at 10 Berkeley St but I found I'd collected a lot of things in seven weeks – bottles of drink, tins of tea and food, a mountain of writing paper, an eiderdown, two vast bath towels, three Vuillard lithographs, two Rouault lithographs, one Picasso etching, one Degas reproduction of a sleeping youth, a wireless, a typewriter, a kettle, an assortment of books, cardboard boxes and some clothes.

Today lunch with B. at Shanghai. Went shopping, spent afternoon with him and had tea at Polish Rest. He has left Reuters after a storm or two – sent in his resignation. It will be good for him to have a rest.

Mottisfont, Tuesday March 2

Looking at old put-away curtains and chair covers for flat. Walked across spring country. First blossom, I think of G. First green, I think of G. Very tired. Haven't taken sleeping draughts for six weeks, but last three nights slept badly so am short of sleep. Letters from Martin immersed in chess and Sinhalese life and Raymond setting about getting his commission. Richmond and Blueie vouching for him – so help them God. He is so improved though, they probably won't rue it.

London, Thursday March 4

Dined with Sibyl – but it wasn't an ordinary Ordinary – at the Dorchester. The dinner was for Oliver Lyttelton and there were: Sibyl, Oliver, Diana C., Desmond MacCarthy, Herbert Agar, Harold Nicolson, Eddy S.W., Venetia

(continued) Black Memorial Prize for fiction 1940. Achieved popularity in France but was never taken seriously by British critics. Worked in Room 17Z at the Admiralty with Maud.

and the Duke and Duchess of Devonshire. The dinner was agreeable and didn't drag like the Ordinaries usually do, I suppose because it was planned simply as a dinner party. Oliver seemed a little shy – and he is a shy man and uncertain of himself – to start with but later embarked on his stories and the people to whom they were new were delighted. At the end of dinner Sibyl moved me next to the Duke of D. I suppose we got on to North Africa because he took a letter out of his pocket and put it in front of me. It was signed 'Harold' and read 'My dear Eddie, Everything you told me about the French is true. Yours ever Harold.' Harold MacMillan is attached to General Giraud[30] in North Africa.

London, Friday March 5

Lunched with Boris at Shanghai. The last time I saw him I asked him half-jokingly, half-seriously, whether he'd ever done anything he was ashamed of. He had taken this very seriously, poor Tartar, and ruminated and fussed, and when we met he demanded to know what I had meant. I had a difficult time making him believe my question had been an idle one. But this idle question set him thinking and then talking. He told me an amusing story about an El Greco head belonging to General Stirling,[31] whose chapel in Scotland Boris decorated. General Stirling had a very good collection of pictures, among them this El Greco – El Greco's daughter I think. Once when Boris was there, he asked B. to have it valued. B. got Borenius[32] to go up to Scotland for £50 and expenses. Borenius valued the picture at £3,500 adding that if the General got an offer of £4,000 he should jump at it. Some months later the General decided to sell and said to B: I leave it to you, try and sell it and if you can't get more I will be content with £3,000. Boris went to Konody,[33] the expert. Konody had a big art library and looked up the picture at once. He was very interested and excited and said they should go together to Lord Rothermere [Harold Harmsworth, 1st Viscount (1868-1940)] who was

30. General Henri Giraud (1879-1949). After escaping German prison, put in charge of French troops in North Africa after Allied landings. Appointed commissioner of French north and west Africa following Francois Darlan's assassination. *De facto* successor to de Gaulle but retired from politics in 1944 after continual disagreements.
31. Brigadier-General Archibald Stirling of Keir (1867-1931). In 1925 Boris was commissioned to make a mosaic of angels raising the figure of Christ for the apse of the private chapel at Keir House, Dunblane, Perthshire.
32. Carl Tancred Borenius (1885-1948), Finnish art historian working in England. Prolific author and expert on early Renaissance Italian art.
33. Paul George Konody (1872-1933), art critic and writer.

buying pictures and paying large sums for them. Konody stipulated he should have 10%. B. and him went off to see Lord Rothermere who received them in rather a hurry. 'How much does General Stirling want?' asked Lord R. Before Konody could answer Boris said £8,000. 'Done,' said Lord R. or words to that effect. Konody sat *bouche béaute*. When they were alone Konody said, 'It's mad to give General Stirling £8,000. He isn't expecting more than half. Why don't we split the extra £4,000?' But Boris thought otherwise. It ended with Konody giving B. half the commission on the whole sum, namely £400, as B. had pulled off the deal and the figure was £5,000 more than they were authorised to accept by the General. The General was very pleased and later sent B. a cheque for £300 as a token of thanks. Boris wrote back and refused and this situation went on for a little. Finally B. took the £300. B. thought the General had guessed he'd had a share in the commission with Konody and understood his diffidence in accepting the General's present.

Another story followed, a fine piece of wile, very successful and which pleases B. to this day because there is a side of him which likes wile, subtle plots and dealings. It's the un-European side. The story starts with Sam Courtauld beginning to be known as an art patron and living in Berkeley Square. He discussed with B. a scheme he had for building a gallery out at the back to house his pictures and B. was to do mosaics for him in the building. There was quite a lot of talk and maybe drawings. Then Sam changed his mind and sold the house. But being nice and kindly – as he is – he felt B. would be disappointed at the vanished opportunity and said, 'If ever you get the chance of some big public job, I'll back you.' B. conceived the idea of doing some work at the National Gallery. He went to [blank] and suggested he should do some floors and that Sam would pay. There was a meeting of the trustees. None of them knew or cared much about mosaics but they said, 'Go ahead.' No question of price arose. Their approval given, B. went off to Sam, said the Trustees were all for the scheme and that Sam had told him he might come to him if he wanted a backer. Sam was quite pleased. He too said, 'Go ahead' and didn't bother to ask the price. The drawings were got out, the details settled and still no one asked what the cost would be. Finally, when all was fixed up, Boris told Sam the price would be £8,000 – £5,000 for the two sides, £3,000 for the centre. B. thinks Sam was very surprised, though he said little, and that he had vaguely thought the cost might be £700.

London, Wednesday March 10

Had a three-quarter hour German conversation class at the Berlitz School at 12. Complimented as usual on my accent. I suppose all teachers do that.

I have had the same in French and Italian, not in Russian though. Dined with I. at Pommier's. My job is slowly being fixed up – no security grounds against me anyhow! But my name has to be passed by a variety of different departments. Talked too much about myself.

London, Thursday March 11

Lunched with B. at Istanbul to meet Henry Lamb[34] who used to be his greatest friend – English friend – but from whom he has become estranged. Maroussia was there too looking handsomer than the first time I saw her. When she laughs her face reminds me of Greek comic masks. Henry Lamb is a disappointment. A small, thin, rather old man, with sharp features and eyes, and thin grey hair. He wore khaki and if his badges of rank had been different he might have been an elderly general. He talked rather impatiently to B. – critically and sharply – as if he were ashamed of him or as if he were ashamed of himself. He is very tetchy and ready to take offence. When I hadn't heard of the school he told me he was sending his daughter to he said, 'But you must be the only person in England who hasn't heard of this school' and was positively offended. He was equally surprised when he was boasting a little about an account by [Astolphe de] Custine he'd read on Russia. He thought hardly anyone else knew about it. I said I'd got it and read some of it. I think he is very anxious to impress. Something must have tormented him all his life.

London, Tuesday March 16

Had a German lesson at Berlitz. Teacher's husband had been on scandalous voyage which took rounded-up enemy aliens to Australia in 1940. She seemed a sensible and truthful person. The short account she gave appalled me. Prisoners looted, bags bayonetted open, watches, wedding-rings and valuables stolen, and the captain of the ship little better than the escort. Revolting. She said that the prisoners were nearly all ill when they got to Australia.

London, Wednesday March 17

Peter Quennell, Eddy and Raymond M. dined with me at the Ivy. Peter Q. warmed up with drink and became <u>very</u> amusing. He is anti-nonsense,

34. Henry Lamb (1883-1960), painter. Influenced by Augustus John, Lamb was a founder of the Camden Town Group in 1911 and the London Group in 1913.

humbug, chi-chi, anti the fashionable, sweeping hypotheses that parents ruin their children's lives, and that all boys suffer misery and incalculable lifelong harm at school, and such like creeds swallowed whole and accepted uncritically by the intelligent young and their elders. Raymond still wallows in all this. Eddy too, but less so. Peter Q. must have had his fill of this too but seems to have discarded the more indigestible positions. He was at school with Claud Cockburn of the *Week* and Graham Greene. In answer to Raymond's rather sloppy suggestion that they must have been very miserable at school he said: not at all, school life had been most ordinary, normal and painless. When the Algerian Burgundy was having a little effect, he gave excruciatingly funny imitations of Eddie Marsh talking aloud to himself when he was staying with Eddie long ago. How Eddie went to bed in the next room, a cigar in his mouth, a glass of whisky in his hand, and then started talking aloud, Shakespeare, other snatches of poetry, partially audible anecdotes of his own, a high cackle of laughter, more poetry and so on. Fearfully funny and rather cruel. Quennell wrote a slim volume of poems when he was 22. Raymond said they were very good. Q. said the Muse had deserted him ever since. He offered her every inducement to return, she could come back on her own terms, a separate pillow, a latch-key of her own. But she'd never done so.

London, Friday March 19

B. dined. Told the story of Lamb and Dorelia, John's wife.[35] They had known each other for many years, then came the 1914 war and Lamb returned with new lustre, and was made a good deal of. By then, Dodo was being severely tried by John, drunkenly shameless, openly unfaithful and crudely inconsiderate. His illegitimate children crowded round. She remained dignified in this chaos; advised and took charge of small babies not her own but was very miserable. It was then that Lamb's opportunity arrived and he became, after many years of close friendship, Dorelia's lover. This greater intimacy was a failure from the start for two reasons. As a lover he was unsuited to her, always restless and nervous, whereas she wanted emotional sympathy and a certain measure of calm after her agitating and restless life. Then, because of his changed relationship with D., he started throwing his weight about in the circle consisting of her children, John's children by other women, and friends who clustered round her and over whom she presided so

---

35. Dorelia McNeill (1881-1969), common-law wife to Augustus John. Model for both John and his sister Gwen John. Close friend of Helen Maitland, Boris's second wife.

beautifully. She did not care for this, nor did the children. The harmony was gone and soon the affair was over. She broke with him completely though she continued to see him. Sometime later he met and proposed to his present wife Patsy. Dodo would not believe he was in love with her but thought he was simply marrying out of worldly considerations and because he was susceptible to rank. B. thinks this wrong. Patsy was so extremely pretty and charming that there was nothing odd in him falling in love. Lamb brought her to see Dorelia but it wasn't a success, neither of them liking each other, and the estrangement was complete. Lamb more or less disappeared from the remarkable John world and B. accuses him of having changed his values or of trying to become a country gentleman. B. described the fantastic and fascinating communal Bohemian life that centred round John and Dorelia, their children and friends, the long table over which Dorelia presided, the great dishes of food prepared by her and two or three women friends who lived with her, and the crowd of young men and girls, some living in caravans, some sharing bedrooms. B. said John never cared much for Lamb. He'd treated him disdainfully. Lamb was B.'s first English friend. They met studying at the same studio in Paris and Lamb introduced B. to Helen, B.'s future wife. I think that in some strange way B. and Lamb are a kind of obsession to each other, or like lovers who have never, even after the rupture, been able quite to get away from each other.

On March 20 Maud officially took over Flat 2, Upper Grosvenor Street and began to furnish and decorate it.

London, Monday March 22

B. came to tea. I told him I would probably soon be at work. He warned me I wouldn't be able to stand the long hours. I said I must try. Indeed, I don't know what I should do with myself if I gave up this job. The thought of it has been my rallying point since I. suggested it in August. If my health gives I must take up something less exacting. I am adrift. I don't feel the future holds much. When I let myself think clearly, I know how painfully lonely I am. I try not to think. I have lots of little plans and occupations to keep my mind engaged.

Mottisfont, Sunday March 28

Came here on Friday morning for lunch. Woolley came and talked to me about the river, channels, drains, ditches and water levels and I consented to open hatches, take away tumbling bays and dig out ditches. The WAEC

[*War Agricultural Executive Committee*] help to the tune of 50% and supply the labour in the shape of Italian prisoners. Yesterday collected Rural Pennies and did village work. After lunch, the day being soft, shining spring I walked alone in the watermeadows and looked at channels and the Rectory Water. I was overcome with melancholy.

Mottisfont, Sunday April 4

Yesterday I took a walk in Spearywell Wood to inspect some larch and fir copses the authorities want to cut down but there were too many Italian prisoners about. Their guard has been dispensed with and they seemed to pop up from behind every bush and I felt awkward and came away. As they collected in the road to wait for their lorry to come and take them back to camp, the village women came out of their cottages and stood gaping at them wishing, I fancy, that they could talk a bit of Italian. The prisoners started picking large bunches of primroses, the women stood staring. Spring is underway.

London, Thursday April 8

Lunched with Riette on Tuesday. John Follett there and Philippe de Rothschild not long escaped from France. He spent a week in the Patriotic School. I asked whether the stay had been oppressive. He said it was alright during the daytime but at night it was impossible not to feel nervous and depressed. There were stories of people who'd committed suicide because they couldn't stand the strain of what appeared to be another concentration camp.

Yesterday I had a telephone message from the NID to go and register. Went to the Labour Exchange, Sardinia Street. Long and confused interview. No record of my job there. Tried to turn me down because I hadn't diplomas or degrees. Told her I thought my job was already fixed up. Interviewer pleasant but only interested in diplomas. Dined with I. at the Belle Meuniere. He was thin, nervous and in need of a rest. His face was drooping. Told me there had been an immense amount of red tape in the putting through of my job.

Mottisfont, Sunday April 11

Friday came here with Mama. We had a talk about her anti-Semitism. She says she doesn't know why she is anti-Semitic, finally came to the conclusion it must be her German background, though when she was young her parents didn't mind her having Jewish friends and don't seem to have been anti-Semitic. G., and the children too, noticed her adverse bias and she talks mostly rather condescendingly about Jews and never, since these persecutions started, with any feeling. I find this very strange since she was married to a Jew, owes every penny she has to him, and benefited by his warm heart to support most of the members of her family. On the other hand she has Jewish friends. This talk came about because my aunt Agnes Mühsam has disappeared from her address in Berlin and letters have been returned 'address unknown'. Mama was completely unmoved till I expressed horror at what she might be going through and then her sympathy began to work feebly.

London, Tuesday April 13

Went to party given by Philippe de Rothschild in Riette's flat. It was an all French party, the only foreigners being Riette, myself, Garrett Moore and his wife, and a young American officer. The party was very lively and the frogs made a lot of noise. Brandy and coffee were going on when I arrived. A big man with a wooden leg in uniform brought out a battered guitar and sang songs in French, Russian and English. One had a refrain 'She married a man who had no balls at all. Whaaaat? No balls at all!' Kessel was there with his mistress Germaine Sablon, a well-known singer, and his protégé Druon. Germaine Sablon sang admirably and passionately. There was a song understood by the French to describe the relationship between France and Germany. France is the poor village girl, Germany the *seigneur* [*lord*]. Several of the women cried when Sablon sang it in Riette's drawing room. Sablon became excitable and there were a lot of criss-cross arguments between the French. She is intransigent, ultra anti-collaborationist and ultra anti-Vichy and Pétain. She turned on the American, who was sitting harmlessly and silently on the floor, and scolded him as a representative of America for having backed Vichy, kept a representative there and for the Darlan set-up in Algeria. Eventually she called out to him, 'Yes, and when you Americans land in France you will be shot by the French people.' This startling remark was hushed up as well as it could be by everyone who heard it, some with light laughter, others with nervous noises.

Mottisfont, Palm Sunday April 18

Yesterday I caught the 3.25 train meeting Ian at Waterloo. He is very tired and in need of rest. Played records after dinner – *Lac des Cygnes* and *Francesca de Rimini*. Today Mr Wort, bee friend, came from Romsey and we opened up the hives. All well. But I was stung several times on the hand. More record playing. I. went out fishing.

London, Tuesday April 20

Yesterday made a cheese and after lunch went for a walk with I. My hands began to swell from the bee stings and during the night I suffered a kind of Chinese torture from tingling and irritated nerves in my arms, passing half of it awake and in a state of nervous fret. I put off going to London till this afternoon. Left I. reading, roaming and resting.

Mottisfont, Friday April 23

Yesterday morning I went round in a taxi buying food as I usually do before going to Mottisfont. Fish is almost unobtainable here. So I bought fish – although the fish shops in London are almost empty too – and coffee, ravioli and spaghetti in Soho. Took 11.30 train here. Blueie joined me at Winchester. Ian was finishing his rest. The room was scattered with books he'd been reading and he'd hacked away and opened up a little whirlpool near the river. Mama, Violet and Raymond B.-C. and Alexie arrived later. Today was Good Friday but I didn't remember it till the evening. I. left in the afternoon. As he took my hand to say goodbye, he pressed an Admiralty badge into it without warning. Blueie must have wondered what the fumbling could have been about. Violet took me aside and said what an amusing talker I. was.

London, April Thursday 29

Dined with I. at Belle Meuniere and he took me to a *conversazione* at Cyril Connolly's in honour of Frederic Prokosch,[36] the American writer. A semi-circle spread out in front of the fire and held Cecil Day-Lewis,[37] Stephen Spender and his wife, Eddy S.W., Raymond M., Peter Watson,[38] Cyril Connolly's mistress, young and pretty Mrs [Lys] Lubbock,[39] Elizabeth Bowen,[40] Prokosch and later Peter Quennell. Before we came there had been talk on that favourite subject the Sergeant i.e. Stuart Preston.[41] Everybody

36. Frederic Prokosch (1906-89), novelist and poet.
37. Cecil Day-Lewis CBE (1904-72), poet and novelist. Poet Laureate 1968-72.
38. Victor William (Peter) Watson (1908-56), art collector and benefactor. Cofounded and funded *Horizon* magazine, edited by Cyril Connolly.
39. Formerly married to an actor, Lys Lubbock lived with Connolly for most of the 1940s. Diligent and loyal, she worked at Connolly's magazine *Horizon* but is remembered mostly for her cooking and house-keeping. She left him after 10 years.
40. Elizabeth Bowen CBE (1899-1973), novelist and short story writer.
41. Stuart Preston (1915-85), writer and art critic for *New York Times* 1949-1965. Came to London in 1942 as part of General Eisenhower's staff and eased himself *(continued)*

was longing to find a flaw in that successful, pleasant, most extremely social young man but very little could be brought up against him. Only one little story of a small solecism when he asked Eliz. [Glenconner], almost as soon as he'd met her, how 'the Glen was'. Ian and I left fairly early to the alarm of Cyril Connolly who thought his party was going to collapse and begged me to get out very quietly. His face changed from good-humoured geniality to a look of positive hatred when I said I was tired and begged him to forgive me for leaving his party so early. I'm told he takes his duties as host very seriously. He is agreeable but not nice. I. leaves for America next week.

Mottisfont, Sunday May 2

Raymond telephoned from Donnington Castle near Derby to say he is earmarked to go abroad without a chance of appearing before the Selection Board. This is incorrect procedure, apparently. Pending a decision on whether he is to appear before the Selection Board, he shouldn't be sent abroad. He made his application two months ago. The War Office is a giant tortoise. He has seen his CO but was afraid nothing would come of it, so telephoned me to see what I could do. I have been racking my brains who to approach. It's so important. Duff hasn't a happy touch in these affairs and I hardly know any soldiers. Today made last minute preparations to leave everything in good order and start work at the Admiralty, so help me God.

London, Wednesday May 5

Yesterday I telephoned to Crinks about Raymond's predicament. I couldn't think of anyone better to interest in poor R. He was immediately sympathetic and active. I sent R.'s letter giving me details round to Crinks and he promised to do what he could with all possible speed. Today I have been in bed, writing and telephoning and arranging 101 things. The horrible nervousness has gone. Work starts tomorrow. I long to be equal to it. I wish I had a little more confidence in myself. I wonder what G. would think about this.

(continued) into English intellectual and aristocratic society through his good-looks and charm or, according to Maud, 'debonair and excelling in the right division of his time and attention between the right people.' Known as 'the Sergeant'.

SIX

Ian Fleming and the Admiralty

JUNE 1943 – AUGUST 1944

In which Maud starts working at the Admiralty;
Ian discusses marriage with Maud;
Mottisfont is requisitioned as a hospital; and
the D-Day landings in Normandy take place.

The tide of war is beginning to turn in favour of the Allies. In North Africa,
they have driven back the Axis powers at El Alamein, taken Tripoli and
forced the Germans and Italians to surrender in Tunisia. In Russia, the
Soviets' second winter counter-offensive has led to the decisive surrender of
German troops at Stalingrad. In the Pacific, a number of victories, including
at Guadalcanal, have put the Allies on the offensive. The next step is to gain
a foothold on continental Europe.

Maud is now working as an unpaid assistant, six days a week, in the
Naval Intelligence Division's (NID) propaganda liaison unit, known as
Room 17Z, at the Admiralty. The Scottish journalist Donald McLachlan,
who interviewed Maud for the role in February, is leading Room 17Z in close
coordination with Ian Fleming and other senior naval intelligence officials.
The unit provides the government's Political Warfare Executive (PWE) with
secret information that can be used in the PWE's subversive propaganda
campaigns to undermine moral and sow confusion among enemy forces. In
particular, McLachlan is working hand-in-glove with Sefton Delmer,[1] the

1. Sefton Delmer (1904-79), known as Tom to his friends, journalist. During the Second
World War, he was recruited by the Political War Executive to organise subversive
propaganda operations against Germany, aimed at creating confusion and undermining
enemy morale. In 1941 he launched the black propaganda radio station *Gustav
Siegfried Eins*, followed in 1943 by *Atlantiksender* and then *Soldatensender Calais* (later
Soldatensender West), among many others. Born in Berlin, Delmer spoke fluent German
and studied modern history at Oxford.

head of the PWE's clandestine propaganda operations located in the village of Milton Bryan in Bedfordshire.

At McLachlan's suggestion, in March 1943 Delmer had launched the counterfeit German military short wave radio station 'Atlantiksender' as part of the Admiralty's all-out offensive against German U-boats. In November 1943, this would evolve into the medium wave channel 'Soldatensender Calais' (later 'Soldatensender West'), expanding the transmission to German forces and civilians in Western Europe and Norway. According to McLachlan, about 75 per cent of the information broadcast was true, and often exclusive, while the remainder was 'ingenious and plausible fiction'.

Room 17Z is also coordinating with the BBC's daily radio German-language naval programme which is given access to information denied to other media. Maud's role involves collecting and passing on intelligence from the NID, including material from interrogated prisoners-of-war, and to field inquiries. Room 17Z is located in an underground room at the Admiralty on Horse Guards Parade.[2]

Maud has now moved into the flat on 39 Upper Grosvenor Street. She usually spends her day off, Sunday, at Mottisfont, travelling down to Hampshire on Saturday afternoon and up to London on Monday morning. On days with no social engagements, she has both lunch and dinner in bed at the flat.

There is a gap in the diary entries from May 6-18. This is unusual for Maud who usually fills in missing entries with the help of her engagement diary. It's likely that she signed some kind of secrecy agreement on starting work, leading her to write few details about her role and nothing at all about her first few days at the Admiralty.

London, Tuesday May 18

Morning and afternoon at office. Dined at Sibyl's Ordinary at the Dorchester. It was my first dinner out on a working day. I wasn't particularly tired. Sibyl said: 'You are doing something very secret.' 'No, ordinary stuff,' I said. 'Interesting, but not exciting.'

---

2. With continual references to Horse Guards Parade, Maud's diary entries indicate that she worked in the old Admiralty building. However, later in the war she mentions that her office is in Sanctuary Buildings, on Great Smith Street, so the office may have moved or she may have had a second office there.

London, Wednesday May 19

It's nearly a year since my darling, loved G. died. I think of this every day and remember the terrible fortnight a year ago before G. died – those dreadful days at Bournemouth, G.'s suffering and patience, my despair and then those last days which appal me whenever I think of them. The office as usual. I did my first bit of writing for a file.

London, Thursday May 20

Went out shopping early. Then the office. I read like a glutton. Lunch in bed. Miss St George came and I gave her bills to pay and letters to write for me. Saw Delmer in the office this afternoon. He has an unusual voice, rather a soft voice. Dinner in bed as usual. There are short raids, one or two almost every night.

Mottisfont, Sunday May 23

Went to office yesterday till 2.45 then escaped to Waterloo where Elvira [Baroni, *Italian maid*] had proceeded me with my luggage and a basket of fish for the servants at Mottisfont. Sibyl Colefax travelled too. Later Stuart Preston, Alice [Astor] and Peter Quennell arrived. Q. is a strange fellow, a good talker, very anti chi-chi and fashion and Bloomsbury highbrow stuff. And very amusing. I think of the devil whenever I look at him. Today lay out in the sun. I was revived by the warmth and the light. Q. was flattering about the house and went round looking at it outside and in from the moment he arrived, walking sharply and lightly. Stuart was interested too and asked 100 questions.

London, Monday May 24

The short weekend rested me. I went back to work *con amore*. Raymond rang up tonight from Scotland. He was swept up there with the others, caught up in the terrible War Office mesh. The others are going off abroad but R. thinks he has managed to straighten out things once again. The War Office, owing to Crinks's good offices, have given orders that R. wasn't to be sent abroad pending the decision of the Selection Board.

London, Thursday May 27

Work. Crinks, Riette [Cochrane-Baillie] and Philippe de Rothschild came to dinner. Crinks filled the passage with his great frame. Philippe started paying me flowery compliments as soon as he arrived and when I turned to Riette and said, 'He's started again,' he laughed and said, 'I am being Frenchy again. I forget I am in England. I haven't been here long enough to remember you don't talk like that here.' He is disarming and I like him.

London, Friday May 28

G. died a year ago. I feel appalled. I can never forget. This is my day off. I saw to hair, lunched alone with Alice in the garden and later took the train to Chenies. Owen the agent met me at the church. It was painful. I looked at my dear G.'s urn which has the inscription on it now. My name is on it too and my bones will be in it one day I hope. I didn't stay long. I saw everything was alright. My heart is heavy. R. arrived [*in London*] on nine days leave. He found a message telling him to report at Derby for his Selection Board.

London, Friday June 4

Work. R. to lunch in my bedroom, well and brown and full of excellent stories about the Selection Board. The 20 young men were kept busy from the moment they arrived with every sort and kind of test – physical, mental, tactical and psychological. This lasts for 48 hours. No indication was given by the Board as to who had done well and who hadn't.

Mottisfont, Sunday June 6

Caught 5.30 here with Boris yesterday. Today long morning in bed, walked about with B., lay in the garden and drank in the sun, and later helped to hive and swarm and take a nucleus from an active hive. B. pointing at the house said: 'You are always thinking about this elephant.'

London, Monday June 7

I like getting back to the office. McLachlan is nice to work for, kind and fair, very quick and clever, and with a head teeming with ideas, just as it should be. Charles Morgan, who is writing an official history, comes in three or four times a week, talks very little, works very quietly, his face pulled to one side as he writes. He has rather a handsome head. Angela Whiteman[3] is a

---

3. Angela B. Whiteman (1919-2009), appointed Assistant Civilian Officer at NID Room 17Z on 10 August 1942. German studies at Oxford interrupted when war broke out. After war, worked with the Allied Control Commission in Occupied Germany.

very efficient girl of 25 or so who knows all the work of the office, names, addresses, numbers, departments and business. She isn't very clever but she is good at her job. Miss C.B.[4] is very plain but good in her painstaking way. Both the women and McLachlan open up when they are alone with me. Angela likes grumbling and Miss C.B. gossiping. Serpell,[5] the only other person in the room, is a clever young man who holds his own with McLachlan and has a number of good ideas of his own, usually of rather a different order. He is less of an enthusiast. He seems a little formidable but I am told he is very shy and so am I in office surroundings.

London, Tuesday June 8

Work as usual. I am beginning to be steadily busy. At first I read a great deal – any file I could get hold of – so as to soak myself.

London, Wednesday June 9

R. came to lunch. He leaves tomorrow. I hope he doesn't get caught in the swirl of army movements and carried away overseas before he knows the result of his Selection Board. I must own I hope he won't have to go overseas yet. The PM is back from America, Gibraltar and Tunisia. Everyone is waiting for the invasion of Europe. The loss of life will be the terrible part of what everyone is hoping will happen soon. I think they forget about the casualties and think we shall march with a reverse or two – but not very bad ones – to Berlin in next to no time.

London, Monday June 14

I. came to dinner, worn out with work, with his travels to America and with a restless night or two. I too was exhausted. We struggled to talk. In the end Ian fell asleep on my shoulder.

---

4. Barbara Cavendish-Bentinck was a part-time office assistant, appointed 17/10/1941.
5. Lt. Christopher H. Serpell (1910-1991), journalist. *Yorkshire Post*, *Times* and BBC correspondent. Seconded from the navy and appointed to NID on 30 March 1942. His duties were listed as 'Political Warfare' in the National Archives. Maud became godmother of his daughter Camilla in January 1944.

London, Thursday June 17

Work all these days, getting to the office about 10.30 and leaving soon after 7. Enjoying all of it. Last night Peter Quennell came to the flat and we went together to the Albert Hall where Alice [Astor] and I were sharing a box for a charity. Camilla and Christopher Sykes – Christopher just back from Persia – were my guests. The place was packed. The performance, a long string of old musical-hall songs. The most popular turn was George Robey and Violet Loraine[6] as themselves singing 'If you were the only girl in the world'. The audience without any fuss joined in and the scene was one of charm and poignancy.

Mottisfont, Sunday June 20

The prospect of two clear days all alone [*day off plus Whitsun Bank Holiday taken at a later date*] was heavenly and 48 hours appeared an eternity. But all too quickly the hours telescoped into each other and duties and obligations popped up their grim faces and I found myself beginning to hurry again. Hurry is what destroys and kills me. I paid a number of visits in the village yesterday but I lay out on the lawn too in a bathing dress to catch the sun which I never see. Today I lay in the sun again, rummaged about the house, inspected bees and kitchen-garden, missed G. often, felt the full melancholy of the house and the beautiful day.

London, Thursday June 24

Dreadfully tired and nervous of not lasting out. Sleeping badly of course. Yesterday B. came to the flat, just as I was going back to the office after lunch, to put a rod in a cupboard and one or two other little jobs. He is good and does these things. It's a great help. It's difficult to get a carpenter. He comes with a bag of tools and sets to work in a deliberate, methodical way. Today felt ill and tired.

London, Sunday June 27

Yesterday work again and a tearing cold started and raged all day. I sat and ached. Spent this morning in bed. Oliver Harvey came for a drink at 12.30

---

6. George Robey (1869-1954) and Violet Loraine (1886-1956) starred opposite each other in the 1916 musical hit *The Bing Boys are Here* singing the duet 'If you were the only girl (in the world)', which became become a signature song of the First World War.

and I put B.'s case before him and asked him whether the FO could find a place for him or if he could think of any other organisation that would. He said it would be difficult because of White Russians bother but he would make inquiries. Went to work after lunch. McLachlan and Angela Whiteman are away on their holidays. The office is quieter without McLachlan, and duller. Raymond telephoned a few days ago. He is still near Glasgow, fears he has failed to get a commission, and thinks he may be going overseas.

London, Wednesday June 30

I. dined yesterday, well and in good spirits and questioning me about the office. He says: you mustn't do too much, you must GO AWAY – and pities and admonishes me. But I tell him not to pity me, that he has saved my life, or given me a new one, that I am engrossed in the work and as happy as I could be under the circumstances. He is tender-hearted and feels partially responsible. We talked a lot about the Admiralty. He has various very significant jobs and is an important person. The work is the work that would suit him. I knew him first when he was 23, a clerk at Reuters and starting out – or dashing out – into the world, a life. That is more than 11 years ago.

London, Saturday July 3

Yesterday was my day off and it seemed like a day of one's childhood, endless, full of delights and surprises. On paper, it sounds prosaic enough. I got up late. I arrived at the hairdresser at 12. I met Boris for lunch at Shanghai, as often before. After lunch we walked about the streets. It was hot and I was craving for sun and air after seven days underground. After shopping in Soho we walked slowly to the National Gallery – much against Boris's inclination – to see a Steer show. Once there B. was quite amused and got a little shaken up from the sight of a lot of pictures he thought awful. I was immensely disappointed. They show each other up badly. Steer was <u>never</u> a great artist. The early beach scenes are the best. On the way to the flat I drew B. into the Redfern Galleries where he had a few more jolts and reactions. He said: 'You must take me more often; it's good for me, even though I know what I am going to think beforehand.' We dined <u>out-of-doors</u> at the White Tower. There was a constant, amusing, trickle of people along the streets and we sat on the pavement till dusk. It was a happy day, as far as I can ever feel happy without G. and with the memory with me for life of his illness, those last years of anxiety, and his death.

London, Thursday July 8

Margot, Cardie and Osbert Peake came to dinner. Margot scolded me lovingly for having neglected her. She told me she was dedicating a new book she hoped some publisher would accept to me, among a number of other people – refugee friends, Bulgarian Ministers and Greek card-playing friends. We talked about Vansittart-ism, which she strongly condemned. We said: What would you do? And she answered, 'Nobody agrees with me but I would make it up with the Germans.'

Raymond isn't being sent abroad for the present. He has arrived back in Matlock and is to do a course for three months and then appear before the Selection Board again. I am very relieved. Reeve, the old butler, was taken seriously ill on Sunday and every evening I have roared myself hoarse on the telephone trying to get onto Mottisfont or in touch with doctors.[7]

On July 9/10 the Allied invasion of Sicily commenced.

Mottisfont, Sunday July 11

Yesterday great news: Landing in Sicily. McLachlan couldn't sit still for long and Serpell who has been ill reappeared. They kept popping out of the room to pay visits and get further news. I came down here by the 5.30 very tired. Today Colonel Bishop came. I got him to witness my will and we talked about his running the shoot for me this autumn as I shan't be able to do so myself.

London, Wednesday July 14

To London by 8.47 train on Monday, carrying roses and raspberries and bringing milk. Elvira met me with a taxi at Waterloo (this is the usual arrangement now), dropped me at the Admiralty and went on to the flat. The Russians who have been attacked south of Moscow are holding their own. This is the first summer they haven't reeled back for hundreds of miles. It may still come but I don't think so. Today went to Zwemmer's, saw there some etchings by Matisse and Picasso and had them sent on approval. Picasso always walks away from Matisse.

---

7. This is typical of Maud. When the gamekeeper, Jack Peach, was taken ill in 1957 Maud rang from Italy to arrange for him to be moved to a private ward and to be examined by specialists from London, according to his son Bob (conversation 7 June 2016).

London, Friday July 16

Van, Sarita, her son Collie Barclay[8] and Ian lunched. I wanted Ian and Van to meet, and I. was anxious to as well. Ian jumped into my taxi at the Admiralty and we got to the flat in good time. The Vans were slow at starting and I thought it was going to be a failure but later Van and I. started on their subjects, time passed, I. missed his daily directive meeting and we got up from the table at 3.30. They talked about many curious things. And Van gave us an account of the reasons why he accepted the post of Diplomatic Adviser, why he stayed on when it turned out to be a bogus job, and how and why he left.

London, Friday July 23

Palermo has fallen. The outskirts of Rome were bombed this week and San Lorenzo Fuori[9] hit. The enemy sent up howls. Let the outskirts of Rome be attacked if there are military objects of importance but not touch the centre – or anywhere near it. At the beginning of the week, I was worried by the thought of the invasion of the Italian mainland and the billeting of officers in numbers on Italian towns. That they might try and 'collect' from houses, gardens or churches and that this must not be allowed to happen and guidance given in advance. I mentioned this to Charles Morgan but his view was that a letter of that sort would imply that our officers were in the habit of stealing.

Mussolini was deposed and imprisoned soon after the invasion of Sicily.

Mottisfont, Monday July 26

Adele called me with the news of Mussolini's fall. All I could say, half asleep under the bed-clothes was: 'You don't say.' This historic happening only evoked those three humdrum monosyllables. And yet I have lived to see the rise and fall of a dictator. 'Bullfrog of the Pontine Marshes', Winston called him and 'Pinchbeck Caesar'. Yesterday a gosling got into the river and couldn't get out. We shooed it up and down the river and finally I plunged in like a spaniel.

8. Sir Colville Barclay (1913-2010), painter. Posted to special operations in the Royal Navy in Second World War.
9. 'Basilica of San Lawrence outside the Walls' in Rome, founded c.580.

London, Wednesday July 28

Yesterday Mussolini was already half-forgotten. Happenings in Italy obscure. Riette, Philippe, Eddy S.W. and Stuart Preston came to dinner and sat talking till 12. Philippe said an ambiguous thing which he didn't know how to explain. He said heavily with a sigh: 'And yet, after all this, at the end of the war, when Germany is beaten, France will have got nothing.' What did he mean? I don't think he quite knew himself. I don't think he meant territorial gains. What does he think <u>we</u> shall have gained? Nothing material. Spiritually, yes, I think a lot.

London, Tuesday August 3

Worked over the bank holiday. The war still goes on – Russians advancing, us gnawing our way forward in Sicily. German towns being appallingly bombed.

London, Friday August 6

Oliver Lyttelton, Cardie, Philippe and Violet Cripps came to dinner on Wednesday. Oliver was in tremendous form and told a lot of funny stories. There were a whole series about Syria – the Vichyites returning to France with their arms and honours of war, the *Marseillaise* being played again and again by a band of Australians on the quayside and, high up, on the hill General de Gaulle and Oliver negotiating in a villa, Gen. de G. rather mystified by the strains of the *Marseillaise*.[10] The party played bridge till after 1 – which nearly killed me and then Philippe stayed on to talk till I turned him out.

Bognor, Friday August 13

Came here yesterday. Found the delicious little house and Diana in all their charm. Katherine Asquith,[11] Evelyn Waugh[12] and Desmond MacCarthy

---

10. As Minister of the Middle East, Lyttelton was responsible for negotiating with de Gaulle the command arrangements for the French colonies and armies during the war. The rendition of the *Marseillaise* to the departing Vichyites would have rubbed de Gaulle up the wrong way during these sensitive talks.

11. Katherine Asquith, *née* Horner (1885-1976), married Raymond Asquith, the son of H.H. Asquith. Roman Catholic convert 1924. Under her influence, Gilbert's brother Conrad, a lifelong agnostic, converted to Roman Catholicism on his deathbed.

12. Evelyn Waugh (1903-66), novelist. Maud never took to Waugh and the feelings appear mutual. Waugh describes a visit to Mottisfont as 'all dishevelled war widows playing Canasta' (letter to Nancy Mitford 28 May 1950).

staying. E.W. never spoke and his ugly, spiteful, stodgy face was the only blemish to the evening. Desmond read aloud passages from a life of Haw-Haw and other propagandists. Waugh was longing to interject pro-German sentiments to irritate us but didn't get the chance. Today Waugh left early and Duff arrived. I was very exhausted and became faint when I was talking to Desmond before lunch. The room was hot because they had lit a fire and he was asking me about G.'s asthma and illness – Desmond is asthmatic too. Suddenly I became faint and had to confess to it. He did everything a fainting person could hope to have done for them. He told me to lie on the floor, he put a pillow under my head, he found smoothly and noiselessly a glass of whisky – yes, and a second – which he made me drink and finally when he saw that I was alright, he said, 'Now I am going to read aloud to you.' He picked up a book of Chekhov's short stories and read the 'Chorus Girl' to me. I can't imagine a happier way of fainting! And I thought, what a nice way it would be to die – lying faint and hearing someone one loved or who was as rare and sympathetic as Desmond reading aloud.

Bognor, Sunday August 15

Duff read aloud after dinner on Friday from a life of Isabella Burton. There were flippant jokes in it about Catholics and the Catholic outlook but I don't think Katherine minded. We lay in the garden most of the afternoon and Peter Quennell, invited by me, arrived. He was nervous because he thought Duff might be fiery and he hardly knew Diana. But things went right straight away. Diana fell for him and Duff liked his company. There was talk after dinner, mostly by Desmond, who described visits he'd made to the great in his youth. He talked about [Oscar] Wilde's niceness to people, charming manners with the clergyman's wife or the dull man or woman in the room, and how he made something sparkling of anything said by them and handed it back to them.

Today we lay in the garden and I talked a good deal to Peter, who asked me for the second time since I have known him, whether I thought he drank too much. For the second time I said: Yes. And for the second time he looked disappointed and rather offended. He is very attractive to women, so Desmond says, so I feel, so I see Diana feels. His face, though, in spite of a sort of desperate beauty, looks mean and he brings a feeling of restlessness into the room with him.

Bognor, Monday August 16

John Julius and his friend Milo Cripps, Fred's son, arrived after dinner having bicycled 30 or 40 miles. John Julius is very natural, clever and charming. The night was perfectly beautiful. We stood in the garden looking at the sky, the moon, the sea, and smelling the strong night smell of the lavender. Overhead, invisible, and in unending procession the bombers set out for Italy and Germany. As I was looking one passed at a great distance just below the moon and then two, like midgets, across its lower half. The bombers roared continuously for three-quarters of an hour. During the night there were three alerts and, during the first, a good deal of firing, some thuds, loudish machine-gunning and sounds of aeroplanes taking evasive action.

London, Friday August 20

Yesterday I dined with Cyril Connolly at 49 Bedford Sq. where he has two floors of charmingly shaped rooms. At dinner there were Mrs Lubbock, who lives with Connolly, Stephen Spender and his half-Russian wife Natasha, Alastair Forbes,[13] Raimund von H., Peter [Quennell] and Philip Toynbee came in at the end of dinner. The food – how one talks of it – was excellent, cooked by the morning-only char who stays on once a week and cooks a very good dinner. On these weekly occasions, Connolly, Mrs L. and Peter, who lives with them, use their week's meat ration entertaining their friends. Most other nights they eat out. Talk was pleasant and controversial. Alastair Forbes, a very handsome young man of 26 or so, talked in an informed serious way about politics chiefly. Connolly has a wonderful imitation of Sibyl Colefax. Today dined with Philippe de Rothschild at the Coq d'Or. He talked about women and sex in that devastatingly analytical French way. The word 'love' was made to include any and every whim and performance. I like him best away from that subject.

The following entry of a work trip is oblique owing to Maud's cautious use of blanks and initials to identify places and people. She was almost certainly visiting the site of subversive propaganda operations at Milton Bryan, run by Sefton Delmer of the Political Warfare Executive. Part of the Woburn Estate in Bedfordshire, the five-acre compound comprised a two-storey, redbrick building and numerous outlying prefab huts to house studios, offices, a

13. Alastair Forbes (1918-2005), writer, journalist. From 1941-45, leader writer, feature writer and book reviewer for *The Observer*, then columnist for *The Daily Mail* and later book reviewer for *The Spectator* among others.

canteen and barracks for intelligence teams, journalists, administrative workers and vetted refugees, prisoners of war and other nationals of occupied countries. The site was surrounded by a high wire-mesh fence and patrolled by armed police with dogs. It was here that Delmer launched in March 1943 the fake German military radio station 'Atlantiksender', among many other counterfeit broadcast and print media initiatives. Every night 'Atlantiksender', and later 'Soldatensender Calais', transmitted live broadcasts of music and 'black' news that ingeniously intermingled truth with fiction to demoralise and weaken the enemy. It drew heavily on intelligence provided by the NID, such as Kriegsmarine movements, the results of bombings on German ports and cities, and personal details about German crews obtained from interrogating prisoners-of-war.

Prior to the outbreak of the Second World War, Herbrand Russell, the Duke of Bedford, offered the Woburn Estate to the government for war work and it was requisitioned after his death. The country headquarters of the Political Warfare Executive hid behind the park's high walls and many installations and residences in the estate's outlying villages were taken over for secret operations or housing. Delmer and his closest team lived in The Rookery in the village of Aspley Guise. Although not part of the Woburn Estate, the decoding centre Bletchley Park was also nearby, creating a critical hub of intelligence activity in the area.

London, Thursday August 26

Worked on Tuesday till 6.30. Then went by train with McLachlan to Blet. [*Bletchley railway station*] where Mrs [*Katherine McLachlan*] met us. Stayed the night with them at Woodcote [*McLachlan's house in Apsley Guise*]. Russell ground. I leant out of my window, watched the stars, smelt the night air, thought of G. and my Russells, and cried. How strange G. would think all this. As we passed them [*on the way to Woodcote*], Mc. said, 'Those are the London Gates' [*into Woburn park*]. I didn't say I had been through them. There was the usual Mc. confusion in the morning but, as usual, everything worked out alright. D. [*Sefton Delmer*] fetched me in his car. In the back sat Cyrus,[14] and the Ch.,[15] whom I didn't yet know. D.'s charm is enormous

---

14. Mr. Cyrus is named in a file in the National Archives as having a visitor's pass to The Rookery in Aspley Guise where Sefton Delmer lived with his wife Isabel and 'the Chief' (see following footnote), together with other close members of Delmer's team. However, I have not managed to identify Cyrus's role.

15. This almost certainly refers to 'the Chief', or 'Der Chef' in the original (*continued*)

and his face very unusual and fascinating. And his voice too. We arrived at [*blank*] off., almost in a little village [*Milton Bryan*]. And again Russell soil. I thought of this, of G., of Ian, of my fate many times. I was then taken round, shown everything, introduced, treated royally. Extraordinary, unreal, very interesting. I spent some useful time checking up on my own job. I stood and talked and got very tired. By lunch time I was dead. This last hour I spent with Ha.[16] Finally I broke away, to the lavatory, and drank a great dollop of whisky. Lunched in the canteen sitting between Ha. and Ch.[17] whom I liked. Ugly twisted face, profoundly melancholic. After lunch, my sightseeing over, I lay in a rough grass field near the huts and read *Petits Poèmes en prose* [Charles Baudelaire] which I had borrowed from Mc.'s bookshelves and reflected and thought again about the ground I was lying on. A wren in an OHMS [*On His Majesty's Service*] car took me to W. [*Woburn Abbey*] where I changed into another car and drove to B. [*Bletchley*] and there, quite exhausted, caught a train to London.

I. came to dinner and heard a full account. When I said how royally I had been shown round he said, 'Ah, they looked on you as someone from the Admiralty. It's respect for the Admiralty. They don't often see people. And someone from the Admiralty is important to them.' I felt rather proud to think I had represented the Admiralty for a few hours. We talked a lot. I was half-dead with fatigue and such strange impressions and sent I. away before midnight.

Mottisfont, Sunday August 29

Worked till 5 yesterday then took 5.30 train here with Boris. I was very tired. Found Tony and Sally here for their holiday. And a new butler. Poor Reeve died a fortnight ago. He was an old friend and had shared all our country life with us from Heveningham [*Hall, leased by Russells in 1928*] onwards. Boris finished cutting down the bamboo clump – he started it three weeks ago – which Cecil Rhodes had planted. There is plenty more of it along the spring-bank. An old crab-apple on the north side of the house was planted by Sir Hudson Lowe.

(*continued*) German, the broadcast name of a fake, highly patriotic Prussian officer who presented the counterfeit German radio station, *Gustav Siegfried Eins*. Der Chef was played by Peter Seckelmann, a German refugee who left Berlin in 1938. Launched in May 1941, *Gustav Siegfried Eins* was Sefton Delmer's first clandestine radio station.
16. Squadron Leader Edward Halliday, project manager, who designed the Milton Bryan studios.
17. As 'Ch.' is not preceded by 'the', this may refer to Clifton Child (b.1912), who was in charge of intelligence at Milton Bryan. Previously a corporate in the Royal Signals Corp and in the Foreign Office's Political Intelligence Department.

London, Thursday September 2

Lunch and dinner in bed Monday, Tuesday and Wednesday because of exhaustion. Tuesday morning I didn't go to the office but telephoned to say I was ill. Yesterday evening Dr Rossdale came and gave me a partial overhaul. This evening B. came to dinner. He said, 'My love has too much agony' and 'I shall never love again.'

London, Saturday September 4

Yesterday early, mainland Italy was invaded by the Eighth Army [*led by the British general Bernard Montgomery*]. I am glad it was the Eighth Army and not the Americans. The mainland of Europe. Hair and manicure before the office. Alice, Stuart [Preston], Cyril Connolly, Mrs Lubbock and Gerald Berners dined. Cyril C. is very amusing. His imitations are admirable. I like him better. Though totally different in every other way, when he is amused he has a half-smirk, half-smile which is exactly like Osbert Sitwell's.[18] This half-smirk is very characteristic of Osbert. It's the visible sign of his innate feeling of superiority. I don't know whether this is so with Cyril.

Mottisfont, Sunday September 5

Mama and I came here yesterday. Tony and Sally are still here. It's a pleasure to see Tony in the country. He's like a bird set free. This afternoon two American billeting officers spent nearly two hours here with a view to taking over a good part of the house as a rest home for airmen. American No. 1 tried to win me over by saying he would get me into the American Red Cross and put me in charge of my own house as hostess. Also he would pay the servants. How many gardeners did I keep? Five? He would pay those. Didn't I mow the lawns? Not since the war? Did the machine run on gasoline? Yes? Well, he would let me have gasoline. I declined all these invitations. Saw the gamekeeper Peach[19] and the riverkeeper [Robert] Coxen.

On September 8, the signing of an Armistice with Italy is announced but the

18. Sir Osbert Sitwell (1892-1969), writer. Maud met Osbert at a dance during the First World War and was close friends with him up until her marriage in 1917.
19. John Robert 'Jack' Peach (1898-1973). Served in Gilbert's regiment, the Grenadier Guards. Worked as gamekeeper for Gilbert when the Russells leased Stanway House in Gloucestershire in early 1930s and was subsequently hired at Mottisfont.

country falls into Civil War with some forces remaining loyal to the Axis
powers and others joining the Allies.

London, Thursday September 9

Yesterday there was great suppressed excitement and whisperings in the office. Angela Whiteman and I didn't feel quite certain whether it was only because an Italian Littorio-class battleship had slipped out of Taranto or whether it was because the Italians were caving in. There are often great flutters over smaller things than armistices. By teatime, though, we knew without being told. Serpell said Fleming was speaking on the BBC German Naval Programme at six. The script was only ready a few minutes before. At six we tuned in, heard first the announcement of the Armistice with Italy in German to the German seamen, and then Ian's talk to them. It was very well done. His voice is excellent – firm, vigorous and dignified. I was pleased with the performance and told him so later when he came to dinner. When I left the Admiralty there was no excitement in the streets. The British public aren't fools though the newspapers try to make them so. I. was exhausted with the week's excitements. He was satisfied but not the least bit exuberant. Today an exciting, restless day in the office. For the last one and a half hours, I was left quite alone and had to deal with Press Division's tantrums [*possibly because intelligence material provided by NID 17Z and used on the BBC's German naval programme could not be broadcast by other BBC services or UK media*].

Mottisfont, Sunday September 12

Friday another busy exciting day. Everybody flying about. We are making further landings in Italy and the Germans are seizing all they can. Friday night came the news that they had entered Rome. I am afraid Italy will become a battlefield after all. Yesterday feeling of restlessness and excitement continued in the office. Mc. went off on leave and I came here on 5.30. Mama came down earlier. Today after lunch, like bad pennies, the Americans turned up. The idea now is to take two-thirds of the house for 'high-ranking' officers and their domestics. They asked me to leave blankets, linen, china, glass, kitchen utensils and silver for them to use.

London, Thursday September 16

Yesterday Boris came to dinner. Poor, poor Boris. He is miserable at having no job and feeling unwanted and eating into his capital. And indeed it's a crisis for him. He thinks his art won't be wanted after the war, saying that it's luxury art. MacColl[20] has been urging him to take up painting again. B. wanted my advice. I didn't know what to say. I felt he might never be able to make a living by it and that he would have a thousand disappointments. His conscience and his affection have always made Maroussia a first charge on his resources and the studio in Hampstead is hers and a couple of policies.

London, Sunday September 19

Yesterday work from 9.30 till after 7 with Serpell. The others were away. Salerno was a worry for some days. The Americans were all but driven into the sea. Mussolini has been rescued by German paratroopers from his mountain eyrie. Very dramatic. Very funny. Rather silly of us to let poor, big-hatted *carabinieri* [*Italian police*] guard him.

London, Tuesday September 21

I. came to dinner, worried and rather unhappy about his job, the slowness and unimaginativeness of most people he has to deal with, the caution and avoidance of responsibility. His old boss suited him admirably. This one doesn't at all.[21] He is conventional and hasn't an idea. And he doesn't like fighting battles. Old DNI was very different it appears. Poor I. He was dismayed and talked about Hawaii and leaving the Admiralty as soon as the war is over. He thinks we shall sink back into slothfulness, indifference and become ostriches again just as we did after the last war. And that in a future war we shan't have time to collect ourselves and hold out till things are ready. We shall be smashed straightaway. There will be a Pearl Harbour on London and other vital spots without a declaration of war. Rocket bombs or their more modern successors will destroy us in a few hours. He talked as if he believed in this horrible prediction. He wears himself out.

20. Dugald Sutherland MacColl (1859-1948), Scottish watercolour painter and museum administrator. Close friend of Boris's.
21. In November 1942, Rear-Admiral Edmund Rushbrooke (1892-1972) replaced Admiral John Godfrey (1888-1970) as Director Naval Intelligence. Fleming is thought to have based James Bond's boss 'M' at least partly on Godfrey.

On September 22, Maud goes to Mottisfont for nine days of leave.

Mottisfont, Monday September 27

Terrible depression thinking of G. and that I can't bear life without him unless I am busy working. I don't want to die but I think of death. Mottisfont is terribly lonely without G. Saw the agent on Friday and had a long talk about the estate. Taught Adele to make a cheese. Claud and Ath, John Follett and Violet B.-C. staying. Asked Claud's advice about writing to Lady Louis Mountbatten, whose husband has just been appointed Commander-in-Chief South East Asia, mentioning Martin. Claud thought the idea good. I love having the Russells round me. They bring back some of my life to me.

London, Friday October 1

I wrote to Edwina Mountbatten giving her, briefly, Martin's history, saying he might be doing useful and interesting work but I didn't know – and if he wasn't, perhaps Admiral Mountbatten might be able to place him. Don't like doing this but if I don't nobody else will. Yesterday visited in the village. Saw Italian prisoners draining land near Oakley and spoke stumbling Italian to them. Leave over. I was unhappy almost all the time and weighed down.

London, Wednesday October 6

Started work again last Saturday feeling ill, exhausted and head ached. Nearly didn't go but thought I'd better and indeed was glad I did because both men were alone as Angela was ill and C.B. away. Feeling of illness wore off gradually. Juliet Duff, Eddy and B. dined. After B. had left Eddy said he must have been a dreadfully difficult husband and what poor Helen had to put up with! I don't believe he was a difficult husband for one moment, but I daresay he made – and he told me he did – dreadful scenes when Helen told him she was going to leave him for Fry. Today Edwina Mountbatten telephoned to say Lord Louis had gone off to India with my letter about Martin in his pocket. She said she couldn't promise anything because if Martin was doing useful work, Lord Louis wouldn't feel justified in moving him.

London, Thursday October 7

I. came to dinner looking tired and harrassed. His job seems a series of combats at the moment. He regrets the old DNI every moment of the day. We talked and talked. He likes hearing all about life in 17Z – the personalities, the jokes, the minor tragedies; Mr Morgan's luncheon dates and the ordering of tables; the bores who drift in for a bit of talk and news; and our great hunts when the fox breaks cover, hounds give tongue and off we all go madly across country, taking our fences in our various ways. The gallant Mc. well to the fore, the checks and disappointments, the troubles, the barbed wire of Press Division, Air Ministry and others. Mc., undaunted, casting hounds onto the scent again – baying voices – all off again.

London, Wednesday October 13

Miss C.B. of 17Z came back to lunch with me on Monday. She's a character, a card. She's conducting a private hunt at this moment on the origin of the Free German Movement in London. She is middle-aged, disillusioned, affectionate, loyal, hard-working, doesn't make a fuss, sceptical and at the same time inclined to believe any old nonsense without using her judgement – as many elderly women do. That night I took the last of four anti-catarrhal injections and had a violent and unpleasant reaction three-quarters of an hour after the injection; aching bones and head, a tightening of the jaw-bones, shivers, horrible acne and slight spasms. Most of these beastlinesses subsided within an hour but shivers and temperature remained. Yesterday no Admiralty of course. Lay like death. Dr Rossdale came and said it was a protein reaction.

Maud spends the rest of the week at home recovering.

Mottisfont, Sunday October 17

Yesterday B. came to lunch and sweetly and kindly took me to the station and put me on the train as I felt weak. He is my best friend. Ian would do many things for me, but not these small warming things. Alexie is here for a long weekend.

London, Wednesday October 20

Yesterday to London on 11.20 train. Went tottering to the Admiralty after lunch and spent three hours there. Serpell away with a sinus, McLachlan looking very tired, the others well except Mr Morgan who retired snuffling. I haven't missed much. Times were uneventful. Progress in Italy very slow. Today Boris came to an early dinner because there are small raids every night and he likes to get back to Maroussia who is very nervous.

London, Friday October 22

Yesterday dined with Sibyl at Lord North Street. Sat next to Major [Desmond] Morton[22] – Winston's man. He had an excellent story about Winston. The French had been especially difficult and Winston had had a row with them. Morton found the PM pacing up and down, late at night, in a dressing-gown and with a cigar in his mouth. He was delivering an oration to an empty room, a tremendous denunciation of the French: 'Not once but many are the times I have warned the British Public against putting their faith in the French, to whom corruption, treachery, assassination etc. etc.' On and on he went with his magnificence. Then, looking up, he saw Morton standing aghast with his mouth open and said, with a smile, 'You mustn't take me too seriously' and continued his denunciation. He was getting it off his chest. Morton thinks as I do that Russia doesn't dream of making a separate peace. She would only try and do so if she were collapsing and that doesn't seem likely anymore.

London, Tuesday October 26

I was determined to see the late First Sea Lord Sir Dudley Pound's[23] funeral. The two women in the office weren't interested. Mr Morgan said he hated funerals and thought he would spend the time at his Club. Mc. said he loved spectacles and was going to try and see it from some window. By various happy chances and a little persistence I saw it from the steps of a statue close to Horse Guards Arch. I saw the rather sad procession start off in a little yellow fog which subdued all colour and made almost invisible all uniforms. The only figure that stood out most extraordinarily was Winston's. He wore a coal-black frock coat and a superbly brushed top hat. He walked alone, walking like a great bull moving its head from one side to another. His silhouette was immensely vigorous, masculine and powerful. There was a moment when the only sounds were the rolling of the drums, the hum of fighters overhead and the pretty, clear, somehow anachronistic chime of the Horse Guards bell, a strange, painful combination of sounds.

---

22. Major Sir Desmond Morton (1891-1971), army officer who served in Foreign Office as intelligence officer 1919-39. A friend of Winston Churchill's and appointed his personal assistant in 1940.
23. Admiral of the Fleet Sir Alfred Dudley Pound (1877-1943). First Sea Lord 1939 to September 1943, when he resigned due to poor health, dying shortly afterwards.

London, Saturday October 30

Day in bed with cold in spite of four anti-catarrhal injections. Got up to have dinner with I. Talked about every kind of thing as usual: Admiralty, personalities, happenings, the funeral, love, death, marriage, houses, Tahiti – or any escape island – and the formidable future till after 12 o'clock. I. told me he is sending orders round that people are to be careful of their health. There will be a lot of sickness this winter and people are to avoid, by staying away for a few days, being more ill than they need be.

On November 6, the Soviets recapture Kiev in the Ukraine.

Bognor, Sunday November 7

Came here early after lunch on Friday having asked for a few days off from the Admiralty as I feel so weak and can't get well. Diana and Oggie [Olga Lynn] were on the train. Enid Jones[24] and Desmond MacCarthy came later. Yesterday Duff came for lunch. He thinks the war in Europe will be over this winter. When I asked 'Why?' he said, 'What have they got to fight for, what hopes can they have? They will be beaten out of Italy in time and pushed back to Germany on the Russian front. Their production is decreasing, ours increasing. And there is the air-bombardment. They must see there is no hope of winning.' Desmond MacCarthy says Harold Nicolson is back from a visit to Sweden and that several people tried to get in touch with him to put out peace-feelers. Duff told a story about Singapore which he said was the most shattering moment of the war for him. For a month and more he'd been idle there, his report (which was the sole reason for his being sent out) having been taken back to England four or five weeks before. His idleness irked him and he telephoned the PM to say so and ask what his orders were. On that particular morning the reply came saying he was to stay on as Resident Minister. He dressed and went off to see the Commander in Chief and said, 'I have a piece of news for you. I have been asked to remain here as Resident Minister and to form a Council.' The C. in C. replied, 'I have a piece of news for you. The *Prince of Wales* and *Repulse* were sunk this morning.' Only a few days before they had seen these wonderful ships arrive, escorted by seven destroyers and had felt thankful.

Trying to follow a regime based on common sense, I went to my bedroom after 11.30, leaving them talking. I excused myself saying I liked going to

24. Enid Bagnold (1889-1981), novelist.

bed early. Duff said, 'She is like Charles Lamb who said he made up for coming late by leaving early'[25] – for I like getting up late and do whenever I can.

Bognor, Monday November 8

Yesterday at lunch talk turned to our nannies and Desmond had a story I liked. He asked his nurse when he was a little boy whether she'd ever told a lie. He knew she was very good but thought she might have told three or four. Her answer was, 'I can't remember. I have told ever so many.' Desmond said, 'I knew she was a very good woman – I understood it and felt it – so ever since then I have never been really surprised when good people did things they shouldn't have done.' As he said this his face was a little shy and very gentle and humorous. I am here alone this afternoon. I asked to stay till tomorrow. It's peaceful. I feel calm. If I knew I should see Gilbert again there is nothing I could want. See G. again and not be parted.

London, Wednesday November 10

I. came to dinner and we talked till after 12. He warned me to leave London if he gave the word. I slept uneasily because of this, wondering how I could have the face to do so. And thinking of other people.

London, Wednesday November 17

Doria Scott, Duff and Oliver [Lyttelton] dined. Duff has just been appointed ambassador to the French Committee of National Liberation in Algiers. An awkward moment with the French is on over the Lebanon and Duff said, 'It's very lucky this happened before I arrived. If it had happened while I was there, everybody would have said, "There you see, that's what happens when Duff Cooper goes anywhere – first Singapore, now Algiers and the Lebanese trouble."' He had a charming story about that troublesome word Amgot [*Allied Military Government for Occupied Territories*]. The PM told Sir Alec Cadogan[26] he had heard Amgot meant 'heap of shit' in Turkish and would

---

25. 'I always arrive late at the office, but I make up for it by leaving early'. Charles Lamb (1775-1834), essayist, writer.
26. Sir Alexander Cadogan (1884-1968), diplomat and civil servant. Replaced Robert Vansittart as Permanent Undersecretary for Foreign Affairs 1938-46, enjoying the confidence of both Eden and Churchill.

he find out if this were so. Sir Alec inquired and reported thus: 'I have made inquiries and find Amgot does not mean heap of shit. On the other hand my informant tells me that Amch (pronounced <u>very</u> gutturally) means in Turkish – as every schoolboy knows – arsehole, and Ghhot – as every schoolboy knows – cunt. Do you want to take further action?' The prime minister was put in a good frame of mind for the rest of the day. He laughed and laughed. I was staggered to find that Oliver too thinks the war in Europe will be over before the spring. He thinks everything is moving fast. I can't believe it will. He was quite confident, more than confident – certain. I think they are all wrong.

Mottisfont, Sunday November 21

This morning I came down here for 24 hours. The calm and beauty struck me anew. While I had lunch the American major billeted in the house came and sat with me and later brought his girlfriend in too. He said nicely and frankly, 'When we came over here we thought we were going to finish things off in no time,' and he added, laughing at himself, 'but now I'm afraid we shall be here for years.'

London, Thursday November 25

Today was a long exhausting day. I went down to Mottisfont by the 9.30 train. Major Sebree and three Americans met me at Winchester. I rushed them over the house – they only had three-quarters of an hour for it – and I saw they fancied it. They pressed me to lunch at Shaftesbury with them in one of the houses they have taken over but I said no thanks, and walked instead by the river. I caught the 2.50 train to London.

London, Wednesday December 8

Major Sebree, the American, came on Monday and talked more about Mottisfont and I produced the plans for him. He couldn't <u>promise</u> to leave me three or four rooms. I felt distracted at the thought of having to pack everything I have into the flat and in dismay at the confusion of lost papers and things I have to get at, apart from sadness at the thought of not having Mottisfont to live in. Finally I decided to ask Crinks to write to Archie Sinclair and put my case, ask what powers the Americans have, and plead to be allowed three or four rooms.

London, Thursday December 9

Dinner at the Dorchester in the nature of a farewell to Duff and Diana. Three tables and about 25 *convives*. Some of the people there: Lords Anglesey, Hood, Hinchingbrook, Rothermere, Queensberry, Lord and Lady Gage, Oggie [Olga Lynn], Baroness Budberg, Chips Channon, Ronnie Tree, Juliet [Lady Juliet Duff], Alfred and Lady Beit, Ann O'Neill, Desmond MacCarthy and a few others. I sat between Charlie Anglesey and Sammy Hood but was moved later on to sit between Duff and Francis Queensberry. Fr. Q. told me about the Queensberry Club for the troops which he started and runs in Soho. 45,000 members, pays its way like hell. Vast success. Dancing, shows, food, no drink, always full, all nationalities. Ann O'Neill was in very good looks, fatter than she used to be and all but beautiful. The party broke up earlyish as all these parties do.

London, Sunday December 12

Yesterday Major Sebree tried to induce me to get my letter back from the Air Ministry. I asked Crinks's advice. He said: no, do nothing. Dined with Sam Courtauld at Marietta's in a private room. It was a party in honour of Christabel's birthday. I sat between Boris and Sam, and then was moved and sat between Arnold Foster and Sir Eric Maclagan,[27] an agreeable old boy, most disagreeably ugly – a sort of withered, Quakerish, Liberalish, sick-man. We talked about Victorian customs and manners and he had a good story about his great-aunts. Their father had taken the three girls aged 16 to 22 to Rome and they were ascending the staircase round the Dome of St Peter's, early in the nineteenth century. Suddenly their guide, who had gone on ahead, came running back and told them with great excitement that in a moment they would meet coming down a world-famed celebrity, no less a person than Lord Byron. I daresay the young women were agog but their Papa was aghast at the thought of Don Juan, that worse than Satan, passing so close to his doves. He ordered them to turn their faces to the wall which, poor things, they had to do. So they never saw Lord Byron but how they must have trembled as he limped past them.

London, Monday December 20

Lisel Müller came to lunch. Tante Fritze, now 79, had a slight stroke in the autumn, recovered partially but is very weak and failing mentally. Tante

27. Sir Eric Maclagan (1879-1951), museum director, art historian.

Agnes Mühsam and her son Hans Werner disappeared from Berlin six or more months ago. Like other Jews. They are probably dead. Otto Franck [*Lisel's brother*] who was in Yugoslavia till sometime this year has disappeared too. I think there may be a chance he is in hiding. Lisel heard indirectly a year or so ago that her husband was alive. He was then an interpreter, she thinks, in the German army. He speaks Arabic so he may have been in North Africa.

London, Tuesday December 21

Major Sebree came to see me again and again we discussed Mottisfont as a rest home for bomber crews. Archie Sinclair wrote to Crinks that he could tell me that there was little doubt I would be left in my corner of Mottisfont and that the Americans 'seemed to have taken the law into their own hands.'

Mottisfont, Saturday December 25

Alexie, Mary, Anthony, Paul, Peter and their nannie staying for Xmas. At 6.30 yesterday the village choir sang carols from the dining-room. Great improvement. They sing quite musically. Today Xmas day. After lunch I heard the King's Broadcast from the stables where I was visiting the Goulds [*who looked after the evacuee children*]. Then church 3.30 with Mama. Fine old carols, plenty of them. *O Israel* which I specially favour.

London, Sunday December 26

B. and Elvira met me at the station relieving me of luggage, game and produce and dropping me at the Admiralty. I was alone with Mc. all day. Towards evening came the news of the engagement with the *Scharnhorst*.[28] Ian came to dinner, back from the Cairo conference [*a meeting of the British, US and Chinese leaders on Asia Pacific strategy and post-war Asia on November 22-26*]. The meetings were held at Mena House [*the Cairo hotel by the Pyramids*]. The surroundings were like an armed camp, soldiers, guns, anti-aircraft guns etc. guarding the precious delegates – the PM, President and Chiang. When Ian was taken ill with influenza, he sank back exhausted in bed and lay blissfully resting, looking through the window at the blue sky and eating delicious food. He was very struck by the desert, sand and camels.

28. The Royal Navy sank the German battle-cruiser *Scharnhorst* off northern Norway on December 26, 1943 as it was trying to intercept an Allied convoy of supplies to the Soviet Union.

He flew out over the North African battlefields and came back tossed about in a cruiser.

London, Thursday December 30

On Monday the *Scharnhorst* sinking kept us very busy.[29] Serpell was away and Angela Whiteman too. Only Mc., C.B. and I in the room. If I had been Serpell I should have rushed back. Then came the news of the sinking of the blockade runner and more excitement. Tuesday another very busy day. Serpell back but Angela still away and C.B. only in the morning. News of destroyer action in the Bay. I read the official Admiralty communiqué on the *Scharnhorst* over the telephone to the BBC German Naval Programme and while I was doing it stupid Charles Morgan, who never uses the typewriter, went to it and laboriously hammered away while Serpell tapped away in another corner of the room. I was exhausted with work and the excitement and felt my voice going. Today still lots of work at the Admiralty. Angela reappeared having missed most of the fun. But I don't think most of these people mind. Only Mc. reacts as I do, froths and fizzes over with inward excitement. I. of course is the same as Mc. and I – tension, excitement, hammering energy.

London, Saturday January 1, 1944

Work began to slacken yesterday but my inward excitement remained as I thought back over the events of the week. Dined in bed and after dinner read through some of Gilbert's letters to Flora. He became clearer to me again and I saw again the sweetness, gayness and comic side of his character. Just before midnight 1943-1944 I came across his letter to Flora and Diana announcing our engagement and written exactly 27 years before. He described me most sweetly but I felt surprised that he described me as highly-strung – which I generally manage to conceal so that people talk of my 'calm'. I didn't know he'd seen it after knowing me such a short time. I don't think I thought he ever really knew about it. Alas, alas, my husband and 25 years with him all gone and disappeared. I sometimes think how wonderful it would be if the bell rang and I went to the door, opened it and saw him standing there smiling, saying, 'Well, I'm back.' And I should say, 'Oh, oh, you've come back at last.'

---

29. Among subversive activities coordinated by Room 17Z, Frank Lynder, Milton Bryan's German naval specialist, did a bogus personal account of the sinking of the *Scharnhorst* pretending to be a surviving crew member (Howe, p. 182).

Mottisfont, Monday January 3

Yesterday Admiralty for eighth day running in the morning. Boris came to lunch, neurasthenic, depressed, difficult. Poor Boris. No work and this painful, tormenting love for me. He took me to the station. I only just managed not to quarrel. He has started painting again. He has decided to starve, if need be, and stick to art. He is right. Today had a quiet day at Mottisfont with Alexie and a walk through the watermeadows looking at the many channels, carriers and drains the Italians have dug out and cleaned up.

Mottisfont, Sunday January 9

Eddy S.W. came to dinner on Friday and told me how at the beginning of the war he'd made his home with the Kenneth Clarks. Both sides were enthusiastic to start with and he felt he'd found a second home. But after a while, Lady C. became restive and eventually he left. He said, 'I always put all my eggs in one basket; I do it all the time.' I daresay he would be enervating to have with one all the time. Elvira makes special preparations when he comes to dinner. I think she has designs to see me chatelaine of Knole! [*the Sackville family's grand stately home in Kent*].

London, Thursday January 13

Ian dined and talked about his plans for the future, whether to take a newspaper job with the *Daily Telegraph* and go on hustling and bustling all his life, or whether to live in a cottage, take off his collar and tie, and write a novel or two. Then pros and cons of marriage. I said he would be happier married and shouldn't leave it too long – not after 40. It will be difficult for him to disengage from all his present S. activities for he is up to his neck in them. He is worn out almost every time I see him and wants to talk about cottages, seashores, Tahiti, long naked holidays on coral islands and marriage.

London, Friday January 21

Went to the Leicester Square Galleries on Tuesday. Saw a small pretty oil by Delacroix and reserved it.[30] I bought the Delacroix on Wednesday. Off duty

---

30. Undated note to diary entry reads: 'This Delacroix was sold by Percy Muir Turner to Sir Michael Sadler. I bought it at the sale by his Executors.' Sotheby's found the Delacroix 'not to be genuine' after Maud's death and valued it at £200.

at 4 on Friday, went to flat and rested and was fetched by Crinks and taken to a revue where I laughed for the first time for months. I never laugh now, that's the trouble. Smile yes, chuckle yes, but hardly ever laugh. We dined sumptuously at the Ritz on oysters, champagne, two saddles of hare and a pudding. Crinks sold everything he possessed in 1939. He had a great many interesting and beautiful things. He said, 'I got fed up and told Sotheby's to get rid of everything I've got.' He didn't keep one single thing.

London, Monday January 24

Ian dined and talked till midnight. He's always anxious about me, my health, my sleeping, my happiness.

On January 27, Leningrad is relieved after a two and a half year siege.

Mottisfont, Sunday January 30

Came here yesterday. Raymond M., Eddy S.W., Mrs Lubbock, Cyril Connolly and Philip Toynbee staying. A lot of literary talk, several quick tiffs, over at once, between Cyril and Raymond, Eddy and Raymond. A lot of lunging in a friendly way and a good deal of laughter. I liked two stories about Brian Howard.[31] He was at a restaurant, rather drunk and had been talking wild, indiscreet, war stuff in a loud voice. An angry Colonel got up, came to his table and said in an icy voice, 'Your name, Sir.' 'Mrs Smith,' answered Howard. In the other story Howard was walking in his rolling manner along the street and a man who was working below pavement-level popped his head out and said, 'Hello Gertie.' '<u>Lady Gertrude</u> to <u>you</u>,' said Howard. Cyril told a story of how he and Mrs Lubbock coming out of the Ivy together in the blackout, heard a man just in front of them saying, 'I must say I quite agree with Virginia Woolf. I don't like that smarty-boots Conn<u>o</u>lly,' (putting the accent on the second syllable and pronouncing the O as in hole). What riled C. most was the agreeing with Virginia Woolf.

Hanson who has been our chauffeur for 20 years died 10 days ago of cancer. His death was most sad and painful to me. He had a delightful personality. Children adored him and grown-ups made friends with him at

31. Brian Howard (1905-58), poet and writer for *New Statesman*. One of the so-called 'Oxford Wits', a group of literary and intellectual aesthetes at Oxford University in the early twenties, including Harold Acton, Cyril Connolly, John Betjeman, Alan Pryce-Jones and Christopher Sykes.

once, preferring to sit on the front seat next to him than inside that old, high, big Rolls Royce. I connect him with the early years of my happy married life, before big country houses came into it, and when we had small houses at Westgate or Sandwich for the children. He helped undress them on the beach, took them paddling, mended toys and my earrings and, when we left London for one of these places, loaded the car with the children's toys and books, a dog or two, tortoises, the aquarium with the crocodile and a smaller one full of frogs and salamanders. Those were sweet times. I mourn him as a friend.

London, Wednesday February 2

I have received a letter to say Mottisfont would probably be requisitioned as a small hospital [by the War Department rather than for US officers].

Boris has been ill again, with another chill. I promised Maroussia medicines and she came to fetch them after lunch. Her face is very handsome, savage, animal and barbaric.

London, Sunday February 6

Yesterday I. came to dinner, looking well and busy with a dream, the dream being a house and 10 acres on a mountain slope in Jamaica after the war.

London, Tuesday February 8

I was very tired and took yesterday off. What we all suffer from is lack of fresh air. We sit underground, work by electric light and have virtually no fresh air. Once every afternoon I go up and walk on Horse Guards Parade for five minutes and save my life. Tonight dined with Glenconners. Oliver Lyttelton there. Had to go at 10 to a meeting of the Defence Committee with the PM. Oliver looks haggard and says he is only just alive. Winston, he says, is in remarkably good form but did say the other night at 1.30 that he was rather tired and thought he would go to bed and that is very unusual. Oliver teased Christopher [Glenconner], rather heavily and bluntly, about having swallowed, like so many others, the Nazi hook and bait before the war. He was rather uncomfortably downright. It's true that Christopher's cousin Ernest and his firm were in with the Germans and Christopher began to lean that way but the hook was never more than just in his mouth. If the war hadn't come when it did, it might have got further. A desire to see fair play to a beaten enemy combined with practical advantages might have been too much for Christopher.

Mottisfont, Friday February 11

To Mottisfont on Wednesday. Engines broke down and we arrived at Winchester two hours late drawn by two gasping duds. This happens all the time now. Shortage of engines and no time to overhaul them thoroughly. Yesterday Colonel Bishop came and discussed requisitioning. Later Colonel Atkinson ADMS [*Assistant Director Medical Services*], sleepy, vague and a much sharper underling came along and we went over the house deciding on the rooms. I am being left with mine and Gilbert's bedrooms, Adele's and Rose's, the morning room and the billiard room and Rex's room to store furniture in. They were tempted to take Rex's room as a ward because of its size and airiness. After many hesitations they decided against it, fearing it would be impossible to stop damage if it were a ward. I am lucky to have to deal with Bishop who is most fair and reasonable.

A letter arrived from Kitty [*living in Ouchy, Switzerland*]. It was uncensored, posted in London, must have been brought by hand [*to England*]. She recounted her efforts to find out whether Tante Emmy [*Maria Nelke's sister*] is still alive after the many bombings of Berlin. Her flat was untouched as late as January but she did not appear to be in it. She is nearly 80, poor old thing. She should have moved to the country a year ago.

Mottisfont, Saturday February 12

Found a letter on my tray stamped Supreme Commander, South East Asia Command – that means Admiral Mountbatten – and thought he must be writing to say he was employing Martin. Disappointment. He wrote to say that the numbers of his establishment were rigidly controlled, that he was afraid he could do nothing, but that he had, all the same, made inquiries about Martin and that these had been unsuccessful, because presumably Martin was no longer in Colombo but had moved elsewhere. I wish to God he'd never written. I didn't expect him to. And now he has put this idea in my head of Martin having been moved. Martin's last wire was sent early in November.

London, Wednesday February 16

Ian, Oliver Lyttelton and Peter and Poppy Thursby[32] came to dinner. I. and Oliver are always funny together. They like each other, laugh at each other,

---

32. Poppy Thursby, *née* Baring (1901-79), daughter of Sir Godfrey Baring. Married Peter Thursby in 1928.

banter and wrangle and behave like two very young men who, attracted and half in love with each other (perfectly chastely as young men are), can't leave each other alone and are always teasing and tearing each other about like puppies. They first met staying with us at Stanway and the fun started straightaway. They wrangled away up to bed and into I.'s room. Gilbert, when he came to mine, said, 'Oliver and Ian have fallen in love with each other.' Oliver is 16 or 17 years older. I didn't remind him that when I saw him in the autumn he said he thought the war would be over by the spring.

Maud takes a fortnight's leave from the Admiralty to handle the requisitioning of Mottisfont.

Mottisfont, Sunday February 20

Up early on Friday and started sorting and stacking books trying my best to be economical with space. Yesterday the same – mostly books. Today 101 things and moving wine in a wheelbarrow from the outer cellar to safer places. The butler pushed the wheelbarrow. Adele and I stacked 300 bottles. No breakages. I think a lot about Gilbert and my heart aches. Earlier this week I cabled to Martin saying I hadn't heard from him for over three months and could he please telegraph.

Mottisfont, Sunday February 27

The requisition started officially on Monday 21st and five furniture movers arrived. They stacked the furniture in Rex's room leaving a passage right round the room and a bigger passage down the middle. Certain things had to remain accessible, like cupboards with hangings, pillows, perhaps blankets in them. I have done all the moving, rearranging, sorting and stacking of books myself, the putting away of all objects, china and glass, ornamental and kitchen.

There have been five bad raids since I left London and quite a lot of places hit. The raids have been very noisy and widespread, it seems. We've had three alerts with distant heavy gun fire here. The Germans are taking anti-invasion steps.

Mottisfont, Monday February 28

Sunday took a telegram from Martin over the telephone, saying he was well, busy and might be going to Delhi next month. So he's still in Colombo.

London, Wednesday March 1

Dined with Sibyl at Lord North St sitting between Sam Courtauld and Graham Sutherland.[33] Others there: Mrs Graham S., Francis Queensberry, Sir Kenneth and Lady Clark, Day-Lewis with his beautiful face, Rosamond Lehmann[34] whom he loves and she him so I've been told, and T.S. Eliot who I'd never seen before and didn't identify till the end of the evening. I looked at his face across the dinner table, thought it very odd and wondered who on earth he could be. He didn't talk much to either of his neighbours. His face is ugly and arresting and very melancholy. I happened to notice his hands which are small and beautiful. The dinner was very early – 7.15 – because of the new crop of raids. Sibyl was so anxious to start it punctually that at the beginning of the evening there was a feeling of tension. I noticed a great difference since I was in London a fortnight ago: considerable nervousness and anxiety which infected me very quickly so that I too wanted to be home early. One hears the same on all sides. People seem much more nervous than three years ago. Three years of strain have worn their powers of resistance and the results of wartime feeding are showing themselves.

London, Friday March 3

Returned to the Admiralty and was really disappointed to find McLachlan away on a fortnight's sick leave. The room is half-dead without him and much less goes on. People seldom bother to come in and see Serpell. He writes better talks for the German Naval Programme than Mc. but his mind works differently and not in the way that is so useful to our section. The day seemed long, dull and tedious and I found little had happened in the last fortnight. This was the first boring day I've had there.

London, Tuesday March 7

Ian dined. I said, 'You are preoccupied and worried.' He said, 'Well, the Second Front is enough to worry anyone.' Among other things, he is the head of the Naval Secret Service – agents, their names, jobs etc. He tells me it wouldn't matter me writing in my diary about our section activities and the personalities but I don't feel quite certain about that. He asked me if I was happy, what I wanted. I said – as I have said before – to be married again,

---

33. Graham Sutherland (1903-80), artist. Official Second World War artist.
34. Rosamond Lehmann (1901-90), novelist. Nine-year affair with poet Cecil Day-Lewis 1941-50.

have a companion, can't bear being alone, alright as long as I am working, but melancholy at Mottisfont. He talked about marrying me, I had qualities he wants to find. I said, 'No, ages makes it impossible.' He said, 'If I was five years older.' 'No,' I said, 'If you were at least 10 years older.' For he is sixteen and a half years younger than me. If he were 10 years older I would marry him, but it's no use a woman of 52 trying to keep pace with a man of 36. After a few years he might fall in love and want me to release him. I should do it and be alone again after much pain and drama, a good deal older, and in still greater need of compassion. He is very good to me.

London, Wednesday March 15

Yesterday Alexie, Harold Tennyson and John Amberley[35] – Bertie's son – dined. Claud had described him as very small, not bad-looking and clever. I was quite unprepared by this frugal description of the young man's very striking appearance. A very noisy raid started after dinner and for once I felt anxious and very nervous. I don't know why this should have been but this morning I heard Muriel Wright, I.'s girl, had been killed. Strange things happen. I heard in my room at the Admiralty that she'd been killed by debris flung up from a crater in the road coming through her roof and falling on her in bed. Most of the room was untouched. Appalled for I. and found it difficult to concentrate. I know he will be overcome with remorse and blame himself for not marrying her and for a thousand other things none of which he is to blame for.

London, Sunday March 19

The Muriel Wright business has affected me. I know what I. will be thinking and how he won't stop tormenting himself.

London, Monday March 20

Boris dined. We quarrelled as we always do about Russian feats of arms and English feats of arms. He cannot bear any criticism of the one or I of the other. When England was suffering her worst reverses, he thoughtlessly and tactlessly attacked and criticised England and the English Army and soldiers incessantly. I said nothing. When Russia suffered some of her most

35. John Russell, later 4th Earl Russell (1921-87), eldest son of Bertrand Russell and his second wife Dora Black. In later life he was diagnosed with schizophrenia.

ghastly reverses I said nothing, but since the days of her most spectacular advances I have occasionally criticised, with a little malicious pleasure, the battles that led to those defeats – not often though – but more often since the present uninformed view that the German retreat is a sort of rout instead of a very remarkable – up until now – withdrawal. B. screams with anger. How national we all are.

London, Tuesday March 21

Dinner with Oliver and Maudie Harvey and Charles Morgan. Both Oliver and Morgan agreed that de Gaulle was a remarkable man. Oliver said, 'He is a sort of Joan of Arc. But our method of treating him is quite wrong. It should always be in the grand manner. It's a great pity Winston and he can't hit it off. It's hopeless now. Winston made de Gaulle. He is like a father who sees his son grow up and become independent and doesn't like it.' Morgan said he'd had one or more long talks with de Gaulle. De Gaulle had said exactly what sort of a set-up he wanted in Algiers and what his and Giraud's spheres were to be and, according to Morgan, it had worked out exactly as de Gaulle had said he wanted it. M. had said, 'What form of govt do you hope for in France?' 'A Republic,' said de G. 'Not a dictatorship?' 'No.' 'And what,' said M., 'do you yourself want to be?' De G: 'Président du Conseil.' Morgan, persisting: 'You don't want to be a dictator in a New France?' 'No,' said de G., 'Président du Conseil.'

London, Wednesday March 22

B. rang up to say his money is exhausted and he must now accept my offer of help – which I had begged him to do for months, but which he'd always refused, to my grief, as I knew he and Maroussia were starving and stinting themselves. We didn't discuss anything but I sent him £1,000 with an immense sigh of relief.

North Drive Lodge, Wentworth, Sunday March 26

Yesterday Eddy S.W. and Freddie Ashton came to lunch. Freddie natural, frank, outspoken as usual, a real person. On Friday night there was an immensely loud raid lasting one and a half hours, the loudest night London has had though the damage wasn't great. Our defences raised hell. The roar of the rockets was the most frightening but the different guns and rocket-guns made a vast, unearthly orchestra. We all felt exhausted and shattered by the noise and fear. Afterwards I came here, Mama's new house at Wentworth, and was most agreeably surprised. It's pretty, modern, luxurious, clean and comfortable. It's perfect as a wartime house or as a house for a woman of 75. The country is heaven after last night's hell.

London, Monday March 27

Came back from Wentworth yesterday afternoon. I came to dinner, first time since Muriel Wright's cruel death. We didn't talk about her at all. I left it to him if he wanted to but he said nothing and I didn't probe. But he talked about his health and that his fingers trembled. We talked about things like that – hair, health, skin, twitching, fingers trembling. He's going to Scotland for a week's get-away. Today Crinks, Cardie, Clare [Tennyson] and George [Howard] dined and played bridge. The three men are wonderful types – all belonging to the easy pre-war days of Newmarket, casinos, golf-courses and White's or the St James's. Now they look most strange, especially Crinks and Cardie. As they walked out of the little flat door I was struck by their comic appearances, hats and clothes. They would make a tremendous hit, Crinks and Cardie, on the screen, poor dears. I love them both and George too. They belong to my good days and my life with Gilbert.

Mottisfont, Monday April 3

I thought Mottisfont would look changed but when I drove up in the half-light on Friday it looked, thank god, just the same. I went through bare passages to my room, passing Gilbert's room which is now an office, and had dinner in bed. Woken by the nurses' dogs barking and yapping on the lawn. After lunch Dr Franklin, the MO, took me over the rooms, most of them looking pretty uncomfortable, cold and bare. He is quite a nice old boy of about 60. There is a sister in charge, 10 or 12 VADs [*Voluntary Aid Detachment*], a couple of Fanys [*First Aid Nursing Yeomanry*], a male cook, some orderlies but no patients yet and most of the rooms seem to have been set aside for the staff. Lunched and dined in the stables in a room in the butler's flat. Rose cooks in the little kitchen in the flat. Today Woolley came at 11.30 and we talked about the estate, farmers, Catchment Board and War Agricultural Executive Committee. Wrote, went to the kitchen-garden, which is in fine trim, and had tea, at their invitation, with the doctor and nurses in the cook's bedroom, now the nurses' sitting room. I am glad this house plays a small part in the history of the times.

London, Tuesday April 11

Mama lunched, always in trouble with her servants. It's chronic. Dined with Emerald [Cunard, *society hostess 1872-1948*] at the Dorchester. Diana [*back from Algiers to spend holidays with her son John Julius*] described life in Algiers which she enjoys though she says the novelty may wear off. The discomfort, however, in their big villa was very great at first, and the cold Arctic. Nothing can be bought, absolutely nothing. The lesser foreign diplomats lead miserable lives without any of the luxuries they are used to and allowed no petrol. They can't move. She says Algiers is an armed camp: no French there, only English and Americans. She tried to buy a car there – an ordinary French car. The price asked was £175. Here an average price would be £50. She walked away saying she must consult her husband so as to get out of it whereupon the Frenchman who had taken her there said: 'Never mind, I will buy the car, and I will lend it to you for a year.' Diana delighted, accepted. She's keeping a diary, she says, in the form of letters which she sends back. As this was said across the table I didn't ask if they go to Conrad. I imagine they do. Diana has her own individual style: outspoken, direct, and a little rough, very business-like, practical and amusing. I think her diaries might be excellent.

London, Wednesday April 12

I. dined. Still we don't mention Muriel. He's just back from a week's rest in Scotland and looks better. I am seeing about his rations. Found Muriel used to. Before he was sent to Scotland I said, 'What are you doing about rations now?' He said, 'It's all in a muddle and I can't cope with it but you're not to bother.' He was in a state and I saw he wouldn't feel like bothering about any mortal thing connected with himself. So I said nothing but took round marmalade, sugar, butter etc. of my own and said I would look after him till he wanted someone else to. By and by he sent his ration card and so that's settled.

Ruthin Castle, North Wales, Sunday April 16

I left for my rest-cure [*at Ruthin Castle*] on Thursday. Arrived very tired and got gratefully into bed for a complete rest. Have been having those slight temperatures I had for so long in 1932 and into 1933. I have been horribly tired, overburdened with a sense of care, duties and obligations. By luck I thought of this place which Cardie had talked about to me. He said he'd spent Xmas here. I asked 'Why?' 'Because I couldn't get to Monte Carlo,' said Cardie. I thought: well, it must at least be comfortable. Today I lay in bed, too delighted to be away from all responsibility and all my ties. When I arrived I was low, dismal and melancholy and every evening I feel sad and lonely but I daresay that will pass. I miss Gilbert.

Maud shelters from life in bed, reading newspapers and books – Boswell, Johnson, Creevey and Nancy Mitford – and writing letters. She is full of morbid thoughts about death and loneliness.

Ruthin Castle, Thursday May 4

I wish I could die like my grandmother Conrad did who was active and interested in life till she was 80. Then one day she lay down on her sofa for a rest after lunch as she always did, and never woke up. Her maid found her quite peacefully dead. How perfect. I don't care for living without Gilbert, that's the trouble.

London, Friday May 5

Arrived in London at 6.40 and found Boris on the platform with a porter. I had ordered a hired car to meet me and all this seemed a strange luxury and B.'s presence a reflection of the days when I came back from abroad to Gilbert and home.

Mottisfont, Sunday May 14

B. came and took me to the station on Friday. He spoils me. This was my first sight of Mottisfont full of patients. There are six beds in the gallery. There are soldiers everywhere: 60 in the house, another 12 in the long room over the stables, and there must be staff of 20 or 30, plus a Field Ambulance Unit camping under the big trees near the house.

Friday night I felt the extreme strangeness of the occupation. It was a hot and beautiful evening, the Field Ambulance had put up its tents – six under the big plane, one under the neighbouring cedar and one under the Chaucerian oak beyond. From 9 until dark at 10.30, one of the members of the unit stood playing an accordion, a slim figure with a dark head silhouetted against the romantic background of the Abbey Water. He wasn't a great musician but had a big repertoire. The others crouched or lay round him. The river behind them ran swiftly and glassily. From the house came sounds of life and occasional shouts. The windows lit up slowly and the whole scene was so strange and romantic that I was seized by a feeling of restlessness and found it hard to settle down to sleep. Today I went over the hospital with the Sister. The rooms are tight-packed with beds. The only rooms not used as bedrooms are the hall, which is a sitting room; the boys' sitting room, now the MO's consulting-room; the study, now the office and record room; the cloak room, used to store blankets and linen; and the servants' hall used as a dining-room by the doctor and hospital staff. The long hayloft (used by the Army a couple of years ago as a dormitory) has walking cases and so has the harness room. The four remaining evacuee children are in the dormitory opposite and the bombed-out Gould family and their children in the servants' flat over the garage and in the gunroom. The butler's flat is kept by me: Miss Bishop, our lady gardener, is in one room; Adele has another for the dairy; the kitchen is Rose's charge; and the remaining room used by them as a sitting-room or by me as a dining room.

London, Tuesday May 16

Started Admiralty again. McLachlan stared at me as if I had come back from the grave and Angela blushed and seemed quite excited. Serpell is away ill and the section very quiet. Ian came to dinner and talked marriage and the sort of person he should marry and the sort of person I should.

Mottisfont, Sunday May 21

Yesterday Admiralty and then caught an appallingly crowded train to Mottisfont. There was a careful check-up by the police of identity cards at Winchester as all that area is in the Coastal Ban area and the country stuffed with troops camping under trees and in the woods. There are more beds in the gallery, six or eight ambulances under the trees. Three-quarters of the cases that come in are malaria cases and the men from the Eighth Army who fought in Sicily. They look tremendously fit, sturdy, self-reliant people and give one a different feeling about the Second Front's chances. It's very refreshing.

London, Tuesday May 23

I had a cable from Kitty saying Tony [*Apponyi senior*] has had a severe heart-attack but that I wasn't to tell the rest of the family. I felt a pang as I thought of Tony, whom I have known all my grown-up life and whom Kitty has loved in a dogged, tenacious way, in spite of his faults, extravagances and deceits. His charm has been his saving and his undoing.

London, Wednesday May 24

Sibyl, Sammy Hood and Harold Nicolson dined. Harold had just come back from a lecturing tour in North Africa. Thinks Diana and Duff are doing their job well. He says Duff is respected and admired and the fact he is intelligent is another asset in French eyes although it's his character and his resignation after Munich that count most. Harold said that de Gaulle, talking about goodwill, said 'The best ambassador you have is the common soldier.' There was talk about the great part the British Council must play in the future and the eagerness there is now in every country to learn, read and understand English. Winston had just made his long review on Foreign Affairs in the House. Harold said his voice sounded dull and rather tired but whenever there was an interruption all his old speed, fire and brilliance returned in a flash.

London, Friday May 26

Ian and Hermann Marx [*Gilbert's partner at Cull & Co*] came to lunch. I. wanted to see him again. He spent a couple of years in Cull and Co. Hermann didn't know quite what a well-informed person he was talking to and boasted once or twice about the importance of his information. Drove back to the Admiralty with I. There alone. Serpell is still ill, Angela having her day off, C.B. was only there in the morning, and I only saw McLachlan for two minutes when I arrived.

London, Sunday May 28

Today is the second anniversary of Gilbert's death. I think of him constantly and I don't get used to being without him. There is nothing more cruel, terrible and irremediable than this separation by death of husband and wife – if I were religious I should revolt against a deity who suffered such misery to exist. During the night I dreamed I went into a room. The feeling of the room made it I.'s at Athenaeum Court, where I go with his rations once a week since Muriel was killed, but in arrangement the room had something of the look of the P/W dormitory I had seen the day before [*she had visited a reconstructed German prisoner of war camp*]. I was astonished to see Martin lying asleep in a bunk. I peered, his face had altered and was fatter, and I began to turn away thinking I must be wrong, but he opened his eyes, smiled and got up. 'How <u>on earth</u> did you get here?' I said. Martin: 'I arrived this morning. I didn't want to let you know beforehand.' I was happy and delighted. The dream began to lose its sharpness. Gilbert appeared walking with his stick and Martin was there too. But the dream had become vaguer. Ian came to dinner. It is his birthday. He is 36. We talked till late.

London, Monday 29 May

An American, Captain Dixon, indescribably boring but good about Germany, has come to sit in our room at the Admiralty for a few days and learn our stuff. McLachlan was in most of the afternoon and the room much more alive. There is a biggish offensive on in Italy. Rome is 20 miles away.

On June 4, the Allies enter Rome.

London, Monday June 5

Yesterday went to the Admiralty and heard that Rome was expected to be occupied that evening. Some fighting in the outskirts. Ian came to dinner looking worn and tired and his speech was blurred as if he'd had a fair number of cocktails. I said, 'You've got something on your mind.' He said, 'It's this invasion.' No news of Rome on the 9 o'clock news so I switched on at midnight and heard that Rome had been entered. It must have been a great emotion for most of the army.

On June 6, the D-Day landings in Normandy take place.

London, Tuesday June 6

Little wonder that I. looked worn on Sunday. It was invasion eve and he was waiting to hear whether it was starting or put off for a day on account of the stormy weather. It was put off for 24 hours. He told me he might be rung up during the evening and had given my number. As I came into the room he said: 'Does this wind worry you?' I thought it was an odd question and answered, 'Well, yes, I've had a headache for three days.' He said, 'I mean, all this rustling and whistling and shushing.' I thought, 'What is his idea?' but never hitched onto the invasion though I sensed something complicated in the question. It shows what a goose I am. There was that, and the fact that Room 39 was locked part of the morning, and that I. had given my telephone number (but he'd done that before), and that Serpell had taken his wife and child to the country three days before – as of course he knew the invasion date. There had been many rumours and reports that London might be heavily bombed by long-range guns, or rockets, when the invasion started.

I didn't guess though. The first I knew was at about 9.40 this morning when the woman from Cyclax who massages my neck said the invasion had been announced at 8. I switched on immediately and listened to the Invasion Broadcast. I felt deeply moved and very conscious of the great drama. During the day there were prayers and I heard that solemn hymn *God Our Help in Ages Past* three times. In the evening broadcasts there were commentaries from the beachheads.

London, Sunday June 11

Friday Boris dined. In an unhappy mood again. When great national events are on I am happier in the company of Englishmen. Yesterday Ian dined and I teased him about that invasion wind. We had a great evening talking and laughing. He is satisfied about the progress. Weather conditions have been bad all the time and we are a bit behind schedule but casualties have been much lighter than was ever dreamed of. I told him I had looked in *The Times* on invasion day (it had of course gone to press before the invasion was announced) to see whether I could find a veiled reference in it to the great day but I had found none, not even in 'Old and True'. Ian told me that some days before, *The Daily Telegraph* had three Most Secret code words in it: Overlord, Crossbow, Mulberry and, I believe, a fourth – a startling coincidence if coincidence it was.[36]

On June 13, the Germans launched their first V-1 bomb attack on London. The V-1 flying bomb, also known as the doodlebug, was designed to cause devastation with up to 100 bombs falling an hour on London in an initial campaign that killed more than 6,000 people, injuring over 17,000.

Wentworth, Saturday June 17

On Thursday night the pilotless plane or the flying bomb was launched against London. The alert started at 11.45 and went on all night and on and off all yesterday. The night was a hell of noise from the guns and the rocket gun, and the pilotless planes humming their way into London. I was stunned with the noise by the morning. This was the first the public knew

36. Overlord was the codename for the Battle of Normandy; Crossbow for the campaign against Germany's long-range weapons programme; Mulberry for the floating harbours used in the Normandy landings; and the fourth word may have been Neptune, the code for the Normandy landings.

of the planes. In fact a few of them had made their appearance on Tuesday night though not in London. I went to the Admiralty on Friday morning and then came to stay here with mama. Last night there was a good deal of noise even here – guns, night fighters, flying bombs and two big sorties of bombers going off to the Continent. Kitty has wired that Tony is convalescent. What a mercy for her.

London, Monday June 19

I took the 11.30 to London on Sunday. The direct line had had a hit so after starting we turned back and looped onto the main Southern Railway line. As we were getting into London, a pilotless plane dived and exploded 100 yards from the line sending up a billowing mountain of smoke and dust. If I had raised my eyes from my book a second earlier, I should have seen it dive and strike. It fell among rows of poor houses. Went to the Admiralty. I. dined, irritated to death about the new weapon and all the talk about it, and the nervous vexation and <u>fear</u> it causes. We laughed and jabbered about it as if by doing so we got rid of the horrors. Last night the anti-aircraft guns, thank God, were stopped and the things attacked by night fighters – a much better idea. So I slept quite soundly. The Guards Chapel and Wellington Barracks was hit during Morning Service yesterday and 35 people were killed.

Mottisfont, Friday June 23

Yesterday lunched with Cathleen Queensberry. All-woman lunch. Continuous talk about the pilotless plane, a lot of it nonsense. Everyone seemed very nervous. Fear keeps people awake, not the noise because there isn't very much unless one is near an explosion. A lot of Piccadilly windows were blown out a night or two ago by a flying bomb going off against the wall of Buckingham Palace close to Constitution Hill. Last night there was constant activity by the pilotless planes and I slept badly. My windows are bowed, very large and the bed no great distance from them and one of the lesser dangers is the danger of flying glass. So whenever the contrivances pass overhead, I pull the eiderdown right up and lay a pillow over my head and shoulders. This doesn't make for a restful night. I arrived here very exhausted after the strain of bad nights. But Mottisfont was looking so pretty and the evening was so lovely, calm and composed that in half an hour I felt refreshed and that beauty is not all dead.

On June 27, US troops liberate Cherbourg, France. Meanwhile the Soviet Union has launched a major attack to liberate Byelorussia and gain a foothold in Romania and eastern Poland.

Mottisfont, Sunday July 2

Cherbourg fell some days ago to the Americans. The advance in Italy continues. The Russians launched a big attack a week or more ago and have advanced rapidly. The offensive started on June 22nd, the day the Germans invaded them three years ago. Stalin orders salutes to be fired by the Moscow guns each time an important town is captured and this has been happening for 15 months now. The Russians must like the din. I can imagine how sick Londoners would get of it and how tiresome and stupid they would think it.

Went to Ian's flat on Friday and met a woman, Mrs Jameson, I had found to mend his clothes. We looked through the cupboards and she ran her expert eye over the suits. A pilotless plane rumbled its way into London and went off with a rather louder pop than usual. When a few minutes later I made for Soho and lunch with B. I found a traffic jam at the end of Piccadilly, some windows out in Piccadilly Circus and a crowd of people peering down one of the side streets. A bomb had just fallen that end of Brewer St, another had gone on and over Soho, falling just beyond. That afternoon there were a number in the air. I have only <u>seen</u> one and that was from South Audley St. It looked very high – because it's so small – and seemed to be going very fast for the same reason. It <u>is</u> fast though – 300-350 miles per hour.

London, Monday July 3

Ian dined. He can't sleep well in his glass-bound flat. He says he hears the contraptions coming from a great distance as well as the outer London gunfire. People have become very glass conscious. He went off to sleep at the Admiralty in the basement. Last week I went through the same anxiety about glass when I was in bed at night. So one night I got out a spare mattress and laid it in the tiny lobby, just outside my bedroom, and there I sleep as well as ever I sleep in a bed. I feel safe from flying glass and I can't hear much, which, ostrich-like, is a comfort.

London, Friday July 7

Met Mrs Jameson at Athenaeum Court and sorted out clothes of I.'s that need cleaning, carrying them away in my arms. I. is off abroad for a few days. New uniforms and equipment lying about. He has a private army of 300 men. When I came home from the Admiralty the evening was lovely so, tired though I was, I went to the park. The grass smelt fresh, the trees were heavy with leaf and I walked to the bandstand and stood for a long time watching and listening. An alert was on as usual. The bandstand, newly painted and sprightly, stood in its circle of summer-leafed plane trees. The audience had shrunk because of the all-day alerts but small clusters of people sat on iron chairs round the bandstand or outside the enclosure under the trees – people of all sorts and kinds, young and old, soldiers and civilians. The Royal Signal Corps band was playing and there was a very tolerable pianist as well. As I came up they were standing and singing the shanty *On the Banks of Sacramento*. Later they played two Viennese waltzes and part of a Grieg piano concerto. The scene was so strange, moving and so unreal – the white bandstand, the charming civilised elegant waltzes, the Americans lolling about, the uniforms, the drone of the pilotless plane, the beauty of the evening, war and peace all mixed up inextricably.

Mottisfont, Sunday July 9

Part of the road between here and Winchester is always congested with tanks, lorries and troops camping under trees to right and left off the road, waiting to go on to Southampton and overseas. It's a scene behind the lines, an army on the march and gives me a feeling of being not very far from the front. This time a great many black troops were settling in for the night, as well as white troops with their hundreds of vehicles, tanks, tank-carriers, guns and other armoured vehicles.

London, Wednesday July 12

Stuart Preston, James Pope-Hennessy[37] and Rosemary Lyttelton (*Oliver Lyttelton's daughter*] dined. The evening was charming and James Pope-Hennessy's laugh contributed largely to it. His face is a bit Japanese – narrow dark eyes, pale skin and delicate features. He talks gaily and amusingly and there is something in the tone of his voice and in his enunciation which reminds me of Rex. Stuart again hinted he was leaving England almost immediately and becoming sentimental, more slow-voiced than ever and

---

37. James Pope-Hennessy (1916-74), biographer and writer. Initial choice as Maud's literary executor until his brutal murder. Maud was also friends with his brother John (1913-94), an art historian who was director of the V&A and the British Museum.

heavy, all of which I always enjoy seeing. It's the moment when he becomes more human and more loveable. We joked him [sic] about his leave-takings and J.P.H. said he had heard all this once before only to find that Stuart had been no further than Himley [*Hall*] where he had spent two days with the Dudleys [*the home of Lord and Lady Dudley in Staffordshire*].

London, Thursday July 13

Admiralty morning and afternoon. Serpell is on sick leave, C.B. having her holiday, so there's only Angela in the room and McLachlan for short periods once or twice a day. Emerald, Peter Q., Cyril C., and Christopher and Camilla Sykes dined. Christopher, alas, is a paratrooper. I asked 'Why on earth a paratrooper?' He explained that if one is 36 one is considered derelict and can't get into anything so that when he got back from Persia last year, finding he was thought too old for almost anything, he volunteered to be a paratrooper – that branch being on a voluntary basis and accepting people of all ages and conditions. His face is as charming as ever; a soft, late Italian saint.

London, Monday July 17

Ian dined and told me about his week in Normandy. As usual he didn't make much of it saying: 'It was just like what you've seen in the papers, nothing happened. The French were on very good terms with us in the little town I was in. There was a football match and I had to tell my people they <u>must</u> <u>not</u> win by more than a couple of goals.' There was a presentation to the members of a fishing boat who had put out in bad weather to try and find an airman who had bailed out over the sea. After a long search they found him. His men, his 'army', are marine-commandos.[38]

London, Friday July 21

Sensation of the day on Thursday was the announcement of an attempt on Hitler's life.[39] Serpell rang up Delmer asking what it all meant. 'It's the excuse for a purge,' said Delmer. After dinner I listened to *Soldatensender Calais*

---

38. A special unit of commandos, known as 30 Assault Unit, tasked with obtaining German naval intelligence.
39. On July 20, 1944 the German army officer Claus von Stauffenberg and other conspirators failed in an attempt to assassinate Hitler by placing a bomb in a briefcase at a military conference at the Eastern Front military headquarters in East Prussia.

[*subversive propaganda radio station run by the Political War Executive with input from NID 17Z where Maud worked*] which was heavily jammed on the subject of the assassination. I expected to go to the country today but McLachlan telephoned to say it was inconvenient. Had lunch with Raymond and Mama at the Carlton Grill. Raymond thinner, very fit looking. He hasn't been accepted by the Selection Board which visited Kingussie. He said he hadn't 'got on with them'. After lunch Admiralty as usual. The most confused, conflictive and hysterical propaganda is being put out by the Germans. If I were in the German army I should feel very puzzled, insecure and depressed. I suppose a Grand Purge is on.

Barhatch, Sunday July 23

Yesterday two letters from Martin whose new job he owes to Mountbatten. He's in Kandy, has helped to start a chess club at Colombo, has had an article on economics published in a local paper, seems to be living in a hut and is buying, poor boy, pictures by Sinhalese artists. Let's hope they aren't too big. Admiralty and then here to stay with Diana [Russell] in her calm house with its Victorian atmosphere: lavender bays; dozens of vases with a few flowers in each standing side-by-side along the ledge of a book-case; careful, dead examples of Italian embroidery or appliqué done by Diana herself and framed or turned into screens or fire guards; debased Morris choice of colouring and covers; many bookshelves of serious books all bought, I should think, in Lord Arthur's day or even in Lady William's early married days; and in every room family prints or engravings of friends and contemporaries of Lord Arthur. Diana was sprightly and alert in spite of her lame leg and comparative immobility. Last night she made me listen, much to my amusement, to *Soldatensender Calais* and she made many comments and conjectures.

London, Tuesday July 25

Dined with Sibyl at the Dorchester sitting between Raymond M. and Eddy. Raymond began to talk to me about Boris and that it seemed hard he hadn't any work to do. I found he thought, erroneously, that B. asks enormous sums for his work. I tried to put this right. £2,500 for one of the two smaller floors at the National Gallery didn't seem much to me, I said, when people like John Lavery[40] or Augustus John charged £1,200 or more for full length portraits,

---

40. Sir John Lavery (1856-1941), painter. Official First World War artist, famous for portraits.

on which they didn't spend a twentieth part of the time B. spends on his floors, nor did they employ six or eight assistants. Raymond volunteered praise of B.'s work and said he would love him to do some small thing for him, such as a table top. I think I must get at him about B. doing the remaining floor at the National Gallery. During dinner Eddy told me Rex had been killed in Normandy. I felt a great pang; but I knew he would be killed. Everybody knew it. Lovely Rex; difficult, strange, rare, unhappy Rex.

London, Friday July 28

Eddy dined. I believe he really is thinking of marrying. He talked in that vein and made a number of allusions to the type he admires in women. They must be big and blonde it seems. Raymond M. told me the other night that Eddy hasn't said a word to him but that he thinks he is bent on marriage to a woman of 40 or so, an old friend, whose husband is missing. Raymond says he dreads loneliness in old age. It comes back to me that Eddy had an enthusiasm for me last summer, used to ring me up often and constantly suggested meeting or dining, but I seldom did so because I was too tired.

All this time the flying bombs have been coming and I have slept in the tiny lobby outside my bedroom. One doesn't hear the alert and all-clear so clearly or the approach of the bugs, and I am much safer from flying glass.

London, Monday July 31

I. dined and talked to me about the German new 'secret' weapon: the rocket. Said he <u>thought</u> it wasn't ready and might never be ready in time but one couldn't know and if it started I was to get out <u>at once</u>. I was to keep a bag packed and leave London immediately without warning the Admiralty or anyone. I said, 'What about you?' He said Winston had decided the govt and the ministers weren't to be evacuated. It would look too bad *vis-à-vis* the people. He told me to make my way to Wentworth, said he might get there some time and promised to let me hear from him. He said it would be a relief for people to know other people were safe. This talk was serious and reminded me of the talks one used to have just before the war about what one would do when the Germans started bombing. The same feeling of dread and uncertainty. I. was quite serious. I read a certain amount of secret stuff about these things but of course he knows more.

London, Thursday August 3

The PM has made another great war speech [*detailed report on war to House of Commons on August* 2]. He warned those of the public who have nothing to do in London to leave. He expressed considerable optimism about the length of the war – over soon, he is inclined to think.

My life is a day to day affair. I eat, sleep and work; do some shopping; look after my face, hair and nails; read the newspapers; and see two or three people, and that is all. No reading, gallery or theatre going, and no uplift.

Yesterday Admiralty all day. Hurried back to lay the dinner for Ian. An alert went just as he was about to leave so I fixed him up in the flat for the night.

Today no shopping, no dates, no Elvira [*maid*] so I slept long and late and was at the Admiralty at 2.30.

SEVEN

Boris Anrep and the National Gallery Mosaic

AUGUST 1944 – AUGUST 1945

In which the Allies win the war in Europe and then the Asia Pacific;
Maud and Boris hatch the National Gallery floor plan;
Boris makes the Holy Trinity mosaic for Mottisfont; and
Maud's significance to Ian is revealed.

The Allies have successfully landed in Normandy and are intent on breaking
through the German defences, taking a firm foothold in western Europe and
pushing on into Germany. Meanwhile, the Soviets are advancing against the
Germans on the eastern Europe front. In the Pacific, US successes have led
the Japanese prime minister to resign. The Allies are now preparing to land
on the southern coast of France.

At the Admiralty, Room 17Z's full-time paid assistant, Angela
Whiteman, is unwell and told to rest for three months, providing more
scope for Maud.

London, Wednesday August 16

Ian dined on Monday and did he breathe a word of the invasion of the Riviera[1]
which happened the next day? No, not a word, the miserable beast. When
I got to the Admiralty on Tuesday I said to C.B. as usual: 'Any news or are
things stagnating?' 'News?' she said, 'I should think so. The Mediterranean
Coast has been invaded. There has been little opposition, things are going
wonderfully and I have been rung up all morning with inquiries about the
ports of Marseille and Toulon.' Dined in bed that evening and listened to

---

1. The Allied invasion of southern France, codenamed Operation Dragoon.

white and black news.[2] I am alone in the Admiralty during the afternoons unless C.B. blows in to visit or encourage. One or two days McLachlan has been in and his personality is refreshing to have in the room after Serpell's amicable effectiveness.

London, Saturday August 19

On Thursday I., Christopher [Sykes], Camilla [Sykes] and Nancy[3] and Peter Rodd dined. The men wrangled and argued, goaded on by I., and drank a prodigious amount. I. was rather drunk, noisy, nonsensical and provocative. He was enjoying himself which I love seeing as he leads such a serious life now, lives with so many mysteries and carries so many burdens. When talking about France and the French Empire, I. called Indo-China 'the saddest piece of France'.

Today B. came to the flat. We drank a wonderful morning drink invented then and there by him consisting of gin, cider, whisky, cherry brandy and white wine. Off we went like lions to the Food Office where I had some re-registering to do. Then lunch at the Shanghai where we talked about post-war mosaic plans for B. and plotted hard. There are two possibilities: the Mosque in Regent's Park and the completion of the National Gallery floors where one of the landings remains to be done. Who is to be approached about this? First we thought Raymond M., then K. Clark, then perhaps Keynes and Sam. On the subject of the floor, B. said first the Seven Ages of Man presented in the modern manner. But this didn't appeal much to him and he jumped on to the Seven Virtues and Vices and began exploring the possibilities. He warmed to the idea and I saw life taking hold of him again.

Mottisfont, Friday August 25

Crinks, Oliver Lyttelton and Nancy and Peter Rodd dined on Tuesday. Crinks was in tremendous spirits and madly funny all evening. I have never seen him so gay. Oliver was funny too. They were like two very young men, ragging, mimicking, singing and whistling. For some time, while we played bridge, they kept up a comic conversation in Dordogne French. They were in tearing form and riotous spirits. The rapid progress of the war and my

2. 'White' is propaganda that is only based on the truth: e.g. BBC broadcasts. 'Black' news mixes the truth with calculated fiction to achieve subversive ends: e.g. the PWE's *Soldatensender Calais*.
3. Nancy Mitford (1904-73), novelist and biographer. Married Peter Rodd in 1933. One of the renowned Mitford sisters and 'Bright Young Things' of the inter-war years.

wine were responsible. The evening was reminiscent of the happy days at Blickling or Stanway [*country houses leased by the Russells in Norfolk and Gloucestershire respectively*] or here. On Wednesday Paris was entered or liberated or freed or whatever you like. A remarkable campaign is being fought with the Americans moving outwards and onwards in widening circles. It's an extraordinary achievement. Oliver gave [US General George] Patton great praise for the manner in which he is supplying his rapidly moving armour. Boris came and dined and we listened to the news and the *Marseillaise*. Perhaps Boris will be back in Paris in a few months' time. I shall miss his love and constant companionship.

London, Sunday August 27

Admiralty all day. There was an outbreak of sniping when de Gaulle entered Paris and I heard the BBC broadcasts [*of the sniping*] direct from the different spots. Very curious they were. I listened to the strange, interrupted, jerky, dramatic accounts of the incidents. The firing could be distinctly heard.

London, Thursday August 31

The armies are moving at great speed in France. Great excitement opening the newspapers every morning. The Romanians have asked for an armistice and the Bulgarians are following suit.

C.B. is away on leave and Angela only comes in the morning. At last I am getting the chance of doing most of the routine office work, and pacifying, or coaxing or putting in inquiries myself.

Mottisfont, Sunday September 3 – At war for 5 years.

Americans over Belgium and Luxembourg borders. Ourselves near Belgium border too. Gothic Line overrun in Italy. Russians passed through Bucharest. Very few flying bombs during the week. German armies in France disorganised. Yesterday B. came to the flat and we went to a News Reel to see de Gaulle's march down Champs Elysees and the extraordinary movements of the crowds when shooting started. They piled up like waves meeting and sank and fell like waves subsiding. Gaulle looked tall, compared to the others, awkward, dignified and – for him – moved. We talked again about the National Gallery floor and how and when to approach K. Clark and the directors. He showed me photographs of the Bank of England floors which I thought very well done.

London, Monday September 4

I did a stencil for the first time for the NID Weekly Directive Notes[4] – easy enough really but I have little typing practice. I. dined – looking haggard and tired. I gave him a talking to about not drinking or smoking too much and about trying to take it easy. He is supposed to go to America with DNI [*Director of Naval Intelligence*] on the 24th and is sick at the idea, bored to death.

The following entry describes another work trip to the Political Warfare Executive's centre of subversive propaganda operations at Milton Bryan in Bedfordshire. Milton Bryan's work has grown and it is now producing the Nachrichten für die Truppe, *or 'News for the Troops', a daily German-language newspaper dropped by air over Germany, France and Belgium from May 1944. It was considered 'grey' propaganda as although it did not state it was an Allied publication, it did not take any lengths to pretend to be German.*

Woodcote, Wednesday September 6

Caught train to Blet [*Bletchley railway station*]. There I found a Ford Brake packed close with a strange collection of people and knew at a glance they were my gang. But there was a muddle about names and at first the driver wouldn't accept me. Finally he telephoned for orders and I got in. Petrified silence followed. Finally my fellow travellers began to talk and soon German was the order of the day. Arrived at [*blank, Milton Bryan*]. Miss Leader[5] met me and I was taken round by her. The place had been enlarged and there were new rooms. One produces *Nachrichten für die Truppe*, another plans of the bombed quarters of German cities etc. Last year I saw the mechanical installation[6] which even Miss Leader had never seen though she is one of the oldest inhabitants. The Sergeant[7] blew in and out to show me things

4. These formed the basis of policy for British naval publicity worldwide.
5. Miss Leader was Maud's main contact at Milton Bryan, with whom she would share 'Pink Slips' containing the day's intelligence.
6. Sefton Delmer's cherished Hellshreiber, a radio-operated teleprinter machine, which received press releases from the official German news agency, the DNB, and routine German propaganda ministry directives at the same time as newspaper editorial staff in Germany. Delmer's teams would rapidly insert a twisted version of the news into the subversive radio *Soldatensender Calais'* frequent news flashes.
7. Frank Lynder (b.1916), known as 'The Sergeant', the German naval specialist at Milton Bryan. The son of a Breman bookseller and publisher, Lynder had a Jewish mother and left Germany in 1938.

and took me across to one of the studios where H...[*Edward Halliday*] was manipulating the affair and S. broadcast.[8] The whole place, the people and everything in it are fantastic, the buildings and rooms small and plain – like the Citadel[9] which I went down to last week – and everything as ingenious and perfected as is possible. H. is a very extraordinary type; proud, vain, difficult, firebrandish and demonical. Among the strange collection is one of Peter Quennell's wives and a conventional-looking, white-haired English gentlewoman of about 60. McLachlan picked me up at 8.30 and we drove over to Woodcote where we had dinner and talked.

Mottisfont, Sunday September 10

Yesterday B. came here with me. Train more crowded than ever, eight people sitting and four standing in our compartment and most others. Corridors packed. Weather sharp and Septemberish with clear stars. Walked through village after dinner in the dark. Boris happy. Great happenings this last week. Brussels and Antwerp taken, Ostend and Dieppe, and the Allied Armies of the North wheeling eastwards and drawing up to the German frontier. Flying-bombs finished, everybody breathing more easily, the end of the war in sight.

London, Wednesday September 13

There was an idiotic govt statement last week covering the flying-bomb period and as good as saying that all danger from the air was over.[10] As soon as the public read the statement, they packed their bags and climbed into home-bound trains. This was a couple of days before the appearance of V2 [*German's V-2 rocket, the world's first long-range, guided ballistic missile*] which arrived with a thump in the afternoon.[11] Early yesterday morning, V2 arrived again and woke up most of London. Everybody I met asked what it was, including Sibyl. The general feeling is that it's the much advertised German secret weapon.

8. There were a number of different presenters. One of the most famous was Berliner actress Agnes Bernauer, who left Germany in 1936, broadcasting under the codename 'Vicky'.
9. The visible military citadel just behind the Admiralty on Horse Guards Parade where the Operational Intelligence Centre, fighting the war at sea, led its operations.
10. Duncan Sandys (1908-87), the chairman of a War Cabinet committee for defence against German flying bombs, informed the House of Commons on September 7, 1944 that the threat of enemy reprisal bombs was at an end, to the annoyance of the Air Ministry.
11. The first V2 bomb actually arrived on September 8, the day after Sandys' announcement (see footnote 10 above).

Wren 3rd Officer Donkin[12] has come to Room 17Z to take Angela Whiteman's place. She hasn't any experience of office work and her typing is as slow and rather less attractive than mine. But she looks reliable.

London, Thursday September 21

Ian came to dinner on Sunday, leaving for three days in France the next day. He is a lonely man. I am always afraid that when he is attracted by some girl he looks for not only youth and attractiveness but many of my virtues, vices and oddnesses and these he can never hope to find in anyone young, and quite likely in no one else but me.

The new girl 3rd Officer Donkin at the Admiralty is as duncy as I was to start with. The scope and variety of our work is difficult for a beginner to get the hang of. On Tuesday at the last moment a hunt had to be made for a complete list of all the U-boat commanders ever given out by the BBC. Needless to say this couldn't be found. The First Lord was said to be champing and afraid of a question being asked in the House. Our interlocutor threw his weight about and it all looked a bit hysterical to us. I always rather enjoy these scares although they generally happen when one is on the point of packing up for the night.

Today I. had proposed himself to dinner saying he would be back from France in time. I had a feeling he wouldn't turn up, nor did he. As I was eating my dinner rather drearily, Marie, the new maid, said, 'Did you ever know Madame Dupont?' 'No,' I said. 'Ah, poor Madame Dupont. The Flight Commander used to see her often. He was very charming. He used to say to her 'If I haven't rung you up by 9.20 – forget me.' And one day he didn't ring up. Ah! Poor Madame Dupont.' This story hardly cheered me!

The Bothy, Culham Court, Henley, Sunday September 24

Yesterday I. came to lunch. The flat is a sort of home or refuge from the war for him. He urges me to make plans for myself for after the war but I can't and don't want to. Any thought of my future makes me very unhappy.

B. came to take me to the station. My craved for leave had started. B. got into the train and accompanied me to Twyford where I had to change. There he put me on the next train and went back to London. Arrived at Raymond's

---

12. Third Officer WRNS Miss Sheila Donkin was appointed on September 9, 1944, to Room 17Z.

[*Mortimer, at The Bothy, near Henley*] – a romantic deep Provençal-pink cottage with Gothic windows, close to a mysterious looking piece of water, in reality a backwater of the Thames. Yews and big trees overhang the little clearing to the river. The prospect is one of romantic neglect. Eddy S.W. is staying, and Desmond Shawe-Taylor[13] who writes on music. He is Irish, very agreeable and has a more robust sense of humour than R. or E. The house is cottage-sized. The door opens into the sitting room, there is a kitchen and upstairs, two bedrooms. I had one, the three men slept in the other. Raymond has managed to build on a bathroom. His cook is very good.

The weekend was charming. Today the men worked busily all morning writing their articles. After lunch we listened to a concert and went for a walk along the meadows following the Thames. After dinner we listened to a BBC item which is expected to interest the public in good music – or bully it into consenting to listen. Eddy, talking to Shawe-Taylor, said he would very much like to translate Goethe – a translation in verse. This seems very ambitious and Shawe-Taylor suggested, as an alternative, a prose translation with the German on the opposite page. Eddy looked a little mortified.

London, Monday September 25

Travelled to London with Eddy, Raymond and Shawe-Taylor. Boris came to an early dinner in the flat, bringing sweets, flowers for me to smell in the train to Scotland and Rosamond Lehmann's new book. I wonder sometimes how I should get on without him. I asked him what Maroussia had said when she heard he'd taken me to Twyford. 'She laughed like a lioness,' said B. He said too, 'I am _so_ glad the war is going to last another six months. I needn't go to Paris yet.'

On September 26, Maud spends a fortnight with the Glenconners at their home Glen House in Scotland.

Glen, Saturday October 7

I would like another fortnight here away from responsibility and the weight of Boris's love. I value it, I treasure it. But treasures are sometimes heavy.

---

13. Desmond Shawe-Taylor (1907-95), music critic. Together with Eddy Sackville-West and the art critic Eardley Knollys, Shawe-Taylor set up home in 1945 at Long Crichel in Dorset, where they were later joined by Raymond Mortimer and Derek Hill. Maud was often a weekend guest at Long Crichel.

He would like me to link myself more closely with him. He would like me to take a flat in a small house in Paris. He plans a long journey round the Mediterranean with me to see mosaics and Byzantine art in general. He has another scheme to bind us, a shop in which we would sell beautiful peasant pottery. This would mean many shorter journeys – to France, Italy, Spain and Portugal, possibly to Hungary and Romania. They are all good ideas but I feel as if I am slowly being swallowed up. I am deeply fond of him but I am too old to enjoy being swallowed up![14] Nor could I break completely with my old life, the only thing that would really satisfy him. Not that he has asked me to do so but his schemes for himself and me would ultimately result in that. Neglected friends are often friends lost to one for ever.

Maud's leave finishes and she returns to London and the Admiralty.

London, Sunday October 15

Serpell and Donkin are on leave, so C.B. in the office in the morning and I in the afternoon. McLachlan blows in when he must – which is rarely enough. Thank God Angela has left. I have got the hang of the thing at last. Yesterday I was alone on duty all day and was kept busy most of the time. Captain Clancy came in to discuss a project. He is fascinated and mystified by our activities. He looked round the room as if he thought every piece of furniture was not what it seemed to be but served as some strange cover. Finally he mumbled half to himself: 'You do funny things down here.'

This evening dined with Elizabeth and Christopher [Glenconner]. The Spenders were there. He says his grandfather was a German Jew. Certainly his beauty is foreign though he is fair. He is charming, serious-minded, sensitive and full of feeling. And good. He talked about the Freud family – the descendants of [Sigmund] Freud and how fantastic and abnormal they all were. He mentioned how Lucian[15] once forced his way into a theatre and onto the stage. The corollary was the police court where the magistrate, peering at him said, 'Are you a grandson of the great Freud?' (which he pronounced Frood). Lucian thought he'd said, 'Are you the grandson of the Grapefruit?' and answered firmly and quite naturally, 'Yes.'

14. At a later date, Maud added a title 'The python' at the top of the page with this entry about Boris.
15. Lucian Freud (1922-2011), German born British painter, grandson of Sigmund Freud.

Mottisfont, Sunday October 22

Rummaged for letters of Rex's. Edith Olivier[16] wants any interesting ones for a book she is doing on Rex. Mine aren't very interesting but one is pretty, with fine spider-like pen drawings of Gothic traceries in the corners.

London, Saturday October 28

After tea I went to a film *Hotel du Nord* with Christabel. A V2 exploded rather noisily in the far distance as I was in the street. A girl of 10 or 12, walking with her relations in the half-dark street, threw herself down in terror, howling in a dreadful way, and was dragged up again by them. I felt disturbed.

London, Monday October 30

Went to *Hamlet* with Alexie but only stayed for first act as I. had announced his return and wanted to dine. Gielgud as Hamlet. Goodish. I. had plenty of stories about America. Travelled there and back by sea with the DNI. A Canadian Wren lost her heart to him on the outward journey, deserted from her unit, poor romantic, but eventually was talked by him into returning to it. Coming back to England, he said, was as depressing as those dread days in little boys' lives when the holidays end and the fun and the good times, and they have to go back to drab, drear school. He brought many presents – hot-water bottles, zip fasteners, powder puffs, sweets and a large piece of French soap.

Wentworth, Sunday November 5

On Thursday Christabel, Eddy and Raymond M. lunched. Raymond expects to go to Paris any moment. I suggested that he talk to working-class people, not literary, cosmopolitan or upper-class French which is all anyone seems to have done so far. Christabel said she would make a list of people she hoped Raymond could make inquiries about for her. 'Your friends in the Velodrome?' Raymond maliciously said. He always thinks that Christabel and Harry would have become collaborationists if England had been overrun. Today, what rain. At dusk I couldn't sit writing or reading anymore and plunged out into it.

16. Edith Olivier (1872-1948), writer. Hostess to a small circle of artists and writers at her home in Wilton, Wiltshire. Confidante to Rex Whistler.

London, Tuesday November 7

Ian dined. I told him about the unsettled state of the section, the plans, the new work, the likelihood of Angela Whiteman returning, the general mess and confusion, and so on. He said that with the winning of the war in the west almost all sections were going through the same period of listlessness and unrest and we must pull ourselves together. This advice braced me. He told me he was off abroad again at the end of the week, this time to the Mediterranean and all around it. He expects to be away a month but is so sick of the Admiralty, the dullness and stupidity choking it, that he hopes he will be away much longer. I have an idea his enemies have been at work while he was in America and that he has come back to find them armed and entrenched. Poor I., the wolves are after him.

London, Wednesday November 8

Boris dined. Talking about Rosamond Lehmann's last book *The Ballad and the Source*, I told him that the atmosphere in it reminded me of a slight brush with perversion I had when I was a girl of 20 or 21. I had just arrived in a country house. There was a small party of girls and young men and one of the girls was Marjorie Cochrane, who I knew slightly. After tea she proposed going for a walk and we set off together, wandering through the woods. When we got back to the house she took me to her bedroom, saying she wanted to change her blouse or skirt. And she proceeded to do so. I noticed her vaguely, half in and half out of her chemise, and I felt faintly uncomfortable because, though I was innocent, I wasn't ignorant. It began to dawn on me that this was an unusual hour at which to change all one's clothes unless one was dressing for dinner which was not what Marjorie was doing. I stood there faintly uncomfortable and awkward. She showed her white breasts and then I looked away while she finished her undressing and redressing. That was all. Boris said he'd only had one slight experience of that kind. He and Lytton Strachey were lunching with (I think) Ethel Sands.[17] A noisy, boring woman sat between him and L.S. to whom she talked all through the meal. 'Lytton looked across her at me with the eyes of a wounded doe,' said B. When they left, he and B. got into a taxi together. A few moments later 'Lytton put his hand on my thigh and said – it was some funny expression – "I leave it to you."' 'What,' I said, 'did you do?' 'I just patted his hand,' said B., 'like this' and he gave my hand a benevolent pat.

17. Ethel Sands (1873-1962), artist and hostess. She was one of Boris's first patrons, in 1917 commissioning a mosaic floor in her home at 15 The Vale, Chelsea.

'Just think of it,' said B., 'that bony body and that thin, floating, red beard.'
Boris is much happier again, happier about getting down to work, happier about me. Some months ago, feeling in despair and having no one to confide in, he made an appointment to see a clairvoyant. He described the whole business to me the next time we met; the draped room, the low lights, the tent-like enclosure, the glass bowl, the robed and mantled clairvoyant and the whole sad, sordid business. He told her his troubles and she gave him practical, worldly advice on how to interest, attract and hold the hard, worldly, spoilt and gad-about kind of woman she gathered I must be from his dejected state and the rough sketch he gave of my character. Don't ring her up, keep her waiting, don't write, neglect her; these were what she told him but happily he hasn't acted on. My heart ached for him when he told me this, in some ways, most humiliating story. I understand it all.

On November 9, Maud goes to Mottisfont for 10 days to deal with estate matters. She meets with the agent Woolley to discuss the management of the estate; talks to the gamekeeper Jack Peach about the shoot; walks along the river with Robert Coxen to inspect the dredging works; and goes around the garden checking each plant with the gardener George Buckell.

Mottisfont, Sunday November 19

On Friday I motored over to lunch at Wilton. Bee and Reggie [Pembroke] rather aged. There is still standing on the mantelpiece a large, heavily-typed card which Bee and Reggie put up during the black days of 1940. It reads: 'Please understand that there is no one depressed in <u>this</u> house; we are not interested in the possibilities of defeat; they do not exist.' They are Queen Victoria's words at the time of a serious reverse during the South African War.

Bee went off to a meeting, and I to see Edith Olivier about the book Batsford is going to bring out about Rex, and his work, and which she and Siegfried Sassoon are doing the narrative for. Rex's drawings and sketches are all lost, mislaid or so scattered that it's going to be a problem to find them. She wants photographs of the big room but it never was done, partly owing to the war, partly owing to Rex wanting Cecil to photograph it and then becoming irritable and capricious when Cecil tried to fix a day. Edith Olivier has a queer jerky manner of speech which I daresay is due to shyness. I daresay she is rather amusing, if one knows her well, and isn't a bit frightened of her witchiness, as I am.

I find Mottisfont hospital is called a Camp Reception Station and the patients are not supposed to stay for more than eight days. In fact they often stay 21. Bronchitis and quinsy[18] have been the latest illnesses. Three Frenchman and a Pole have been and gone and there are six Italian P/Ws now. The other day from the window of the morning room I could see the MO, Major Bond, scything the lawn (for pleasure) and two Italian P/Ws sweeping up behind him in a very leisurely fashion. One whistled continuously like some unmusical bird – no melody, just rather clear, sharp, notes – and spent most of his time playing with a white puppy.

London, Monday November 20

To London. Train was already in the station and I held it up till my luggage was brought across. Two things remarkable about this. First that a train can come in on time in wartime (abnormal on this line) and second that the guard and engine driver consented to hold the train in these democratic days when to ignore the individual is the rule.

London, Saturday November 25

Today I had planned a quiet morning Xmas shopping but everything conspired against me – especially the telephone and Sylvia Henley who rang up and insisted on me coming to [*her daughter*] Juliet's wedding breakfast that morning. It was put in such a way I couldn't refuse so I went and rather enjoyed it. There I saw a number of old friends like Margaret Stanley, Blanche Serocold [*née* Stanley] and Clemmie Churchill – people who belonged to the earlier days of my marriage and always give me a feeling of warmth. There too was a Churchill daughter or two and Rosalind Pitt-Rivers.[19] I was welcomed so warmly by all these people that I felt touched. Then Admiralty.

London, Tuesday November 28

Sylvia and Clemmie Churchill lunched. C. talked a vast amount – too much – but she's shrewd and a good judge of character. There was a lot

18. Quinsy is a rare and potentially serious complication of tonsillitis (also known as peritonsillar abscess).
19. Rosalind Pitt-Rivers, *née* Henley (1907-90), biochemist who discovered T3 thyroid hormone. Conducted nutritional study of Bergen-Belsen concentration camp prisoners in 1945. Sylvia Henley's daughter.

about Winston's 70th birthday on Thursday and whether she should go to the expense of spending, I think she said, 6/- a head on red roses for him. We talked a lot about Duff, Diana, the Embassy in Paris [*where Duff has been appointed Ambassador*], and a bit about Venetia who is going there as Diana's Social Secretary. I thought Venetia might do the job well but both Sylvia and Clemmie said that Venetia's one wish, always, is to please the person she is fond of. As she is devoted to Diana, she will never criticise her but always fall in with her whims and wishes.

Mottisfont, Sunday December 3

Today warm and wet. Very high temperatures most of October and November and quantities of rain. The spring, which dried up from April to October, is pouring out water – as I like to see it do. The Home Guard had its final parade today. The Mayor of Romsey took the salute and now it's disbanded.

London, Monday December 4

After lunch to Wildenstein's Gallery where there is an exhibition on 'From Constable to Cézanne' organised by Derek [Hill]. My small Delacroix is there – a pretty minnow among sea trout, salmon and a whale or two.

London, Tuesday December 12

Lunched with Boris and Maroussia at the Etoile to meet Mrs Stirling of Keir, B.'s first patron, for whom he is doing a mosaic of the Sacred Heart. She has always been very kind and considerate to him and I was curious to meet her. We drove away alone together afterwards. She said the trouble about B. was that he was no businessman, he always asked much too little for his work.

London, Wednesday December 13

Raymond M., Juliet Henley (now Daniel), Stephen Spender and Clive Bell lunched. The electricity was fused so we sat in our coats as people do in Paris. Raymond had just returned. Described the conditions: black market – oysters, orchids, chrysanthemums and luxuries coming into Paris but no milk or meat. Tremendous prices paid in restaurants (black market prices), no heating, no baths, no petrol, except petrol sold by the American Army (so it is said) to the black marketeers, electric light only available for a few hours. Raymond used to go to the Embassy to see Cecil Beaton who was staying there, then making an excuse about washing his hands, made for the bathroom where he had a quick bath. The only way of getting one.

Generally feeling under the weather and depressed, Maud takes a fortnight off from the Admiralty. She spends a week at Mottisfont, followed by Christmas at Wentworth with her mother and Raymond. On December 16, Nazi Germany commences the Ardennes counter-offensive, catching the Allies by surprise.

London, Sunday December 31

Over Xmas a heavy hoar-frost covered ground and trees and a dense white mist shrouded everything. News of the serious German attack in the Ardennes began to trickle through and suddenly the war looked as if it was going to last for years.

On Thursday I dined with Sibyl at Lord North St and sat between Terence Rattigan, the playwright, and Chips Channon. Among others there the Greek Minister Aghnides and Major [Desmond] Morton. Talked afterwards to Sir Lionel Ismay,[20] a nice goggle-eyed, swarthy soldier. He went to Paris with Winston in October. Said it was <u>very</u> dangerous. PM should never have been allowed to go but no one can ever stop him. Nothing would have been easier than to shoot him from any one of many hundred windows. Ismay was close behind him and determined, if shooting started, to put out his foot, trip up the PM and bring him to the ground. He said the PM, who is very emotional and cries equally from pleasure or from sadness, cried and sobbed from the moment he set foot in France. They landed at a new airfield. Ismay thought the PM would be interested in the airfield and ask a number of questions but he was too busy crying. And as they walked through the streets of Paris tears poured down his face. 'Everybody cried at some time or other,' said Ismay. 'I cried when a detachment from the Brigade of Guards passed. They walked not exactly arrogantly but as if to say, "Of course we're here again. Oh, yes, we had to clear out of France in 1940 but we always knew we were coming back again."'

Because of the horrifying troubles – civil war – in Greece, I fancied the Greek Minister [Ambassador Thanassis Aghnides] might look pale and distraught. Not at all. When Major Morton mumbled a commiseration he

20. General Hastings Lionel Ismay, 1st Baron Ismay (1887-1965), army officer and public servant, chief military assistant to Winston Churchill during the Second World War, enjoying his complete trust. Secretary General NATO 1952-57.

said laughingly: 'We Greeks always fight among ourselves and we always shall.' Very many English people are most miserable and sickened at the thought of British troops firing on Greeks but not so the Greek Minister.[21]

After the New Year, Maud returns to the Admiralty.

London, Saturday January 6 1945

Yesterday lunched with a stranger, a new John Russell, at the Jardin des Gourmets. He works at Sanctuary Buildings [*where the Admiralty had offices*] and had been urged a long time ago by Stuart Preston to introduce himself to me. I was struck by him. I believe he is that rare thing, a man with a personality of his own and not a potpourri of other people's. He is fair, straight-backed, narrow shouldered, aged 25. He says witty things in a conversational way. He looks very observant – of character, of personality. In other matters, aloof and unobservant as Rex sometimes was. He talks rather slowly because of a dumbfounding stammer which, however, often completely vanishes. He writes on painting and painters and works of the nineteenth century.

John Russell became one of Maud's dearest friends, to whom she entrusted her diaries and some personal correspondence on her death (see page 36).

London, Tuesday January 9

Went to dinner with the new John Russell, sharing a car with Edith Sitwell[22] down to Paulton Square. In the car Edith confessed to the fact she was wearing a hat. This was news to me. In the dim light I thought I saw her hair coiled in great plaits, tier above tier – like an immensely high tiara – as the Romans used to wear their hair. Only when the light was better could I see that she was wearing a hat of silver tissue built up with plaits of silver. It suited her very well and was the only original thing about her dress on this occasion. On our way we collected Osbert [Sitwell], awkward with gout, from Carlyle Square. The new John's dinner was given in a friend's house – Esther Darlington's – and the other guest was William Plomer[23] whom

21. In a controversial decision British forces were ordered to secure Athens after violence broke out between leftists and rightists targeting the power vacuum left by the withdrawal of German troops.
22. Dame Edith Sitwell (1887-1964), poet and critic. Notorious for her exotic dress.
23. William Plomer (1903-73), author, poet and literary editor.

I'd never met before. The house was newly-painted, newly-got-into, very sparsely furnished and completely devoid of cosiness or atmosphere. The hostess and William Plomer were so busy with the cooking and serving, and new John so active fetching chairs, bringing coffee and so on, that the Sitwells and I saw little of them. Edith was looking her beautiful gothic self. I always like her. Osbert was more insistently anecdotal than ever. He cut into any conversation with: 'Did I ever tell you?' Then followed an anecdote, always rather funny, but not much wanted.

London, Thursday January 11

Lunch with Mama at Claridges. Four generations represented – mama, myself, Mary and her boy Paul. Mary expects another child in May. She is wise to have a bigger family and not bother herself too much about whether she can afford it. G. and I longed for a big family, but owing to some delicacy or inability[24] of mine, two was all we had, sad to say.

From January 1-17, the Germans withdrew from Ardennes and on January 17 Soviet troops capture Warsaw, Poland.

London, Wednesday January 17

The Russian winter offensive seems to have started at last. We are reducing, steadily, the Ardennes bulge and if only we can still manage to go over to the offensive in a fairly biggish way, great things might yet happen.

Clare and Mark Tennyson came to see me before lunch. Mark has just returned with his destroyer, *Etruscan*, from the Mediterranean where he had a number of successful engagements off Greece and the Greek Islands. At Mytilene he put a Brigadier ashore to cope with ELAS [*Greek People's Liberation Army, effectively controlled by the Greek Communist Party*] who were terrorising. After firing a salvo into the air, they put the Brigadier ashore. ELAS disappeared in a flash into houses and cellars and out came the inhabitants who had been hiding in their cellars and gave the Brigadier and the ship's crew a great welcome. Mark said he'd never been so warmly entertained or seen such kindness and hospitality. After five days they withdrew. 'What happened then?' I asked. 'I should think ELAS rushed up from the cellars again', said Mark, 'and the others hurried back into theirs.'

---

24. Maud inserted the words 'or inability' after 'delicacy' at a later date. I haven't been able to find out what this referred to.

On another occasion, after *Etruscan* had set fire during a night engagement to a German destroyer, which the Germans managed to beach, the sound of shooting came from across the water. The ship's crew were mystified as to what was happening. When they came within view of the shore, they saw the crew of the German destroyer – most of whom had managed to get to the beach – being mown down by ELAS and slaughtered. This incident shocked Mark. 'They were unarmed men,' he said. 'They should have been taken prisoner, not shot.' I am glad to think these distinctions still count. I forgot to ask Mark how he knew the Greek guerrillas belonged to ELAS and not to any of the other parties.

London, Thursday January 18

I lunched at the Ivy with Clive Bell. Peter Quennell was there and Desmond MacCarthy appeared about 2.30. Clive is wonderfully dated and his mere presence is a kind of escapism. He lives by virtue of values most of us have forgotten or have brushed aside in the turmoil and the fray. Desmond is an old man but he is not especially dated. Clive shot his cuffs, he emphasised and mouthed as he used to and his hair was turbaned round his head as of old. Desmond had a story I liked very much about Heine[25] who said with a sigh on seeing a young and pretty Polish woman: 'Si jeune, et déjà Polonaise.'[26]

London, Sunday January 21

Went with mama and Alexie to see a Marx Brothers film and laughed a lot. I feel deprived in my life of laughter. When the chance presents itself, I laugh like a lunatic.

London, Wednesday January 31

Boris called for me and we walked out to dinner with Sam at Manetta's. Christabel had told me the night before who was going to be there. The

---

25. Heinrich Heine (1797-1856), German poet, journalist, essayist and literary critic. Born into a Jewish family, Heine converted to Protestantism in 1825 because, he explained, it was the 'ticket of admission into European culture.' His radical political views led to many of his works being banned in Germany. In an insight of what was to occur in Germany in the 1930s he famously wrote: 'Where they burn books, they will ultimately burn people as well.'
26. 'So young, and already Polish'

party sounded a fine jumble with Sir Kenneth and Lady Clark the uncertain quantity. B. was appalled at the thought of meeting them as he doesn't much like Sir K. and the same goes for Lady C. He said if they offered to drive him home to Hampstead, where they too live, he would refuse. We discussed whether he should seize the occasion to mention the National Gallery mosaic to Sam if he happened to find himself alone for a few moments with him. B. suggested making some sort of allusion to a possible mosaic commission to the room at large and getting views on Virtues and Vices. I was rather against this. It seemed premature. I felt it was awkward mentioning the subject in front of Sam, who was B.'s patron for the other floors and might think B. was fishing for another commission, without making it clear that the commission had come from elsewhere. And _that_ I didn't want suddenly made public. I don't want any publicity. I tried to explain this to B. I felt B. was going to be voluble and indiscreet and hoped I wouldn't be next to him. Well, I _was_ next to him, with Sam the other side, and he _was_ indiscreet, and the Virtues and Vices got bandied about as I feared. I sweated and hoped Sam didn't think Boris was throwing out hints to _him_. I don't know what Sir K. thought.

The evening ended with a final Russian clumsiness from my poor bear. When Sir K. asked Boris whether he could give him a lift home, Boris refused loudly and triumphantly, saying that he couldn't accept as he had an engagement with a lady. There was general laughter and when we all started saying goodbye and asked, as one does, which way are you going, it appeared quite plainly that B. was trying to take me home. But by then I had accepted a lift from Barbara Freyberg. That dinner was agony. And B. behaved just as Russians are constantly shown behaving in novels and plays – clumsily, noisily, embarrassingly and agonizingly. And after it was all over the poor wretch realises what he has been doing or saying and nearly dies of shame.

London, Sunday February 4

B. fetched me at Claridges and we went to a film and afterwards up to his studio in Hampstead for dinner. I have been there only once before many years ago, soon after it had been bombed. So this was an adventure. I expected to see it as it looked years ago and was surprised to find a warm room, light, a fire burning, armchairs, tables, ornaments, pictures, some leaves in a vase, a table laid for dinner, and all the outward signs of normal life. 'How strange and unexpected this is,' I thought. I imagined B. and M. lived in a kind of ruin with piles of dust and bricks around them, living little better than animals. But here they are in a warm, civilised room. The walls are plain, pale-coloured brick and on them a remarkably good drawing by B. done many years ago; a large ikon of the Archangel Michael with a beautiful cloak and the most fascinating pair of spindly legs; and a picture made of *papier-mâché*, or carved out of wood, of a ship and plenty of blue sea and sky. The window is immensely high and has stone-coloured satin curtains which were much damaged by glass when the house was blitzed. There is a small table with a little group of the Russian Royal family on it. From the room, an open staircase leads up to a balcony overlooking it – a kind of gallery. We dined in the lower room and had an extremely good dinner. B. had prepared a *compote* – slices of apple with small pieces of bitter-orange peel in it – and he was very pleased with it. The room B. uses as a studio is on the other side of the entrance hall. The mosaic of the Sacred Heart [*for Mrs Stirling*] was being assembled on a large table. A good part of the head was done and I was startled by the brilliance of the pieces and the juxtaposition of the colours. I liked seeing Boris at home. The surroundings suit him. The rooms are warm and hospitable. I liked looking across the table at Boris and seeing just behind his head the Archangel Michael, with his brilliant cloak and spindly legs. The evening was happy and strange.

When I got back here I found a message asking me to ring Hilde Lubelska up at once and guessed it was to say Tante Fritze had died. And so it was. She died early that morning of old age.

London, Tuesday February 6

Today Sibyl, Osbert Peake and George Dix[27] lunched here. Osbert said the French ought to have a closed season for the shooting of collaborationists – say May 1st – they oughtn't to go on indefinitely. People ought to know when they could start settling down, he added laughingly. He was in very good spirits. Said he'd paid a visit to the Mint in his capacity as a Treasury Official and in the visitor's book he saw Gilbert's and my name.[28] Remarked how few people visit the Mint. Our names are in the same book as Sir Isaac Newton's.

27. George Dix (1912-99), art dealer and collector. Opened in 1967 art gallery in New York.
28. It was a family tradition to visit the Mint as Maud's mother Maria grew up over the Mint in Frankfurt and then Berlin. She used to take her children, grandchildren and great-grandchildren to visit the London Mint.

London, Tuesday February 13

Lunched with Cyril and Eddy at the Etoile. Cyril seemed shy or oppressed, or perhaps simply disappointed the lunch wasn't more glamorous. He has been in Paris. There was so much talk about Charles Morgan that Cyril, who had agreed it might be quite amusing to meet him, now says he feels he couldn't possibly do so. How silly these literary chaps are. He's envious. He can't forgive Morgan for being so esteemed by the French. Cyril talked of the furious letters editors get and quoted one he'd had the other day beginning: 'Homosexuals like you ought to have your backsides kicked from there to Sodom.'

On Sunday I wrote a formal letter to B., which he could show if a V2 destroys me, asking him whether he would do the remaining National Gallery floor for £4,000 or, if the directors weren't agreeable to the whole floor being done, then £3,500 for the main, central part of the landing.

From February 4-11, Churchill, Roosevelt and Stalin met at Yalta in the Crimea to discuss the reorganisation of Europe after the war. Among other demands, Stalin insisted that the Soviet Union kept the territory in eastern Poland that it had annexed in 1939.

London, Friday February 16

Utek and Urla Podleski lunched on Wednesday at Etoile. Both very depressed about the result of the Yalta Conference and the decisions taken about Poland. Utek said, 'Why should we fight anymore? We have lost our country. After the war is over where shall I go?' He longed not to return to the front and had been to a doctor hoping he would be found unfit. He has fought with great bravery in all the stiffest fighting from D-Day onwards and has the Virtuti Militari [*Poland's highest military decoration*].

London, Sunday February 18

A week or so ago I saw Field Marshal Montgomery for the first time. He was driving along Whitehall in a large car. I made the taxi slow down, peered out and saw the car draw up at the War Office. It was the Big Man but fatter than I expected. He walked across the pavement in a coy, self-conscious manner as if he expected to be recognised. There was something distinctly feminine in his coyness. But he remained unrecognised, the passers-by were preoccupied.

The Crimean conference is over. France wasn't represented. The photographs show Winston looking like a very gay clown, the President a wraith and Stalin a softened ruffian.

Today lunched with Boris at Shanghai. Tomorrow he is to dine with Kenneth Clark to whom he wrote some days ago saying the chance had occurred to finish the National Gallery floor. Clark wrote back saying how splendid and asked B. to dinner. Boris wants to make panels of the Virtues and Vices – but a new edition of them, <u>modern</u> virtues and vices. We discuss them. Boris has ideas but it's not easy. The modern versions either sound banal or on a very much lower plane than the originals. The titles too are important. The word must look and sound well. Common sense, humour, live and let live, spunk (hideous word) are some temporary favourites. I am sure they will all be changed. I have asked B. to keep my name out of this as much as possible but I feel sure he will keep on blurting it out. He can't understand my reasons and asks but why are you ashamed? I am not ashamed but he doesn't understand.

London, Wednesday February 21

Went to *Uncle Vanya* with George Dix. First time I'd seen the play and it seemed remarkably good. The audience laughed during the shooting scene and all the crying that followed. It's asking too much of an English audience to do anything else, brought up as it is to exercise self-control, hide feeling, not cry in public and put the best face it can on an awkward situation.

London, Friday February 21

Boris came to the flat and then we went to the White Tower where Desmond MacCarthy and Diana C., on a visit to London, joined us. Diana seemed glamorous to me in her French clothes, elegant hat, veil, earrings and faint smell of good scent. She looked very handsome and much younger again. She had nothing new to say about Paris but she talked very animatedly and busily thinking, I suppose, that we hadn't heard much about Paris. B. looked at her, fascinated, though he has known her for years and afterwards asked a lot of questions about her – what her life was like, what had made her so 'nervous', why she talked and rattled away as she did. He thought she was like an actress – and so she is in some ways. Diana's appearance – as it were from another world and another kind of life – unsettled and agitated both B. and me.

London, Monday February 26

Admiralty after lunch as usual and was told that I. had rung me up. He came to dinner at Claridges full of stories about his travels. He has been away four months, visited a number of places in the Mediterranean. Then India and Ceylon where he saw Martin, who made a good impression on him. When I told him that Martin had written and said, 'It was wonderful to see someone from home.' Poor I. suddenly realised what that sort of thing can mean and muttered, 'I ought to have done more for him.'

He told me about a singular coincidence that occurred to him in Ceylon, making him feel as if he was entangled in a witches' mesh. On the beach at Mount Lavinia, a Sinhalese came up to tell his fortune. Ian asked if there were any women in his (I.'s) life who had influenced it very much. The fortune teller said yes, two. His mother and another woman, a widow. He couldn't tell in what relationship she stood to him; he couldn't see it clearly. She'd given him (I.) money, for what purpose the soothsayer didn't understand. That same evening, I. dined in Colombo. The talk was about ghosts and I., when asked, said he'd only had one experience of that sort that he ascribed to a heavy dinner. He described a sort of nightmare he'd had at Mottisfont when a great bat seemed to fly out from behind his bed, circle the room and disappear again into the wall behind his bed. 'Probably the result of eating lobster thermidor,' he said. Dinner over, the little party went to the movies and almost immediately a documentary film was shown called 'Two Ancient Abbeys'. Ian was dumbfounded when one of the Abbeys turned out to be Mottisfont and there he saw the well-known aspects of the house, the steps leading down from the morning room, the cellarium, the dining room with Reeve moving round the table, and my bedroom. He felt as if he were the object of sorcery.

Forston, Dorchester, Sunday March 4 [*Staying with Alice Astor*]

Crinks [*Liberal politician Harcourt Johnstone*] died suddenly of a stroke on March 1st. I am really unhappy about it. I thought of him as one of my best friends and loved his eighteenth century personality, though it included prodigality, arrogance and on occasions, dreadful rudeness, especially to servants – faults which are not in fashion anymore and which for that reason seem doubly unattractive. He certainly liked rich and extravagant living and I think he would have hated the post-war world in which he would have come to seem, more and more, an archaic figure. He was very generous and big-hearted and one went easily to him for advice. He was shrewd and clear-headed where his own affairs weren't under discussion but when they were he quarrelled with wine merchants, art dealers, shops, servants and bankers. As his obituary notices remark, he hated sham and pretension.

London, Wednesday March 7

Returned from Forston on Monday and went straight to work at the Admiralty where I found Serpell had rearranged my work and stuck me with a neglected job of Donkin's and rewarded her with pleasanter work of mine. Boiling rage. Today I. came to dinner bringing a number of presents collected on his journey: two pairs of stockings, a box of almonds and nuts, a packet of Bromo [*loo paper*], four small books, powder-puffs and a satin scarf from Honolulu. He sat talking very late. I didn't tell him about my Admiralty grievances. They are irritating for me but too small-scale to worry him with. During the evening he said, 'You are the only person who seems alright, everybody else has come and poured out their troubles to me.' After being with I., I always feel a more sensible, less petty and more courageous person.

In early March, Maud writes formally to Kenneth Clark offering to commission Boris to complete the last landing at the National Gallery. Clark replies that the proposal will be considered by the Directors at the next meeting.

London, Monday March 12

On Saturday Raymond and Alexie came to lunch. Raymond's course is finished and he is now an officer, Royal Fusiliers. Looking very well, dressed in new civilian suit. He gets over 200 clothes coupons for his role of officer and gentleman. Talked, laughed and seemed happy.

London, Tuesday March 13

Dined with Cyril. Lys was there, of course, pretty and flowerlike, Stephen Spender, Desmond Mac. and a couple whose name I didn't catch. It transpired that Natasha, Stephen's wife, was in the process of having her first baby. After dinner S. telephoned to the nursing home and was told 'in about one and a half hours' which he took calmly enough and sat on talking. After he left, the telephone rang and it was the nursing home to say his child had been born. 'May one ask what it is?' said Cyril in his odd, wobbly voice. It was a fine boy, they said.

London, Friday March 16

On Thursday I. dined, questioned me about the section and I told him what it had been like the last year, and that I didn't care for it anymore. I've had a charming letter from K. Clark saying that the [National Gallery] Trustees were delighted and most grateful [*regarding the commission of Boris's last pavement*].

London, Monday March 19

Admiralty 3-5, then to the studio to dine with Maroussia and Boris. It was pleasant and the food was absolutely delicious. We discussed B.'s list of human qualities for the National Gallery floor, trying to think of new ones or to find a more attractive synonym for some quality we had agreed on. The trouble is that words are such living things and their sense or suitability so exact that even a synonym evokes a host of new impressions and new trains of thoughts. Left the studio in a great gale of wind and rain and B. walked me down to Golders Green Tube Station as it was too wet and boisterous to wait patiently at the bus stop. I struggled in the wind and rain, laughing, holding onto B.'s arm and trying to prevent his umbrella from getting blown inside out. He said, 'You are like a drunken sailor.'

Mottisfont, Palm Sunday, March 25

Yesterday Montgomery and his armies crossed the Rhine in four places.

Barhatch, Easter Sunday April 1

Went to see Flora [*Gilbert's sister*] at East Hills. She lives entirely in her long sitting-room, sleeping, writing and eating there. It is completely packed with junk, curios and one or two better things – an empire clock under a glass dome, a wooden-cased Georgian clock. The walls are crammed with prints and bad pictures, the bookcases packed with books, most of them from Audley Square or Russell houses. There is hardly a good thing in the room and everything is in such confusion. It is ludicrous but rather delightful. Every object has its history, clearly remembered and often discussed.

London, Thursday April 5

I. proposed himself to dinner. Had been spending a week's leave with Esmond Rothermere and Ann O'Neill who have taken Lord Moyne's house at

Littlehampton, and was so fed up, bored and aggravated by the atmosphere, the frivolity and the chatter that he packed up and left four days before his leave ended. He complained about that crowd and said why had I let him see such people, why hadn't I said what I thought about them? To which I answered: I didn't want to run down people he liked seeing, and that men who worked hard and seriously all day long often needed the relaxation of gay, light chatter, and that Duff and Mr Asquith, and countless other men, have found that sort of society a great rest. In any case Ann isn't stupid nor the others – only perhaps people with little guts and very little sense of duty or obligation – unless a photographer is on the spot. I. said, 'That is the wrong world for me. I can't imagine why I ever see them. I am Presbyterian and Scotch.' He said, 'You are to blame.' I said, 'If it helps you, you can always say so.' Then he looked moved and protested.

London, Sunday April 8
Yesterday Alexie and Raymond dined. R. looks remarkably well. He took his men out on an exercise and appears to have enjoyed it immensely. How strange, after all those agonies three years ago. Today long morning in bed reading that the army is nearing Bremen and Hanover. Can't take a fraction of this in. We are gorged on victories.

London, Wednesday April 11
On Monday I went to Leicester Galleries where Hugh Walpole's pictures are being sold and there I bought a small Landseer[29] landscape – mountains and a lake – and a small Alfred Stevens[30] of a ship sailing away over a dirty yellowish sea with a vast amount of sky overhead.

London, Friday April 13
Boris lunched at the flat and the weather being quite wonderful – there is a heatwave with temperatures of 68 and 70 and more – we went to Kew which was a dream of green, clouds of white blossom and pale blue misty distance. All the blossom was out and the magnolias. We brought our tea and had it by the river, watching the ducks flying round and settling between us and the

29. Sir Edwin Landseer (1802-73), painter.
30. Alfred Stevens (1823-1906) Belgian painter. In a note added later, Maud says the picture was sold in the 50s.

tugs and barges. It was a dreamlike afternoon. From there we went by bus to the studio where Maroussia gave us an excellent dinner. The [*Sacred Heart*] mosaic has made great progress. I like the striped garment but found fault with the arm which seemed to have no bone, consisting only of heavy draped material and a fine bony hand. B. paid a lot of attention to this criticism and began to try alterations at once. Maroussia was called in from the other room to advise and suggest too.

London, Sunday April 15

Yesterday I. came to dinner. I cooked some cutlets for him and managed by overcooking to reduce them to a mere mouthful. Today got up very late, ate a light lunch and went to the Admiralty.

Roosevelt died suddenly on the 12th. He had been in bad health for some time though he worked till the end and travelled to Yalta in January. He was a great man. His value to us was 1) always anti-fascist and 2) he knew his own countrymen intimately and how to get them to do the most unlikely things. In political affairs he was exceptionally astute. He was very courageous and patient. He had a fine idealistic type of American face.

London, Wednesday April 18

Mama's birthday. 76. She wouldn't let me arrange a family dinner and wouldn't even come to lunch as her sister, my Tante Emmy, has her birthday on the same day and she is alone, without a maid, in her flat in Berlin – if, indeed, she is still alive. She is, or would have been 81, and has insisted on staying on in Berlin through all the bombing. I don't think one leaves one's house easily at 81.

London, Thursday April 19

Lunched with B. at Shanghai and picnicked in the flat. He was in a heavy, sad, apprehensive mood as he always is if he knows he isn't going to see me for several days. He said, 'You didn't know what you were letting yourself in for when you took me on' and 'I am quite capable of a shooting act.' Sometimes these heavy broodings and half threats alarm me. The Russian soul is different to the Western European equivalent. For one it's poisoned with suspicion. The great moments are greater, the dismal ones more dismal and the soul staggers between the two.

London, Sunday April 22

I. dined and cooked some of the dinner. He gave a fascinating account of the capture by [Robert] Harling and some of the Assault Unit of two important German physicists living incognito in a German country house long bypassed by the Americans. The house belonged to a cultivated, very cosmopolitan, aristocratic German, of the Von Papen kind, who received Harling and party in the most snare [sic] manner and staggered these simple souls with his knowledge of England, English country houses, nicknames of the great, relationships, scandals and political intrigues. He wasn't at all their idea of a German and Harling was bowled over. But he nabbed the two physicists all the same and all their immensely valuable papers and records – he kept his head for that – and the lorry was loaded up. After the search was concluded and the valuables collected Harling and the German sat out in the courtyard, where Harling had a gun mounted as a precaution and a threat, and they talked and talked, and so the day passed. I believe Ian has got Harling to write a detailed account of his adventure, but no matter how detached it is it will never give a hint of what the German extracted from poor Harling!

The Allies are continuing to make huge military gains in Europe. The Soviets take Berlin, US troops reach Nuremberg, Mussolini is captured and hanged, and the Italian front collapses. There are reports that Heinrich Himmler is trying to negotiate peace with the Allies.

Mottisfont, Sunday April 29

Buchenwald and Belsen were overrun a fortnight ago and their hells opened up. I am prepared to bet that Osbert Sitwell and those who don't want to face the fact of German sadism still won't allow themselves to be convinced. The week has been one of tremendous happenings. I feel blunted and can't take things in. It seems strange to live through such times and to be able to register so little. Many people feel the same. We are blunted and dulled, and over-used to happenings, great and small, of the most extraordinary kind; glutted with drama and tragedy, blood and thunder, dreadful miseries and sufferings, heroic tales, fantastic occurrences, fortitude, courage and death. Among these we crawl, most of us, preoccupied with the small details of daily life, busy keeping our place in queues, buying rations, catching crowded buses or planning small pleasures. We are poor limited creatures.

On April 30, Hitler commits suicide.

London, Thursday May 3

Admiralty 4-5. My work there is over and I started tearing up papers. Then went to a News Reel to see the films of Buchenwald and Belsen. They are little worse than the photographs. The figure which struck me as the strangest is that of a skeleton of a man sitting among a heap of rags which he appears to be sorting and wearing on his head a sort of pointed dunce's cap. He seems unconscious of the world around him, indeed the world seems to have ceased to exist for him. No doubt his mind had left it even if his body hadn't.

London, Saturday May 5

I. should have come to dinner yesterday but wasn't back from Germany. So I dined alone and then listened to every broadcast I could get hold of. And so I heard of the German surrender to Montgomery of NW Germany, Denmark, Holland, Frisian Islands, Heligoland and their fleet. A description of this great act taking place near Lüneberg was broadcast. After this stirring news I went on tuning in to all the news. Finally, when I tried to go to sleep, I found it quite impossible. The war over for us in the west! These long six years, the fears and anxieties, the troubles and small worries, Gilbert not alive to rejoice, the boys still likely to be in the army for some time, all this and much else passed through my agitated mind.

On May 7, all German forces unconditionally surrendered to the Allies.

London, VE Day Tuesday May 8

Oggie Lynn, Boris and Eddy came to lunch. At 3 we listened to the PM's broadcast announcing the end of hostilities and a moment later Raymond rang up from Liverpool St to say he'd just arrived in London, expected to have 24 hours leave, and would come along when he'd disposed of his men and their luggage. This he did and another lunch was served. Then R. and I went to Whitehall and came up out of the tube in the sea of a vast crowd which was filling Whitehall, especially opposite the Ministry of Health where windows were decorated with baize and flags. A few moments later the PM and the War Cabinet came out on the central balcony and the PM addressed the crowd through loud-speakers: 'This is your day' etc. We heard him well but unfortunately couldn't see him. The crowd was enormous, the day very hot and damp. We wound our way through Parliament Square and went into the Abbey. At that moment the 6 o'clock service started so we sat down near the tomb of the Unknown Warrior which formed a kind of shrine. People were pressing round it all the time. We sat in the cool till the service was over and the greater part of the crowd had disappeared. Then out we went into the blazing sunlight and decided to walk home rather than take the tube. We walked past Horse Guards Parade and it struck me I would like to visit the Admiralty, partly out of sentiment for the place and the day, partly for more private and personal reasons. So I left R. sitting on the steps of the Guards Memorial and went in for a few minutes. I got back to the flat, footsore, wet with heat and exhausted. R. and I dined alone but Alexie joined us later. They went off to see the illuminations at night but I was much too tired. I am immensely glad the war in Europe is over but not elated.

London, Thursday May 10

Yesterday Alexie joined me at home. We went out about 4 or 5 and found a small crowd in Grosvenor Square and were told the PM was about to pay a visit to the American Embassy. We stood in the crowd and cheered him as he drove up. I had no idea how useful police horses are in manipulating and pressing back a crowd. I had the huge white haunches of one of them between me and the PM's car as I surged forward with the others at the moment of his arrival. I happened to be passing back through Gros. Sq. as the PM drove away and this time I had a close-up view in an empty street. I stood in the roadway and his car passed within five or six feet of me. He was sitting on the hood of his small open car with his feet on the seat. He looked expressionless and distant like a rugged, time-worn idol and under the surface pink of his face he looked white. He seemed exhausted. He didn't see me or any of the six or seven people standing about and waving at him. He seemed withdrawn.

That night Cyril, Lys, new John Russell, Stephen Spender and Elizabeth Bowen dined. The talk was mostly topical – the heat, the sights, the illuminations, the Royal Family and our feet. And indeed feet was one of the main topics of VE and 1 Day because people had walked and trudged and stood about so much in the very hot weather and, in many cases, their shoes were old or ill-fitting due to wartime conditions.

Today I went to the Admiralty and tore up more of my papers. Dined with Natasha and Stephen Spender in their new house in Loudoun Road. Her relations Mr and Mrs George Booth were there, a man whose name I never heard, and a German – not a Jew but a refugee from Germany in the late 30s. He was a decent sort of young man but humourless and very German. He said Belsen and Buchenwald had been constantly in his mind these days and he'd tried to find occasions in the histories of other countries when the public conscience had been so inert, lulled, or deadened that persecutions and cruelties had occasioned no outcry. Casting round he seemed to have derived considerable satisfaction from the discovery of the horrible conditions of child labour in England a century ago. Here, he said, was a historical parallel to the state of mind that could permit a Belsen. I felt it wasn't any good trying to alter the German character. It's unalterable.

London, Friday May 11

I. dined and told me all about his journey to Schloss Tambach, near Coburg, from Paris with Mitchell that very rough diamond: how kind and excellent the Americans were without exception, how cold it was, how they raced along and finally how they arrived at the Schloss and seized the complete German Naval Documents and Records – complete up to January 1945 when the documents were evacuated there in charge of a couple of admirals. He described the extraordinary situation in the Schloss and the outbuildings – the owners still there, the Americans who'd been too soft and polite and left them in their rooms, doubling up rather uncomfortably themselves and not establishing themselves definitely as the masters of the situation. They asked instead of giving orders. Everything was very confused. Every building was packed and stuffed with people: escaped prisoners, displaced persons, foreign workers, Americans, Russian women. The whole thing was chaotic. However the documents were there safe and sound and constitute a great prize.

London, Tuesday May 15

B. and I stayed at Mottisfont [*over weekend*]. We talked and walked, discussed the National Gallery commission and listened to songs and music from Moscow. But I wasn't feeling well. The cessation of my work and the end of the war have reduced me to thinking about myself and my lonely state again. I think constantly of Gilbert – the spring, the flowers he liked, remind me of him and my life with him. I feel lost and unsettled again. There is nothing and nobody to come back to. Soon I shall have to start resuming the life I laid down when I went to work at the Admiralty. I shall have to bother more about Mottisfont. I shall have to make plans of one kind and another. I don't care for the thought of an idle life. Filling my life with social engagements till I die seems a sad and dismal way to spend it. I wish I could find someone I liked and marry again. I wish I could have died with G. He seems immensely far away from me now. This is a cruel business.

London, Thursday May 17

Lunch with Xandra Howard-Johnston [*née Haig*]. Dawyck [*Xandra's brother Douglas Haig*] looked appallingly delicate but he was in high spirits and talked freely about his experiences. He was one of the 'Special Prisoners' earmarked by Himmler and was moved with the others from his prison camp to Königstein on the Elbe. Dawyck was obviously infected with anti-Russian propaganda and looked on their armies with horror. He described the last hours before their arrival. It was a race whether the Americans or the Russians would get there first. Then on the horizon to the east small dots appeared and these gradually became lorries, carts, tanks or men, till finally, without any apparent control or discipline, the Red Army was there. I asked how the Russians behaved. 'Without any discipline. They took anything they wanted off anybody they met – wrist watches, coats, boots. They broke into cellars, they carried off the women into the barns.' 'Did you see any beating up or killing?' said I. 'No,' he said. The relief, he said, when the Americans arrived was tremendous. They arrived in their traditional way, war correspondents, loudspeakers, chocolates and chewing gum right up with the first tanks and infantry.

Wentworth, Monday May 21

On Friday I. dined and gave me a gold locket. He told me how narrow a squeak we had last year with V1 [*the 'flying-bomb'*]. If Eisenhower hadn't said go ahead on June 6th – though the weather wasn't ideal – he would have had to put D-Day off till August as the weather was unfailingly bad on the few days on which tide, moon etc. were suitable during the eight weeks following June 6th. V1 started about June 20th. If there had been no Normandy landing by that date all the V1 [*launch*] sites in that region would have come into action against London and the south coast, as well as those that actually did, and the destruction would have been immense with who can tell what deferment of D-Day.

On Saturday I came down here very tired and tormented with worries about the new world we are hoping to build. The Russians seem to be playing a most unscrupulous double-dealing game of power-politics. Their attitude to Poland makes me sick. Then there is Tito in Trieste, polite and threatening at the same time with Russia at his elbow. One can only feel miserable at all this and the lack of decency of behaviour and all this ruffianliness. B. says much of it is done to have bargaining counters. It may be so but friends don't behave in that way.

London, Thursday May 24

Urla telephoned to say her mother Hilde had died that afternoon after four days of illness. She'd had a rare illness for some years. When she was young, she was extremely pretty, very small, tiny bones, delicate skin and lovely eyes. She was devoted to her children and made a comfortable home for them.

London, Friday May 25

I tried to see the German submarine which is tied up in the docks near the Tower but I found a queue of three or four hundred people. I went and bought my meat ration, tried without success to get a skirt invisibly darned, and got back here at 12 to find Boris already in the flat preparing to hang a picture. While the raids were on I only had reproductions and lithographs here, but lately I have brought up a Picasso watercolour and a Degas drawing and it was this picture B. hung while I acted as mate.

London, Saturday May 26

Went to a News Reel. I try to go twice a week to see all the current news, the occupation of Germany, the arrest of German generals, admirals, Nazi bosses and officials – every possible topical thing. I have no reason to feel kindly towards the Germans but it's impossible not to feel pity at the sight of some of them; their ghastly world in ruins, their lives wrecked, their faces – often ugly, unpleasant faces – dreadful in their misery. I don't feel elated. My make-up is Christian and humanitarian. I know many of them <u>must</u> be punished but the idea doesn't fill me with glee, however much they merit punishment. We are all sinners in varying degrees.

London, Monday May 28

Went to Hilde Lubelska's cremation at Woking taking down in the car with me her sisters Lisel and Lotte, a German pastor and two unknown friends. It was odd listening to prayers in German. It seems remarkable that the sisters should have wanted a German clergyman, however disassociated from the hated Nazi regime, after everything the Jews have suffered at the hands of the Germans. But I suppose they still feel very German themselves though purely Jewish.

London, Thursday May 31

George Dix, Camilla [Sykes], Xandra [Haig] and Peter Q. lunched. Peter is very entertaining. He asked me whether I had enjoyed Palinurus [*Cyril Connolly's book* The Unquiet Grave *written under the pseudonym Palinurus*]. I said yes. All that self-revelation was fascinating. Peter said laughingly that he'd been amazed when reading it at the depths of suffering it revealed, and astonished to think he had, all these years, been under the same roof as the sufferer without realising what he was enduring. We talked about Cyril and his first marriage and the indescribable squalor of his bedrooms. Peter described going into one of them in the morning in the days of Cyril's marriage. The room was littered, clothes lay on the floor. There was some wild animal kept at large in the room and this animal could only do its affairs in a pan of water. This pan was on the ground full of water and the beast had made use of it during the night. Cyril and his wife lay on the bed 'like stranded whales'. Peter's strange face, dry voice and strange laugh provided at least half the fascination of this story.

Mottisfont, Sunday June 3

Gilbert's birthday on Friday. All this week I have been thinking of him and mourning him. He died three years ago on Monday. Three years ago on Wednesday he was buried at Chenies. Gilbert seems a universe, the whole of time away from me.

The first time I saw I. after VE Day he gave me the Admiralty Signal announcing VE day to all Divisions and asked me to get it framed for him. He had extracted it from the board it was on or the folder it was in and decided he'd worked hard enough to deserve it. It reads [*here Maud wrote a copy of the signal in her diary that is shown on page 297*].

London, Wednesday June 6

I went to Sylvia's to a small cocktail party for Rosalind [Pitt-Rivers, *Sylvia Henley's daughter*] to celebrate her return from Belsen. She was in one of the special parties sent out to combat starvation. She is a sturdy, tough type but Belsen has taken a stone or two off her weight and she looks not far from being a nervous wreck. She was there three weeks. She said one never got over the smell. She attended post-mortems but they were nothing compared with the horrifying sights of the living.

Clare [Tennyson], Christopher [Glenconner], Sammy [Hood] and the K. Clarks came to dinner. Lady C. was as agreeable as possible. I don't like her but she was extremely agreeable. He is remarkably unattractive in spite of his intelligence. They sailed into the room and whether out of shyness, or because they thought it was expected of them, or because it's an ingrained habit, their eyes flew straight to the walls to see what was hanging on them, almost before they'd said their how-d'you-dos. On the walls there were hanging a Degas drawing and a Picasso watercolour and on two little bookcases there stood the small Delacroix and the small Landseer. The Delacroix was immediately recognised, held up, admired and I was told that Sir K. had almost bought it himself. He said, 'You got it £50 below its original price because of me. I told Philips it was too expensive and because it didn't sell at once and because he thought I was going to buy it, he reduced the price.' The Landseer then came in for its share of attention. 'Look, Jane, look what Mrs Russell has got here! The Landseer we liked so much and wanted to buy but it had already been sold!' More admiration. But I am being malicious. They liked both pictures quite genuinely. I don't know why I can't help mocking them. He says he is retiring at the end of the year. He's tired of the job.

London, Monday June 11

Sylvia [Henley] came to lunch and told me that Venetia [Montagu, Sylvia's sister] has had her breast removed. Cancer, no tumour, but swelling of the glands under the arms. She was characteristically abrupt, outspoken and rough – or tough – in manner when she told Sylvia about it. She said, without any preparation, 'I'm going to have my breast amputated on Monday.'

London, Thursday June 14

Lunched with Clive at the Ivy, Bertie Russell on one side of me, Cyril on the other, Mrs Hamish Hamilton and Lys were there too. Bertie looks much older, his hands especially look very gnarled but his little body is as straight as ever, and he still walks lightly and in an alert manner. I've never had much private talk with him but this time we talked a lot and got on. He makes his humorous points with great speed; the story is being told and almost before one is aware of an opportunity having presented itself, the dart is there, neatly planted. He and Clive listen sympathetically to and like each other's stories and jokes. But they don't care so much for Cyril's. Nor does Cyril care so much for theirs. There is a slight feeling of awkwardness between them. They belong to such very different generations and seem conscious of it. I find myself able to laugh at the jokes of both sides, being placed, happily, between the two generations. Bertie and Cyril each told an indecent story.

Bertie hesitated for a moment and had to be pressed to tell it. It was filthy. Cyril didn't have to be pressed to tell his story but then he knew the women of the party much better than Bertie did. Each laughed, a little awkwardly, at the other's story. We sat long at lunch. The two other women left and as I was following slowly, passing Bertie who was sending for his hat and coat, I heard him mutter through his teeth: 'Stay' or perhaps it was 'Wait' which I supposed was addressed to me. This, as it were, secret whisper – the kind of noise and order one usually reserves for intimate friends – surprised me; but I thought I had better wait outside. In a moment, Bertie joined me and off we walked together. I was going shopping in Museum St and Bertie walked there with me, seemed inclined to spend the afternoon in my company. But I intended to sell some unwanted jewellery and thought I could do it best alone. So I asked him to give my love to his wife, and said goodbye.

London, Thursday June 21

I. dined. He was restless. He told me Ann O'Neill had brought him together with Elizabeth Leveson-Gower,[31] a rich only child, an orphan, who will inherit the Earldom of Sutherland on the Duke of Sutherland's death. She is 24. I thought her quite pleasant and obviously she would be a good marriage for him. Ann had rung him up a few days after the dinner and urged him to ask the girl to dine with him. He had done so. Elizabeth L.G. had told him she was going away for the weekend but why didn't he come too? She would get him asked. And this she'd done and he was taking her out for lunch on Saturday and motoring down to the country with her. All this he told me, a bit excited, unsettled. I said it sounded very suitable. And so I'm sure it is. But I felt sad because he is my oldest friend, a strong link with my past life and the one person I could say anything to – and often do. After dinner we listened to an election broadcast of the PM's and then put on some records. But it was a sad evening.

London, Monday June 25

B. came to the flat for tea and took me to the station where I found Mama, Alexie and Tony waiting for the Continental Train. There we were, on the same platform, after an interval of six years waiting for the Boat Train again. I didn't recognise Kitty at first. She looked so much older, very grey, very

31. Elizabeth Sutherland, 24th Countess of Sutherland, born Leveson-Gower (1921-). Married in January 1946, Charles Janson (1917-2006).

foreign and very distinguished. We took her to Claridges and there was a lot of talk as at most reunions. We were all lively and an endless question and answer chatter followed. There was a family dinner in Mama's bedroom. Mary came to it, looking rather weak and sallow as her baby is only three weeks old. Gilbert's absence made me feel only half present so used were we to being together on the occasion of many family gatherings. Kitty has been head of the British Section of Wounded and Missing P/Ws since August 1940. When they were busy she used to take the train into Geneva from Lausanne at 7.15am and didn't get back till late. Tony who has always managed to get his own way with her continues to do so now by being an invalid for life who must not be worried or upset and must be allowed to do as he likes. What luck for him.

London, Tuesday July 3

I. came to dinner. His meeting with Elizabeth Leveson-Gower was a failure and he never went down to the country with her after all. He talked about Ann O'Neill who has just married Esmond Rothermere and told me he'd slept with her a few times, though he'd always denied this before. But though he denied it, I was never in any doubt but that he had.

London, Wednesday July 4

Dined with Ulick [Alexander] at Claridges. He says the King talks as if Princess Elizabeth might marry at any time. Sunninghill Park has been brought by the Crown as a home for her when she does. The King is going to return to London from Windsor which will then only be used, as it was before the war, for Easter and Ascot, in all for about four or five weeks a year. In spite of it being lived in for so few weeks, it always had 40 housemaids busy looking after it as well as carpenters and cabinet-makers. Buckingham Palace is, so Ulick says, in a dreadful state. It needs painting almost throughout and the King wants to put in radiators and hot and cold water in most bedrooms. This will cost at least £130,000 and take five years to do as the Royal Family will be living in it and it will have to be done piecemeal.

London, Thursday July 5

I went down to the Admiralty and handed in my two passes signing a declaration to the effect that I would never divulge in any form what I had learnt during my work there – neither openly nor covertly in the guise of a play, a novel etc.

I felt a pang at leaving as I loved working there. Went to Room 39 for the last time and I saw I. for a moment. A year ago V1s were roaring overhead, life was very different, duty was clear and life sharp and valuable.

London, Wednesday July 11

On Monday Lisel Müller came to lunch. Her husband is alive and a P/W in American or British hands in Austria. A returning soldier brought a short note from him. We talked about her boy's education. I am glad to say she doesn't think of returning to Germany, even if it were possible.

Today I took fruit to Urla Podleska [neé Lubelska]. Jan has been given a scholarship by the late Polish govt in exile of £20 a month so as to study art at the polytechnic. The Polish govt were generous enough to pre-date the grant which otherwise would have been perilously near the time of their dissolution in London. Utek is in Germany and is going to try and get to the Military Camp in which Urla's father is living temporarily. And I am trying to find out how he can be got to England.

London, Friday July 13

I. came to dinner. He is likely to be offered a new job he thinks he won't be able to refuse. It would carry with it the rank of commander if he cared to remain in uniform. Goodbye then to Jamaica and a lazy life, negroes and palms and the dreams that have sustained him during the hard work of these last years. I felt a pang for him. He will go on, straight on, without rest or pause, he will never get free. He will wear himself out and lose his youth. His muscles will melt away, his back will get bent, he will sweat away at this job for ever till his dreams fade and none are left to take their place.

London, Monday July 16

Last night when I came to London [*from Mottisfont*] I found all the street lighting on again – the first time for six years. The sight was lovely and stimulating and I thought, 'Now the war is really over.'

Dined with the Kenneth Clarks. Emerald, the [Garrett] Moores, Clive, Freddie Ashton and Granville-Barker[32] were there. The Clark house in

---

32. Probably Harley Granville-Barker (1877-1946), theatre director and playwright. Although he spent most of the Second World War in the US, he came to the UK in 1945 before returning to Paris where he had made his home for many years.

Hampstead – Upper Terrace House – is an old and pretty house. Plenty of pictures, a large Gainsborough landscape, the white-skinned, red-haired Italian nude by Renoir, a well-painted Delacroix prison (?) scene and a beautiful drawing of a horse's buttocks by Degas. Emerald was tedious after dinner. She said, 'We must make Mr Bell talk to us about art. I want a lecture on art. What is Mr Bell like? I always hear he talks so brilliantly but when I meet him I never hear him talk about art and surely Mr Bell knows a great deal about art?' This went on and on. Emerald has known Clive slightly for 30 years.

As soon as the men appeared after dinner Clive was lassoed and manoeuvred without much effort into a discussion with Granville-Barker, for our benefit, on ART. Clive did his best. The white Renoir opposite was discussed. G.B. didn't like her waist and buttocks and didn't think the Greeks would have either because she was so un-athletic in shape. Also, he said, art should have a moral foundation and a mission and here Renoir and most of the moderns failed. There must be a revival of missionary zeal, another Ruskin and another Morris. We jumped on him and said that most art had a religious foundation and what he was thinking of was Puritanism in art and ethics. The others left first in Emerald's car. Clive, Freddie and I remained deliberately behind and a few minutes later started off down the hill under a starlit sky feeling gay and released.

London, Tuesday July 17

Raymond came up for the day – he, Kitty, Mama, Mary and Alexie lunched. Though it was probably our last sight of each other for a long time he barely said goodbye. It's awkwardness, I daresay. [*Raymond was being sent to India with the Royal Fusiliers at the end of the month.*] Left a basket of raspberries at Margot's and a letter for her. She is dying. I think of her very often and wish I could see her as if by doing so I could comfort and warm her.

I dined with Boris and Maroussia and saw the mosaic of the Holy Trinity that Boris is doing for Mottisfont (*see colour plates*). The hand of God is Boris's own hand. He'd exaggerated the length and vigour of the thumb. I complained. At first he defended it. Then I said it seemed to have a life of its own, apart from the hand to which it belonged, upon which B. said, 'That's a good criticism.'

Mottisfont, Monday July 23

I had three letters from Boris, two of them written under the stress of painful emotions after a fainting-fit at Waterloo after seeing me off, followed by a collapse of the nerves. He seems to have been so miserable and so ill that he went, when his faint was over, to a doctor and poured out his troubles and gave voice to all his torments. The doctor seems to have been wise and shrewd. Told B. he didn't pity him if he was such a fool as to throw so much weight into his sex emotions; that at his age he should know better. He started laughing and then B. began to laugh too. B. writes, 'I feel I am too young for my age, too impetuous and too self-centred. I am ashamed, very much ashamed' and 'I am in dread of our ardent relationship coming to an end, all passionate longing dispersed.' I give him so much: he has little to complain of except that I don't love him and that I cannot help. I cannot alter that. It's a beautiful thing to be able to feel as B. does so ardently, desperately, painfully, selfishly and unselfishly at 58.[33] Half the world is dead by then, hearts dead. The first letter was an out-pouring and a purging, the second a poem, the third a half-ashamed excusing. My poor Tartar.

London, Thursday July 26

I. came to the flat, we had a cocktail and then went to the Rothermere's election party at the Dorchester. It was the first time I. and I had been anywhere together for many years. 80-100 people must have been there – Diana and Duff, Ed Stanley, Violet Cripps, Nancy Rodd, Herbert Asquith and his wife, Christopher and Clare, Peter Q., Emerald, Sibyl, Raimund, Caroline Paget, Virginia Cowles, Sir John and Lady Ava Anderson[34] and many others. Sir John Anderson remained completely unmoved as the results poured in. Either he'd foreseen them, or he has the finest self-control, or else he is a block of wood. I think he must be a block of wood. Ava A. on the other hand was a pitiful spectacle. She looked like a waif, an orphan, a refugee and finally like an old hen which has been run over but, miraculously, not killed by a car and which proceeds slowly to pick itself up, try its legs and fluff out its feathers again. The Socialists will be in for five or 10 years and where now is Sir John's premiership? I couldn't resist laughing a good deal at the results and some of the long, foolish faces and so did Ed Stanley who was positively wild with excitement and said, 'That will teach those old fools a thing or two' and 'Now they'll have to get rid of those duds behind

---

33. Boris was actually almost 62, making me wonder whether he was hiding his age so as to appear more attractive!
34. Lady Ava Anderson, *née* Bodley (1896-1974). Married in 1941 John Anderson, who at the time of the election was Chancellor of the Exchequer under Churchill and regarded as a possible future prime minister.

the scenes who were clogging up the wheels of the party machine.' There was a vast supply of drink. I. and I found vodka, real good vodka. I left him to wander around on his own but he kept on coming back to me.

Barhatch, Sunday July 29

At 6 the wireless announced Margot's death. I loved her and would always have forgiven her anything. She was exacting, tiring and often trying to be with. If it hadn't been so, I would have seen her very often because I was so fond of her. It was nearly always a business asking her to dinner these last years because many people who knew her weren't anxious to meet her, others wouldn't have amused her, and one had to arrange for a car to fetch her and take her away. But once all this had been got through the evening generally went off pretty well. She hardly ever failed to say some trenchant, witty things and her warmth and affection evoked one's own. I think I feel more pain at her death than I would at any other woman's – Iris's [Tree], Elizabeth's [Glenconner] or Clare's [Tennyson]. I am sure she died gallantly and made as little fuss as one can. I daresay she made a joke in her harsh voice before she became too weak and once again and for the last time cursed all fools.

London, Monday July 30

I. came to dinner. He has refused the new job. He feels he must break away. So Jamaica is on again. I am sure he is right not to let himself grow old, unhealthy and apoplectic sitting for ever in London on mysterious committees and having no leisure, no freedom, no unbuttoning.

London, Tuesday July 31

Sylvia drove me to King's where I saw Conrad [*ill with phlebitis*]. He looked very big in bed – not much changed but unhealthy. He has been in bed about three months. I don't think he will live long. He and G. were devoted and whenever I see him my married life and my sadness without G. are brought back vividly to me.

London, Thursday August 2

B. came at 3 yesterday and brought with him the first sketches for the panels of the National Gallery floor. Not the subjects but the design. We discussed two alternatives, one rather dully regular, the other cock-eyed and more *mouvementé* [*eventful*]. I see from the floor plans that this floor is much bigger than the others. This being so, I must pay him much more: £6,000 or £7,000.

Today I went to the studio to see my mosaic embedded in cement [*Holy Trinity mosaic for Mottisfont*]. I found B. ready, in old work-clothes, with the cement mixed. The process took about two and a half hours. I saw the cement trowelled into the waiting timber frame, a single strand of strong wire pushed into the cement, parallel and an inch or two away from the frame, then a strongly-knit iron mesh or trellis pushed flat into the centre of the 'picture', then cement over it again. All this was allowed to harden a bit after being stamped even with a block. Then fresh cement was added, stamped flat and pressed into every corner and worked absolutely level. Then the mosaic was lifted easily, adhering to its sheet of stout paper, and placed face downward in the cement (it's made in reverse), then hammered over with a block to embed it sufficiently. The sides round it were carefully made up with cement, tightly packed, as the mosaic is to have a cement frame. Finally the mosaic was sponged over, the paper was peeled off, and there lay the mosaic, dirty, stuck with bits of glue and messy with sand and water, but unveiled. After that there came a lot of tidying up, replacing of stones, washing and sponging and the fixing was complete. Maroussia criticised the colour of one half of the heart. Boris agreed saying 'Damn Maroussia' and groaned. As I thought he looked tired I offered to take out the stones before they became too firmly set and this I did with a knife. Even in this small thing there is the right method. We drank to the mosaic and each other. I put five stones into the mosaic on the vaporous background. They are five small dark blue stones that came from the great mosaics in St Sophia and which B. had been given.

London, Tuesday August 7

Kitty came to tea to tell me that Alexie had confided in Mary that she is thinking of marrying new John Russell. They 'fell in love at first sight', she considers herself engaged but is going to wait till October to give herself time to consider. They are probably going to take a flat in Cyril Connolly's new house in Regent's Park. I was enormously surprised because though I had thought that John might want to marry her, it never struck me that she might want to marry him. I thought it might be nice for her to have an admirer but I didn't give a thought to her marrying him.

London, Wednesday August 8

Mama, Kitty, Mary, Tony, Alexie and Sally came to dinner. It was K.'s last night in England. Over the last few days a number of people had discovered she was in England – P/Ws she'd helped, Austrian and Hungarian emigrés and a number of other people including Queen Geraldine Apponyi-Zog. She hadn't had a minute to herself and been begged to find out about missing relations and friends in Russian-occupied Europe and in our zone. She'd been given endless slips of paper with names and addresses and commissions on them and she was bulging with bank notes – money paid back to her by P/Ws she'd helped. These, at the last moment, she forced on me with many hurried injunctions. And so she said goodbye.

London, Thursday August 9

B. came to the flat and later we took the train to Mottisfont. Boris had the mosaic with him and we unwrapped it when we arrived. It looked charming with all its delicacy and gaiety of colour in the morning room but when we took it to the chapel porch, the grim severity of the monastic remains and the ugly barbarism of the stuccoed wall quite killed it. It was disappointing. I would have liked it over the door in the chapel porch leading into the basement. But it would have been cruelty to have placed it there – a sentence of death. So we took it back to the morning room and there it still is.[35]

Mottisfont, Friday August 10

Alexie arrived in the evening with news that London was beginning to celebrate the surrender of Japan though official confirmation was still lacking. We interrupted our dinner in the stables to run down to the Gould's room below to listen to the 9 o'clock news. Still there was no official news but everything pointed to a finish.

The Atom Bomb made its first appearance a few days ago [*on Hiroshima on August 6, Nagasaki August 9*] dropped by the Americans over Japan. Its existence and use has come as a shock to most people. Moral considerations are invoked but behind it all lies fear. Strange thought: one day a madman may touch one off over the earth and the verse of the poets will whirl away into space and their bones become liquid gas.

---

35. The Holy Trinity mosaic stood on a bookshelf in Maud's bedroom at Mottisfont until 1970 when she arranged to have it imbedded in the wall of the Red Room, where Boris used to sleep.

London, Tuesday August 14

To Margot's Memorial Service at St Margaret's. The whole affair seemed ludicrous in connection with Margot and she would have loathed it, all except the hymn O *God Our Help in Ages Past*. A drill outside in Parliament Square provided a constant dulling, distant rumble which prevented the In Memoriam address from being heard by most of the congregation. What little I did hear sounded the sort of thing she would have liked. Plain, direct and unconventional. Tears came to my eyes as I thought of her.

I. came to lunch. The newspapers are offering him handsome jobs. That life will be best for him provided he can have four months to himself in Jamaica or elsewhere every winter. He said *apropos* of Jamaica: 'Why don't you take a house there too?'

During the afternoon the news vendors chalked up on their blackboards: 'Japan accepts surrender terms'. There was a general feeling the war was at an end though there were no crowds in the street and no excitement. I bought some small flags and placed one behind the little black bust of Nelson in I.'s room. And I fetched the Admiralty signal on VE day 'Splice the Main Brace' from the shop where I had it framed; and there it is in I.'s room in its red frame and the Union Jack and the bust of Nelson (*see below*).

Mottisfont, Wednesday August 15

Victory over Japan. End of the war. I had the flag pole on the roof put back into position and I flew the family flag, the big one, though I think it should probably not, technically, be flown unless there is a male member of the family in the house. The soldiers hung flags in the gallery and I put a couple of small Union Jacks in the morning room. In the evening there was a short Thanksgiving Service in the church and a small impromptu dance in the parish hall. B. and I walked past it after dark and peered in. By then it looked pathetically dreary. There had been no drinks and all I could see were a few women and small children sitting round the walls and a few tired elderly men.

Mottisfont, Thursday August 16

B. continued to work at the panel provisionally called 'Daring' which depicts Winston, emblematic of the youth of England, defending Britannia and the White Cliffs from the Dragon (*see photo in colour plates section*). B. had meant to put a cane or a tommy-gun or simply a cigar in his hand. I suggested the characteristic V sign which, in actual fact, was about all we had between us and defeat in 1940 and 1941. We had a happy time together, full of plans and talks, arguments and discussions, asking and giving advice. He seemed quite happy all the time and not anxious to get home. That was because he had his table, pencils and paper. Though I was very happy, all the time – almost all the time – over his shoulder I saw Gilbert. That may be because, in a sort of way, he has taken G.'s place in my life as far as anyone can and because, in a strange way, there is a sort of similarity.

Epilogue

Although Maud was able to help many of her German Jewish relatives obtain visas to England, her aunt Agnes Mühsam and Agnes's son, Hans Werner, did not get out of Germany in time. They delayed departure because Hans Werner was worried about what awaited him abroad and Agnes did not want to leave him behind alone. Agnes was deported to Theresienstadt camp in Czechoslovakia where she died in 1943, while Hans Werner was sent to Neuengamme forced labour camp near Hamburg. As the Allies advanced into Germany, the Nazis evacuated the surviving prisoners from the camp onto ships and these were unwittingly bombed by the British. Hans Werner was among the many who died as a result, just days before Germany's surrender. Agnes's daughter, Lieselotte, committed suicide at Irun on the Spanish border with France in 1941 as she was being deported by train into German hands in Vichy France. Agnes's other daughter Ilse survived the Budapest ghetto in Hungary. Another family victim of the Holocaust was Tante Fritze's son, Otto Franck, who is believed to have been deported by train from Skopje in Macedonia to Majdanek concentration camp in Poland, or shot by Germans when they were retreating from Yugoslavia.

Raymond came back from the Far East and was discharged from the army in 1946. For a number of years he trained to become a professional harpsichord player, giving a number of public concerts, before pursuing a myriad of other interests. His world-class collection of early keyboard instruments was donated to Edinburgh University after his death in 1964 in line with his wishes. Martin delayed his return to England after the war to continue research for a book on a group of Sri Lankan painters known as the '43 Group, led by the artist George Keyt. Owing to Martin's patronage and lifelong interest, many of the 42 Group obtained international recognition for their art. On returning to England he went into the City and eventually became a banker.

Maud and Ian remained close friends up until Ian's marriage to Ann Charteris in 1952. In 1946 Maud gave Ian £5,000 to buy a home in Jamaica; he bought the 15-acre property for £2,000 and budgeted £3,000 to build a house. He originally thought of calling it Shadylady after a sensitive plant that grew profusely on the land but decided on Goldeneye, the codename for a wartime operation. The house is now famous for being the retreat where Ian wrote his James Bond thrillers every January and February.

Maud and Boris were lovers until Boris's death in 1969. In December 1945, Boris planted a chestnut tree and Maud a beech tree, side by side, at Mottisfont, 'symbols of our happiness together', wrote Maud. For Boris, the tree-planting ceremony had a spiritual significance akin to marriage. He returned to his studio in Paris in 1946 to work on the National Gallery commission, which was completed in 1952, but the couple frequently saw each other. Maud continued to play an important role in Boris's work, visiting the studio on every visit to Paris and commenting on mosaics in the making.

In 1946 Boris made the *Angel of Mottisfont* mosaic in his Paris studio, brought it over to England and fixed it at Mottisfont in November of the same year. 'B. is pleased with the work. And so am I. Really pleased. The colour is admirable and unusual, the angel is excellently conceived for the place it has to occupy and the place itself turned from a crude, awkward, architectural excavation into a shrine, delicate and mysterious,' Maud wrote in her diary on November 10, 1946. When asked what the angel signified, they both answered that the angel 'represented the Guardian Angel of Mottisfont and was protecting the house.' People began immediately noticing a likeness in the angel to Maud and although this was obviously Boris's intention, it is not clear that she was initially aware of this.

Boris moved permanently into Maud's new flat in Hyde Park Gardens, Bayswater, in 1961 at the age of 78. After Boris died, Maud buried his ashes and pieces of mosaic in a bowl under his chestnut tree at Mottisfont, in line with his wishes. During his life she had championed Boris and his work, and after his death she continued to care for his legacy, putting together and leaving an important archive about his life and work with the Victoria and Albert Museum in London.

Despite her ongoing relationship with Boris, Maud led an independent life, travelling abroad frequently and maintaining her old friendships as well as making new ones. Musicians, artists, writers and critics made up the bulk of the new friends, often a generation younger than her, reflecting her own eager interest in the arts and keeping up with the times. She was a regular visitor of the Cork Street and Burlington Street art galleries, continuing to collect art, and held musical evenings in her London home. Family also remained a central concern and she attentively followed the development of her numerous grandchildren, great nephews and a great niece with genuine interest and, when possible, a guiding hand. Nonetheless, she sometimes regretted what she thought had been a wasted life and remembered the war years as 'the great years of my life, worthwhile and all important.'

Maud resumed her famous house parties at Mottisfont after the war and Laurie Lee finished *Cider with Rosie* there in 1958. She closely oversaw the management of the estate and was deeply involved in village life up until her death. In 1957, she donated Mottisfont, together with a large endowment, to the National Trust to ease the responsibility of managing such a large estate singlehandedly. She continued to live there until 1972 when the effort of maintaining the house to her own high standards became too much for her and she moved to a smaller house in the same village. She felt no sadness at her departure: 'The countryside, the village and the people are what count most with me.'

After she died at home in London on May 27, 1982, Maud was cremated and her ashes were placed in the same urn as Gilbert's in the family crypt at Chenies, Bedfordshire, in accordance with written instructions in her will, following a short private memorial service. On June 13, 1982, villagers at Mottisfont showed their appreciation for her devotion to the village with their own service in her memory at the local church which, despite her atheist views, she never stopped attending and supporting.

THE RUSSELL FAMILY

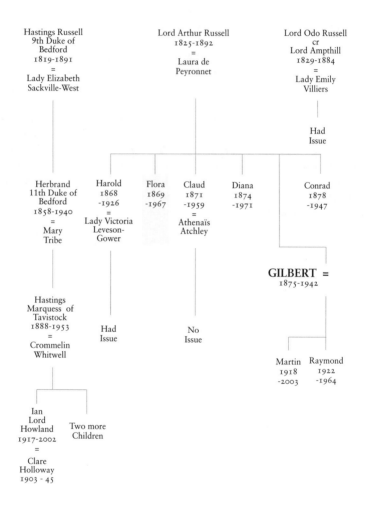

Hastings Russell
9th Duke of
Bedford
1819-1891
=
Lady Elizabeth
Sackville-West

Lord Arthur Russell
1825-1892
=
Laura de
Peyronnet

Lord Odo Russell
cr
Lord Ampthill
1829-1884
=
Lady Emily
Villiers

Had
Issue

Herbrand
11th Duke of
Bedford
1858-1940
=
Mary
Tribe

Harold
1868
-1926
=
Lady Victoria
Leveson-
Gower

Flora
1869
-1967

Claud
1871
-1959
=
Athenaïs
Atchley

Diana
1874
-1971

Conrad
1878
-1947

GILBERT =
1875-1942

Hastings
Marquess of
Tavistock
1888-1953
=
Crommelin
Whitwell

Had
Issue

No
Issue

Martin
1918
-2003

Raymond
1922
-1964

Ian
Lord
Howland
1917-2002
=
Clare
Holloway
1903 - 45

Two more
Children

THE NELKE FAMILY

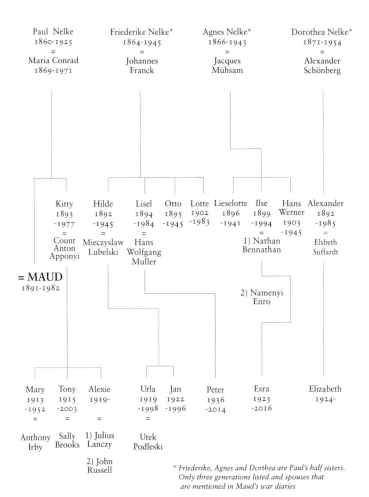

Paul Nelke	Friederike Nelke*	Agnes Nelke*	Dorothea Nelke*
1860-1925	1864-1945	1866-1943	1871-1954
=	=	=	=
Maria Conrad	Johannes	Jacques	Alexander
1869-1971	Franck	Mühsam	Schönberg

Kitty	Hilde	Lisel	Otto	Lotte	Lieselotte	Ilse	Hans	Alexander
1893	1892	1894	1895	1902	1896	1899	Werner	1892
-1977	-1945	-1984	-1945	-1983	-1941	-1994	1903	-1985
=		=				=	-1945	=
Count	Mieczyslaw	Hans				1) Nathan		Elsbeth
Anton	Lubelski	Wolfgang				Bennathan		Suffardt
Apponyi		Muller						

= MAUD
1891-1982

2) Namenyi
Enro

Mary	Tony	Alexie	Urla	Jan	Peter	Esra	Elizabeth
1913	1915	1919-	1919	1922	1936	1923	1924-
-1952	-2003		-1998	-1996	-2014	-2016	
=	=	=	=				
Anthony	Sally	1) Julius	Utek				
Irby	Brooks	Lanczy	Podleski				
		2) John					
		Russell					

*Friederike, Agnes and Dorthea are Paul's half sisters.
Only three generations listed and spouses that
are mentioned in Maud's war diaries

Acknowledgements

It has been a huge privilege to spend the past few years delving into my family history and to produce a book about my grandmother Maud Russell. I am extremely grateful to my brother Julian Russell, sister Laura Beresford and cousin Lavinia Grimshaw for letting me take family papers, correspondence and my grandmother's diaries to Chile, where I live, to enable the research and the transcription and editing of the diaries that cover the Second World War. I owe all three a lot more besides including their steadfast support for this project. A special mention must also go to John Julius Norwich whose Foreword wonderfully evokes the era of Mottisfont in bygone times and Maud's personality. He has also been extremely generous with his time, answering many questions and giving feedback on an early draft.

When I began this project I knew very little about my German Jewish ancestors and was never sure whether the story that my grandmother helped relatives leave Germany in the 1930s was fact or fiction. The quest to find descendants of these relatives and to hear their stories was the most compelling part of the research for this book. I am particularly thankful to have met my cousin Esra Bennathan who was born in Berlin in 1923. Esra told me about the life of my German Jewish relations before the Second World War and also about the fates of his grandmother Agnes, aunt Liselotte and uncle Hans Werner who died in the Holocaust. I would also like to acknowledge the help of my cousins Anthony Apponyi, Rosie Apponyi, Joel Bennathan, Emma Blacker, Frances de Rees, Paul Irby, Peter Irby, Charlie Irby, Sarah Irby, Caroline Irby, James Mayor, Caroline Muller, Judith Nowak, Irena Podleska and Christina Podleska for talking to me about their branches of the family and/or providing photographs. I am delighted that this mission to track down my missing relatives has led to regular family gatherings bringing in relations from Chile, Portugal, Switzerland and Poland as well as all parts of Britain. My big regret, however, is that Esra and my charismatic and encouraging cousin Charlie Irby died before the book's publication.

Another surprise for me on reading the diaries was to discover the depth of my grandmother's 25-year relationship with Boris Anrep. Here I would like to thank Boris's grandson Ben, and two Boris experts, Lois Oliver and Jane Williams – the latter recently completed a PhD on Boris at the University of

Reading – for talking to me about Boris and his work. Likewise, I have been touched to learn of my grandmother's deep friendship with Ian Fleming and am grateful to his niece Kate Fleming for her input.

The book has also benefited from discussions with Kate Hawnt, who is doing a PhD on Raymond Russell at the University of Southampton as part of a larger project on the History of the Modern Harpsichord. Kate's admiration for Raymond has made me look with new interest at my uncle, who died shortly after I was born.

Research for the book has provided me with a great excuse to regularly visit Mottisfont. It is heartening to see how the staff and volunteers at Mottisfont are skilfully using my grandparents' footprint in the house to bring the place to life. I am also very grateful for their unfailing support for this project. In particular I would like to thank the current and former Mottisfont general managers, Louise Govier and Paul Cook respectively, and Kerry Bignell, Anna Pizzey, James Rothwell and John Burns who have been enthusiastically on hand to answer my questions. From the village, contact with Valda White, Bob Peach, Brenda Osman, Peter Southwell and Andy Simmonds have helped me build up a picture of Maud and her interaction with residents of Mottisfont and Dunbridge. A cup of tea with John Clark, a child wartime evacuee at Mottisfont, brought the house to life during the war years.

It has been enormous fun talking to people who knew Maud for this book. Among these I would like to mention conversations with my 'aunt' (in truth a cousin) Alexie Mayor on growing up in my grandparents' care, and my cousin Rachel Campbell for her shrewd observations on Maud's character of contrasts. I would also like to thank Richard Shone, of the *Burlington Magazine*, for his insights into Maud as a foremost modern French art collector. Polly Toynbee, Rupert Wollheim and Bruno Wollheim, the children of Maud's friend Anne, helped me flesh out my grandmother's character, as did a conversation with Anne Norwich.

I am also grateful to the libraries, archives and records offices that opened their doors to me on my fleeting visits to the UK. I immersed myself in books on Maud and her circle at the British Library or the London Library. At the National Archives in Kew I found out about Maud's wartime work in Room 17Z at the Admiralty and Woburn Abbey estate helped me piece together her opaque references about work trips to the Political Warfare Executive's secret radio operations in Milton Bryan. The Salisbury Museum in Wiltshire gave me access to their Rex Whistler Archive and the Hampshire Records Office to records about the Mottisfont Estate in my grandparents' time. I also visited the Wiltshire and Swindon Records Office to read Edith Olivier's journals. *The Oxford Dictionary of National Biography* and Wikipedia were my two main sources for footnotes.

I must also thank the following for allowing the inclusion of illustrations in their possession or for which they hold the copyright: Desmond Banks, The Ferens Art Gallery and Bridgeman Images for the portrait of Maud Nelke by William Nicholson; the National Gallery, London, and Ben Anrep for the 'Defiance' and 'Folly' mosaics by Boris Anrep; the V&A Museum, London, and Ben Anrep for 'Maud Russell Sitting in Bed' by Boris Anrep; the Tate Gallery and Ben Anrep for 'Nude in the Ruins' by Boris Anrep; Mary Beard and Anna Christophoroff for the portrait of Boris Anrep by Leonide Inglesis; the Matisse Estate for the portrait of Maud Russell by Matisse; and The Cecil Beaton Studio Archive at Sotheby's for the photograph of Maud Russell by Cecil Beaton. A particular debt is owed to the National Trust for providing the images of Mottisfont, including the exterior of the house, the Whistler Room, and Boris Anrep mosaics.

One of the greatest rewards of the last two years of family research has been getting to know my grandfather Gilbert, who died long before I was born. Family members have always spoken about him with high regard but reading his funny warm letters to Maud and his sisters has turned him into a real person for me. Likewise, this project has opened up to me my grandmother's rich inner world. I am eternally grateful to David Burnett of Dovecote Press for taking on the task of publishing this book so that their story can be more widely shared. He has been immensely supportive through the arduous publication process and provided valuable feedback, creative ideas and produced with care and dedication a beautiful book. I'd also like to acknowledge the hard work and professionalism of Ildi Clarke who took on the massive task of indexing and of Peter Lightfoot for the family tree.

I thank all my friends who have patiently listened to me talk about this project. I would especially like to acknowledge the Santiago Writers Group, Ruth Bradley, Jessica Davies and Anna Dobai for their input, Quena Flores for help with photography and Fernanda Vidal for helping me believe this book was possible. The support of Max Bañados and the enthusiasm and interest of our children Tom and Nicole in this project has been a constant source of reassurance and pleasure. I am lucky to have such a loving circle of friends and family.

EMILY RUSSELL
Santiago, Chile, March 2017

Bibliography

Anrep, Boris, letters to Maud 1934-1969, Maud Russell Family Estate
 Unpublished correspondence and papers, National Gallery Archive
Asquith, Lady Cynthia, *Diaries 1915-18* (Hutchinson, 1968)
Beaton, Cecil, *The Years Between: Diaries 1939-44* (Weidenfeld and
 Nicolson, 1965)
Beevor, Anthony, *The Second World War* (Black Bay Books, 2012)
Blakiston, Georgiana (ed.), *Letters of Conrad Russell 1897-1947* (John
 Murray, 1987)
Blow, Simon, *Broken Blood: The Rise and Fall of the Tennant Family*
 (Faber and Faber, 1987)
Cecil, Hugh and Cecil, Mirabel, *In Love and War* (The Pimpernel Press,
 2015)
 In Search of Rex Whistler (Frances Lincoln, 2012)
Cooper, Duff, *Old Men Forget: The Autobiography of Duff Cooper*
 (Rupert Hart-Davies, 1953)
Davie, Michael (ed.), *The Diaries of Evelyn Waugh* (Phoenix, 2009)
Declassified papers on Wartime Propaganda, Naval Intelligence Division
 1939-47, ADM 223/477, National Archives
Delmer, Sefton, *Black Boomerang* (Secker and Warburg, 1962)
Farjeon, Annabel, *The Adventures of a Russian Artist: A Biography of
 Boris Anrep* (unpublished English manuscript provided by Boris Anrep
 Family Estate)
Howe, Ellie, *The Black Game: British Subversive Operations against the
 Germans during the Second World War* (London, 1982)
Lees-Milne, James, *A Mingled Measure: Diaries 1953-72* (John Murray,
 1994)
Lycett, Andrew, *Ian Fleming* (Weidenfeld and Nicolson, 1995)
McLachlan, Donald, *Room 39: Naval Intelligence in Action 1939-45*
 (Weidenfeld and Nicolson, 1969)
Norwich, John Julius (ed.), *The Duff Cooper Diaries* (Weidenfeld and
 Nicolson, 2005)

Oliver, Lois, *Boris Anrep: The National Gallery Mosaics* (National Gallery, 2004)

Olivier, Edith, unpublished journals 1938, 1939 and 1944, Wiltshire and Swindon Archives

Partridge, Frances, *A Pacifist's War* (Hogarth Press, 1978)
  Everything to Lose: Diaries 1945-60 (Gollancz, 1985)
  Good Company: Diaries 1967-70 (Harper Collins, 1994)
  Hanging On: Diaries 1960-63 (Collins, 1990)
  Other People: Diaries 1963-66 (Harper Collins, 1993)

Pearson, John, *The Life of Ian Fleming* (London, 1966)

Rankin, Nicholas, *Ian Fleming's Commandos* (Faber, 2011)

Renton, Claudia, *Those Wild Wyndhams* (William Collins, 2014)

Robinson, John Martin, *Requisitioned: The British Country House in the Second World War* (Aurum Press, 2014)

Russell, Diana, unpublished memoir of family life, Maud Russell Family Estate

Russell, Gilbert, unpublished correspondence with family 1900-42, Maud Russell Family Estate

Russell, Maud, engagement diaries 1919-1938, Maud Russell Family Estate
  Unpublished papers and correspondence with family and friends 1917-77, Maud Russell Family Estate
  Unpublished diaries 1905-08 and 1938-77, Maud Russell Family Estate

Scrapbook on Mottisfont Abbey and papers and correspondence on the Mottisfont estate, Hampshire Records Office

Shone, Richard, 'Matisse in England and Two English Sitters', *The Burlington Magazine*, Vol. 135, No. 1084 (July 1993)

Taylor, John, *Bletchley Park's Secret Sisters* (The Book Castle, 2005)

Thomasson, Anna, *A Curious Friendship: The Story of a Bluestocking and a Bright Young Thing* (Macmillan, 2015)

Whistler, Laurence and Fuller, Ronald, *The Work of Rex Whistler* (Batsford, 1960)

Whistler, Laurence, *The Laughter and the Urn: The Life of Rex Whistler* (Weidenfeld and Nicolson, 1985)

Whistler, Rex, unpublished correspondence in The Rex Whistler Archive, The Salisbury Museum

Index